UNEVEN RE-DEVELOPMENT:
Cities and Regions in Transition

Restructuring Britain

Uneven Re-Development: Cities and Regions in Transition
edited by Doreen Massey and John Allen

Divided Nation: Social and Cultural Change in Britain
edited by Linda McDowell, Philip Sarre and Chris Hamnett

A State of Crisis: The Changing Face of British Politics
edited by James Anderson and Allan Cochrane

The following are the associated Open Texts published by Sage Publications in association with the Open University:

The Economy in Question
edited by John Allen and Doreen Massey

The Changing Social Structure
edited by Chris Hamnett, Linda McDowell and Philip Sarre

Politics in Transition
edited by Allan Cochrane and James Anderson

Open University Course D314 Restructuring Britain

This reader is one part of an Open University course and the selection is therefore related to other material available to students. Opinions expressed in it are not necessarily those of the course team or of the University.

Restructuring Britain

UNEVEN RE-DEVELOPMENT:
Cities and Regions in Transition

A Reader

edited by

Doreen Massey and John Allen

at the Open University

HODDER AND STOUGHTON
LONDON SYDNEY AUCKLAND TORONTO
in association with the Open University

British Library Cataloguing in Publication Data
Uneven re-development: cities and regions
  in transition: a reader.
  1. Great Britain. Economic development.
  Geographical aspects
  I. Massey, Doreen, *1944–*   II. Allen,
  John, *1951–*   III. Open University
  IV. Series
  330.941'0858

ISBN 0 340 49393 3

First published in Great Britain 1988

Typeset by Wearside Tradespools, Fulwell, Sunderland
Printed in Great Britain for Hodder and Stoughton Educational, a division of Hodder and Stoughton Ltd, Mill Road, Dunton Green, Sevenoaks, Kent, by Richard Clay Ltd, Bungay, Suffolk

Contents

Acknowledgments

The editors and publishers would like to thank the following for permission to reproduce copyright material in this volume:

Edward Arnold for 'A "modern" industry in a "mature" region: the remaking of management-labour relations' by Kevin Morgan and Andrew Sayer published in *The International Journal of Urban and Regional Research*, Vol. 9, pp. 383–403; Associated Book Publishers (UK) Ltd for 'Spatial development processes: organized or disorganized?' by Philip Cooke published in *Class and Space* by N. Thrift and P. Williams, Routledge and Kegan Paul; Basil Blackwell for 'The geography of international economic disorder' by Nigel Thrift published in *A World in Crisis? Geographical Perspectives* ed. R. J. Johnston and P. J. Taylor (1976) pp. 12–76; Cambridge University Press for 'Employment change and the role of the producer service sector' by P. A. Wood first published under the title 'The anatomy of job loss and job creation; some speculations on the role of the "producer service" sector' in *Regional Studies*, Vol. 20, No. 1, pp. 37–46; Macmillan for 'The deindustrialization of the city' by Steve Fothergill *et al.* published in *The Geography of De-Industrialisation* ed. R. Martin and B. Rowthorn and for 'Producer services and the post-industrial space-economy' by P. W. Daniels published in *The Geography of De-Industrialisation* ed. R. Martin and B. Rowthorn; *Marxism Today* for 'The unions: caught on the ebb tide' by Tony Lane published in *Marxism Today*, September 1982; the Open University for 'The geographies of self' by John Allen, 'Uneven development: social change and spatial divisions of labour' by Doreen Massey and for 'Industrial capitalism in transition: the contemporary reorganization of the British space-economy' by Ron Martin © the Open University; Pion Ltd for 'Labour market changes and new forms of work in "old" industrial regions' by Ray Hudson first published under the title 'Labour market changes and new forms of work on old industrial regions: maybe flexibility for some but not flexible accumulation' published in *Society and Space* **6**(4). Unwin and Hyman for 'The geography of the fifth Kondratieff' by Peter Hall published in *Silicon Landscapes* ed. P. Hall and A. Markusen.

Section I Setting the scene

Introduction

This book forms part of the Open University course *Restructuring Britain*.* The purpose of the course as a whole is to explore the current debate about the nature of change in the UK today. The course is divided into three parts concerned with, respectively, the economy, social structure, and politics and the state, and for each part there is an Open Text and a Reader. The part on the economy comprises this Reader and the Open Text *The Economy in Question*, edited by John Allen and Doreen Massey (London; Sage/The Open University, 1988).

'Restructuring' has come to be a vague, indeed rather a catch-all, term. It is used here to indicate at least the possibility of major change. For there is no doubt that recent decades have witnessed major transformations in economy, society and politics within the United Kingdom. What is more, and this is a central concern of the course, these changes have been integrally bound up with transformations in the urban and regional geography of the UK. Three questions, then, run through this Reader. First, what kind of a change is the UK economy going through? What kinds of concepts of periodization are most helpful? Secondly, what is the relationship between historical periodization of the economy and changes in the form of spatial uneven development within the country? And, thirdly, even among those who argue that there has been structural change there are differences between them as to what this means. So how do the various theoretical frameworks interpret the notion of structural change?

Are we, then, at some kind of a turning-point? Do the current transformations mark a structural change? Many though not all of the contributions to this Reader argue that they do. Their view of what kind of structural change it is varies, however. Hall's position (Chapter 2) is that what we are passing through is a change of direction as part of the regular sequence of long waves in economic history. What lies in front of us is the upswing of the fifth Kondratiev. For him the key mechanisms are the bunching of innovations and the process of technological change. And the key dimensions of change are in technology and in sectoral shift, from mature industries to sunrise sectors. Daniels (Chapter 5) approaches the issue entirely in a sectoral framework, and on a broader schema. In his analysis the crucial change is in the balance within the economy between manufacturing and services. It is a shift from an industrial to a post-industrial (or post-affluent) economy, interpreted theoretically within a 'post-industrial' framework. Here, therefore, the key dynamic is the restructuration of the economy from goods production to information-

---

* Details of this course, D314 *Restructuring Britain*, are available from the Student Enquiries Office, The Open University, PO Box 71, Milton Keynes MK7 6AG.

handling activities. It is the latter, which are, he argues, predominantly concentrated among service rather than manufacturing industries, that are now moving towards a more pivotal position in the overall economic structure. There is no question of cycles or long waves here. What is at issue is a long, historical, gradual and linear process in which the last great structural shift was the evolution from agricultural to manufacturing-based economies.

Thrift and Martin (Chapters 1 and 10), in contrast again, each interpret the character of the current period through a loosely defined 'regulationist-school' framework. It is the end of Fordism which we are travelling through, and the struggle of post-Fordism to be formed. As far as the economy is concerned, the key shifts in this view are in the labour process and in the organization of production, but these elements are embedded in a much wider concept of society as a system held together by a regime of accumulation and an associated socio-institutional structure (to use Martin's terminology). Shifts between historical periods are neither cyclical nor simply linear. The internal dynamics of each period – Fordism in the present case – will lead to its own self-stifling and the necessity for new forms of organization if accumulation is to continue.

Cooke (Chapter 11) explores the thesis that we are operating in an even longer time-frame – that of a shift from organized to disorganized capitalism – but argues, as does Massey (Chapter 12), who uses a spatial division of labour framework, that there have been a number of different 'restructurings', of changes in direction, in recent decades, so that if this is indeed a major turning-point it is not a sudden or simple one.

Not everyone agrees, however, that the current changes are anyway quite so dramatic, or certainly not in the sense of a recent systems change. Fothergill, Gudgin, Kitson and Monk (Chapter 3) see the much discussed phenomenon of the decline of the manufacturing city in the perspective of many decades and point to its turn-of-the-century beginnings. Hudson (Chapter 7), tackling the issue of changes in the labour process and in the organization of production and conditions of work, challenges the regulationist view. He points out that even if Fordism as a labour process were once dominant nationally, which may anyway be debatable in the case of British industry, it was not so in all regions of the country. From the perspective of workers in the north-east of England some of the current changes to their working conditions and practices might seem in some cases more like the reinforcement of pre-Fordist characteristics or in others only now the arrival of Fordism.

What all the authors do agree on, however, is that there is a relation between changes in the organization of the economy (whichever aspect they focus on) and changes in its geography. If what we are analysing at one level is forms of periodization of the British economy, at another level the exploration is of the relation between that periodization and different forms of uneven development. For not only the economy of the UK but also its geography have been undergoing a major reworking over recent decades. And not only can the same questions be asked of these geographical changes – have they been, or are they, structural shifts? – but there is also the issue of what is their relation to the shifts in the economy at national level.

Behind all the contributions in this volume there lies an argument, though formulated in highly contrasting ways, that there is such a relation and that it is important. Moreover, the argument is often not only that changes in the economy will have spatial effects, but that geographical reorganization is part and parcel of changes in the economy. Thrift, whose article opens this Reader, writes: 'There is no need to stress that the chapter is geographical. All the changes described are inherently geographical. Indeed, they depend upon the existence of geography.' He goes on to argue that at the heart of the new world-economic order is the process of internationalization of capital. This internationalization, moreover, is a strategy which has been adopted by different types of capital in order to achieve a range of immediate and longer-term goals. Whether it be to expand the geographical sphere of accumulation, to combat falling rates of profit and/or to pit workers in different countries against each other, capital is here analysed to be taking advantage of spatial differentiation and spatial separation. Moreover, understanding these processes which span the world is essential for understanding many of the main elements in the changing internal geography of the United Kingdom.

Other chapters follow up the changing geography of some of these elements. Both Hall and Cooke examine the effects of technical change, though in different ways. Hall's focus is on long waves and he argues that each long wave in the UK has had a distinct regional geography, that there has been a regional as well as a historical bunching of innovation. It is that which is at the heart of the major shift from older industrial areas (the 'north', the inner cities) to the south-east of the country, and especially the outer areas of that region. Cooke introduces the concept of 'technological paradigm', which goes beyond technology, to include ideological, social and political factors. Moreover he embeds technological paradigms within the more fundamental structures (in a capitalist economy) of the law of value and competition. Distinct technological paradigms, he argues, have distinct spatial connotations, and he uses this framework to analyse the restructurings of the UK space-economy since the mid-1960s.

From different perspectives, both Martin and Daniels also argue that the major socio-economic turning-points which they identify have spatial impacts. Martin argues that each combination of accumulation regime and socio-institutional structure has produced different geographical implications. Daniels and Wood (Chapter 4) explore the geographical effects of the increasing relative importance of service industries within the employment structure. Daniels relates current patterns very clearly to the processes of internationalization outlined by Thrift, and the implications of this for the increasing dominance of the south-east over the rest of the country. In this context, both he and Wood explore the possible futures, in terms of service employment, of cities and towns in different parts of the country.

Other articles deal explicitly with the more active role of geographical character and spatial form on the nature and outcome of current changes. Fothergill, Gudgin, Kitson and Monk argue directly that in explaining geographical patterns and changes (in their case the geography of manufacturing employment growth and decline) it is necessary to analyse the interaction of national trends and the characteristics of localities. Both must be active elements in any explanation. Allen, in his analysis of the changing geographies of service (Chapter 6), does precisely this, firstly embedding intranational changes in their international framework and then exploring how companies, depending on the nature of their internal structures, take advantage of spatial differentiation, in other words of existing forms of uneven development. Morgan and Sayer (Chapter 8) make similar points in their analysis of the location of a 'modern' industry in a 'mature' region, and they push the argument further in pointing to managerial strategies for actively transforming the characteristics (in this case primarily the labour characteristics) of the localities in which they invest. Again with considerations of labour and industrial relations as the central focus, Lane (Chapter 9) argues that recent geographical shifts, and in particular the major losses of manufacturing employment in the big cities, are an important component of the set of new conditions facing trade union organizers in the restructuring British economy.

Finally, back at a more general level Massey argues that the spatial organization of an economy and society both can be part and parcel of any 'turning-point' and can affect the social characteristics of constituent social groups. And Hudson, even more strongly, pursues his theme about the regionally uneven development of Fordism to argue that such uneven development may precisely have been both an element in the last-ditch attempt through decentralization to prolong the life of that regime of accumulation and a factor in its ultimate crisis.

The Reader is organized into Sections, each of which deals with a different aspect of the economic changes in the UK. Section II is concerned mainly with manufacturing, and Section III with service industries. Section IV focuses on the labour market, management–labour relations and the changes facing trade unions. Finally, Section V looks at the dynamics of uneven development more generally. Within each of these Sections the papers have been selected or commissioned in order to present, overall, a range of views. Each Section therefore also has a brief introduction which highlights the characteristics of the views presented and draws out the contrasts between them.

The sequence starts with the chapter by Thrift, which follows this introduction. The chapter analyses those roots of the changes in the UK space-economy which lie at the international level. Thrift begins by referring to Aglietta and the regulationist school, and follows them in arguing that the world-economic crisis was brought on by essentially national phenomena. However, the most important element in the attempted solution adopted has been internationalization. There is thus, immediately, a clear relation between economic crisis and spatial reorganization, the second being seen as one means of solution to the first. In the process are emerging 'the beginnings of a new world spatial division of labour often called the "new international division of labour"'. Such developments have major impacts on both developing and developed countries and, among the latter, perhaps especially so on very open economies such as that of the UK. Indeed, at the end of the chapter Thrift raises the question of 'whether a coherent national economy still exists'.

The first half of Chapter 1 analyses in detail a range of these processes of internationalization. The second half explores some of their implications for the constituent parts of the international division of labour. This achieves two things in relation to the chapters which follow. Firstly, it introduces many of the elements which will be examined in more detail later, and hints at some of the intranational spatial impacts, within the UK, of some of the international processes – the increase in unemployment, the decline of manufacturing employment, the increase in part-time work, especially for women, the patterns of international migration, and the rise and rise of a tier of dominant 'world cities'. But, secondly, by looking also at some of the ways in which these same processes are affecting developing countries, this discussion serves to remind us that from the decline of manufacturing in our cities and regions, to the rebuilding of docklands everywhere, the uneven development, and re-development, of the UK space-economy is tied in to a set of forces which are also having their effects elsewhere in the world, be it First World or Third.

1 The geography of international economic disorder

Nigel Thrift

The 1970s will long be remembered as the decade in which the world economy entered a prolonged period of economic crisis. The economies of the industrialized market countries dipped into recession first in 1974–5. They recovered slightly but then in 1979–80 plunged into recession once again, a recession from which a slow recovery is only now [1986] under way. The economies of the developing countries followed those of the industrialized market countries into recession, at least in part because of linked effects such as the depressed demand for their goods from the industrial market economies (World Bank, 1983). Even the economies of the socialist countries of eastern Europe were not immune from the general downturn. In the last five years their overall economic performance has declined, and again, in part, this decline can be traced to international factors (Neuberger and Tysson, 1980). Only some of the oil-exporting countries seemed likely to weather the storm, but even their economies have recently taken a turn for the worse, hit by declining real oil prices.

The world-economy in crisis has presented an unhappy prospect for each of the three principal groups of actors on the world stage – the multinational corporations, the banks, and the governments of countries. They have all been forced to adjust their roles in the general atmosphere of greatly heightened competition. The result has been a reshuffling of the world-economy as certain of the actors in each group have proved more successful than others. Out of this reshuffling has come a new world-economic order which, after the period of turmoil in the 1970s, it now seems possible to outline. That is what this chapter attempts to do.

The first part of the chapter gives a highly compressed and necessarily selective account of the main changes that have taken place in the world-economy as a result of the crisis. The emphasis is very much upon the role of the multinational corporations and the banks in bringing about a new world-economic order, although the power of the governments of industrial countries is not forgotten. The second part looks at what has happened to people's jobs as a result of all the changes. It looks at the rise of unemployment and at new kinds of jobs. Particular consideration is given to the way employment opportunities in some parts of the world have become more closely tied to employment opportunities in other areas through the rise of the so-called 'new international division of labour' (its growth facilitated by state action), through international migration and the rise of a new international services economy. There is no need to stress that the chapter is geographical. All the changes described are inherently geographical. Indeed, they depend upon the existence of geography.

It is important first to clarify a number of issues. In this chapter the phrase 'world-economy' refers to the capitalist world-economy and the phrase 'new world-economic order' refers to the new capitalist world-economic order. No consideration is given to the socialist countries which some commentators (for example, Wallerstein, 1979, 1983) place within the orbit of the capitalist world-economy and the capitalist world-economic order. Such countries are certainly increasingly linked to it (see, for example, Bora, 1981; Kortus and Kaczerowski, 1981; Gutman and Arkwright, 1981), but the case has yet to be convincingly made that they are an integral part of it. Second, since what follows is such a compressed account it is inevitable that changes in the world-economic order will be presented as remorseless, unitary movements forming an ordered and coherent whole. The reality, of course, is rather different. The changes taking place are still, even now, quite tentative processes which can conceivably be reversed. This is no surprise, for they are organized by humans. And the new world-economic order is not an ordered whole. Certainly, it has some semblance of order. Otherwise it would not work. But it is not 'an order established *in order* to be coherent' (Lipietz, 1984b, p. 92). Third, and following from the second issue, it is important to stress that no attempt is made in what follows to give one determinant of the change to a new world-economic order absolute priority at the expense of any other. In particular, many writers have been guilty of emphasizing the role of one or two of the groups of actors on the world-economic stage to the detriment of others. For some writers, for example, the multinational corporations and the banks have fused into an overarching 'world capital' which transcends all national barriers (for example, Harris, 1982). For others, what goes on inside national barriers must be given priority and multinational corporations are a sideshow (for example, Aglietta, 1982; Lipietz, 1984b). Each of these reactions is equally incorrect. The world-economy is the outcome of a whole series of countervailing forces operating at a whole series of scales, no one of which makes sense without the others.

Finally, some questions of definition. In this chapter the phrase 'developed countries' generally refers to the 24 countries that belong to the Organization for Economic Co-operation and Development (OECD), namely Australia, Austria, Belgium, Canada, Denmark, Finland, France, West Germany, Greece, Iceland, Ireland, Italy, Japan, Luxemburg, The Netherlands, New Zealand, Norway, Portugal, Spain, Sweden, Switzerland, Turkey, the United Kingdom and the United States. The phrase 'developing countries' generally refers to those designated as low-income or middle-income developing countries by the World Bank in its annual *Development Report* (World Bank, 1983).

1.1   The world-economic crisis and the new world-economic order

Economic experts are still arguing about the reasons for the world-economic crisis of the 1930s (see, for example, Kindleberger, 1973; Brunner, 1981). It comes as no surprise, then, to find that they cannot agree on the causes of the present crisis. Perhaps the only thing they *are* willing to agree on is that it is not simply the result, to cite the conventional mid-1970s wisdom of the McCracken report, of 'an unusual bunching of unfortunate events' (OECD, 1977, p. 103). As the immediate recession of the mid-1970s has lengthened into a period of prolonged crisis, so most economists have seemed more willing to agree that 'something fundamental happened' (International Labour Organization, 1984, p. 36).

So what is this fundamental something? It is important here to distinguish between, on the one hand, certain temporally contingent factors which have the effect of triggering periods of recession and, on the other hand, the set of processes – that fundamental something – which meant that a crisis would happen at some time. Among the temporally contingent factors, the most important was undoubtedly the 'oil shock'. In 1973–4 petroleum prices quadrupled. They fell by a sixth between 1974 and 1978 and then increased again, by 80 per cent in real terms, during 1979–80. Some perspective on the magnitude of this shock can be gained from just two facts. First, world trade in fuels increased from $29 billion in 1970 to $535 billion in 1980. Second, paying for the 1970s' fuel-price increases was equivalent to the countries of the world having to find the money to buy all the exports of another United States (Mitra, 1983).

But, important as the oil shock was in triggering the period of crisis and then sustaining it, it seems likely that it would have happened quite soon because of other fundamental processes. More particularly, it seems that in the late 1960s the rates of profit of many firms operating in the industrialized market economies began to fall. This general fall, which was essentially a *national* phenomenon, can be traced to the breakdown of a particular 'intensive' regime of capital accumulation (Aglietta, 1979) which had become typical of the economies of many of the industrialized market countries and which reached its peak in the 1960s. This was based on massive increases in productivity, brought about through widespread mechanization and sustainable by equally massive increases in demand for the goods produced, generated by the linking of wages to productivity through the regulation (Aglietta, 1979; de Vroey, 1984) of state or state-mediated institutions such as collective bargaining and systems of welfare. For all effects and purposes, this system of mass consumption – the 'powerhouse of demand' as it has often been called – excluded countries other than those of the industrialized core: 'Capitalism had temporarily resolved the question of markets on an internal basis. One could even say that the exports of manufactured goods to the periphery were only just covering the cost of raw materials' (Lipietz, 1984b, p. 99). Certainly, the 1950s and 1960s saw a large increase in the number of multinational corporations in the world, mainly those of North American extraction, but their attentions tended to be restricted to the other developed countries.

With the general fall in the rate of profit two things happened. First, many firms were forced to reorganize in order to make a profit again. They might, for example, have had to change their production techniques, consider new products, reorganize their administrative and financial structures, and, in particular, think about producing and marketing in new locations. Not the least of the many stimuli behind this reorganization were the heightened conditions of competition brought on by the recession. Second, as these firms have groped towards a new regime of capital accumulation, so a new system of regulation, based upon new national and international institutions, has shown signs of coming into being. Out of the old order comes the new.

To summarize, that fundamental something underlying the economic crisis has been capitalism 'putting its books in order' (Margirier, 1983, p. 61). Whereas the world-economic crisis was brought on by essentially *national* phenomena (albeit triggered by an international event), the solution adopted by many corporations and banks was essentially *international*.

At the heart of the new world-economic order, then, is a very simple process – the internationalization of capital. Faced with falling rates of profit, firms were forced to 'automate, emigrate or evaporate' (*New York Times*, cited by Frobel, 1983). Many nationally based firms chose the path of emigration (usually mixed with a strategy of automation as well), for an obvious reason. Multinational corporations have been more profitable than other enterprises in the crisis and the gap between the rate of profit of multinational corporations and that of nationally based firms has actually grown during the years of the crisis (Andreff, 1984). This is not to say that the profits of existing multinational corporations were not hit by the crisis. But the rate of profit of these corporations has recovered, not least because many of them have become even more international than before. Thus the internationalization of capital describes the processes of both nationally based firms becoming multinational and multinational corporations becoming more multinational.

The internationalization of capital

What does the 'internationalization of capital' mean? Above all, it means the export of capitalist relations of production, not just of money. Capitalist relations of production are created on a world scale through direct investment by firms which create subsidiaries abroad, organized on capitalist lines. Multinational corporations are the main vehicles of this capital export and as they have increased in both number and size so they have taken on much greater importance in the world-economy than they had in the 1950s or 1960s.

The total flow of foreign direct investment abroad increased by about 15 per cent per annum (in current US dollar terms) in the 1970s and more than trebled between 1970 and 1980. In spite of the economic crisis, outflows of foreign investment continued to increase year by year. Indeed, the pressures of competition from the economic crisis stimulated the multinational corporations to channel direct investment in new ways, most especially through the internationalization of production and through the formation of global profit strategies which led to some of the larger international corporations being transformed into a new species – 'the global corporation'.

The export of capitalist relations of production can take three main forms, each of which has been important at a particular stage in the development of the world capitalist economy but all of which are still important now (Michalet, 1976; Brewer, 1980). First, capital export can be aimed mainly at obtaining raw materials. This has often meant that capitalist social relations were only formed in the mining and agricultural sectors of the developing countries. This kind of capital export was extremely important up until the Second World War and continues to be so, although it is of declining relative importance. For example, Table 1.1 shows the relative ownership of world aluminium, alumina and bauxite capacity in 1982. The six biggest transnational corporations (Aluminium Company of America (United States), Pechiney-Ugine-Kuhlmann (France), Swiss Aluminium (Switzerland), Aluminium Company of Canada (Canada), Reynolds Metal Company (United States) and Kaiser Aluminium (United States)) between them controlled 44.5 per cent of world aluminium capacity, 50.4 per cent of world alumina capacity and 46.3 per cent of world bauxite capacity (United Nations, 1983). Figure 1.1 shows the extent of Pechiney-Ugine-Kuhlmann operations outside France at the end of 1973. Currently, Pechiney-Ugine-Kuhlmann is involved in prospecting or exploiting all the large bauxite deposits in the world (apart from those in the Caribbean where North American companies prevail). It has a share in all the main aluminium complexes near strategic bauxite deposits (Guinea, Greece and Australia) and it has smelting plants in Europe, America and Africa (Savey, 1981). But increasing competition from the big North American producers in the recession has meant that the corporation has had to seek out new markets. The purchase of a smelter in South Korea in 1973 marked its entry into the south-east Asian market and the corporation is now also active in the USSR.

The subject of markets leads to consideration of the second form of capital export, which is aimed at penetrating the markets of countries that cannot be effectively penetrated by exports, for example because of tariff barriers. This form of capital export, which is oriented towards the manufacturing sector, was the dominant form even before the Second World War and is still dominant today. It leads to a spatial structure in

Table 1.1 Ownership of world aluminium, alumina and bauxite capacities, 1982

Owner	Aluminium		Alumina		Bauxite	
	Total capacity (000s tons)	Share world capacity (%)	Total capacity (000s tons)	Share world capacity (%)	Total capacity (000s tons)	Share world capacity (%)
Big six multinational corporations	7 962	44.5	20 113	50.4	51 789	46.3
Other multinational corporations and investors	3 801	21.2	8 642	21.7	22 606	20.4
Goverments of developed countries	1 497	8.4	1 571	3.9	323	0.3
Governments of socialist countries	3 730	20.9	7 026	17.6	15 600	13.9
Governments of developing countries	893	5.0	2 523	6.3	21 622	19.3
Total	17 883	100.0	39 785	100.0	111 940	100.0

Source: United Nations, 1983, p. 210

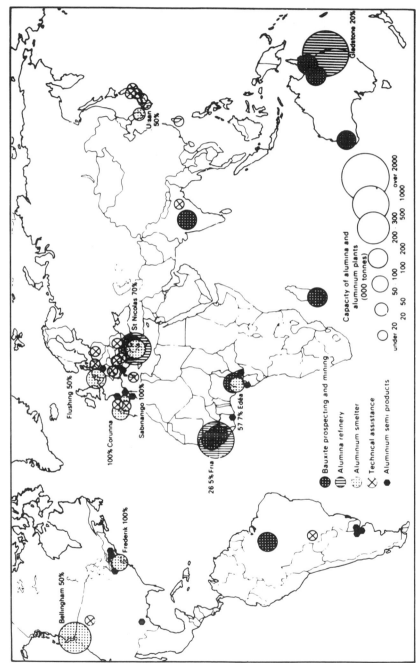

Figure 1.1   Pechiney-Ugine-Kuhlmann's aluminium operations at the end of 1973 (% denotes share of refinery or smelter owned by Pechiney)

Source: Savey, 1981, p. 309

which production facilities are replicated in several countries. The reasons why a multinational corporation will almost certainly decide to internalize production in order to obtain entry to the market of a country, rather than license a local firm to make its products, are [several] [. . .] For example, a multinational corporation may find it impossible or too expensive to arrange with a local firm a contract which affords the multinational corporation effective protection from legal action. (Such a reason is often invoked when new technology is involved or if the local producer is likely to make an inferior product and so damage the multinational's corporate image.) Or the multinational may be unable to persuade the local firm to pay a royalty for making a product which gives a better return than that which can be obtained if the multinational makes the product itself. But the most usual reason is that other multinational corporations making a similar product have already established themselves in the same country. Rivalry with them becomes a very serious consideration [. . .] Rees (1978) documented just such imitative rivalry among the five largest American tyre-producing multinationals – Goodyear, Firestone, Uniroyal, BF Goodrich and General Tire – in the 1960s and 1970s. In particular he showed how three of these corporations – Goodyear, Firestone and General Tire – fought each other with a move–counter-move strategy [. . .] In several cases, each corporation set up plants in the same country within a few years of one another. In the Philippines, Firestone and Goodyear set up in the same year.

Finally, and of particular importance since the late 1960s, capital export has been aimed at exploiting cheap labour to produce goods for re-export to the home country or to third markets (including not only other countries but also other plants in the corporation). This strategy leads to the creation of integrated hierarchical production organizations which cut across national boundaries and is often called the 'internationalization of production'. An example of this most recent form of capital export can be found in the actions of the British multinational, Coats Patons, over the last ten years. Coats Patons is prominent in textiles, a fiercely competitive industry. In the 1970s its profits in the developed countries were threatened by imports from firms in the developing countries who could hold their unit costs down because labour costs were so much cheaper. Coats Patons' response was to move many of its production facilities to such countries, where they too can take advantage of the lower labour costs (see Table 1.2), and by 1979 it had built up a sizeable labour force in the developing countries (see Figure 1.2).

These are the main forms of capital export, but it is important to point out that, in reality, they are difficult to separate from one another. Thus parts of the operations of Pechiney-Ugine-Kuhlmann and even of the tyre companies may be aimed at obtaining raw materials whereas other parts are aimed at penetrating markets for the products made from the raw materials. Similarly, multinational corporations may be simultaneously seeking out reserves of cheap labour and new markets.

Table 1.2   The Coats Patons table of comparative labour costs at 21 April 1981

	Single shift		Double shift		Treble shift	
	Total cost per hour (£)	Index	Total cost per hour (£)	Index	Total cost per hour (£)	Index
UK (base)	2.678	100	3.186	100	3.481	100
Italy	3.259	122	3.499	110	4.943	121
West Germany	3.561	133	3.696	116	3.913	115
Canada	3.596	134	3.564	112	3.613	109
United States	3.134	117	3.134	98	3.157	90
Portugal	1.076	40	1.177	37	1.799	42
Colombia	0.950	36	1.121	35	1.304	26
Brazil	0.840	31	1.009	32	1.065	31
Peru	0.611	23	0.620	19	0.637	19
India	0.342	13	0.345	11	0.416	11
Philippines	0.276	10	0.276	9	0.282	8
Indonesia	0.166	6	0.169	5	0.168	5

Source: *Financial Times*, 29 June 1981, p. 11

The integration of the three different forms of capital export under the one corporate roof has become more and more common because the largest multinational corporations have become even larger, adding on more and more subsidiaries. Indeed, some of the larger multinational corporations now operate in the markets of virtually every country in which it is possible to make a profit. For them the challenge is no longer expansion into the markets of new countries. Rather, it has become how to organize their world network of subsidiaries in such a way as to make the best possible profit. Until the late 1960s the challenge of organizing and putting into effect such a global profit-making strategy would have been formidable. But technical developments, most notably in telecom-munications and data-processing, organizational developments, especially the setting up of 'regional headquarters offices' (see Dunning and Norman, 1983; Grosse, 1982), and the rise of an international capital market have enabled this challenge to be met by some of them at least. The result has been the growth of a new type – the global corporation [. . .] – which will often carry on all three forms of capital export at one and the same time in an integrated way. They tend to promote global brand names, and production within them is organized on a regional or even global basis. The result of this integration of production, and of the constant shifting of materials, components and information that is entailed, is the dramatic enlargement of markets internal to the corporations (see Rugman, 1981, 1982). Just how widespread these internal markets now are can be traced through figures on intra-firm trade across national boundaries. For example, for the United States in 1977, 39 per cent of total imports and 36 per cent of total exports could be classified as intra-firm trade. The

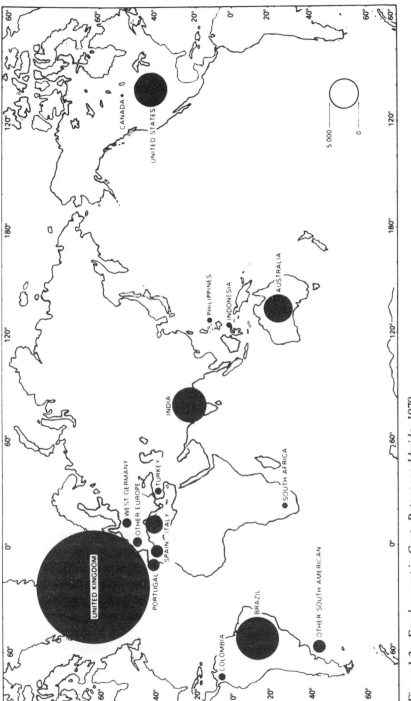

Figure 1.2 Employment in Coats Patons worldwide, 1979
Source: Taylor and Thrift, 1982, p. 8

proportion of intra-firm exports in the total exports of the UK increased from 29 per cent in 1976 to 31 per cent in 1980. One UNCTAD estimate is that as much as *30 per cent* of world trade is now within corporations (United Nations, 1983).

A good example of how a global corporation came into existence and now goes about its business is provided by the European operations of the automobile manufacturers, Ford, currently the third largest company in the world and for long a multinational corporation. Even in 1930 the corporation was assembling its cars in 20 countries [. . .] In 1950 Ford's European organization consisted of three main and quite separate manufacturing and assembly plants serving the three main retail markets of France, the UK and West Germany and four more 'completely knocked down' assembly plants serving the subsidiary markets of Belgium, The Netherlands, Denmark and Ireland [. . .] The company's organization in 1960 was mainly an elaboration on this theme of national market concentration but with France abandoned as a market and the number of component manufacturing plants increased in the UK and West Germany. However, in 1967 Ford of Europe was created in an attempt to integrate the corporation's European operations. Among the factors involved in this decision were the desire to spread investment (especially because the British subsidiary was prone to labour unrest), the shortage of labour near the existing plants, the high cost of separate model development in a number of markets and the new market opportunities created by the founding of the EEC. By 1970, signs of this new kind of integration were already apparent and by 1978 integration of the European operations was becoming a reality. For example, the introduction of the Ford Fiesta created new and complex patterns of movement within the corporation, integrating plants such as Belfast (carburettors and distributors) and Bordeaux (transmission and axles) with the assembly centres in the UK, Germany and Spain (Bloomfield, 1981).

Prominent among the changes between 1970 and 1978 was the opening of a plant at Valencia, Spain, in 1972. This shows the risks of greater integration for the workers employed in a global corporation. Such corporations can choose a location for a new plant which, if it is successful, becomes the measure for all the other plants in the corporate network. Ford invested in Spain for two reasons: to gain access to the growing Spanish car market – import duties into Spain were prohibitive – and to take advantage of low labour costs. The success of plants like the one at Valencia now threatens other older plants at Dagenham in the United Kingdom and Cologne in West Germany, which find it hard to reach the new corporate norm that Valencia has set because their labour costs are inevitably higher (Cohen, 1983).

Changes in the origin and destination of foreign direct investment

The advent of a new form of capital export and of the global corporation should not be allowed to obscure some far-reaching and important changes in the origins and destinations of direct investment during the crisis (see Table 1.3). For, although the total flow of foreign direct investment increased at about 15 per cent per annum (in US-dollar terms) in the 1970s and, indeed, more than trebled between 1970 and 1980 (United Nations, 1983) there were very significant changes in the direction of flow.

Before 1970, US-based multinational corporations accounted for nearly two-thirds of the outflow of foreign direct investment. But by the end of the 1970s the US corporations' share of the total had dropped to less than half (see Table 1.3). The corollary of this decline was a rise in the relative position of corporations based elsewhere. In particular, Canadian, West German and Japanese corporations stepped up their rate of foreign direct investment. Of these three the Japanese case is probably the most significant, especially if accumulated direct investment is considered (see Table 1.4). Already by the 1960s Japan had become a major economic power in the world, but in general its corporations produced at home and exported abroad. However, in the 1970s Japanese corporations went multinational as never before, spurred on by the state of the home market, by the accumulation of the international resources of capital needed to pay for expansion, by the threat of protectionism in many countries to which Japanese exports were directed, and by the active involvement of government through the offices of MITI (the Ministry for International Trade and Industry) (Yoshihara, 1977; Franko, 1983).

Another significant outflow of foreign direct investment has come from the increasing number of multinational corporations based in the developing countries (see Lall, 1984; Wells, 1983). Its significance is not based upon the actual proportion of foreign direct investment in total – which is still small – but upon the fact that such investment exists at all. Up to 50 developing countries now have some direct overseas investment. As might be expected most of this comes from the 12 or so newly industrializing countries. Nearly 10 per cent of the top 500 non-US-based corporations in the world are now based in the developing countries, and most of these are multinational. Hyundai, the South Korean shipbuilding firm, is now bigger than Michelin or Rio Tinto Zinc. Taiwan's Walsin Likwa, an electronics group, is bigger than Distillers or De Beers.

The important changes in the destination of foreign direct investment during the crisis can be neatly summarized as a double capital movement (Teulings, 1984), towards both the United States and the developing countries. Before 1970, the United States accounted for only about 8 per cent of the total world inflow of direct investment. But, by the end of the 1970s, its share had increased to almost 30 per cent (see Table 1.3) [. . .]

Table 1.3   Foreign direct investment by selected countries, 1970–2 and 1978–80

	Outflow				Inflow			
	1970–2		1978–80		1970–2		1978–80	
	US$ million	%	US$ million	%	US$ million	%	US$ million	%
Developed market economies								
Australia	113	0.8	344	0.8	1 030	9.1	1 820	5.3
Austria	25	0.1	90	0.2	84	0.7	197	0.5
Belgium	171	1.3	699	1.7	384	3.4	1 371	3.9
Canada	316	2.4	2 617	6.3	807	7.1	1 138	3.3
Denmark	76	0.6	11	0.0	131	1.1	64	0.2
Finland	53	0.4	106	0.3	27	0.2	30	0.0
France	455	3.4	2 359	5.6	612	5.4	2 902	8.4
West Germany	1 161	8.7	4 262	10.2	1 220	10.8	1 257	3.6
Italy	242	1.8	42	0.1	976	8.6	42	0.3
Japan	481	3.6	2 552	6.1	155	1.4	173	0.5
Netherlands	564	4.2	2 210	5.3	575	5.1	1 038	3.0
Norway	21	0.1	120	0.3	93	5.8	315	0.9
South Africa	22	0.1	89	0.2	237	2.1	–204	–0.6
Spain	35	0.3	221	0.5	231	2.0	1 270	3.7
Sweden	217	1.6	551	1.3	86	0.7	145	0.4
United Kingdom	1 597	11.9	5 756	13.8	982	8.7	3 756	10.9
United States	7 649	57.4	19 547	46.9	929	8.2	10 205	29.6
Developing countries								
South-east Asia	20	0.1	152	0.4	530	4.7	2 389	6.9
Latin America	17	0.1	229	0.5	1 130	10.0	4 902	14.2
Total[1]	13 245	100	42 245	100	11 151	100	33 878	100

[1]Totals do not add up owing to the number of countries which have been omitted.

Source: from United Nations, 1983, p. 19

Table 1.4   Accumulated direct investment overseas by country, 1970 and 1978

	1970		1978		
	US$ bn	Share (%)	US$ bn	Share (%)	Increase (%)
United States	78	52	168	42	115
United Kingdom	20	13	35	9	75
West Germany	7	5	29	7	314
Japan	4	3	27	7	575
Switzerland	8	5	25	6	213
Others	33	22	116	29	252
World total	150	100	400	100	167

Source: Kirby, 1983, p. 40

The developing countries were the other recipients of foreign direct investment. But this growth has been concentrated in a small number of such countries – Hong Kong, Brazil, Singapore, South Korea, Taiwan, Argentina, Mexico and Venezuela – again, those with a developed base, the newly industrializing countries. Of the total inflow of foreign direct investment into the developing countries, just six (Argentina, Brazil, Hong Kong, Malaysia, Mexico and Singapore) accounted for between one-half and two-thirds of the total.

Within these flows of direct investment into particular centres, multinational corporations based in particular countries still tended to have particular regional biases. Thus US-based corporations are still biased towards Europe; Japanese-based corporations are still biased towards Asia, and are the largest investors in South Korea, Thailand, Malaysia and Indonesia. Developing-country multinational corporations are biased towards other developing countries.

The internationalization of finance

The expansion of production overseas in the 1970s and 1980s, whether as a result of the search for new markets or for cheap labour, has been matched by a parallel and complementary expansion of producer services, especially finance (Versluyen, 1981; Brett, 1983; Coakley, 1984). The expansion of finance cannot be seen as simply an enabling factor. Rather it is part and parcel of the whole process of internationalization of capital that has been caused by the world-economic crisis. It has three main components, which will be considered in turn.

The internationalization of domestic currency

The modern international financial system is based upon the creation of a number of new international markets for domestic currency which can be borrowed and lent. These markets have become possible because of the advent of floating exchange rates and the creation of a series of 'pseudo currencies', especially Eurodollars. In 1944 the Bretton Woods agreement was signed, setting up what was essentially a US-run international financial system with three poles – the World Bank, the International Monetary Fund and, most important of all, fixed exchange rates, with the US dollar serving as the convertible medium of currency with a fixed relationship to the price of gold. This system worked only so long as sufficient international reserves of currency could be found to finance the growth of world trade through the 1950s and 1960s, and so long as the United States was the dominant economic power in the world (Daly, 1984). But by the 1960s the system was under pressure. Countries and companies could not find sufficient international reserves and the United States was no longer such a dominant economic power. In 1950 the United States produced 62 per cent of the total manufacturing output of the ten major western economies and 26 per cent of world exports. But by the beginning of the 1970s the figures were respectively 44 per cent and 19 per cent (Parboni, 1981). The result was that the Bretton Woods system crumbled. In particular, by the late 1960s fixed exchange rates effectively disappeared and every domestic currency became convertible into every other. Exchange rates 'floated' and, as a result, all domestic currencies could themselves become a medium that could be bought and sold and out of which a profit could be made. Soon exchange rates began to change far more frequently than other prices, and now exchange rates are changing in Tokyo when London businessmen are abed and then in London before New York businessmen wake up.

The establishment of a pool of Eurodollars, which are simply dollars held in banks located outside the United States, has been the other crucial factor in the development of the modern international financial system (see Aliber, 1979; Mendelsohn, 1980; Sampson, 1981; Coakley and Harris, 1983). The origins of the Eurodollar market are shrouded in mystery. It is thought to have started when, in the late 1940s and early 1950s, the Chinese and the Russians doubted the safety of holding dollar reserves in the United States (where they could be confiscated) and so transferred them to banks in Paris and London. Later, towards the end of the 1950s, as the United States government began to run a balance-of-payments deficit, paying out more than it was receiving and doing so in dollars, so the newly created dollar owners deposited their dollars in banks in Europe rather than in New York. Because the European banks were far away from any potential United States jurisdiction and (increasingly importantly) away from United States control over interest rates they were able to pay higher interest rates on these dollar deposits than the American banks. Then three things happened which made the market in

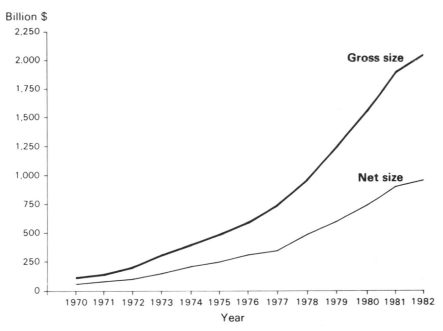

Figure 1.3 Eurocurrency market size, 1970–82
Source: World Financial Markets, *Morgan Guaranty, New York*

Eurodollars take off (see Figure 1.3). First, during 1963 and 1964 President Kennedy, worried by the increasing flow of dollars abroad, announced an Interest Equalization Tax and a Voluntary Credit Restraint Programme, which were intended to reduce capital outflow. Instead, international borrowers looked to Europe and the Eurodollar market. (Prominent among these borrowers were United States multinational corporations raising loans on the Eurodollar market so that they could continue to expand abroad.) Second, from 1971 the United States government began to finance its budget deficit by paying in its own currency, flooding the world with dollars and helping to fuel the inflationary process worldwide. It is estimated that world monetary reserves increased *twelvefold* between 1970 and 1980 (see Parboni, 1981). Finally, there was the 'oil shock'. When the members of the Organization of Petroleum Exporting Countries (OPEC) simultaneously raised the price of oil they also acquired huge reserves of dollars from their sales of oil, reserves which had to be invested. Many of these dollars were invested not in government bonds but in banks outside the United States, dramatically swelling the banks' Eurodollar deposits.

The international banks, and other institutions, had to find somewhere to put all the money they suddenly found in their coffers. This was no easy task. It was difficult to find borrowers in the shape of existing governments, government-backed corporations and multinational corporations willing to take out new loans and soak up the surplus. One outlet was to create new markets. For example, the Eurodollar market became considerably more sophisticated in order to allow a greater range of borrowers to participate. Three distinct categories of lending can now be found (Coakley and Harris, 1983). There are short-term loans (often overnight) called interbank loans which are made between one bank and another and by multinational corporations. There are medium-term (three to ten years) syndicated dollar credits; these are loans of dollars from banks outside the United States, made by syndicates of banks. And there are loans which can be long term. These are Eurobonds, IOUs issued by a borrowing state or corporation to raise Eurodollars which can be sold and resold. Another development in the Eurodollar market has been the inclusion of other Eurocurrencies, domestic currencies like Japanese yen, British pounds sterling or German marks held in banks outside the country of issue. But the dollar still reigns supreme in the Eurocurrency market – about 80 per cent of which will be in dollars in any one year. Other financial markets have also been created such as the *futures* market, which trades in contracts. The main futures markets are, in their order of importance, in treasury bonds, in soya beans, in corn, in gold, in stock index controls and – in Eurodollars.

Another outlet the banks found to soak up their surplus was the 'better-off' developing countries. The problem was that these countries could not, for a number of reasons, pay off the debts that they incurred in borrowing from the banks and there is now a widespread crisis of debt among them, especially those in Central and South America like Mexico, Brazil and Argentina [. . .] For example, by 1982 Brazil's debt service had reached the level of its total exports. This crisis of debt is not likely to be solved so long as interest rates continue at their present high levels [. . .] It is no surprise that the governments and populations of many Latin American countries are beginning to balk. As one banker put it, 'Somehow the conventional wisdom of 200 million sullen South Americans sweating away in the hot sun for the next decade to earn interest on the debt so Citicorp can raise its dividend twice a year does not square with my image of political reality' (Delamaide, 1984, p. 123).

The internationalization of the banks

With all the money that was being pumped into them, the international banks became truly global in the 1970s, aided by advances in telecommunications and data-processing. In the race to become global the United States banks were the most successful. The number of foreign branches of US-based banks increased from 124 to 723 between 1960 and 1976 and their assets grew by 1816 per cent (Sampson, 1981). But the United States banks were soon followed by the British and French banks (with their experience of dealing with former colonial countries) and later by the German, Italian, Arab and Japanese banks. Like Japanese multinational corporations, the Japanese-based banks have become a major force in global banking, first by forming Japanese companies abroad as they went multinational and then by competing for other business and especially the Eurodollar market (Fujita and Ishigaki, 1985). They are now second only to the US-based banks [. . .]

But a problem now affecting the internationalization of the banks is developing-country indebtedness. For the banks, having lent so much money, are now themselves locked into the problem of debt. If the Latin American countries were to renege on their debts, a number of the global banks could fail. This, in turn, might halt the further internationalization of banking and even put a question-mark over the further internationalization of capital (Lipietz, 1984a).

The internationalization of the capital markets

Occurring in parallel with the internationalization of currency and banking has been the internationalization of the capital markets. All the infrastructure necessary to sustain the new international financial system, from stock exchanges through futures exchanges to tax havens, has proliferated (Gorastiaga, 1983). The result has been that the international financial system is now a 24-hour-a-day business, with dealing in currency, shares and bonds migrating around the world with the passage of the sun.

The internationalization of the state

The influence of the state is the final pole in an explanation of the economic crisis of the 1970s and 1980s. It is, of course, quite possible to build up a theory which either gives the state an undue amount of power to resist capital or reduces the state to an agent of capital. The reality is rather different. States are the result of a long-drawn-out conflict between different social groups to wrest different elements of power from one another. At different times and in different countries states play different roles. Four such roles can be identified, each of which has had some influence on the course of the world-economy in the 1970s and 1980s, and has both contributed to the internationalization of production and finance and hastened the integration of states into the new world-economic order.

One role has been as a market. For example, a considerable part of the move of multinational corporations towards the United States in the 1970s, especially those involved in the electronics industry, can be explained by their desire to obtain lucrative United States government defence contracts. Another role has been restrictive: as the crisis has deepened, so it has touched off a rising tide of protectionism – the erection of new tariff barriers, the insistence on local labour, and so on. It has been argued that this increasing protectionism is one of the main reasons why Japanese corporations went abroad in such numbers in the 1970s. It was realized that the protectionist policies would make it more and more difficult for Japanese corporations simply to export. Instead they would have to produce within them. Certainly, this has been one of the motives behind Japanese expansion in a number of industries in Europe and the United States, most notably in the automobile industry.

A third role has been enabling. States can and do provide packages of measures to attract foreign direct investment. The activities of foreign investment agencies in nearly every country of the world are legion. The battle in 1983 and 1984 to attract a Japanese (Nissan) automobile plant into Britain is only one notable example. Then again, the state can act to help multinational corporations based in their country to expand into other countries, either indirectly by providing export advice and insurance, or directly through an explicit internationalization strategy as in the case of the Ministry of International Trade and Industry (MITI) in Japan and the efforts made by the South Korean government. Finally, the state can act as a competitor to other foreign direct investors. For example, it can compete for funds from the banks. The United States does this so effectively, in order to finance its budget deficit, that it has pushed up real interest rates around the world. Or the state can compete even more directly through state-owned multinational corporations. Thus in 1978, out of the largest 483 industrial companies in the developed market economies, 37 were state-owned and nearly all were multinational (Dunning and Pearce, 1981) [. . .]

Finally, it is important to remember that states do not have to be restricted to their own boundaries. A number of international state organizations exist, all the way from the United Nations, with its various industrial bodies, through the 24-member OECD to the IMF and the World Bank. These international organizations can be used to extend a country's economic power abroad, promoting its exports or the influence of its multinational corporations. Thus it is difficult not to see the IMF as an explicit arm of United States economic policy, there to open up the economies of recalcitrant countries to United States exports and to United States multinational corporations, to discipline the economies of these countries to the needs of 'the market'.

Summary

Three main net effects of these changes will continue [beyond the 1980s]. The first is the acceleration of capital movement. Capital has become more footloose, both in time and space. Take the case of time first (see Figure 1.4). Before the 1970s, exchange rates changed only once every four years on average, interest rates moved perhaps twice a year, companies reviewed the prices of their products once a year and made decisions on investment even less frequently. But in the 1970s and 1980s all this has changed. Exchange rates change every four hours, interest rates change more frequently, prices can be adjusted much more swiftly, companies

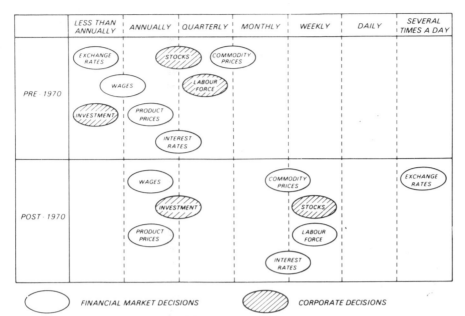

	LESS THAN ANNUALLY	ANNUALLY	QUARTERLY	MONTHLY	WEEKLY	DAILY	SEVERAL TIMES A DAY

Figure 1.4   The pace of the world economy speeds up
Source: The Economist, *24 September 1983, p. 11*

FINANCIAL MARKET DECISIONS   CORPORATE DECISIONS

make investment decisions every year. In other words, the whole economic system has speeded up. Capital has also become more footloose in space. Because of the speed-up in time multinational corporations now review the productivity of their plants much more frequently and if plants do not produce the required level of profit they are likely to be shut down. At the same time multinational corporations can, through the medium of acquisition, move more swiftly into new markets or production, gaining control over existing plants or opening up new plants as they go along. Thus there is a constant process of strategic rationalization in which plants are set up and shut down more frequently than before, with all the consequences this has for the countries in which these plants are located.

The second net effect is the growing interpenetration of capital as multinational corporations based in different countries have spread worldwide. To take but two examples, the largest amount of Japanese direct investment still goes to the United States, and European multinational corporations have increasingly channelled their direct investment into the United States as well (Dicken, 1982). On a smaller scale, European direct investment has increasingly been directed to the UK and vice versa (Dicken, 1980). Thus the core industrialized economies have become more tightly integrated. In the process the world-economy has moved from being an economy with but a single economic pole – the United States – to one that is multipolar.

The third net effect is that the borders of capitalist production have moved a little further out. There has been no wholesale industrialization of the Third World, as the increasing poverty of most of Africa attests. Rather the border of capitalism now encompasses a few developing countries – the newly industrializing countries – partly through their own efforts and partly through the attention of the multinational corporations. And the international debt crisis could still block even this small advance. This is hardly:

> a picture of ascendant Southern industrial power. Rather local governments in the [newly industrializing countries] have attempted to maximize the possibilities for their indigenous capitalists, within a set of international economic and political constraints which makes preserving a space for indigenous capital a delicate business. This is not possible without permanent struggle. Perhaps South Korea has succeeded; probably Brazil, Taiwan, the Philippines, Argentina and Chile have not. (Roddick, 1984, pp. 126–7)

1.2   The world market for labour

These changes in the structure of the world-economy have brought prosperity to some people and agony to many others (literally, in the case of some people working in developing countries with authoritarian regimes). The main cause of these mixed fortunes has been the changes in people's chances of getting a job.

There is still a very real difference between employment opportunities in the developed and the developing countries [. . .] Therefore, initially, the very different circumstances that can be found in each bloc will be enumerated. But as a consequence of the form of internationalization of capital that has taken place during the crisis some new links have now been forged between employment opportunities in the developed and the developing countries respectively: I will discuss four of these below.

The developed countries

The world-economic crisis of the 1970s and 1980s took place against the background of some quite important changes in the characteristics of the labour forces in the developed countries. The most important was the number of women (especially married women) joining the labour force. The proportion of women increased in nearly all the OECD countries over the period of the crisis. A second important factor was the 'baby boom' that lasted from the end of the Second World War until 1960. The generation born then entered the labour market at the very time that opportunities for employment started to plummet.

By far the most visible effect of the world-economic crisis on the structure of opportunities for employment in the developed countries has been unemployment, which has increased dramatically. As firms restructure or go out of business in the climate of fierce competition which is typical of an economic crisis, so workers are laid off.

From 1960 to 1973, unemployment rates in North America varied between 4 and 7 per cent. In Europe and Japan they were never higher than 2 or 3 per cent. But after the first oil shock in 1973 unemployment rose quickly in nearly all countries until the end of 1975 (see Figure 1.5). Then it remained relatively stable in most countries until 1979, when it again rose rapidly [. . .] In all, in the 24 OECD countries there were about 30 million persons out of work in 1983 (International Labour Organization, 1984), and 31 million in 1984. The OECD *Employment Outlook* reckoned that some 20 million jobs would have to be created in the OECD countries by 1990 just to keep unemployment at [1986] rates and as many as 35 million jobs to get back to the levels of unemployment of 1979 [. . .]

Added to this general upward trend in rates of unemployment and the numbers unemployed [. . .] are three other trends which have caused great concern. First, the numbers of long-term unemployed have been increasing in nearly all the developed countries [. . .] Second, in many countries unemployment is not only underestimated, which is generally the case with official figures, but it is thought that the number of those who are unemployed but not counted in the official figures is increasing. Third, unemployment has had particularly severe effects on certain social groups. Those who are least likely to be unemployed are men between 24 and 54 years of age who have a good education or training. These people tend to fill what is often called the primary segment of the labour market, the segment with full-time jobs, promotion opportunities and incomes steadily rising with age. In contrast the young, the old, women and minorities are more likely to be members of the secondary labour market – the segment with unskilled, poorly paid, insecure jobs – that is, if they are employed at all. The young and the old are more likely to be unemployed in every developed country. So are women. So are minorities. And any combination of these characteristics drastically reduces a person's chance of being employed. In short, on the average in every developed country:

> ten persons out of 100 are unemployed. Of these ten persons, five are young and three of these are women. [Further] among the unemployed queuing up for unskilled jobs, the successful applicants will first be adult males (between 24 and 54 years of age), then women of the same age, followed by young persons; the last will be minorities and older workers. (International Labour Organization, 1984, p. 46)

If unemployment is the most clearly visible effect of the world-economic crisis, this does not mean that the crisis has had no other effects on the structure of opportunities for employment. In fact, the economic crisis has undoubtedly hastened the demise of manufacturing employment and the rise of service employment. Manufacturing employment has declined in nearly all the developed countries since the oil shock of 1973. The main exception has been the electronics sector, where demand for computers, office equipment and videos has kept employment up. Employment in services has grown in nearly all the developed countries since 1973. In the

Percentage of
total labour force

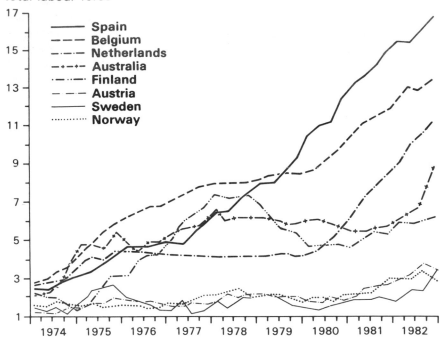

Spain
Belgium
Netherlands
Australia
Finland
Austria
Sweden
Norway

Percentage of
total labour force

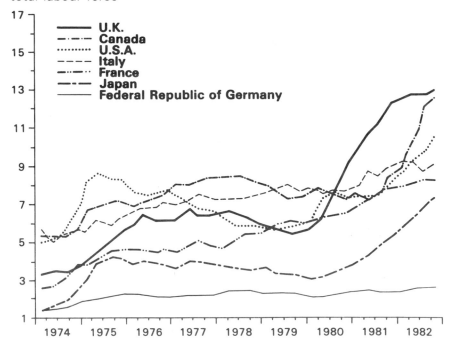

U.K.
Canada
U.S.A.
Italy
France
Japan
Federal Republic of Germany

Figure 1.5   Standardized unemployment rates in 15 OECD countries (quarterly data, seasonally adjusted)

Source: International Labour Organization, 1984, pp. 38–9

OECD countries, for example, employment in services, on average, had risen to 63 per cent of total employment by 1981. Employment in services in the United States and Canada is now as high as two-thirds of total employment and well above 50 per cent in most other countries. Part of this increase is, of course, a relative effect of the decline in manufacturing employment but there has also been an absolute increase in numbers employed in some parts of the service sector since 1973, most particularly in government and in financial and business services.

Of course not all the growth in the services sector has been a direct result of the world-economic crisis. The role of the service sector in the economies of developed countries was increasing before the 1970s. But the crisis has hastened its growth – employment in the services sector grew much more rapidly in the OECD countries between 1973 and 1980 than from 1960 to 1973. And in some cases it has had more direct impact. For example, in many countries the greatest growth in government employment has been in social services concerned with promotion of employment: 'Owing to slower economic growth and a rise in unemployment, many governments have expanded activities in the field of employment promotion, vocational guidance, training and security' (International Labour Organization, 1984, p. 49). Similarly, although much of the growth in employment in financial and business services during the 1970s was the result of banks and other financial institutions expanding their branch networks, some of the growth in employment was also the result of the rise of international banking and the increase in the information-gathering and other producer services demanded by multinational corporations.

It is important to note that much of the increase in service employment consisted of an increase in the number of part-time workers. By 1981, part-time work accounted for more than a quarter of all employees in employment in Sweden, 20 per cent in the UK and more than 10 per cent in most of the other OECD countries. Most of this part-time work is concentrated in service-sector industries which need flexibility from their employees to meet their peaked patterns of business activity during the day (for example, in banks and restaurants) or during the week (for example, in shops). The majority of this part-time work is done by women. Nowhere is the figure for female part-time employment below 60 per cent and in a number of the developed countries it is well above this figure. In the United States, for example, by 1981 the figure was nearly 70 per cent and in the UK it was over 90 per cent for the same year. Further, the proportion of women in part-time work is increasing.

The second effect which the world-economic crisis has had on the state of employment opportunities has been to hasten the rise of an informal economy. According to Pahl (1980) the informal economy has two major components. The first is the household economy. Production in the household has increased enormously in the last 20 years in the developed countries as households have switched from buying services to producing their own. More precisely, households now increasingly buy goods, which are in effect capital equipment, to which they then add their own labour. So there has been a rise in do-it-yourself, in vegetable gardening, and so on. We no longer go to the laundry or employ servants; instead we use washing machines and vacuum cleaners which we operate ourselves. This is the rise of the so-called 'self-service economy' (Gershuny, 1978). The second component is the underground or clandestine economy (de Grazia, 1984), which consists of the production of goods and services that evade systems of public regulation and taxation. It takes three main forms. The first is the undeclared employment of workers, especially illegal immigrants (to be found among outworkers in the clothing industry and workers in building, agriculture, the hotel and catering trades, housework, etc.). The second is undeclared self-employment (to be found among workers in dressmaking, in car repairs, in household repairs, among those running a market stall, etc.). The final form is undeclared multiple jobholding (to be found especially now among teachers, businessmen and policemen). The numbers employed in each of these forms of employment are all on the increase.

This might not matter if the underground economy were small, but it is not [. . .] Clandestine employment is, of course, the only job that many workers have, especially the unemployed, migrant workers, pensioners and housewives. There are [. . .] over 500 000 clandestine immigrant workers in Europe and 5 million in the United States. Estimates vary concerning the number of the unemployed who have jobs, from 80 per cent in some *départements* of France to very few in parts of the UK (see Pahl, 1984). If the figures of those who have a clandestine second job are added in to the total then the numbers become very large indeed. In West Germany it is reckoned that 2 million workers, or 8 per cent of the workforce, have a second undeclared job. In France, Sweden and Belgium the proportion of the workforce so employed varies from 5 to 15 per cent. In the United States and Canada some estimates are as high as 25 per cent (International Labour Organization, 1984).

It is difficult to know precisely how the world-economic crisis has affected the informal economy but it has almost certainly fuelled its growth. Faced with competition, many firms have resorted to clandestine employment to reduce labour costs, and there are many more unemployed who are prepared to work at what they can find in order to eke out a living.

The developing countries

In the developing countries employment problems are far more serious because of the massive expansion of the labour base which makes the post-war baby boom in the developed countries seem insignificant [. . .] Certainly, it seems clear that the crisis did have an impact on the labour forces of the newly industrializing countries, which are more tightly linked to the world-economy. In these countries the crisis was transmitted through the manufacturing sector in the shape of labour demand for manufactured goods from the developed countries. But there are countervailing trends, in particular the related shift of manufacturing industry into developing countries, which make the exact effects difficult to quantify.

The truth is that figures on unemployment in the developing countries are hard to come by, difficult to compare because of differing definitions and applicable only to the wage labour force [. . .] In general, the unemployment rate does not seem particularly high by comparison with rates in the developed countries. However, the *underemployment* rate (those who are in employment of less than normal duration) is very high. In the Asian economies, for example, it is estimated that 40 per cent of rural workers are underemployed, as are 23 per cent of urban workers.

As in the developed centres, so in the developing countries, the world economic crisis has had effects on the structure of employment opportunities [. . .] The first important effect has a close parallel with the growth in the developed countries of the so-called *urban informal sector* of employment (Bromley and Gerry, 1979; Sethuraman, 1981). It seems certain that the world-economic crisis has speeded the expansion of this sector.

The urban informal sector consists of what is often the largest part of the urban labour force in the developing countries, workers who carry on their livelihoods outside the domain of public regulation and taxation. The activities that are included in this sector are too diverse to itemize one by one, but they include small-scale commodity production (for example, of bicycles) and repair shops, street vending (the selling of food, cigarettes and drink), the operation of low-income forms of transport (such as tricycles, scooter-based three-wheelers and jeeps), and a whole range of activities that are often illegal, such as prostitution and running drinking dens. The urban informal sector has come about, in part at least, because the activities that it comprises are the only activities that many rural–urban migrants – who stream into the cities of so many developing countries – can gain access to. Since the urban population of the developing countries is expected to double over the next two years, in great measure owing to rural–urban migration, it seems highly unlikely that the sector will diminish in size and highly likely that it will continue to grow. The world-economic crisis has directly affected this growth, especially through increasing the rates of migration into the cities in many countries as agricultural poverty has become more severe.

The second way in which the world-economic crisis has had effects on the structure of employment opportunities has been through manufacturing employment. Manufacturing has continued to grow as a proportion of total employment in nearly all developing countries and it has grown particularly fast in the newly industrializing countries. This growth has come about in part through the expansion of indigenous industries trying to satisfy new levels of consumer demand, in part through the demands of a thriving local construction industry, in part through aggressive (and usually state-led) export strategies, and in part through decisions made by many foreign-based multinational corporations to relocate some of their unskilled assembly production to the dozen or so newly industrializing countries, thus apparently providing the beginnings of a new world spatial division of labour often called the 'new international division of labour'.

The global effects of the world-economic crisis on employment opportunities

This new spatial division of labour is the first of four direct effects on employment of the economic restructuring that has taken place during the world-economic crisis which are truly global in character – that is, they are effects which span both the developed and developing countries and which have effects on the employment opportunities of both simultaneously. The other three effects are the growth of free trade zones, the growth of international migration and the growth of 'world cities'. Each of these effects will be considered in turn.

The new international division of labour

By 1980, 44 million workers were in jobs directly provided by multinational corporations (International Labour Organization, 1981). Much of this employment is provided by US-based multinational corporations. Thus the 500 largest United States corporations now employ an international labour force almost exactly the same size as their national labour force. In the period from 1960 to 1980 manufacturing employment outside the United States directly controlled by US-based multinational corporations increased from 8.7 per cent to 17.5 per cent of the total, a 169 per cent increase compared with a 20 per cent increase in the United States (Peet, 1983) [. . .] But, as would be expected, multinational corporations based in other countries have taken an increasingly large part of the total; in 1978 Japanese company subsidiaries employed about 650 000 people around the world (Nakase, 1981).

A new aspect of this pattern of employment by multinational corporations is that so much of it is in developing countries. Multinational corporations now employ 4 million workers, or 9 per cent of their labour force, in the developing countries, and the number of these workers has been growing much faster in these countries than in most of the developed nations [. . .] The increasing presence of workers employed by multinational corporations in developing countries (in manufacturing in particular) has led some writers to posit the existence of a new international division of labour (Frobel, Heinrichs and Kreye, 1980; Tharakan, 1980) – in which the parts of the production process which require cheap, unskilled labour are relocated to the Third World. One reason why this new international division of labour has taken root has been the breakdown of traditional economic and social structures in many developing countries, leading to an inexhaustible supply of cheap labour. Another reason has been that the production process has become more fragmented and more homogenized, making it possible for many sub-processes to be spatially separated and carried out by unskilled workers after very short training periods. A third reason is that as transport and communications technology have developed so it has become possible to carry out complete or partial production processes at many new sites around the world without prohibitive technical, organizational or cost problems.

The trouble with this simple explanation of the new international division of labour is that it is difficult to sustain the argument that it exists as a significant *global* tendency (Thrift, 1980). The most important component to this argument is that there is only limited evidence for the actual *relocation* of employment, that is for the direct physical movement of a plant from a location in a developed country to another in a developing country. Certainly such cases exist, but not in profusion. For example, Gaffikin and Nickson (1984) looked at all the redundancies announced by ten major British multinational corporations in the West Midlands region of Britain from September 1979 to October 1983: not one involved the direct relocation of plants to Third World locations. Another component is that there are real difficulties in interpreting the new international division of labour as simply the result of a search for low-cost wage locations by multinational corporations. Certainly wage levels *are* an important determinant, but other commentators (such as Faire, 1981) have argued that the need to control markets within developing countries is an equally important or even more important determinant of relocation even when this relocation is then accompanied by a significant growth of imports from plants located in these countries (Jenkins, 1984). Yet other commentators have argued that the higher level of labour discipline in developing countries, especially the fact that trade unions are outlawed or incorporated, is an important determinant.

It is clear that the new international division of labour is, in any case, limited in its impact, both by country and by industry. The redeployment of manufacturing employment by multinational corporations in the developing countries has generally been restricted to a very few countries, mainly the newly industrializing ones. Even in the latter the part played by multinational corporations in stimulating employment varies enormously. In Singapore, for example, the share of employment in both foreign-owned and joint-venture firms rose from 33 per cent in 1963 to 69 per cent in 1978. In the Republic of Korea and Hong Kong, however, the proportions were much smaller, at 10 per cent in 1978 and 11 per cent in 1971/2, respectively (see International Labour Organization, 1984; Jenkins, 1984; United Nations, 1983).

Moreover, the new international division of labour is restricted to a few industries, especially textiles and clothing (Clairmonte and Cavanagh,

1981) and electronics (Morgan and Sayer, 1983; Economist Intelligence Unit, 1984), where the economic and technological considerations of making particular products make it more difficult to increase mechanization with existing technologies and much easier to relocate production abroad [. . .] While multinational corporations' involvement in production abroad in textiles and clothing is considerable, in the electronics industry – where the newly industrializing countries have severe problems in terms of gaining access to technology, and sufficient capital for research – multinational corporations' involvement in production is all but total. In the electronics industry the tendency for multinational corporations to shift the assembly and simple testing stages of production to developing countries has been almost irresistible [. . .]

So, seen in the narrow sense as the relocation of elements of the production process to developing countries by multinational corporations searching for low wages, the new international division of labour is of less importance than originally thought. Indeed, some writers have gone so far as to suggest that the phenomenon may even be temporally limited if the costs of automation of these elements of the production process reach the point where they offset the advantages which peripheral low-wage locations may now give (see Jenkins, 1984).

However, the new international division of labour is of much greater significance if to the direct shift in employment from developed to developing countries is added the relative shift in employment between the countries of the world, a shift which favours the developing countries. Seen in this light, the concept has very considerable merit in describing the employment outcomes of the strategies pursued by multinational corporations as they have restructured during the world-economic crisis. Then the spatial pattern of employment more or less follows the spatial pattern of direct investment outlined above.

In particular, there is a general fall-off in the labour force of most multinational corporations in response to the restructuring needed to weather the world-economic crisis. But within this trend of a general decline there is a shift in where the remaining employment is concentrated because employment falls more in certain countries and falls less, if at all, in others. Specifically, employment decreases more in the home countries of multinational corporations, and decreases less, or even expands, in other countries and especially in some of the developing countries. For example, among European multinational corporations there has been a greater tendency for employment to fall in the home country's plants and offices, while staying static in Europe and expanding in North America and some of the developing countries [. . .]

The case of ICI in the years from 1970 to 1983 is indicative. ICI was originally formed in 1926. A large number of products are made and marketed by the corporation, including fertilizers, fibres, general chemicals, organic chemicals, industrial explosives, paints, petrochemicals, pharmaceuticals and plastics. In the 1970s ICI ran into trouble. Too many of its products were in declining markets like fibres, petrochemicals and plastics. The result was that the corporation was forced to restructure its operations worldwide, in the process making the transition from a multinational to a global corporation. It now has factories in more than 40 countries and selling organizations in more than 60.

In the process of restructuring a very different division of labour was produced within the corporation, which is reflected in the employment figures for its regional divisions. In general, there was a decrease in employment within the corporation. Employment rose from 190 000 in 1970 to 192 000 in 1975 but then fell to only 117 900 in 1983, so that over the 1970–83 period there was a 38 per cent drop in the workforce. However, there was a particularly massive drop in employment in the United Kingdom, from 137 000 in 1970 to 132 000 in 1975 to only 61 800 in 1983, a 55 per cent decrease, which contrasted with a relative increase in employment elsewhere. In fact, most regional divisions recorded an absolute loss of employment but a relative increase. However, two divisons – the Indian subcontinent, and Australia and the Far East – also recorded an absolute increase (most of the employment increase in the Australian and Far East division was in south-east Asia).

Reinterpreted in this more general light the new international division of labour is a general tendency which has undoubtedly had serious repercussions on employment prospects of workers in developed countries, particularly in those countries with 'open' economies. These are countries like The Netherlands, Sweden and the United Kingdom whose corporations have historically carried out much of their production overseas [. . .] and which are themselves extensively penetrated by multinational corporations. In these countries the behaviour of just their 'own' multinational corporations has led to extensive job loss.

Export-processing zones

Governments have not stood idly by as the refurbishing of the world-economy has taken place. They have been active participants in all the ways mentioned in the first part of this chapter. But one relatively new phenomenon whose period of growth coincides with the world-economic crisis has been the export-processing zone, an adaptation of the free trade zone which has been common around many ports for some time (Currie, 1979; Marsden, 1980; Salita and Juanico, 1983; Wong and Chu, 1984), and now a response by governments, especially the governments of the developing countries, to the new international division of labour [. . .]

The United Nations Industrial Development Organization (UNIDO) defines export-processing zones as 'small closely definable areas within countries in which favourable investment and trade conditions are created to attract export-oriented industries, usually foreign-owned'. Within export-processing zones four conditions are usually found. First, import provisions are made for goods used in the production of items for duty-free export and export duties are waived. There is no foreign exchange control and there is generally freedom to repatriate profits. Second, infrastructure, utilities, factory space and warehousing are usually provided at subsidized rates. Third, tax holidays, usually of five years, are offered. Finally, abundant, disciplined labour is provided at low wage rates.

The first successful implementation of an export-processing zone was in 1956 at Ireland's Shannon International Airport. Puerto Rico (in 1962) and India (in 1965) were the first two developing countries to follow suit followed by Taiwan, the Philippines, the Dominican Republic, Mexico, Panama and Brazil in the period from 1966 to 1970 (Wong and Chu, 1984). The great expansion in the number of such zones came after 1970. By 1975 there were 31 zones in 18 countries. By the early 1980s at least 68 zones were established in 40 (principally developing) countries. The major world regions in which they are found are in the Caribbean, Central and Latin America, and Asia, although there are also a few in Africa. In the rest of this section particular attention will be given to the cases of Mexico and Asia [. . .]

Export-processing zones have three chief characteristics connected with the type of industry to be found in the zones, the number in the labour force and labour-force composition. Each of these characteristics will be examined in turn.

Most of the industry in the export-processing zones is owned by foreign-based multinational corporations and, not surprisingly, most employment in export-processing zones is in the two industries that have expanded strongly in developing countries (partly as a result of multinational corporations' intervention), namely electrical and electronic goods and textiles and clothing. In Mexico in 1978, 60 per cent of the *maquiladoras*, the assembly-plant factories located in special zones near the United States border with Mexico, were concerned with electronics and electrical assembly, while 30 per cent were in textiles and clothing (Hansen, 1981). In Asia, approximately 60 per cent of employment is in the electronics industry with the clothing and footwear industries second. The advent of electronics companies is fairly recent, which makes the build-up even more impressive [. . .]

The numbers employed in the export-processing zones [. . .] are modest, with a few exceptions. The case of Mexico is well known. In 1980 *maquiladora* employment was estimated to be over 110 000. Juarez alone accounted for 115 plants and 40 000 workers, including major United States corporations such as RCA, Ford, General Motors, Chrysler and General Electric, as well as Japanese companies. Some of the zones in Asia have also generated considerable employment. There are about 500 000 workers directly employed in export-processing zones in Asia. But, of this number, nearly 50 per cent are employed in the zones of Singapore (105 000) and South Korea (121 700). Zone employment is also comparatively high in Malaysia (73 000) and Hong Kong (70 000).

Most employment in the zones, usually over 75 per cent, is of young, unmarried women aged between 17 and 23; in Mexico about 85 per cent of *maquiladora* employment is of young women. In some of the zones in Asia the figures are even higher. In Sri Lanka young women account for 88 per cent of zone employment, in Malaysia and Taiwan 85 per cent, in South Korea 75 per cent and the Philippines 74 per cent (Morello, 1983).

Young women are employed because their wages can be lower than men's and because they are considered 'dexterous' and 'more able to cope with repetitive work'. Very little skill is required of them, certainly, and wages are very low, often less than 50 US cents per hour. Overtime and incentive payments account for a high proportion of wages. Working weeks range from 45 to 55 hours. What is more, in some zones the iniquitous trainee system is used, in which 'trainees' are paid only 60 to 75 per cent of the local minimum wages and are constantly fired and rehired so as to obtain a permanent 40 per cent reduction in the wages bill.

Weighing up the advantages and disadvantages of export-processing zones to the centres in which they are located is no simple task. There is the matter of employment creation. In some areas, the employment advantages have been substantial [. . .] But except in these few cases the impact of the zones on joblessness has been marginal and even in the successful cases most of the employment created has been temporary and lowly paid [. . .] Then there is the matter of the generation of foreign exchange. This can be high: the foreign exchange generated by the *maquiladora* industries in Mexico is fourth after oil revenues, remittances and tourism. But the figures can be deceptive: in 1981 the value of the Philippines' three export-processing zones export total was US $236.2 million but the figure for exports minus the imports into the zones was only US $62.5 million, and this was *before* interest payments and repatriation of profits was taken into account (Morello, 1983).

It is arguable that export-processing zones, through their linkages to local firms, might create extra employment outside. But in fact links to local economies are generally minimal [. . .] Finally, other advantages have been mooted such as transfer of technology and upgrading of workers' skills; little evidence of these can be found. Indeed, the export-processing zones' concentration on electronics assembly and textiles and clothing limits worker training to simple, quickly mastered skills. The more complex production processes remain in the developed countries.

To sum up, export-processing zones are marginal in most, although not all, cases [. . .] Further, competition between zones is now undermining what benefits there were. Competitive bidding for firms between prospective sites has resulted in more and more incentives having to be offered. Tax holidays are now being extended from five to ten years in many zones as evidence mounts that multinational corporations will simply relocate when these holidays come to an end [. . .] So export-processing zones are, on the whole, a much commented upon but relatively unimportant outgrowth of the new international division of labour. Estimates vary, but it is unlikely that they currently employ more than a million workers worldwide – this is a drop in the ocean.

International migration

The export-processing zone represents an attempt to bring work to the workers. Another solution is for workers to go to the work. International migration has been an important part of the world-economic system since before the turn of the century, but the world-economic crisis has influenced international migration in new ways (Portes and Walton, 1981; Petras and McLean, 1981).

The International Labour Organization (1984) estimates the stock of economically active migrants in the world today as between 19.7 and 21.7 million (plus a similar number of dependants living with them). In general, the flow of migrants is from the less economically successful countries to the most economically successful. Thus the United States had some 5 million legal immigrants in 1979, half of whom were in the labour force and two-thirds from developing countries, with a further 2.5 to 4 million illegal immigrants, most in the labour force and nearly all from Mexico. Canada also has a large immigrant workforce. Western Europe has numerous economically active immigrants, perhaps as many as 6.3 million [. . .] The Arab countries employ some 2.8 million foreigners, nearly all of whom are from developing countries [. . .] But many developing countries also have substantial migrant-worker labour forces; those of South America have 3.5 to 4 million migrant workers and those of West Africa have 1.3 million (International Labour Organization, 1984). This migration has considerable economic importance for all the countries concerned, increasing the interdependence of the world-economy [. . .]

Conventionally, international migration is split into four categories: settlement migration, irregular migration, contract migration, and official and business migration. In each of these categories there has been some response to the world-economic crisis and the restructuring it has brought about. However, it is among contract migration and official and business migration that the most important responses can be found (see Petras and McLean, 1981).

Contract migration has grown swiftly during the period of the crisis, involving migration for a period of time which is dependent upon the issue of a contract by an employer in the country concerned. Indeed quite often a group of workers are admitted under a collective contract for the span of a particular project or part of a project. Thus a group of workers may be brought into a country on contract to build factories and infrastructure and they are then replaced by another group who specialize in operations and maintenance [. . .]

Official and business migration has also become more important in the period of the crisis as a result of increasing activity by multinational corporations, and especially of their 'globalization'. This category of migrants includes many types of temporary migrant, in particular the subcategory of businessmen and intra-company transferees. As businessmen have been forced to go from country to country more frequently, and as intra-company transfers of personnel have had to be made more often as multinational companies have grown larger and established themselves in more countries, so these subcategories have increased in proportion. Here patterns of migration closely mirror the internationalization of capital.

However, international migration has also produced problems as the world-economic crisis deepened. The potential number of international migrants is increasing in the poor countries of Asia, Central and Latin America and Africa but the opportunities for employment in the developed countries are falling away. It is no surprise, then, that many developed countries are now trying to rid themselves of the 1950s and 1960s boom who originally formed a useful substratum of the working class but in the recession have formed the leading ranks of the unemployed [. . .]

The growth of the international service economy

The final global effect of the crisis on employment opportunities has been the growth of a new international service economy based upon corporate activities. This growth can be traced to the internationalization of production and especially the growth of global corporations with their large internal markets which require considerable administration. Much of this administration is carried out *within* corporations, especially through new innovations like the regional headquarters office (see Heenan, 1977; Grosse, 1982; Dunning and Norman, 1983). (Regional headquarters offices provide the intermediate tier of management between the administration, much of it strategic, carried out by the head office of a corporation and the administration, much of it routine, carried out by regional branch offices. They are responsible for definable regions of the world such as Asia and the Pacific, and are intended to reduce the internal transactions costs of moving information and making decisions within the global corporation.) However, the growth of the administrative load has been such that it has also stimulated the growth of more and more producer services. These are services which could, no doubt, be produced within the corporation but which, for various reasons, especially because they can be obtained more cheaply outside are externalized and bought in. Producer services, then, are 'activities that assist user firms in carrying out administrative, developmental (research and development, strategic planning), and financial functions, banking, insurance, real estate, accounting, legal services, consulting, advertising and so forth' (Noyelle, 1983a, pp. 117–18). All these services have internationalized too, sometimes following in the wake of the multinational corporations, but sometimes expanding independently of them as well (see Thrift, 1985). For example, banks have internationalized to meet the financial needs of their corporate customers but also in order to search for new customers.

The most important result of the growth of corporate administration and related producer services has been the growth of a complex of corporate activities, which has had important results for employment. For example, in [. . .] the United Kingdom Daniels (1985) [see Chapter 5] estimated that by 1981 as much as 22 per cent of service employment was in producer services.

The main result of the worldwide growth of this complex of corporate activities has been the formation of the so-called world cities [. . .] For various reasons, producer services have tended to develop in a very selective hierarchy of key urban centres round the world in which they have come to dominate economic life. The world cities occupy the top of this hierarchy, and can be divided into three (Daly, 1984). First, there are the truly international centres – New York, London, Paris, Zurich and Hamburg. These contain many head offices, branch offices and regional headquarters offices of the large corporations, and include the head offices or representative offices of many banks. They account for most large business dealings on a world scale. Second, there are the *zonal* centres – Singapore, Hong Kong, Los Angeles. These also have many corporate offices of various types and serve as important links in the international financial system but they are responsible for particular zones rather than for business on a world scale. Finally, there are the *regional* centres – Sydney, Chicago, Dallas, Miami, Honolulu and San Francisco. These host many corporate offices and foreign financial outlets but they are not essential links in the international financial system. Some specialize in providing space for corporate regional headquarters serving particular regions [. . .]

The importance of employment in producer services in these cities should not be underestimated. London, for example, is now a massive corporate complex with 24 per cent of the United Kingdom's office space. In 1977, 525 out of the *Times* top 1000 companies had their headquarters there (Goddard and Smith, 1978); 72 of the largest US-based multinational corporations and 11 of the largest Japanese-based multinational corporations had their regional headquarters in London. In 1983, in keeping with the city's role as a corporate complex and the chief node of the Eurocurrency market, there were 391 foreign banks directly represented in London. A further 69 were indirectly represented, and there were 94 foreign securities houses. In all 38 020 people were directly employed in these financial institutions in 1983 (*The Banker*, 1983) and Daniels (1985) [Chapter 5] has calculated that, in 1981, 467 000 workers were employed in Greater London in banking, finance, insurance, business services and leasing. London is only one such case. In 1982 Hong Kong received 26 per cent of its GDP from financial services and more than 5 per cent of its employment was in finance, insurance, real estate and business services. In the same year, Singapore received 20 per cent of its GDP from financial services, and producer services accounted for nearly 8 per cent of the island's employment.

But the trend towards greater centralization of corporate complexes – which still seems to be going on (see Noyelle, 1983b) – has some negative effects. In particular, while some privileged cities can derive prosperity from being the location of corporate complexes, other cities get only the leftovers, the manufacturing jobs and the lowlier service jobs. Thus the international services economy increasingly bypasses many cities and many workers.

1.3   Conclusions

Perhaps the most important conclusion to draw from this chapter is that, as a result of the world-economic crisis, the world-economy has become more integrated than ever before. There are new links between multinational corporations, banks and countries and the old links have been strengthened.

Take, first, the interconnections between the multinational corporations and the banks. The internationalization of production and finance has forged much closer links between the two. Company finance and profits now depend on interest rate and currency swaps, on Eurobond issues, on financial futures and on foreign exchange options, all usually arranged by the banks. Banks advise on corporate finance, on mergers, on acquisitions. And banks are increasingly the shareholders of the multinational corporations [. . .] Second, the ties between multinational corporations and countries have been strengthened. In nearly every nation of the world the level of foreign direct investment has increased and national economies have consequently become more 'open'. Indeed, country action to prevent import penetration by the use of tariffs and other barriers has only hastened this process. In a few countries like the United Kingdom and The Netherlands, which have particularly high levels of foreign direct investment and which conduct much of their production abroad, it is possible to ask whether a coherent national economy still exists (Radice, 1984). Finally, there are much greater connections now between countries and banks. The present international debt crisis is simply the most extreme illustration of this fact (Lipietz, 1984a).

The greater level of integration of the world-economy should not be overemphasized. The rise of a new world-economic order does not give overwhelming power to the multinational corporation, it does not give the banks total control, and it does not mean the end of national sovereignty. The internationalization of capital, understood in its broadest sense, is a very messy business. It is, as Michalet (1976) has pointed out, a process which produces partial outcomes; it is not an economic apocalypse. But it is still the most important economic event taking place in the world at present and it is having crucial reverberations – economic, social and cultural – on many countries [. . .]

References

AGLIETTA, M. (1979) *A Theory of Capitalist Regulation: The US Experience*, London, New Left Books.

AGLIETTA, M. (1982) 'World capitalism in the eighties', *New Left Review*, No. 136, pp. 25–36.

ALIBER, R. Z. (1979) *The International Money Game*, New York, Basic Books.

ANDREFF, W. (1984) 'The international centralization of capital and the re-ordering of world capitalism', *Capital and Class*, No. 22, pp. 58–80.

BLOOMFIELD, G. T. (1981) 'The changing spatial organisation of multinational corporations in the world automative industry', in Hamilton, F. E. I. and Linge, G. J. R. (eds) (1981a) pp. 357–94.

BORA, G. (1981) 'International division of labour and the national industrial system: the case of Hungary', in Hamilton, F. E. I. and Linge, G. J. R. (eds) (1981a) pp. 155–84.

BRETT, E. A. (1983) *International Money and Capitalist Crisis: The Anatomy of Global Disintegration*, London, Heinemann.

BREWER, A. (1980) *Marxist Theories of Imperialism*, London, Routledge and Kegan Paul.

BROMLEY, R. and GERRY, C. (eds) (1979) *Casual Work and Poverty in Third World Cities*, Chichester, Wiley.

BRUNNER, K. (ed.) (1981) *The Great Depression Revisited*, Boston, Kluwer Nijhoff.

CLAIRMONTE, F. and CAVANAGH, J. (1981) *The World in their Web: Dynamics of Textile Multinationals*, London, Zed Press.

COAKLEY, J. (1984) 'The internationalisation of bank capital', *Capital and Class*, No. 23, pp. 107–20.

COAKLEY, J. and HARRIS, L. (1983) *The City of Capital*, Oxford, Basil Blackwell.

COHEN, R. B. (1983) 'The new spatial organisation of the European and American automotive industries', in Moulaert, F. W. and Salinas, P. B. (eds), *Regional Analysis and the New International Division of Labour*, Boston, Kluwer Nijhoff, pp. 135–43.

CURRIE, J. (1979) 'Investment: the growing role of export processing zones', *Economist Intelligence Unit Special Report* 64, London, Economist Intelligence Unit.

DALY, M. T. (1984) 'The revolution in international capital markets: urban growth and Australian cities', *Environment and Planning A*, Vol. 16, pp. 1003–20.

DANIELS, P. (1985) 'Producer services and the post-industrial economy', in Martin, R. L. and Rowthorn, B. (eds), *Deindustrialisation and the British Space Economy*, Cambridge, Cambridge University Press. (Reprinted as Chapter 5 in this Reader.)

DE GRAZIA, R. (1984) *Clandestine Employment*, Geneva, International Labour Office.

DELAMAIDE, D. (1984) *Debt Shock*, London, Weidenfeld and Nicolson.

DE VROEY, M. (1984) 'A regulation approach interpretation of contemporary crisis', *Capital and Class*, No. 23, pp. 45–66.

DICKEN, P. (1980) 'Foreign direct investment in European manufacturing industry: the changing position of the United Kingdom as a host country', *Geoforum*, Vol. 11, pp. 289–313.

DICKEN, P. (1982) 'Recent trends in international direct investment, with particular reference to the United States and the United Kingdom', in Robson, B. T. and Rees, J. (eds), *Geographical Agenda for a Changing World*, London, Social Science Research Council, pp. 118–61.

DUNNING, J. H. and NORMAN, G. (1983) 'The theory of the multinational enterprise: an application to multinational office location', *Environment and Planning A*, Vol. 15, pp. 675–92.

DUNNING, J. H. and PEARCE, C. D. (1981) *The World's Largest Industrial Enterprises*, Farnborough, Gower.

ECONOMIST INTELLIGENCE UNIT (1984) 'How to make offshore manufacturing pay', *Economist Intelligence Unit Special Report* 171, London, Economist Intelligence Unit.

FAIRE, A. (1981) 'The strategies of economic redeployment in the West', *Review*, No. 2.

FRANKO, L. G. (1983) *The Japanese Multinational*, Chichester, Wiley.

FROBEL, F. (1983) 'The current development of the world economy: reproduction of labour and accumulation of capital on a world scale', *Review*, No. 5, pp. 507–55.

FROBEL, F., HEINRICHS, J. and KREYE, O. (1980) *The New International Division of Labour*, Cambridge, Cambridge University Press.

FUJITA, M. and ISHIGAKI, K. (1985) 'The internationalisation of Japanese banking', in Taylor, M. J. and Thrift, N. J. (eds), *Multinationals and the Restructuring of the World Economy*, London, Croom Helm.

GAFFIKIN, F. and NICKSON, A. (1984) *Jobs Crisis and the Multinationals: The Case of the West Midlands*, Nottingham, Russell Press.

GERSHUNY, J. (1978) *The Self-Service Economy*, London, Frances Pinter.

GODDARD, J. B. and SMITH, I. J. (1978) 'Changes in corporate control in the British urban system, 1972–1977', *Environment and Planning A*, Vol. 10, pp. 1073–84.

GORASTIAGA, X. (1983) *International Financial Centres in Underdeveloped Countries*, London, Croom Helm.

GROSSE, R. E. (1982) 'Regional offices in multinational firms', in Rugman, A. M. (ed.), *New Theories of the Multinational Enterprise*, London, Croom Helm, pp. 107–32.

GUTMAN, P. and ARKWRIGHT, F. (1981) 'Tripartite industrial cooperation between East, West and South', in Hamilton, F. E. I. and Linge, G. J. R. (eds) (1981a) pp. 185–214.

HAMILTON, F. E. I. and LINGE, G. J. R. (eds) (1981a) *Spatial Analysis, Industry and the Industrial Environment*, Vol. 2: *International Industrial Systems*, Chichester, Wiley.

HAMILTON, F. E. I. and LINGE, G. J. R. (eds) (1981b) *Spatial Analysis, Industry and the Industrial Environment*, Vol. 3: *Regional Economies and Industrial Systems*, Chichester, Wiley.

HANSEN, N. (1981) 'Mexico's border industry and the international division of labour', *Annals of Regional Science*, Vol. 15, pp. 1–12.

HARRIS, N. (1982) 'The road from 1910', *Economy and Society*, Vol. 12, pp. 347–62.

HEENAN, D. A. (1977) 'Global cities of tomorrow', *Harvard Business Review*, Vol. 55, pp. 79–92.

INTERNATIONAL LABOUR ORGANIZATION (1981) *Employment Effects of Multinational Enterprises in Developing Countries*, Geneva, International Labour Office.

INTERNATIONAL LABOUR ORGANIZATION (1984) *World Labour Report 1. Employment, Incomes, Social Protection, New Information Technology*. Geneva. International Labour Office.

JENKINS, R. (1984) 'Divisions over the international division of labour', *Capital and Class*, No. 22, pp. 28–57.

KINDLEBERGER, C. P. (1973) *The World in Depression 1929–1939*, London, Allen Lane.

KIRBY, S. R. (1983) 'Towards the Pacific Century. Economic Development in the Pacific Basin', *Economic Intelligence Unit Special Report* 137, London, Economist Intelligence Unit.

KORTUS, B. and KACZEROWSKI, W. (1981) 'Polish industry forges external links', in Hamilton, F. E. I. and Linge, G. J. R. (eds) (1981a) pp. 119–54.

LALL, S. (1984) *The New Multinationals: The Spread of Third World Enterprises*, Chichester, Wiley.

LIPIETZ, A. (1984a) 'How monetarism has choked third world industrialisation', *New Left Review*, No. 145, pp. 71–87.

LIPIETZ, A. (1984b) 'Imperialism or the beast of the apocalypse', *Capital and Class*, No. 22, pp. 81–109.

MARGIRIER, G. (1983) 'The eighties: a second phase of crisis?', *Capital and Class*, No. 21, pp. 61–86.

MARSDEN, J. (1980) 'Export processing zones in developing countries', *UNIDO Working Papers on Structural Change* No. 19.

MENDELSOHN, M. S. (1980) *Money on the Move*, New York, McGraw-Hill.

MICHALET, C. A. (1976) *Le Capitalisme Mondial*, Paris, Presses Universitaires de France.

MITRA, P. M. (1983) 'World Bank research on adjustment to external shocks', *World Bank Research News*, Vol. 4, No. 3, pp. 3–14.

MORELLO, T. (1983) 'Sweatshops in the sun?' *Far Eastern Economic Review*, 15 September, pp. 88–9.

MORGAN, K. and SAYER, A. (1983) 'The international electronics industry and regional development in Britain', *University of Sussex, Urban and Regional Studies, Working Paper* No. 34.

NAKASE, T. (1981) 'Some characteristics of Japanese-type multinationals today', *Capital and Class*, No. 13, pp. 61–98.

NEUBERGER, E. and TYSSON, L. D. (eds) (1980) *The Impact of International Economic Disturbances on the Soviet Union and Eastern Europe*, Oxford, Pergamon.

NOYELLE, T. J. (1983a) 'The implications of industry restructuring for spatial organisation in the United States', in Moulaert, F. and Salinas, P. W. (eds), *Regional Analysis and the New International Division of Labour*, Boston, Kluwer Nijhoff, pp. 113–33.

NOYELLE, T. J. (1983b) 'The rise of advanced services. Some implications for economic development in U.S. cities', *Journal of the American Planning Association*, Vol. 25, pp. 280–90.

OECD (1977) *Towards Full Employment and Price Stability*, Paris, OECD.

PAHL, R. E. (1980) 'Employment, work and the domestic division of labour', *International Journal of Urban and Regional Research*, Vol. 4, pp. 1–19.

PAHL, R. E. (1984) *Divisions of Labour*, Oxford, Basil Blackwell.

PARBONI, R. (1981) *The Dollar and its Rivals*, London, Verso.

PEET, J. R. (1983) 'Relations of production and the relocation of United States manufacturing industry since 1960', *Economic Geography*, Vol. 59, pp. 112–43.

PETRAS, E. and McLEAN, M. (1981) 'The global labour market in the world economy', in Kritz, M. M., Keely, C. B. and Tomasi, S. M. (eds), *Global Trends in Migration*, New York, Centre for Migration Studies, pp. 44–63.

PORTES, A. and WALTON, J. (1981) *Labour, Class and the International System*, New York, Academic Press.

RADICE, H. (1984) 'The national economy – a Keynesian myth?', *Capital and Class*, No. 22, pp. 111–40.

REES, J. (1978) 'On the spatial spread and oligopolistic behaviour of large rubber companies', *Geoforum*, Vol. 9, pp. 319–30.

RODDICK, J. (1984) 'Crisis, Seignorage and the modern world system; rising third world power or declining US hegemony', *Capital and Class*, No. 23, pp. 121–34.

RUGMAN, A. M. (1981) *Inside the Multinationals*, London, Croom Helm.

RUGMAN, A. M. (ed.) (1982) *New Theories of the Multinational Enterprise*, London, Croom Helm.

SALITA, D. C. and JUANICO, M. B. (1983) 'Export processing zones: new catalysts for economic development', in Hamilton, F. E. I. and Linge, G. J. R. (eds) (1981b) pp. 441–61.

SAMPSON, A. (1981) *The Money Lenders*, London, Hodder and Stoughton.

SAVEY, S. (1981) 'Pechiney Ugine Kuhlmann: a French multinational corporation', in Hamilton, F. E. I. and Linge, G. J. R. (eds) (1981a) pp. 305–27.

SETHURAMAN, S. V. (ed.) (1981) *The Urban Informal Sector in Developing Countries*, Geneva, International Labour Office.

TAYLOR, M. J. and THRIFT, N. J. (eds) (1982) *The Geography of Multinationals*, London, Croom Helm.

TEULINGS, A. W. M. (1984) 'The internationalisation squeeze: double capital movement and job transfer within Philips worldwide', *Environment and Planning A*, Vol. 16, pp. 565–706.

THARAKAN, P. M. (1980) *The New International Division of Labour and Multinational Companies*, Farnborough, Saxon House.

THRIFT, N. J. (1980) 'Frobel and the new international division of labour', in Peet, J. R. (ed.), *An Introduction to Marxist Theories of Underdevelopment*, Australian National University, Department of Human Geography, HG14, pp. 181–9.

THRIFT N. J. (1985) 'The internationalisation of producer services and the integration of the Pacific Basin property market', in Taylor, M. J. and Thrift, N. J. (eds), *Multinationals and the Restructuring of the World Economy*, London, Croom Helm.

UNITED NATIONS (1983) *Transnational Corporations in World Development: Third Study*, New York, United Nations.

VERSLUYEN, E. (1981) *The Political Economy of International Finance*, London, Gower.

WALLERSTEIN, I. (1979) *The Capitalist World Economy*, Cambridge, Cambridge University Press.

WALLERSTEIN, I. (1983) *Historical Capitalism*, London, New Left Books.

WELLS, L. T., Jr (1983) *Third World Multinationals: The Rise of Foreign Investment from Developing Countries*, Cambridge, Mass., MIT Press.

WONG, K. and CHU, D. K. Y. (1984) 'Export processing zones and special economic zones as generators of economic development: the Asian experience', *Geografiska Annaler*, Series B, Vol. 66, pp. 1–16.

WORLD BANK (1983) *World Development Report 1983*, Oxford, World Bank/Oxford University Press.

YOSHIHARA, H. (1977) 'The Japanese multinational', *Long Range Planning*, Vol. 10, pp. 41–5.

Section II   Manufacturing employment change

Introduction

The core focus of this Section is the changing geography of manufacturing. Both chapters start from the phenomenon which has dominated debate since the 1970s: deindustrialization. From that starting-point, however, the arguments develop in very different directions.

For Hall, deindustrialization means the loss of manufacturing jobs, a process which he identifies in First World countries as resulting from shifts at international level. His concern is to argue that this happens as industries 'age', as they become less profitable, and that the important thing is to analyse the conditions for the birth of new industries. Such conditions, he argues, will not be found in the same regions where the old sectors flourished. There is therefore a contrast, in countries such as the UK where both types of region are to be found, between regions locked into the traditional industrial – and associated social – structures of the past, and those where the industries of the future are being born. Fothergill, Gudgin, Kitson and Monk have a wider definition of deindustrialization, seeing it more in terms of the changing structure of the economy as a whole, including the shift from manufacturing to services and the failure of the UK economy to grow at a sufficient rate to provide 'full employment'. Their particular focus, however, is on the different ways in which urban and rural areas have been affected by the national decline in manufacturing and the reduction in its share of total employment.

It might also appear, therefore, that the two chapters are asking questions about different kinds of geographical change: that Hall's focus is on interregional change and Fothergill, Gudgin, Kitson and Monk's is on the shift from urban to rural. But that is probably to misread the issue. Rather it is that for Hall the decline of the inner areas of cities is the most recent manifestation of a more general process, which is afflicting other old industrial areas too, whereby new generations of industries customarily grow up in places away from those now in decline. Here, then, there is no particular distinction between urban and regional levels of analysis. For Fothergill, Gudgin, Kitson and Monk, however, one of the keys to explaining interregional shifts in manufacturing employment is the movement of such jobs away from cities: 'highly urban regions have declined; more rural regions have grown.'

Behind these contrasting positions, and explaining them, lie two very different theoretical positions. Hall is one of a number of writers who have used the notion of long waves, based on the debate deriving from the work of Kondratiev, to explain uneven development within individual economies. In this chapter he uses the currently changing economic geographies of the United States and the United Kingdom to explore what might be the spatial form of a new upswing – the geography of the fifth Kondratiev. In contrast to Fothergill, Gudgin, Kitson and Monk, therefore, whose enquiry concerns the reasons for the concentration of manufacturing decline in the cities, Hall's interest is in the geography of growth. His focus continues to be on manufacturing, but on manufacturing based around new technologies. There is some assumption, therefore, though it is implicit, that at least some of the basis of a transformed economic geography of the country will be based on manufacturing. And the key to his explanation of this changing spatial pattern is the geography of innovation and entrepreneurship, the key elements in a new upswing.

Fothergill, Gudgin, Kitson and Monk also examine changes in manufacturing in a long historical perspective. What they identify as crucial, however, is not cyclical upswings and downswings associated with different technologies, but a long, slow process, which may have begun as long ago as the late nineteenth and early twentieth centuries, of the relative decline of urban manufacturing employment. It is a process which has varied in intensity, but as a result mainly of shifts in wider national economic conditions, rather than in any regular cyclical fashion.

So the tempos of change discussed in the two chapters are distinct. So also are the basic mechanisms. For Hall it is the clustering of innovations (both historically and geographically) in successive new technologies which is fundamental to the subsequent cycles of growth and maturity. For Fothergill, Gudgin, Kitson and Monk the central mechanism is the long-term increase in labour productivity (output per employee) in manufacturing, combined with the fact that output per unit of floorspace has remained, according to them, more or less constant. The outcome is a declining number of workers per unit of floorspace. In this context, the very nature of cities as already developed and densely developed areas means that while, like all areas, they will lose workers on existing floorspace, they are likely to get only a small proportion of new development. The result is employment decline.

There is, then, putting these arguments together, a further contrast between the two chapters. This concerns their assessment of the kind of change which is under way. For Hall it is clearly a structural change, in the sense that it is a historical turning-point – the end of one long wave and the beginning of the next. For Fothergill, Gudgin, Kitson and Monk the assessment is less clear. There have clearly been recent periods when the deindustrialization of the city has proceeded particularly fast, but this was the result only of the speeding up of long-term underlying tendencies, not because of any change in direction. (One caveat here is that their analysis is necessarily somewhat constrained by the date at which it was done. The data goes up to the early 1980s and much of it exhibits important shifts in the last years. It is not possible to tell if such shifts mark the beginning of a more major change, and the assumption is made that they are the temporary effects of recession under particular government policies.) The distinct tempos of the changes discussed in the chapters, and the distinct views of the importance of structural change, do not mean that the two approaches are necessarily incompatible. But neither can they simply be 'added together' to deal with different time-spans and different processes. For they exhibit contrasts in other ways too.

Both chapters consider the current relative decline of cities. They agree that what is at issue is a combination of wider changes in industry and the particular character of urban areas. Interestingly both also reject what might be called a simple deindustrialization thesis, that manufacturing jobs are being lost nationally and most of that loss is happening in cities. For Hall, anyway, it is not 'terminal' deindustrialization which is at issue, but a downswing before a new upswing. For Fothergill, Gudgin, Kitson and Monk, even if manufacturing employment stayed stable nationally, without major intervention to provide sites in urban areas the cities would still lose manufacturing employment. For Hall, too, the future for cities, particularly older inner-city areas, is bleak. But the reasons are very different. For Hall the problem of the cities is not the lack of suitable sites, but the fact that they are, physically and perhaps most importantly socially, simply 'repellent' to the new industries and the 'highly-qualified, highly-paid, highly-mobile workforce' which works in them.

In that sense Hall's explanation rests more on 'social' factors than does that of Fothergill, Gudgin, Kitson and Monk. For Hall, while some people are 'highly-qualified . . .', others constitute 'a residual labour force' and 'the hard-to-employ'. There are fundamental differences in 'innovative entrepreneurship', and all these characteristics have a very definite geography. Fothergill, Gudgin, Kitson and Monk advance an explanation that is in a sense more 'technical'. Technological change makes decentralization possible, differences in rates of growth of labour productivity explain the shift from manufacturing to services, floorspace ratios are the basis of the urban-rural shift.

Yet behind all of these things are other social mechanisms. Fothergill, Gudgin, Kitson and Monk point out that their explanation of the relative decline of cities 'is an almost inevitable consequence of the process of economic change within an "advanced" capitalist economy', the result of the operation of market forces, but they do not develop the point. Hall's position seems contradictory. He ascribes the UK's industrial decline in part to its 'subsidizing uneconomic coal mines and steel mills' and argues that what is important is commercial viability – 'there must always be the ability to recognize what will sell'. Yet on his own analysis the successes of Silicon Valley in the USA and Cambridge and the M4 corridor in the UK owe much to government subsidy, whether through university research, government scientific establishments or defence contracts. What is commercially viable, and therefore in Hall's terms what is 'innovative', may actually be what is politically favoured. Indeed, his analysis of the 'post-war success stories' of Germany, France and Japan precisely indicates the importance of state intervention. The same issues of private and social costs and calculations are raised by Fothergill, Gudgin, Kitson and Monk when they talk, for instance, of 'the expense of reclaiming sites which have fallen derelict, and the scarcity of very large sites suitable for development as trading estates *by the private sector*' (emphasis added). Much of current government policy is precisely concerned to pay these costs in order to regenerate private sector investment once again in inner cities.

This raises, finally, the question of the future of inner cities and of big industrial cities more generally. According to Hall the future is not hopeful, but there are possibilities of change through government intervention. One possibility, though assessed as remote, is to generate a new entrepreneurial tradition in the cities. The other possibility is that 'some kinds of work' may be created there: 'low-paid assembly industry of the Third World type; similarly low-paid work in service industries ... to match demands for certain kinds of labour with the supply of them.' It must be stressed that this is not a necessary conclusion from a long-wave analysis (the work of Marshall (1987) and of Rothwell (1982), for example, both of which draw on the long-wave approach, come to different conclusions). For Fothergill, Gudgin, Kitson and Monk the future of cities is different. They make a clear distinction between a manufacturing future and one based more on service industries. The former is only possible both if there is national economic recovery and if there is local public sector intervention to provide for future land requirements geared to the demands of the local area. But even without manufacturing, cities are not to be written off. Even then, they are likely to survive, if reduced in size, as service centres for their wider regional hinterlands.

References

MARSHALL, M. (1987) *Long Waves of Regional Development*, London and Basingstoke, Macmillan.
ROTHWELL, R. (1982) 'The role of technology in industrial change: implications for regional policy', *Regional Studies*, Vol. 16, pp. 361–9.

2   The geography of the fifth Kondratieff

Peter Hall

Geographers, economists, planners and politicians throughout the advanced industrial countries have recently been haunted by the spectre of deindustrialization. Whole regions and cities are suddenly gripped by a kind of economic plague: within a very short order, as their factories massively contract or close completely, their economic base crumples and dies. This disease afflicts not merely regions traditionally vulnerable to the winds of economic fortune, like Central Scotland or South Wales and New England, but also areas formerly thought immune, like Britain's Birmingham and Coventry, America's New York City and Detroit.

2.1   The anatomy of job loss

There has been one good result, in the form of a flood of academic literature – first and still foremost in Great Britain, now developing in the United States – which has thrown light on some of the causes. In particular, geographers – both in Great Britain and in the United States – have devoted sustained and productive research effort to what can be called, in a title from two of them, *The Anatomy of Job Loss* (Massey and Meegan, 1982). Working within a Political Economy tradition, these writers have shown how heavy employment losses in advanced industrial countries, during the recession of the late 1970s and early 1980s, represent a logical reaction of the system of capitalist production to increasing competition and falling profits.

At the bottom of it is a process that economists call the *product cycle*, and that some among them are starting to call the *profit cycle* (Markusen, 1984). In the earliest stages of development of an industrial product – be it cotton textiles, steel or cars – the necessary technical knowledge is limited to a few people in the most advanced industrial countries of the day. Later, the knowledge is progressively diffused to more and more people in more and more countries. These countries, which are at an earlier stage of economic development, often possess a very vigorous entrepreneur class. They are also apt to have large numbers of workers, pouring off the land and into the cities, happy to take work at almost any price. Details like trades unions, health and safety regulations, and pollution controls are often effectively absent. It is not surprising that plants in these countries can readily undercut the Americas and Great Britains of the world. This is especially true because so many of these factories are now owned by mutinational corporations based on advanced industrial countries. As Ford and General Motors open plants in Mexico or Brazil, and the electronics companies open plants almost everywhere, the world increasingly becomes a single factory. A 'world car' may be literally that, with the engine coming from one country, the transmission from another, parts from several others. This is already a reality in Europe; it threatens soon to become the case in North America.

In these circumstances, the product cycle becomes a profit cycle: firms or plants in the advanced industrial countries, faced with competition from the newly industrializing countries, can react only by cutting costs – which means shedding expensive labour. Massey and Meegan demonstrate that in Great Britain job losses have arisen from three causes: *greater productivity* through the introduction of new and more efficient processes; *failure to compete* resulting in closure; and *rationalization* where a multiplant enterprise shuts down certain factories in order to concentrate production on others (Massey and Meegan, 1982). Harrison's work on the New England economy has shown that such processes lead to a shedding of labour that does not, so far, manage to find alternative jobs demanding equivalent skills, and so is displaced into low-skill, service-occupation employments (Bluestone and Harrison, 1982; Harrison, 1982).

The obsession with deindustrialization has brought forth an appropriate antidote, which for a time became almost an American political buzz word: *reindustrialization*. It is easy to see why industrialists, politicians and economists should all, in their mutual anxiety, grasp at such a miracle cure. They should however try to recall their classical education, if any: *re* is a Latin root meaning backwards. Reindustrialization, taken too literally, is a recipe for trying to re-create the glories of a lost industrial past – which, like any other exercise in nostalgia, is a fatal guide to industrial policy. Britain has gone down this road for a long time, by subsidizing uneconomic coal mines and steel mills; it is no accident that in the process, the British economy became the sickest in Europe.

The fact is that economic history, like any other kind of history, never quite repeats itself. Industries and regions, once on the way down, are apt not to come up. And if they ever do, they make it not by rediscovering past economic traditions, but by inventing new ones. New England textile towns lost out to competition from the South, but then made a partial comeback in electronics. Western mining towns became ghost towns and then flourishing tourist resorts. Reading in England was a sleepy biscuit- and beer-making town until it was invaded by decentralized offices from London and high-technology factories from California.

2.2   The anatomy of job creation

In comparison with our knowledge of job contraction, we do not understand – a few limited exceptions apart – the parallel process of job creation. Even in the most severe depression since the 1930s, it is clear that certain regions and certain industries are growing. The contraction of employment in older industrial staples like textiles, deep coal-mining, steel manufacture and shipbuilding is paralleled by an expansion of such newer industries as electronics and aerospace, as well as producer services such as finance, insurance and real estate. But, though to some extent these processes can be traced everywhere, clearly they result in pronounced regional shifts: the new industries tend to grow in places different from those where the old industries are contracting. Central Scotland, the English North East and Merseyside, the Middle Atlantic and East North Central regions, are the contracting economies; East Anglia and the South West region of England, and the American Sunbelt, are the complementary areas of growth.

It seems time, then, to shift focus. Are there parallel forces in contemporary capitalism that lead to the birth and growth of new industrial traditions, just as others lead to decay and death of older ones? The limited recent work gives some clues. In particular, the meticulous work of David Birch on the American economy (Birch, 1979) suggests that the important processes in both expansion and decline consist in the birth rates of new firms and the death rates of both new and old ones. Many firms are born, in every region; but many soon die. However, of those that survive, a few show rapid growth and hence contribute powerfully to total job gain. In older industrial regions like the [US] Northeast, there are fewer firm births to compensate for the high death rate; so there are fewer firms available to expand. In newer regions, for reasons not entirely clear, there are more births of new firms. In Great Britain, some work on older inner cities (Dennis, 1978; Lloyd and Mason, 1978; Dicken and Lloyd, 1978) suggests a similar dominance of birth and death processes; the main reason why these areas are contracting is that many firms die while relatively few are born. In both countries, actual movement of firms or plants is a far less important factor in explaining the overall pattern of regional economic growth.

Here, some episodes from economic history may provide a useful clue. In Britain in the 1890s, both Glasgow and Birmingham prospered – Glasgow on the basis of its great shipbuilding and marine engineering yards, Birmingham on the basis of small workshops that made a bewildering variety of small tools, guns and bicycles. Thence, Glasgow stuck to building ships – even after 1950, when new competitors entered the market and world demand failed to keep pace. But Birmingham constantly adapted: as the market for bicycles became satiated, it switched to cars. In the thirty years after World War Two, Glasgow declined while Birmingham boomed. The Glasgow economic historian Sidney Checkland, pondering the reasons for Glasgow's failure, borrowed a metaphor from Robert Louis Stevenson: the Upas tree of the South Pacific, whose foliage spread so wide as to kill any vegetation in its shade (Checkland, 1975). In the same way, the energies of Glaswegians were so absorbed in building ships that they caused any other enterprise to wither. Checkland shows that in the 1920s Glasgow had infant truck and automobile industries but they died or moved away. Birmingham, but still more London and its surrounding area, stood in sharp contrast. In the 1930s – a period that most Britons still regard as the darkest ever in economic terms – the economies of these areas showed remarkable growth. Whole new industries were created, lining the arterial highways of London's suburbs: processed foods, pharmaceuticals, vehicles, electrical goods, and many others. The 1930s, contrary to popular views, represented one of the more buoyant periods in British economic history.

2.3   Three success stories

More recently, the post-war success stories of three nations, two of them defeated in war – West Germany, France and Japan – illustrate the same point. In 1945, much of Germany's industrial past was buried in rubble. But in the 1950s came the economic miracle, its essence consisting in the Germans' ability to provide the consumer goods that people wanted. One of the most important was an absurdly shaped car, designed in 1934 by the distinguished automobile engineer Ferdinand Porsche for Adolf Hitler as the People's Car. When British car manufacturers toured Germany after World War Two, they were offered the Volkswagen factory; they turned the offer down, saying the car had no future.

Even more recently, the French economy has shown a spectacular rate of growth. Aided by a strong alliance between government and private industry, the French have gambled audaciously on a plan to become one of the most technologically advanced countries in the world. Sometimes this leads to costly blunders like the Concorde airplane, which the French shared with the British. But it also leads to the spectacular new rapid transit system in Paris, the even more advanced one recently completed in Lille, the new high-speed rail link now open between Paris and Lyon, and the plan to give a computer terminal to every French telephone subscriber. The aim of these plans is not just to modernize France; it is to make the country a living showplace of technology, to serve as a base for export orders. And it seems to be working.

But the most spectacular example of such a policy – and, indeed, a model for the French – is Japan. The most significant aspect of the Japanese story is, however, apt to be neglected in some bastions of free enterprise like the contemporary United States and Great Britain: it is the systematic and ruthless partnership between the government, in the form of the Ministry of International Trade and Industry (MITI), and private industry. MITI, in the last quarter century, has systematically sought to identify the large new industrial markets of the future – and has then exploited them, by pouring state money into the crucial initial stage of research and development. Then, at a certain point, it has made its exit, having carefully arranged for one or more companies to take over mass production. It did exactly this with colour television in the early 1970s, to such an extent that Japanese sets overran the American and European markets. In 1983 it is doing the same with home computers.

The moral of all this is clear: economic success lies with the country and the region and the city that innovate, that keep one step ahead of the action. Such innovation has two key elements, both of which must be present for the trick to happen. There must first be some breakthrough, generally but not necessarily technical in character. (It can also be in organization and marketing. Ray Kroc did not invent the hamburger, but he did invent a new way of organizing hamburger sales when he purchased the modest San Bernardino business of the McDonald brothers. Similarly, Kemmens Wilson did not invent the hotel, but when he opened the first Holiday Inn in Memphis, Tennessee, he did pioneer a new concept of standardized hotels of uniform quality, with instant nationwide room reservations.) There must always be the ability to recognize what will sell; in the celebrated aphorism of the great American entrepreneur Henry Kaiser, to find a need and fill it.

2.4 Innovations and long waves

This dual nature of technical innovation is important. It means that technical developments *per se* are not of much significance. They may never become innovations, in the sense of becoming commercially useful; or they may do so only after years or decades of further development. Technical developments without commercial viability include some of the great commercial disasters of economic history, like the aforementioned Concorde airplane. Conversely, relatively simple developments can prove spectacular successes if they meet a need. It was no spectacular scientific breakthrough when – in Atlanta, Georgia in 1886 – a local drug merchant mixed together some ingredients in a formula for a new soft drink. But the customers liked it, not merely in Atlanta but eventually across most of the world.

The dual character of innovation is not a new idea. It was a key concept in a classic of economic analysis: Joseph Schumpeter's *Business Cycles*, written in the late 1930s (Schumpeter, 1939, 1982). His thesis was that every so often in economic history, several innovations in the true sense – that is, commercially utilizable inventions – bunched together to produce a rapid economic expansion. Thus for Schumpeter the so-called Industrial Revolution was just the first in a series. Based on developments in cotton spinning and weaving and in the smelting and refining of iron, plus the steam engine, it occurred from approximately 1785 to 1842. Then there was a second revolution, based on railroads and the Bessemer process in steel; it ran from 1842 to about 1895. The third industrial revolution was based on the chemical industry and on the beginnings of the electrical and auto industries; it started in the mid-1890s and had almost run its course when Schumpeter was writing in the 1930s.

In developing his thesis, Schumpeter leaned fairly heavily on an obscure paper, written in the early 1920s by a Moscow professor who later died in one of Stalin's jails. Nikolai Kondratieff was director of a Moscow research institute, and his paper – published in Russian in 1924 – had been translated and published in Germany in 1926, in a journal Schumpeter had helped to edit before emigrating to the United States. Only in 1935 was it published in the United States (Kondratieff, 1935). Following a Marxist line of analysis, Kondratieff argued that capitalist development followed a regular cycle, of about fifty-five years, from boom to bust and then to boom again. The triggering mechanism – so Kondratieff argued in a mere sentence – was technological development, which created new economic opportunities and thus generated economic expansion. But, after a time, these industries found their markets saturated, and so recession and then depression ensued, until a new wave of innovation set the whole process off again.

Schumpeter refined this theory, arguing that two shorter cycles were laid over the long Kondratieff waves – the Juglar, eight to ten years long, corresponding to the classic 'trade cycle', and the Kitchen, a short cycle only just over three years long. The complex interrelationship between these cycles, he hypothesized, should explain the process of economic expansion and contraction in modern capitalism – the process of creative destruction, as he termed it. Attempting to prove it, he traced the course of economic history since the first Industrial Revolution in meticulous detail, almost month by month. The result seemed positive, though Schumpeter – no believer in precise mathematical modelling, despite his own considerable competence in the field – never subjected it to rigorous analysis.

Economists are disputatious folk. It was small wonder that as soon as such a prestigious professor had embraced the Kondratieff notion, another should try to demolish it. Already, in his 1940 review of Schumpeter's book, Simon Kuznets doubted the validity of the long-wave theory (Kuznets, 1940). In his subsequent life's work, which gained him the Nobel prize in economics, Kuznets did what Schumpeter had eschewed: to gather a mass of data and to model it, so as to establish economic history on a quantitative basis (Kuznets, 1930, 1946, 1966). At the end of some thirty years of work, he concluded that the time series of national income – derived from several advanced industrial countries – provided no evidence for the Kondratieff thesis. Instead, he claimed, they strongly suggested a twenty-year cycle of expansion and contraction.

There the matter might have rested, but for a nagging point about the Kondratieff–Schumpeter theory. It should have predicted a bad slump around 1930, an economic revival in the 1930s (when Schumpeter was writing), a boom in the 1950s and early 1960s, and a descent into depression in the 1970s. It is small wonder that in the 1980s, a number of people are again taking Kondratieff–Schumpeter very seriously. These include the flourishing school of political economists working within the Marxist tradition, for whom the thesis is particularly appealing. The Belgian Marxist Ernest Mandel, for instance, makes the long waves a principal feature of his major tome on *Late Capitalism*, and has subsequently written a shorter book particularly on the subject (Mandel, 1975, 1980). Other economists, working within different traditions – such as W. W. Rostow, orginator of the celebrated theory of Stages of Economic Growth – have also embraced the notion (Rostow, 1978). The global modeller Jay Forrester has suggested that Kuznets's cycles may nest inside Kondratieff ones (Forrester, 1976; see also Forrester, 1981).

A major additional reason why the long waves are again receiving attention is a remarkable book by a German scholar. Published originally in 1974, but not translated into English until 1979, Gerhard Mensch's *Technological Stalemate: Innovations overcome the Depression* is a breathtakingly original and stimulating attempt to provide detailed substantiation of the original Kondratieff thesis. Mensch assembles data for hundreds of technical innovations – that is, inventions that actually came to be applied in industry – from the first Industrial Revolution onwards. He traces in detail the progress from original technical breakthrough to industrial innovation, and emerges with what seems to be a remarkable finding. This is that in some periods the process of application is very slow, while in others it speeds up. The result is what Mensch calls a waggon-train effect, whereby many innovations occur almost simultaneously within a few years. The peak years for such clustering – what Mensch calls radical years of history – were 1764, 1825, 1886 and 1935. These, he argues, almost exactly correspond to the dates of the long waves originally identified by Kondratieff and described by Schumpeter.

But Mensch does not stop there. Because the process is a very regular one, he is able to go on and predict it. He does this not by any simple extrapolation from past data, but by a complex technique that involves looking at the actual pace of innovation in the recent past. According to this analysis, by the mid-1970s fully half of all the innovations for the next Kondratieff upswing had already reached the stage of commercial applicability. The next radical year of history, Mensch announces with a flourish, will be 1989. And the decade of maximum innovation will start in that most symbolic of years, 1984. If the theory holds good, however, the boom will come long after 1984. Past experience indicates that generally an economic upswing will happen between eleven and seventeen years after the peak of innovation. On that basis, the effect on the world economy will not be felt until well into the 1990s. The picture would be one of world depression throughout the 1980s – a daunting prospect.

Recently, Mensch's thesis has been beginning to get a great deal of attention – meaning a great deal of criticism. In summer 1981 the journal of prediction, *Futures*, devoted a whole issue to the subject of long waves, including an attack on the Mensch thesis by members of the Science Policy Research Unit at the University of Sussex, England (Clark, Freeman and Soete, 1981). They claimed that much of the data he used were vaguely dated and that he had left out important innovations that might weaken his argument. Also, following Kuznets and using the available data on economic growth, they could not systematically trace a 55-year wave. In subsequent work the same team have accepted the existence of Kondratieff long waves but have continued to dispute the Mensch hypothesis that innovation bunching is the explanation (Freeman, Clark and Soete, 1982). They incline rather to a thesis that is shared by Marxist writers like Mandel: that the waves are triggered by exogenous forces of an almost accidental nature. Thus both the Sussex team and Mandel believe that the long wave starting around the time of World War Two was partly triggered by the rearmament boom of the 1930s, by the war itself and by the subsequent Cold War.

Meanwhile another most important contribution to the debate has appeared, again in translation, from the Dutch economist van Duijn (van Duijn, 1983). Apart from showing that the theory had been developed by other economists before Kondratieff – notably by the pre-World War One Dutch writer van Gelderen – van Duijn makes a major discovery: that the long waves appear much more clearly from the data if they are assumed to be superimposed on another, even deeper, wave representing the Rostowian curve of economic growth. In the mid-1980s, then, there is a great deal of agreement that the long waves – as well as other, shorter economic perturbations – exist; what is still at issue is their cause, and in particular the question of whether they are generated by some kind of automatic, internal regulating machinery inside the capitalist economic system itself. If that proved true, of course, it would mean that Kondratieff had made a major nonsense of Marx's central thesis of deepening capitalist crisis – which is one good reason, perhaps, why Stalin should have locked him up, and why the latter-day Marxist economists are so concerned to disprove the notion.

2.5   The geography of innovation

What is significant is that all workers in the field do seem agreed that long cycles exist; they disagree only on their length and on the explanation of their occurrence. From this, it seems logical to conclude that different long waves can and do occur in different countries and even in different regions. Accepting for a moment the Kondratieff–Schumpeter framework, then clearly the first and second waves were dominated by Great Britain, though the United States and Germany began to emerge during the second; the third was dominated by these two countries; in the fourth, which can be dated from World War Two until approximately the present time, the United States was predominant with Japan just beginning to appear on the stage. Further, within Great Britain the first wave was dominated by Lancashire, Shropshire and the Black Country; the second by newer regions like South Wales and the North East; the third and fourth by the West Midlands and Greater London.

New industrial traditions, in other words, took root in places different from older ones. Traditional explanations, like available raw materials, might be a factor here – especially in the earlier, more material-dependent, stages of economic growth. But they could not provide the only or even the main explanation why, for instance, the fledgling automobile industry should set itself up in Coventry and in Detroit rather than in (for instance) Glasgow or Baltimore. The evolution of older and closely related industrial traditions (such as bicycles in Coventry) provides one explanation; so does the accidental presence of key industrialists. But perhaps one necessary condition was the very lack of very old-established industrial traditions, such as shipbuilding in Glasgow, which inhibited the growth of new and delicate industrial vegetation: the Upas Tree effect (Checkland, 1975).

Lack of such an inhibiting inheritance, then, can be regarded as a necessary condition for the development of new industrial traditions – but surely not a sufficient one. In the American Sunbelt, for instance, there are many possible areas where new industries might have taken root, but in only a few did this actually happen. The map of the 1980 United States Census, for instance, shows that many Sunbelt areas, especially in the 'Old South', experienced population loss in the 1970s (Hauser, 1981, p. 54). Thus there has to be some other factor or factors. Studies among industrialists indicate that 'favourable business climate' is a factor quoted by many establishing branch operations in the Sunbelt (Weinstein and Firestine, 1978); yet even this cannot explain the spatial variations that occur. Since the sources of Sunbelt economic growth are varied – ranging from high-technology industry to recreation and retirement – one should expect that the precise triggering mechanisms will similarly vary.

One plausible hypothesis is that growth of a relatively small industrial base – especially in innovative, high-technology industry and associated producer services – can create a very large income and employment multiplier effect in the form of construction, real estate, recreation and personal service industries. Much of this multiplier effect will be felt in the immediate local economy, but some will occur at great distances, especially in accessible recreation areas. Thus the growth of ski resorts in the Colorado Rockies or the California Sierra can be ascribed in part to demand generated in the metropolitan areas of Denver-Boulder or San Francisco-Oakland, one hundred and more miles away.

No geographer, as yet, appears to have teased out these connections – important as they are for understanding the contemporary geography of growth. But central to the whole process is the triggering of the new basic industry, which provides the rationale for it. We know from limited studies of the subject that high-technology industry seems to stem from basic R&D either in universities or in specialized research laboratories, both public and private. Malecki's work on American R&D shows it to be fairly well-distributed across the United States, both Frostbelt and Sunbelt, with strong concentrations in larger metropolitan areas (Malecki, 1980a, 1980b, 1981a, 1981b). However, what is more difficult to identify is the distribution of the basic R&D that contributes to new industrial development: what in the jargon are called product innovations as distinct from process innovations. Recent research suggests strongly that these product innovations are sharply bunched in time and that major periods of job creation follow them; in contrast, succeeding periods of process innovation lead first to stagnation, then to contraction of employment (Rothwell, 1982). The unconfirmed suspicion is that product innovations are quite highly concentrated in certain places.

The classic case is of course Silicon Valley. Located between San José and Palo Alto in the San Francisco Bay Area, the Santa Clara Valley is the centre of microprocessor and associated industries in the United States. Since 1950 it has been the fastest growing industrial area in the United States; during the last decade its has added, on average, 25 000 new jobs a year. It sits next door to Stanford University, and that is no accident; as shown by AnnaLee Saxenian, it was the brainchild of Frederick Terman, a Stanford professor (Saxenian, 1981, 1985). In the 1920s Terman started to encourage his electrical engineering graduates to stay in the area and set up small business there. Two of the first, William Hewlett and David Packard, started theirs in a garage near the campus in 1939; it is now one of the largest electronics firms in the world. But most of the firms were set up in the 1950s and 1960s – by which time Terman, by then a senior figure at Stanford, had persuaded his university to build a special industrial park to house them. Thus, by a deliberate set of policies, was Silicon Valley born [. . .]

In England the scanty available evidence indicates that – with the possible exception of the Cambridge area, where a whole host of small firms seems to have spun off from university research – the presence of a major university has not been a major factor in the development of new high-technology industry. In the outstanding British example of the growth of such industry – the so-called M4 Corridor west of London (*The Economist*, 1982; Feder, 1983; Neil, 1983; Thomas, 1983; Walker, 1983) – the key factor seems to have been the dense concentration of government scientific establishments in the Reading–Newbury–Oxford triangle. Previous research indicates that the British South East region, within which the heart of the M4 Corridor lies, has both the highest concentration of R&D (Buswell and Lewis, 1970; Howells, 1984) and a high proportion of innovative firms (Oakey, Thwaites and Nash, 1980).

Of these two possible sources of R&D, universities and research laboratories, it seems clear that both had origins that were often fairly arbitrary. Stanford University was the result of a gift by the railroad entrepreneur Leland Stanford in the late nineteenth century, and is established on land donated when the area was almost completely rural. Government research laboratories, in both Britain and the United States, seem often to have been located for strategic reasons – in particular, relative freedom from air attack – in World War Two [. . .] Very often there seems to have been no pressing location factor; there were no original advantages of intellectual agglomeration, though these may have been produced internally as a result of the expansion of the facility concerned.

2.6   Innovation and the agglomeration effect

The precise point is that once the critical decision had been taken, these institutions became a force for further development, creating intellectual 'external economies' for new firms setting up close to them and even directly depending on subcontracts from them. Once the process was under way, then – as has been documented both for Silicon Valley and for the Highway 128 development around Boston, Massachusetts – a process of regular spin-off occurred, whereby new firms would be created by entrepreneurs splitting away from a parent firm. However, since all the firms depended on the same skilled labour pool and access to scarce information, they tended to remain tied in close proximity to each other: a new, high-technology version of the traditional industrial quarter first described in a classic passage by Alfred Marshall:

> When an industry has chosen a locality for itself, it is likely to stay there long: so great are the advantages which people following the same skilled trade get from near neighbourhood to one another. The mysteries of the trade become no mysteries; but are as it were in the air, and children learn many of them unconsciously. Good work is rightly appreciated, inventions and improvements in machinery, in processes and the general organization of the business have their merits promptly discussed: if one man starts a new idea, it is taken up by others and combined with suggestions of their own; and thus it becomes the source of further new ideas. And presently subsidiary trades grow up in the neighbourhood, supplying it with implements and materials, organizing its traffic, and in many ways conducing to the economy of its material. (Marshall, 1920, p. 225)

That was true of the traditional industrial quarter in the inner areas of the great Victorian cities, such as the clothing and furniture quarters of East London (Hall, 1962; Martin, 1966) and the jewellery and gun quarters of Birmingham (Wise, 1951); it is equally true of a high-technology area like Silicon Valley. What has changed is the original propulsive influence and hence the location. For the Victorian quarters it was the merchant houses, which were traditionally associated with the fringe of the central business district; for Silicon Valley it is venture capital which may be found on a regional or even a national scale, coupled with the knowledge of R&D that stems from the university and more widely from the scientific infrastructure of the area. So the industrial quarter is no longer locked in to the inner city; in contrast, it tends to look for high-amenity areas capable of attracting a highly-qualified, highly-paid, highly-mobile workforce (Berry, 1970). In the jargon of the economists, such places offer psychic income. And, to attract already highly-paid and scarce scientists and technicians, that is an important factor.

Indeed, it could be vital. These new industries do not locate near coal or iron or port facilities, or any of the 'factors of location' that traditionally decorated geography textbooks. Their material inputs, as in the case of silicon chips, may indeed be almost weightless. What is critical is, first, the general atmosphere of scientific excitement and advance; second, an agreeable environment in both a physical and a social sense; and third – arising out of the other two – what the economists call the external economies of agglomeration, which create a powerful inertia effect. For computer scientists, leaving Silicon Valley would be like getting off the world. In the Valley, everyone talks and breathes computers. They even have their local trade newspaper, the *Silicon Valley Gulch*. Cut off from this, like a fish out of water, their creative energies may just die.

2.7   Innovation and the older cities

This has profound implications. For it means that the new industry is likely to be found in regions and in areas quite different from the old. Indeed, the image of the old industrial city – committed to dying industries produced by traditional methods with an ageing workforce resistant to change, with a depressing physical environment that is unattractive to mobile workers, and perhaps lacking the necessary research expertise in the new technologies – is just about as repellent to the new industries as could be imagined. The new industry, then, will seek positively to avoid such places. This may help explain why, despite a history of vigorous intervention in regional policies since World War Two, the British have been so unsuccessful in attracting new industry into the older cities. Insofar as the policy had some success, it was to attract a range of such new industry into the suburban, exurban and new town areas beyond commuting range of these cities. Thus, ironically, it had the effect of hastening the outflow of population from these cities, which by the late 1960s and 1970s had reached American proportions.

We can logically ask whether, in such circumstances, the inner cities in the older industrial regions have any economic future at all. They have an ageing and often outworn infrastructure, which is reaching an age when it demands complete renewal. They have increasingly a residual labour force composed of those who could not or would not join the exodus, and which contains disproportionate numbers of the hard-to-employ. They have a depressing physical environment and often suffer from poor transportation linkages compared with suburban and exurban areas. And they suffer from a lack of innovative entrepreneurship: the Upas Tree effect. They lack the right milieu (Hall, 1981).

They have, in other words, little going for them. Determined policies, accompanied by liberal front-end government money, may succeed in creating some kinds of work there: low-paid assembly industry of the Third World type; similarly low-paid work in service industries associated with recreational or tourist developments (conference and exhibition centres, theme parks); some regional-scale office developments, mainly involved in routine data processing (and subject to technological change that may displace some labour and create a demand for special skills which such areas lack). Some such developments, at least, would appear to match demands for certain kinds of labour with the supply of them. None of them however promises to develop truly entrepreneurial industrial traditions, such as were once nourished in the inner city. That role has passed to the outer city.

The only exception could occur if an R&D tradition, either already existing in the inner city or deliberately implanted in it, could be used on the Silicon Valley model to create a new entrepreneurial tradition. In 1935, after all, the Santa Clara Valley had no high-technology tradition at all; it was a fruit-growing area. Similarly, the Research Triangle of North Carolina, deliberately located between the University of North Carolina and Duke University, has transformed the research map of eastern North America. And in the United States there are universities, like the University of Texas and the University of Colorado, that are edging into the top league and that may spawn new industrial complexes.

The problem is that the University of Texas campus at Austin, and the University of Colorado campus at Boulder, share with Research Triangle and Silicon Valley an exceptionally pleasant environment. Still unproven is whether the same trick can be performed in the very different and less prepossessing environment of the older industrial city. Such an attempt is being made in Pittsburgh, where Carnegie-Mellon University – an old-established university with a strong technological tradition – is developing an experiment in computer literacy for every student, sufficient to guarantee that all graduates will emerge as sophisticated in computer applications. The hope is that in turn they will set up new infant industries within the Pittsburgh area, so giving it an alternative industrial structure to replace the contracting steel and heavy engineering base. Located some three miles from Pittsburgh's Golden Triangle, Carnegie-Mellon can fairly be regarded as an inner-city university. A similar thrust in the direction of high-technology, campus-linked industry is evident at the University of Salford in England, an inner-city campus located in an area of industrial decline in the Greater Manchester conurbation.

Such bold strategies may succeed, but they are likely to take a long time to produce substantial results. At Stanford, as already seen, Terman started his activities in the 1930s; but it was not until the 1950s and 1960s that substantial numbers of new jobs began to be created. On this analogy, an inner-city high-technology strategy might be expected, if successful, to show real results around the turn of the century. And it must be stressed that in the interim, high existing levels of unemployment will almost certainly demand alternative, complementary measures to deal with them. The conclusion is that no single strategy, but rather a combination of different approaches, will be appropriate.

However, even then there is a limitation. Not every declining industrial city has a major university with a strong technological emphasis. It is highly likely indeed that in any advanced industrial economy there will only be room for a strictly limited number of such high-technology industries. To attempt to develop such concentrations all over the country may be self-contradictory and fruitless – particularly as the Silicon Valleys and Research Triangles have a head start.

2.8   An R&D-based regional strategy

The question naturally arises as to the main emphasis of such R&D strategies. That may be expected to differ from place to place, but to draw as far as feasible on adaptation of older industrial traditions. Three major likely areas for future industrial growth have been identified in a number of publications. First, the whole complex of computer applications, information systems and automatic control systems (robotics). These may increasingly differentiate themselves as separate industries, since they are likely to constitute the main economic base in advanced industrial countries. Secondly, the biotechnological group of industries, including agricultural and medical applications. And thirdly, the development of alternative sources of energy coupled with energy conservation devices. It is highly likely that these streams may merge and interrelate, as for instance in the development of computer systems for energy exploration or energy conservation, or the application of biotechnological research to the problem of generating artificial intelligence.

Policies for developing such new industries may range from the highly decentralized and dispersed to the highly centralized and coordinated. In almost all industrialized countries, however, there is some degree of national coordination of R&D efforts. Governments consciously try to cooperate with the private sector in the development of new areas, whether for military reasons (a powerful force in the early development of Silicon Valley) or for reasons of economic development. These governmental efforts, by definition, will have spatial impacts. The question is whether governments could or should pursue a conscious strategy of urban and regional development based on R&D policies.

To do so, as already suggested, will in many cases mean swimming against the economic tide; the question is whether such policies could be successful. The British government, for instance, wanted to base its subsidized private manufacture of memory chips, through the British subsidiary of the American firm INMOS, in an Assisted Area – that is, one of the older and more problematic industrial regions. The returning expatriate members of the company resisted this move and instead located their headquarters in Bristol, an environmentally-attractive city with a good reputation in high-technology industry; later, under government pressure, they agreed to locate the manufacturing capacity across the Severn estuary in South Wales.

This, however, is perhaps an unfortunate example, since the entrepreneurs concerned were by no means new entrants. The right strategy might well be the Stanford or Carnegie-Mellon one: to bias government R&D spending to favour certain inner-city universities in the Assisted Areas. Such a policy, however, would tend to run up against the tradition in most western countries of relative autonomy in the granting of university research funds. In Great Britain the Science and Engineering Research Council, or in the United States the National Science Foundation, all dispose of funds without direct government interference on the principle of supporting the best centres. If government were to intervene it might well provoke loud protest from the scientific establishment and the charge that money was going to second-rate institutions.

There does not seem to be any easy reconciliation of these arguments. The best may sometimes be the enemy of the good. But perhaps there is a way out: in most countries, there are some inner-city centres of excellence in some fields. These should be differentially encouraged through government R&D funding (perhaps through the establishment of regional quotas to the research councils) and this scheme should be coupled with another, to provide venture capital to graduates of these universities to set up new local enterprises. In such a way, without undue violence to scientific susceptibilities, new industrial traditions may be implanted to replace the old.

References

BERRY, B. J. L. (1970) 'The geography of the United States in the year 2000', *Institute of British Geographers, Transactions*, Vol. 51, pp. 21–53.

BIRCH, D. L. (1979) *The Job Generation Process* (MIT Program on Neighborhood and Regional Change), Cambridge, Mass., Massachusetts Institute of Technology.

BLUESTONE, B. and HARRISON, B. (1982) *The Deindustrialization of America: Plant Closings, Community Abandonment, and the Dismantling of Basic Industry*, New York, Basic Books.

BUSWELL, R. J. and LEWIS, E. W. (1970) 'The geographical distribution of industrial research activity in the United Kingdom', *Regional Studies*, Vol. 4, pp. 297–306.

CHECKLAND, S. (1975) *The Upas Tree*, Glasgow, Glasgow University Press.

CLARK, J., FREEMAN, C. and SOETE, L. (1981) 'Long waves, inventions and innovations', *Futures*, Vol. 13, pp. 308–22.

DENNIS, R. (1978) 'The decline of manufacturing employment in Greater London', *Urban Studies*, Vol. 15, pp. 63–73.

DICKEN, P. and LLOYD, P. E. (1978) 'Inner metropolitan industrial change. Enterprise structures and policy issues: case studies of Manchester and Merseyside', *Regional Studies*, Vol. 12, pp. 181–97.

THE ECONOMIST (1982) 'Britain's Sunrise Strip', 30 January.

FEDER, B. J. (1983) 'Britain's Science Corridor', *New York Times*, 24 April.

FORRESTER, J. (1976) 'Business structure, economic cycles, and national policy', *Futures*, Vol. 8, pp. 195–214.

FORRESTER, J. (1981) 'Innovation and economic change', *Futures*, Vol. 13, pp. 323–31.

FREEMAN, C., CLARK, J. and SOETE, L. (1982) *Unemployment and Technical Innovation*, London, Frances Pinter.

HALL, P. G. (1962) *The Industries of London since 1861*, London, Hutchinson University Library.

HALL, P. (ed.) (1981) *The Inner City in Context: The Final Report of the Social Science Research Council Inner Cities Working Party*, London, Heinemann Education.

HARRISON, B. (1982) *Rationalization, Restructuring, and Industrial Reorganization in Older Regions: The Economic Transformation of New England since World War II*, Cambridge, Mass., Joint Center for Urban Studies of the Massachusetts Institute of Technology and Harvard University.

HAUSER, P. (1981) 'The Census of 1980', *Scientific American*, Vol. 245, pp. 53–61.

HOWELLS, J. R. L. (1984) 'The location of research and development: some observations and evidence from Britain', *Regional Studies*, Vol. 18, pp. 13–29.

KONDRATIEFF, N. D. (1935) 'The long waves in economic life', *Review of Economic Statistics*, Vol. 17, pp. 105–15.

KUZNETS, S. S. (1930) *Secular Movements in Production and Prices*, New York, Houghton Mifflin.

KUZNETS, S. S. (1940) 'Schumpeter's business cycles', *American Economic Review*, Vol. 30, pp. 250–71.

KUZNETS, S. S. (1946) *National Product since 1869*, New York, National Bureau of Economic Research (Publications, No. 46).

KUZNETS, S. S. (1966) *Modern Economic Growth: Rate, Structure and Spread*, New Haven and London, Yale University Press.

LLOYD, P. E. and MASON, C. M. (1978) 'Manufacturing industry in the inner city: a case study of Manchester', *Institute of British Geographers, Transactions*, New Series, Vol. 3, pp. 60–90.

MALECKI, E. J. (1980a) 'Corporate organization of R and D and the location of technological activities', *Regional Studies*, Vol. 14, pp. 219–34.

MALECKI, E. J. (1980b) 'Science and technology in the American urban system', in Brunn, S. D. and Wheeler, J. O. (eds) *The American Metropolitan System: Past and Future*, London, Edward Arnold.

MALECKI, E. J. (1981a) 'Public and private sector interrelationships, technological change, and regional development', *Papers of the Regional Science Association*, Vol. 47, pp. 161–38.

MALECKI, E. J. (1981b) 'Government-funded R&D: some regional economic implications', *Professional Geographer*, Vol. 33, pp. 72–82.

MANDEL, E. (1975) *Late Capitalism*, London, Verso.

MANDEL, E. (1980) *Long Waves of Capitalist Development*, Cambridge, Cambridge University Press.

MARSHALL, A. (1920) *Principles of Economics*, London, Macmillan.

MARKUSEN, A. (1984) *Profit Cycles, Oligopoly and Regional Development*, Cambridge, Mass., MIT Press.

MARTIN, J. E. (1966) *Greater London: An Industrial Geography*, London, Bell.

MASSEY, D. and MEEGAN, R. (1982) *The Anatomy of Job Loss*, London, Methuen.

MENSCH, G. (1979) *Stalemate in Technology: Innovations overcome the Depression*, Cambridge, Mass., Ballinger.

NEIL, A. (1983) 'The information revolution', *The Listener*, 23 June.

OAKEY, R. P., THWAITES, A. T. and NASH, P. A. (1980) 'The regional distribution of innovative manufacturing establishments in Great Britain', *Regional Studies*, Vol. 14, pp. 235–53.

PHILLIPS, B. *et al.* (1983) 'Western Corridor: a special report', *The Times*, 30 June.

ROTHWELL, R. (1982) 'The role of technology in industrial change: implications for regional policy', *Regional Studies*, Vol. 16, pp. 361–9.

ROSTOW, W. W. (1978) 'Regional change in the fifth Kondratieff upswing', in Perry, D. C. and Watkins, A. J. (eds) *The Rise of the Sunbelt Cities (Urban Affairs Annual Reviews*, Vol. 14), Beverly Hills and London, Sage.

SAXENIAN, A. (1981) 'Silicon chips and spatial structure: The industrial basis of urbanization in Santa Clara Valley, California', University of California, Berkeley, Institute of Urban and Regional Development, Working Paper 345.

SAXENIAN, A. (1985) 'The genesis of Silicon Valley', in Hall, P. and Markusen, A. (eds) *Silicon Landscapes*, London, George Allen and Unwin, pp. 20–34.

SCHUMPETER, J. A. (1939, 1982) *Business Cycles: A Theoretical, Historical and Statistical Account of the Capitalist Process*, (2 Volumes). New York and London, McGraw Hill. Reprinted Philadelphia, Porcupine Press.

THOMAS, D. (1983) 'England's Golden West', *New Society*, 5 May.

VAN DUIJN, J. J. (1983) *The Long Wave in Economic Life*, London, George Allen and Unwin.

WALKER, M. (1982) 'The boom that's by-passing the new towns of Britain', *The Guardian*, 26 April.

WEINSTEIN, B. L. and FIRESTINE, R. E. (1978) *Regional Growth and Decline in the United States: The Rise of the Sunbelt and the Decline of the Northeast*, New York, Praeger.

WISE, M. J. (1951) 'On the evolution of the jewellery and gun quarters in Birmingham', *Institute of British Geographers, Transactions and Papers*, Vol. 15, pp. 57–72.

3   The deindustrialization of the city

Steve Fothergill, Graham Gudgin, Michael Kitson and Sarah Monk

3.1   Introduction

The industrial city in Britain is the product of nineteenth-century capitalism. Technical innovations in production and the accumulation of capital led to the development of large factories. At the same time it was advantageous for factories to be clustered near the focal points of the rudimentary transport network, such as ports, canals and railway terminals, and workers had little choice but to live close by. Few restrictions were placed on urban development. The result was that cities grew in an uncontrolled and cumulative manner following the cost-and-profit calculations of entrepreneurs. Britain was the first country to become fully urbanized: by the middle of the century over half the population lived in the new industrial cities.

In the late twentieth century all this has changed. The virtually universal availability of power, telecommunications and transport, with minimal geographical variations in cost, has released the magnetic grip of cities on industry. The advent of cheap road transport, in particular, has finally removed the locational advantage of cities. Indeed, there has been a complete turnaround in the fortunes of the industrial city: in the late twentieth century the city is the principal location of de-industrialization.

Three aspects of de-industrialization impinge on the city. The first is the shift in the balance of employment in Britain as a whole away from manufacturing towards services. This process dates back to at least the end of the Second World War. Its cause is the difference in the rate of growth of labour productivity between manufacturing and services. The nature of many tasks in manufacturing production facilitates the introduction of machinery to replace labour; in services this is not possible to the same extent. For any given growth of output the rate of increase in manufacturing employment is therefore lower than the rate of increase in service employment. The effect is a shift in the distribution of the workforce from manufacturing to the service sector. This has occurred in years of both high and low employment, and is likely to continue. It does not necessarily pose a major economic problem. Indeed, if the rate of growth of the economy is fast enough then there may be an increase in manufacturing employment even if the overall structure of employment is moving towards services. This occurred in Britain until 1966: manufacturing employment was expanding, but service employment was expanding faster and services thus accounted for an increasing share of all jobs.

The second aspect of deindustrialization affecting the city is the failure of the British economy to grow at a sufficient rate to provide full employment. Manufacturing and service employment are both below what they would be if all available labour were utilized. Since 1966, manufacturing employment nationally has fallen by around 3 million and the gap between the supply of labour and the supply of jobs has widened, especially since 1979. Unlike the structural shift from manufacturing to services this aspect of deindustrialization creates severe problems, the most obvious of which is the high level of unemployment that now affects nearly all areas. The reasons for the failure to achieve adequate economic growth are numerous. They include the deflationary economic policies pursued by governments, the competitive weakness of much of British industry and the constraints imposed by the underlying imbalance in Britain's trade with the rest of the world. Cities suffer deindustrialization because of these failures but the solutions lie with national economic policy, not spatial policy.

The third aspect of the deindustrialization of cities is specifically spatial: accompanying the national contraction of manufacturing and the reduction in its share of total employment, there has been a large urban–rural contrast in the rate of change. Until the recession at the beginning of the 1980s, small towns and rural areas experienced a long period of sustained expansion in industrial production and employment. Even after the recession, with national manufacturing employment at less than 60 per cent of its level of twenty years earlier, the number of manufacturing jobs in many small towns and rural areas remains greater than in the 1960s. Britain's cities, in contrast, have lost manufacturing jobs faster than almost any other part of the country.

This chapter concerns only this third aspect of deindustrialization. It examines how and why the loss of manufacturing jobs has proceeded faster and further in cities than in small towns and rural areas. The explanation put forward is that the relative decline of cities as centres of industrial production is an almost inevitable consequence of the process of economic change within an 'advanced' capitalist economy. Just as the unrestrained operation of the market economy led to the development of ever larger cities during the last century, in changed circumstances the market economy is eroding their industrial base. The next part of the chapter describes the urban–rural contrast in manufacturing employment change and considers the consequences for unemployment, population distribution and 'inner-city' problems generally. This is followed by a discussion of the national economic trends which have concentrated industrial job loss in Britain's cities. The chapter then looks at how the policies pursued by the Conservative government since 1979 have affected the industrial city, and concludes by considering whether the increasing range of urban economic initiatives adds up to an effective strategy for urban industrial regeneration.

3.2   Urban industrial decline

Table 3.1 shows manufacturing employment change between 1960 and 1981 in six types of area in Great Britain. Each local-authority district (there are about 450) has been classified on the basis of settlement size and employment has been measured using statistics that have been adjusted to be fully comparable through time. The table reveals the considerable locational change that has occurred.

Two points are worth noting. The first is the number of jobs involved. At one end of the urban hierarchy, London lost over half its manufacturing employment – nearly 700 000 jobs – during this period. To put this into perspective, the number of manufacturing jobs lost in London is not far short of the present number of manufacturing jobs in the whole of the West Midlands region, and is considerably more than the total in Scotland, Wales or the Northern region. The second point to note is the consistency of the urban–rural contrast. Across the whole urban hierarchy manufacturing employment change is related to settlement size. As a general rule the larger the settlement the greater the decline. The consistency in aggregate trends mirrors consistency at the local scale: all the conurbations lost more than one in three of their manufacturing jobs during this period, and fifteen out of seventeen free-standing cities lost manufacturing jobs. Stability or growth in manufacturing employment has occurred in relatively remote towns and rural areas as well as in places close to cities, indicating that the urban–rural contrast is more than merely the 'overspill' of jobs from cities to their immediately surrounding hinterlands. The decentralization has also been largely unplanned. Although for thirty years until the late 1970s public policy encouraged the movement of people and jobs to New and Expanding Towns away from cities, these centres of planned growth account for only a small proportion of the shift to towns and rural areas (Fothergill, Kitson and Monk, 1983).

An urban–rural contrast can be observed in all parts of Britain. In every region small towns and rural areas have fared better than larger settlements by a sizeable margin, an indication of the pervasiveness of the forces generating this shift in location. The decline in the number of manufacturing jobs in cities and the relative growth elsewhere has also redistributed jobs between regions. Highly urban regions have declined; more rural regions have grown. It is no coincidence, for example, that East Anglia and the South West have been the regions least affected by deindustrialization. These are the most rural regions in Britain with comparatively little of their industry in cities. The North West, at the bottom of the regional growth league, is possibly the most urban region, with a high proportion of its jobs in the Manchester and Merseyside conurbations.

It is difficult to assess exactly when the relative decline of urban industry began: appropriate statistics do not go back far enough. At least some manufacturing firms were moving out of London during the late

Table 3.1   Manufacturing employment by type of area, 1960–81

	Employment (thousands)		Change 1960–81	
	1960	1981	(thousands)	(%)
London	1 338	650	−688	−51.4
Conurbations	2 282	1 295	−987	−43.2
Free-standing cities	1 331	950	−381	−28.6
Large towns	921	756	−165	−17.9
Small towns	1 631	1 609	−22	−1.3
Rural areas	527	655	+128	+24.3
Great Britain	8 030	5 915	−2 115	−26.3

Conurbations: Manchester, Merseyside, Clydeside, West Yorkshire, Tyneside, West Midlands.

Free-standing cities: other cities with more than 250 000 people.

Large towns: towns or cities with 100 000 to 250 000 people.

Small towns: districts including at least one town with 35 000 to 100 000 people, plus coalfield areas.

Rural areas: Districts in which all settlements have fewer than 35 000 people.

Source: Department of Employment

nineteenth and early twentieth century, but the 1920s and 1930s still saw substantial industrial expansion in suburban areas. From the 1950s onwards it is easier to monitor the changing scale of the urban–rural contrast. Table 3.2 shows the average annual change in manufacturing employment in London and the conurbations during each of the five periods since 1952. The first part of the table shows that during the 1950s their manufacturing employment increased a little. In the 1960s decline set in and accelerated. Between 1966 and 1973 London and the conurbations lost an average of 100 000 manufacturing jobs every year. In the mid-1970s the decline eased a little, but after 1978 the recession led to unprecedented job losses. The second part of Table 3.2 shows manufacturing employment change in London and the conurbations relative to the national average. This is the difference between the employment change in these areas and the change which would have occurred if their employment had grown or declined at the national rate during each period. This provides a measure of the urban–rural contrast in each period because, by definition, the greater the relative decline of London and the conurbations, the greater the relative growth of other areas. The picture is one of virtually uninterrupted decline in Britain's largest cities. In the 1950s the relative decline was more gentle than in the 1960s and early 1970s, and in the mid-1970s it eased again to nearer its 1950s' rate, but it continued throughout the period up to 1981. These figures indicate that the shift of industrial employment away from cities is clearly a long-established trend,

Table 3.2   Manufacturing employment change in London and the conurbations, 1952–81

	1952–60	1960–66	1966–73	1973–78	1978–81
Actual change					
number per year	+20 000	−25 000	−108 000	−73 000	−154 000
% per year	+0.6	−0.7	−3.0	−2.6	−6.3
Relative to UK average					
number per year	−24 000	−38 000	−63 000	−29 000	−28 000
% per year	−0.7	−1.0	−1.8	−1.0	−1.2

Source: Department of Employment

pre-dating the national economic difficulties which have dogged the British economy since the early 1970s.

The loss of manufacturing jobs in Britain's cities has consequences for employment in other sectors of the local economy and for the distribution of population. Some service employers in cities depend on manufacturing firms for their business or on the expenditure of wages earned in local industry. As manufacturing declines in the city, output and employment in local services therefore tend to decline. The loss of jobs in the city encourages the out-migration of population to small towns where there are more employment opportunities. As people leave the city this has a further depressing effect on local service employment, including public services such as health and education in which provision is related to local population levels. Because migration is the principal mechanism through which the labour market adjusts to the changing location of jobs, the increase in unemployment in cities has not been as large as the loss of jobs would warrant. London, for example, has maintained below-average unemployment, despite an above-average loss of jobs, by losing population to other areas: it now has two million fewer people than at its peak in the late 1930s. Thus as industrial employment leaves the city, the city itself moves into decline. Its population growth is halted, then reversed, and counter-urbanization becomes the dominant trend.

A linear extrapolation suggests that by the early decades of the next century few manufacturing jobs will be left in Britain's largest cities. Following the manufacturing-led model of urban decline, discussed above, it would be tempting to suggest that cities might disappear entirely. A more likely outcome is that cities in future will be smaller and function primarily as service centres for their hinterlands rather than as centres of industrial production. Cities continue to offer locational advantages for some service industries, and in the economy as a whole service employment has proved more buoyant than employment in manufacturing. Eventually the high proportion of city employment in services is therefore likely to outweigh the continuing decline of a small residual manufacturing sector, and when this point is reached the cities' decline in employment and population may come to an end.

This is similar to what occurred in Britain's rural areas. Mechanization led to a steady reduction in the agricultural workforce from its mid-nineteenth-century peak and to a loss of rural population. However, by about 1960 agriculture had shrunk to such a small proportion of employment in most rural areas that the number of jobs which continued to be lost in agriculture no longer outweighed the local growth in other sectors, notably manufacturing. Rural decline eased, and a new era of growth began. Exactly when cities might reach a similar turning-point is unclear, but it is unlikely to be soon because manufacturing still provides a large share of urban employment. Indeed, by the time a turning-point is reached the employment and population in Britain's cities may have fallen to such an extent that the urban structure of nineteenth-century Britain will have been substantially modified. The industrial city, in particular, is likely to have lost its pre-eminence.

3.3   The roots of decline

Despite the large volume of theory on regional growth, urban spatial structure and industrial location, there is no generally accepted theory to account for the deindustrialization of the city. In a survey of the literature on urban growth Richardson (1969) commented that what is available constitutes 'less a theory of urban growth than a prologue to the development of such a theory'.

There are two perspectives that might be adopted to try to explain the shift of industry from cities. One concentrates on the characteristics of cities themselves. It has been argued that certain features of city locations – inadequate premises, high rents or militant workers, for example – make them unsuitable locations for contemporary manufacturing industry. (See Scott (1982) for a review of these arguments.) The focus of such explanations is the city itself. A second perspective concerns the changing nature of the national economy. It has been argued, for example, that the decline of industry in cities is the result of the 'restructuring' and 'rationalization' of industry in the face of the deepening crisis of the British economy (Community Development Project, 1977; Massey and Meegan, 1978). The logic of such arguments is that the interests of industrial capital and the maintenance of urban employment levels are irreconcilably opposed. The focus of this explanation is the economic system; characteristics of localities have little influence.

This dichotomy is misleading. The geography of employment growth and decline is in our view determined by the interaction of national economic trends and the characteristics of localities. Trends in the national economy confront firms with pressures they cannot easily resist – for example, to introduce new technology to keep costs down, or to close redundant capacity during a recession. Most firms face these pressures, though their nature and extent vary from industry to industry and from firm to firm. The extent to which each area is affected by these pressures depends on its mix of industries, and on the costs, opportunities and constraints it poses for firms. Taking this view of industrial location it is still necessary to identify the specific national trends and characteristics of cities which result in urban industrial decline. It is impossible to give full consideration to all the possibilities in this short chapter, but two theories that do not seem to offer a satisfactory explanation are worth mentioning.

One is the idea, derived from Keynesian economic theory, that the growth of industry in an area is determined by the growth of the market for its industries' products. Thus areas with a high proportion of their jobs in industries whose national or international market is contracting experience job losses, while an increase in employment normally results from a concentration of 'growth' industries. The mix of industries in each area and the national growth of those industries are the crucial influences, it is suggested. The relevance of this theory to the urban–rural contrast in manufacturing employment change in Britain has been exhaustively investigated (Fothergill and Gudgin, 1979; Moore, Rhodes and Tyler, 1980; Keeble, 1980; Danson, Lever and Malcolm, 1980). The unanimous conclusion is that it cannot account for any part of the urban–rural contrast.

The second theory, derived from neo-classical economics, is that cities are high-cost locations and that in a profit-maximizing business environment production and employment are therefore diverted to towns and rural areas where costs are lower. The evidence relating to this theory is contradictory. For example, average manufacturing profitability in cities appears to be below average (Fothergill, Gudgin, Kitson and Monk, 1984), but not in all cities, notably London (Wellbelove, Woods and Zafiris, 1981). It is generally agreed that urban land costs are higher than in small towns and rural areas, but production costs in total appear to be no higher in cities (Fothergill *et al.*, 1984) or the inner city (Lever, 1981) while labour costs are above the average in some cities and below average in others (Moore *et al.*, 1980). The conflicting nature of this evidence suggests that if cities are high-cost locations the disadvantage is unlikely to be large – otherwise these studies would have revealed more consistent differences – and that any resulting influence on the location of jobs is therefore likely to be modest.

We do not entirely rule out a role for cost differences in generating urban–rural differences in growth. However, if cost factors were the main or only determinant of locational choice the urban–rural contrast would probably be weaker and more patchy than it actually is. A more plausible explanation is that there are locational constraints which differentiate cities from other areas. Two constraints – the availability of land and labour – are the most likely candidates. Until the early 1970s surveys usually found that the availability of labour was a major factor in determining the location of new branch plants (for example, Department of Trade and Industry, 1973). In an era of full employment firms were often short of labour in many areas, both urban and rural, but women's involvement in the labour market was relatively low in many coalfield and rural areas away from cities. Such untapped reserves of women workers almost certainly attracted some industrial jobs out of cities. However, during the last decade or so the availability of labour has been less of a problem in all areas, as unemployment has risen, and female 'activity rates' in most parts of the country have converged towards the national average.

It is therefore to land constraints that we turn for the main explanations for the urban–rural contrast in manufacturing employment trends. In essence, our view is that the continuing replacement of workers by machines leads to a loss of jobs in factories in all areas, while constraints on the supply of industrial land in cities mean that a disproportionately large share of new factory floorspace and new jobs is diverted to small towns and rural areas. Cities then lose out from the rising capital intensity of production; small towns and rural areas lose jobs for the same reason, but they receive most of the offsetting job gains. The full evidence supporting this explanation is published elsewhere (Fothergill, Kitson and Monk, 1984), but its main elements should now be explained.

3.4   National trends: local constraints

Figure 3.1 shows the number of workers per thousand square metres of industrial floorspace in England and Wales between 1964 and 1982. (Comparable figures cannot be calculated for Scotland and Northern Ireland because of the absence of floorspace statistics.) Over this period the average employment density fell by nearly 3 per cent a year from 36.0 to 21.4 workers per thousand square metres. The decline accelerated during recessions and eased during upturns in the economy, but the long-term trend was unmistakably downwards. Adjustments to take account of changes in capacity utilization make little difference to this downward trend. The decline in employment density can be observed to varying degrees in every manufacturing industry and in all locations. However, its significance for the location of jobs had largely been ignored. One implication is that in a factory where floorspace is fixed the reduction in density leads to a loss of jobs, irrespective of the commercial performance of the firm. Similarly, in a city in which the total stock of factory floorspace is fixed, manufacturing employment will tend to fall. Thus a town or city wishing to maintain a stable level of manufacturing employment must continually add to its stock of occupied floorspace merely to offset the loss of jobs arising from the fall in employment density on existing floorspace.

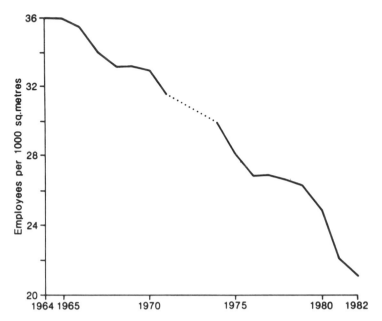

Figure 3.1   Manufacturing employees per 1000 square metres of industrial floor-space: England and Wales, 1964–82
Sources: Department of Employment; Department of the Environment

It is not the explicit intention of firms to reduce employment density. In a competitive economy what is important to firms is the efficient use of resources: how much output they can get from each worker and from each unit of floorspace. Employment density is a residual which emerges from attempts to maximize the productivity of labour and achieve the optimum use of space. To examine the underlying causes the decline in density can be disaggregated into these two components [. . .]

Figure 3.2 shows how these components have changed since the mid-1960s. Output per unit of floorspace [. . .] remained relatively stable until about 1979, with small cyclical fluctuations resulting from changes in capacity utilization. After 1979 there was a sharp decline, reflecting a reduction in manufacturing output which was not matched by a simultaneous reduction in the stock of manufacturing floorspace. The amount of floorspace actually in use probably did decline after 1979, but the stock of floorspace adjusts only slowly to lower levels of manufacturing output, as redundant factory buildings are demolished or changed to other uses. Assuming that the trend after 1979 is largely the result of an exceptionally severe recession, there is little evidence that the ratio between output and floorspace shows a long-term trend in either direction despite the introduction of new production methods. Technical change may thus change the physical requirements of individual industries, but in aggregate its effect on the productivity of factory floorspace appears to be broadly neutral.

Output per manufacturing employee [. . .] has increased substantially.

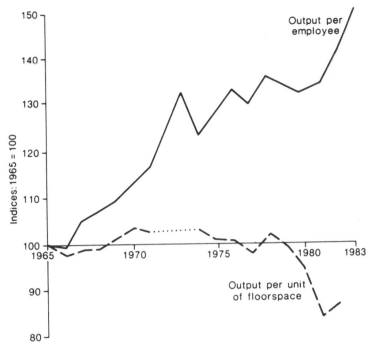

Figure 3.2   Changes in manufacturing output per employee and per unit of floorspace, England and Wales, 1965–83
Sources: Department of Employment; Department of the Environment; National Income and Expenditure Blue Book

We do not propose a lengthy consideration of the factors determining the rate of increase in labour productivity. Our views, however, closely mirror those elaborated by Kaldor (1966) and others, namely that the main determinant of the long-run growth in manufacturing productivity is the rate of growth of demand. The growth of demand which determines the growth of output, allows greater economies of scale in manufacturing production including investment in more capital-intensive methods of production which result in higher labour productivity. In the short run the influences on labour productivity are more complex: in particular, productivity fluctuates with changes in capacity utilization over the trade cycle (Okun, 1962).

From a spatial point of view there are two conclusions to be drawn from these national trends within manufacturing. First, given the long-term stability of the ratio between output and floorspace, an increase in manufacturing output leads to an increase in the demand for factory floorspace. Second, the productivity gain associated with an increase in manufacturing output results, other things being equal, in a reduction in the number of workers per unit of factory floorspace.

Until the recession at the beginning of the 1980s manufacturing output increased, though slowly and unevenly. The resulting increase in the

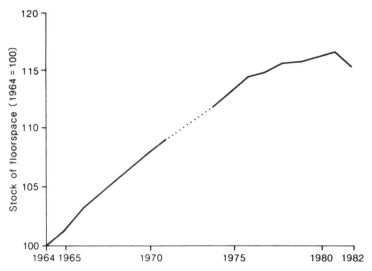

Figure 3.3   The stock of industrial floorspace in England and Wales, 1964–82
Source: *Department of the Environment*

stock of factory floorspace is shown in Figure 3.3, again for England and
Wales. There was an increase every year from 1964 to 1981, though the
rate of increase began to decline in the second half of the 1970s and the
recession reduced the stock after 1981. Comparatively little of the stock is
vacant, it should be noted. Statistics compiled by King & Co., a leading
industrial estate agent, show that in April 1982 only just over 4 per cent
was vacant and on the market, and prior to the recession the figure was
between 1 and 2 per cent. The increase in demand for industrial land has
been even greater than for floorspace. Modern industry prefers single-
storey premises on spacious sites with room for car-parking, circulation of
heavy lorries and, where appropriate, for outdoor storage and future
expansion. This reduces the 'plot ratio' – the ratio between floorspace and
land – in new developments to levels well below that in older industrial
areas.

These national economic trends are important because areas vary in the
extent to which they are able to accommodate physical increases in the
stock of factory floorspace. In particular, cities are usually less able to
accommodate increases than small towns and rural areas, so they receive
few of the job gains but share in the job losses associated with the
reduction in employment density.

There are three ways in which the stock of industrial floorspace is
increased: by extensions to existing factories, by building new factories
and by changes of use (from warehousing for example). The last of these,
changes of use, does not differentiate cities, towns and rural areas.
Increases in floorspace arising from extensions and new buildings,
however, occur at a slower rate in cities than elsewhere. Our research

suggests this has a great deal to do with the availability of land for industry.

In cities, factories are more likely to be on highly developed sites, hemmed in by existing urban development, so that they are unable to extend their premises either on their existing sites or on immediately adjacent land. Table 3.3 illustrates this point using figures for factories with twenty-five or more employees. The figures are the result of two studies: a survey we conducted of industrial premises in the East Midlands and a survey by JURUE (1980) of the industrial building stock in inner Birmingham. It is difficult to know the precise extent to which factory sites in Birmingham and the East Midlands are typical of areas elsewhere, though the percentage change in manufacturing employment in urban and rural areas in the Midlands has been broadly similar to that in similar types of area in Britain as a whole. Table 3.3 shows that the proportion of employment in factories with room for expansion on site, and the proportion with vacant land next to their site, are both more than three times greater in the rural parts of the East Midlands than in inner Birmingham.

Table 3.4 presents figures on land for new factories. This is the land which local authorities consider to be 'available' for new industry, in both the short and long term, and it excludes land reserved for specific firms and land within the curtilage of existing factory sites. As with room for on-site expansion, there is a marked urban–rural contrast. In absolute terms and especially in relation to the size of the manufacturing sector in each type of area, there is less land for building new factories in cities. This is probably because most city land is already in use, because other uses compete with industry for the city land that becomes available, and because of restrictions (such as green belts) on peripheral urban development. The limited availability of industrial land in cities sets a ceiling on the amount of new factory building in these places and means that they

Table 3.3 Room for expansion of existing factories by type of area

	% of manufacturing jobs in factories with:	
	less than 50 per cent of site covered by buildings	vacant land next to existing site
Birmingham inner city (1979)	12*	14*
East Midlands (1982)		
cities	28	44
towns	26	50
rural areas	41	57

*Estimated

Source: JURUE, Industrial Premises Survey

Table 3.4   Available industrial land by type of area, 1982

	Hectares	Hectares per thousand manufacturing employees
London	746	1.0
Conurbations	4 661	2.8
Free-standing cities	4 213	4.3
Large towns	4 418	6.3
Small towns	9 732	6.9
Rural areas	6 439	10.9
Great Britain	30 208	4.9

The following counties are excluded: Derbyshire, Nottinghamshire, Hereford and Worcester, Essex, Oxfordshire, Berkshire, Surrey, Buckinghamshire (except Milton Keynes), Gloucestershire, Devon.
Source: Local authorities

are unable to offer firms the number and range of potential sites that are available elsewhere. Additional problems in cities include the higher price of land, the expense of reclaiming sites which have fallen derelict, and the scarcity of very large sites suitable for development as trading estates by the private sector.

On the whole, manufacturing industry is neither able nor willing to overcome the constraints on the supply of industrial land in cities. Firms without room for on-site expansion mostly cannot buy up the adjacent land they need, even at a high price. In many cases the land market simply does not operate. Surrounding land uses may be roads, railways, canals or rivers, public parks, schools, hospitals or churches, and these cannot be bought when needed. The highly dispersed ownership of private housing also makes it difficult for firms to assemble large plots in cities, and of course planning controls impose further restrictions. Office developments avoid these constraints by building upwards – an unattractive or impracticable option for most manufacturing firms – and in any case manufacturing's land requirements are much greater. Office growth therefore remains in the city, but manufacturing growth is squeezed out.

Urban industrial decline is thus rooted in national trends within manufacturing, and in the nature of cities as densely developed environments where alternative uses compete for a limited supply of land. The increase in manufacturing output leads to an increase in the aggregate demand for factory floorspace; it also induces increases in productivity leading to a loss of jobs on existing floorspace. Given the physical constraints in cities, most of the new floorspace and the jobs that go with it are diverted to small towns and rural areas.

Urban industrial decline cannot therefore be blamed on deliberate decisions by companies to avoid or desert cities. Some firms no doubt do have preferences for rural locations, though others benefit from being in a city and continue to prefer urban locations. Instead, we are suggesting that the urban–rural contrast in manufacturing employment change has its origin in national economic trends affecting a wide range of companies and places. Locational preferences may be relevant to an understanding of change within an individual firm, but in aggregate such preferences probably make little difference to the overall shift in the location of manufacturing jobs.

3.5 The impact of Thatcherism

The economic strategy of the Conservative government in 1979 differed from those of the previous Labour and Conservative governments during the post-war era. The commitment to full employment through public intervention was finally abandoned, and the new government sought a shift in the balance of industrial power away from organized labour. As a consequence, several trends in the national economy altered after 1979, the most significant change being the severe contraction of manufacturing production and employment during the following three years. Since national economic trends are so important in generating urban decline, the impact of 'Thatcherism' on the city needs to be considered.

The contrast in manufacturing employment trends before and after 1978 are shown in Table 3.5. Before 1978 there was a large urban–rural contrast, and small towns and rural areas experienced absolute growth despite the national decline. After 1978 all areas suffered large job losses, but the pattern of change was more complex. Conurbations and other cities continued to fare worse than towns and rural areas, but London's

Table 3.5 Manufacturing employment change, 1960–78 and 1978–81, by type of area

	1960–78 (as % 1960)	1978–81 (as % 1978)
London	−42.5	−15.5
Conurbations	−26.5	−22.7
Free-standing cities	−13.8	−17.2
Large towns	−2.2	−16.0
Small towns	+15.7	−15.2
Rural areas	+38.0	−10.0
Great Britain	−11.5	−16.8

Source: Department of Employment

manufacturing employment fell by a little less than the national average – a reversal of a trend dating back at least to the 1950s. London also lost a smaller proportion of its manufacturing jobs than the conurbations, again the opposite of the trend prior to the recession.

Physical constraints in cities influence where expansion is located in times of economic growth. Falling manufacturing output, such as occurred between 1979 and 1981, reduces the need for increases in factory floorspace because many firms need to cut their productive capacity. In a severe recession, towns and rural areas all therefore suffer from the contraction in employment; physical constraints are less important in allocating jobs between locations. Some investment in new factories and factory extensions continues, even in recession, and this continues to favour small towns and rural areas. However, the magnitude of job loss in different localities mostly reflects other factors, though these are only partly understood.

One reason why London has suffered less than the national average and less than the conurbations is that a relatively small share of its manufacturing jobs is in steel, motor-vehicles and textiles, three industries that were hit exceptionally hard by the recession. Using a simple technique known as 'shift-share analysis' we have estimated that London's mix of industries meant that its manufacturing employment could have been expected to fall by 3 per cent less than the national average between 1978 and 1981. In fact, London's manufacturing employment did not hold up as well as this, indicating that the weak employment performance of London firms which marked the period up to 1978 also continued during the recession. The conurbations, on the other hand, were burdened by a mix of industries that led to above-average job losses during the recession. This accounts for a large part of the divergence between trends in London and the conurbations after 1978. The concentration in London of head-quarters plants with an above-average proportion of jobs in research and development, marketing and administration is another factor which probably helped London avoid the worst of the recession. Branch plants undertaking routine production, many of them in the assisted areas, appear to have been the most prone to closure and redundancies.

The post-1979 recession had further implications for urban industry. Previously the growth of labour productivity was associated with the growth of output. In the initial stage of the recession, falling output led to falling productivity, but thereafter there was a substantial increase in productivity even though output remained depressed. This increase reflected the closure of less efficient factories and changes in labour practices facilitated by the weakening of trade-union power in a period of rising unemployment. Increasing labour productivity reduces employment densities, as we noted, reducing still further the potential employment capacity of urban factories.

The boost to productivity during the recession and the resulting fall in employment density may be once-and-for-all occurrences. The low level of manufacturing investment, compared to the 1970s, suggests that the introduction of new machinery and techniques will not be sufficient to create a sustained acceleration in the growth of labour productivity. Much therefore depends on the Conservative government's success in continuing to force changes in labour practices – in obtaining the same output with fewer workers and the same machines. The extent to which this may occur is uncertain. A sustained increase in labour productivity would, however, reduce employment densities still further, leading to fewer jobs in physically constrained urban factories.

If there is a major recovery in industrial production – engendered by new working practices or by traditional reflation – the consequences for manufacturing jobs in urban and rural areas are likely to differ, at least initially, from those during previous upturns. The severity of the post-1979 recession pushed output far below capacity. Many firms have spare capacity within their factories and for the first time in three decades the level of manufacturing production and employment in cities has probably been pushed well below the ceiling imposed by the stock of industrial land and premises. In the initial stage of a recovery, the expansion in output and employment would therefore be accommodated mostly within existing factories in all areas. There would be little tendency for urban and rural employment trends to diverge. As spare capacity was used up, more growth would be diverted into premises which are currently vacant, many as a result of closure during the recession. Since by historical standards the stock of vacant industrial premises is high in all areas, all areas might again benefit during this stage of a recovery.

But the long-term problem in cities would remain. Once the spare capacity in existing and vacant factories had been utilized, physical constraints in cities would reassert themselves. Small towns and rural areas would gain a disproportionately large share of new factory floorspace and new jobs, and the urban–rural contrast in manufacturing employment trends would widen. Moreover, some of the manufacturing jobs which have been lost in cities since 1979 would have disappeared from cities for ever: the reduction in employment density means that, even at full capacity, most factories will not employ as many workers as they did before the recession.

3.6   Urban policy

The decline of the industrial city is widely acknowledged to be a political problem. Labour's 1977 White Paper on the inner cities placed the blame for deprivation and dereliction on the erosion of the cities' economic base; the subsequent Conservative government has not dissented from this view. Effective action to stem the drift of industry from cities is harder to find. Along with other areas, the Tyneside, Clydeside and

Merseyside conurbations are designated as 'Special Development Areas' by the government's regional industrial policy. This entitles manufacturing firms to grants towards the cost of new capital investment, and the government builds advance factories in these places. These conurbations' assisted status pre-dates the concern over inner-city industrial problems: regional aid was first available in these areas during the 1930s. Also, in the cases of Tyneside and Clydeside, the area eligible for assistance includes not only the conurbation but also its hinterland, including in Tyneside's case almost the whole of north-east England. Regional policy thus impinges on urban areas, but it is not a specifically urban initiative.

In contrast, the government's Urban Programme is directed at inner cities, but not just at industry. Central government makes funds available to a hierarchy of urban local authorities, the most important of which are 'Partnership Authorities', to finance schemes designed to revive inner areas. The finance, which has never been generous, is spread across projects as diverse as aid to community groups and the preparation of industrial sites. Its potentially beneficial effect is, however, more than offset by the withdrawal of grants from the same authorities as part of the squeeze on local-government expenditure.

The establishment of inner-city 'Enterprise Zones' – areas where firms are exempt from paying rates and where planning controls are relaxed – has been the most notable Conservative initiative to promote urban industry. These have been criticized for a number of reasons: for example the zones are exceptionally small, and within cities they are liable to fill up with firms relocating from just outside the zones, with little net benefit to the city as a whole. Other Conservative initiatives include the setting up of urban development corporations in London's docklands and Liverpool along the lines of those operating in the New Towns, the provision of an 'Urban Development Grant' to encourage private sector property development, and a modest relaxation of planning controls on industry. There have also been numerous exhortations to the private sector to put its money into declining inner cities. In addition, an increasing number of local authorities are becoming involved in promoting urban industry. This is done mainly by providing land and small premises, and in a few authorities by direct financial assistance to firms, though the scale of local-authority intervention is severely limited by the funds available.

In all, these policies do not add up to very much in the light of the formidable national trends leading to the deindustrialization of the city. In our view national economic recovery is an essential step towards stemming the loss of industrial jobs in urban areas, especially since the recession of the early 1980s has pushed manufacturing output so far below its potential in all areas. Cities would benefit directly from a recovery. Local firms could expand production and employment within their existing buildings, and further growth would be possible in factories which had space for expansion on site. Investment in new factories would increase, and cities could expect to gain some of these. Also the expansion of job opportunities in small towns and rural areas would enable those who wanted to move out of cities to do so, further reducing inner city unemployment. However, we do not think that the economic policies pursued by the Conservative government since 1979 are likely to create a sustained recovery of this sort; what is needed in particular is an increase in the level of demand through reflationary fiscal policy, and international co-ordination to prevent foreign-exchange crises which might scupper a recovery.

But even if such a recovery were to occur, the relative decline of the industrial city would not be at an end. As this chapter has explained, there are constraints on industrial growth in cities, and the gap between employment trends in cities and other areas could actually be expected to widen during sustained recovery as new factory floorspace was diverted to small towns and rural areas. In the long run, increases in labour productivity and the expansion of output are not compatible with the maintainance and expansion of industrial employment in cities.

To do anything about this aspect of urban deindustrialization – the decline relative to other areas – requires spatial policies. The problem highlighted in this chapter is the physical constraint on industrial expansion in cities. Even in relatively depressed economic conditions, many individual firms and some industries have the potential for growth. However, many factories in cities do not have room for expansion on-site, and at the same time many firms in cities operate in old premises, often multi-storey and designed for products and processes that have long since been abandoned, which impose handicaps on operating efficiency. These obstacles can frustrate expansion. They also mean that in order to increase production and employment many city firms have to move to other areas.

The most useful step would be for urban authorities to get together with the major industrial employers in their areas to plan for their future land requirements, in particular land for expansion next to existing factories. In some instances employers may face no shortage of land. In others there may be straightforward steps – the redesignation of vacant land, for example, – which would permit local expansion that would otherwise be thwarted. To supplement such initiatives urban authorities should ensure that within their areas there is a sufficient quantity and range of sites available for local relocations and for incoming factories. Some authorities already do this as a normal part of their activities; a surprising number do not.

This approach to urban industrial decline will not, of course, bring an end to the urban–rural contrast in manufacturing employment change; to some extent the physical constraints on industry in cities cannot be removed even by energetic planning. But these policies could make a valuable contribution at the local level.

References

COMMUNITY DEVELOPMENT PROJECT (1977) *The Costs of Industrial Change*, An Inter-project Report, London, Community Development Project.

DANSON, M. W., LEVER, W. F. and MALCOLM, J. (1980) 'The inner-city employment problem in Great Britain, 1952–76: A shift-share approach', *Urban Studies*, Vol. 17, pp. 193–210.

DEPARTMENT OF TRADE AND INDUSTRY (1973) Memorandum on the Inquiry into Location Attitudes and Experience, *Minutes of Evidence*, Trade and Industry Subcommittee of the House of Commons Expenditure Committee, Session 1972–3, pp. 525–668, London, HMSO.

FOTHERGILL, S. and GUDGIN, G. (1979) 'Regional employment change: a subregional explanation', *Progress in Planning*, Vol. 12, pp. 155–219.

FOTHERGILL, S., GUDGIN, G., KITSON, M. and MONK, S. (1984) 'Differences in the profitability of the UK manufacturing sector between conurbations and other areas', *Scottish Journal of Political Economy*, Vol. 31, pp. 72–91.

FOTHERGILL, S., KITSON, M. and MONK, S. (1983) 'The impact of the New and Expanded Town programmes on industrial location in Britain 1960–78', *Regional Studies*, Vol. 17, pp. 251–60.

FOTHERGILL, S., KITSON, M. and MONK, S. (1984) *Urban Industrial Decline: The Causes of the Urban–Rural Contrast in Manufacturing Employment Change*, London, HMSO.

JURUE (1980) *Industrial Renewal in the Inner City: An Assessment of Potential and Problems*, DOE Inner Cities Research Programme Report No. 2.

KALDOR, N. (1966) *Causes of the Slow Rate of Economic Growth of the United Kingdom*, Cambridge, Cambridge University Press.

KEEBLE, D. (1980) 'Industrial decline, regional policy and the urban–rural manufacturing shift in the United Kingdom', *Environment and Planning A*, Vol. 12, pp. 945–62.

LEVER, W. F. (1981) *Operating Costs as an Explanation of Employment Change in the Clydeside Region*, paper presented at the 'Industry and the Inner City' Conference, University of Newcastle upon Tyne, May.

MASSEY, D. and MEEGAN, R. (1978) 'Industrial restructuring versus the cities', *Urban Studies*, Vol. 15, pp. 273–88.

MOORE, B. C., RHODES, J. and TYLER, P. (1980) *New Developments in the Evaluation of Regional Policy*, paper presented at an SSRC Urban and Regional Economics Conference, University of Birmingham, May.

OKUN, A. M. (1962) 'Potential GNP: its measurement and significance', reprinted in Okun, A. (1970) *The Political Economy of Prosperity*, Washington, D.C. Brookings Institution, pp. 132–45.

RICHARDSON, H. W. (1969) *Regional Economics: Location Theory, Urban Structure and Regional Change*, London, Weidenfeld and Nicolson.

SCOTT, A. (1982) 'Locational patterns and dynamics of industrial activity in the urban metropolis', *Urban Studies*, Vol. 19, pp. 111–42.

WELLBELOVE, D., WOODS, A. and ZAFIRIS, N. (1981) 'Survival and success of the inner-city economy: the case of Islington', *Urban Studies*, Vol. 18, pp. 301–13.

Section III   Services and employment change

Introduction

The three chapters in this section have a number of themes in common. They are all concerned with what kind of service-based economy is emerging, what type of jobs are being created, and what the geography of all this looks like. In particular, they share an interest in unearthing the kinds of processes that have shaped the uneven geography of service employment change. But before we go too far with these points of similarity, let us also consider some of the fundamental ways in which the chapters differ.

They differ, first, in the way that they characterize service sector development, that is, how they interpret the changes that are taking place in the economy which lie behind the uneven pattern of service development. Secondly, the chapters show considerable variation in the kinds of evidence used to support a particular interpretation. All refer to general employment trends, for instance, but they vary in their reliance upon quantitative or qualitative evidence. Thirdly, the accounts adopt different, although overlapping, ways of explaining the uneven geography of service employment. Naturally, the chapters diverge in other ways, too, but it is these three aspects that we wish to concentrate upon here as, in our view, they are among the most revealing.

One further point that should be borne in mind is that each account of service sector development contains an assessment of what is happening to people's jobs and the kinds of waged work that, arguably, are likely to predominate in the years leading up to and beyond the year 2000.

What, then, can be said about the different characterizations of service sector development in the three chapters? To start with, they have different foci. Each looks broadly at the pattern of service employment change, yet each chooses to focus on certain aspects of the rise in service sector employment. Both Daniels and Wood, for example, are concerned with producer service employment (which includes financial and business services, and more generally those service activities which meet intermediate, not final or consumer, demand), but each has something rather different to say about this group of services.

Wood is concerned to show the interconnections in the economy between manufacturing and service industries and how the growth of producer-related service employment is linked to what is happening to production within the manufacturing sector. He emphasizes the transfer of jobs from manufacturing to services, and from what he calls the corporate to the competitive sector of the economy, as firms externalize parts of service production. In effect, he is highlighting a shift in the (social) division of labour. Daniels chooses to emphasize a rather different aspect of producer services. He also draws attention to the process of externalization, the contracting out of services previously provided in-house by firms. His focus, however, is squarely on what types of demand exist for producer services and the geography of the firms which organize the supply. Above all, he is concerned with the spatial inequalities that arise from the uneven spatial distribution of producer service activities.

Allen also has geography in the foreground of his analysis. His focus, however, is broader than that of either Woods or Daniels in so far as he takes in employment changes in both the public and private service industries and the national and international processes that lie behind these changes. The emphasis in Allen's account is neither that of the division of labour, nor that of the market-place, but rather the changing organization of the relations of production over space. The criterion of breadth, however, on its own, is not an indication of a more fruitful or comprehensive account. It depends, as always, on the substance of the explanation and the coherence of the interpretative framework that informs the content.

Wood's analysis, for example, draws heavily upon the ideas of Gershuny and Miles (1983). In their view service jobs have grown in response to an increased demand for manufactured goods which, itself, is a product of what they refer to as a growing self-service economy. The whole process appears to be led by waves of technical and social innovations that, as in Hall's chapter in the previous Section, owes much to the work of Kondratiev. As one set of 'heartland technologies' displaces another, so new products come on line supported by the appropriate infrastructure. In the post-war period this has enabled more people to take advantage of products such as washing machines and cars to 'service' themselves. In recent years this shift to a self-service economy appears to have taken a new twist as new products and new information-based technologies are developed. In consequence, a related demand for (producer) services has arisen to support the production of these new products which, in turn, has boosted employment within (producer) service firms. And what is important about this framework for Wood is that it points to the clear interdependences between manufacturing production and service employment, and the pivotal role accorded to a manufacturing base.

Daniels, in contrast, works within a framework that accords a more central role to the position of services within the economy. His characterization of service sector development is influenced by post-industrial ideas. According to Daniels, Britain is in the midst of a structural transition from an industrial to a post-industrial, service-based economy. As the economy adjusts to this change, certain industries, especially the main producer services, are seen to move centre stage and play a more significant role in the nation's economic performance. Knowledge and information are among the key characteristics of these industries, a point stressed by post-industrial and information society theorists, and in Daniels' view their location will be of considerable significance to the changing relative fortunes of cities and regions.

Allen draws upon a different set of influences from either of the above two. His account of uneven service development takes its starting-point from Massey's (1984) view that the changing geography of the labour force and of class is best understood through the framework of production relations and how they are organized over space. In this framework the social relations under examination are not post-industrial or technological relations, they are the relations of capitalist production. It is the fact that production is organized for profit that is the central issue here. In stressing this point, Allen places the development of the private service industries in the context of their relative profitability and their geography in the context of the kinds of calculation of profit made by different types of service firm.

All three chapters, therefore, are informed by a different kind of conceptual and substantive framework. Two of the three chapters, Wood and Daniels, are concerned with producer service employment, but the theorization of change they receive is altogether different. Each chapter has something rather different to say about the kind of change that the shift to services represents. Moreover, each is in a broad sense a geographical application of the theoretical view that informs it. With Massey, the geography is an integral aspect of her framework; with the other two, Gershuny and Miles's technological view and the post-industrial theorization, the geography has to be 'built in'. Let me illustrate.

If we take one of the key aspects of the uneven pattern of service development in post-war Britain, the concentration of service jobs, and in particular of high-level jobs, in London and the South East, we find a difference of interpretation in the chapters. Daniels and Allen, for instance, talk about similar sorts of developments – the globalization of (producer) services, the increase in direct investment by multinational service companies, and the concentration of company headquarters in London and the South East. They may use somewhat different terms to describe these developments, but essentially they have in mind the same processes. Yet they do not explain their significance for London in the same way.

For Daniels, these sorts of processes both reflect and are a reflection of the strong pull that London exerts over 'knowledge capital', that is, the professional and managerial skills provided by commercial and financial service firms. It is largely the demand for these knowledge-based activities that is taken to be behind London's growth as a producer service complex. Allen, however, sees the concentration of these kinds of 'thinkwork' in London rather differently. Instead of emphasizing the different types of jobs in London from elsewhere (knowledge-based as opposed to, say, routine-based service work), Allen points to a difference in the type of functions performed in part of London's service-based economy. He refers to the capital city as a centre of strategic control, a centre which includes people who plan and manage the geography of investment and the location of jobs, and also those who are involved directly with the control and organization of work within the overall structure of a company's activities or corporate system. In short, he refers to London as a centre which shapes the relations between different types of service jobs and activities in various towns and cities.

Wood is more cautious about what he has to say about the peculiarity of London, as he is in general about speculating on the emerging spatial pattern of service employment. In one sense, this may be indicative of the framework adopted, in that the spatial impact of the processes that Gershuny and Miles refer to are difficult to discern. Nonetheless, Wood does offer a broad view of the kind of geography that appears to be on the horizon. One likelihood is that the growth of producer service industries will benefit provincial cities and towns in the south, together with some of the non-industrial towns and cities such as Edinburgh, Coventry and Hull in the north. The benefit is seen as disproportionate, with the southern urban locations likely to fare better than their northern counterparts.

For Daniels and Allen the pattern of uneven development that is taking shape as the balance of the economy shifts further towards services is much the same – with urban and provincial locations in the south in a favoured position and job growth occurring in areas different to those most affected by manufacturing job loss. Where they differ again, however, is over what they have to say about the structure of service employment that is being created in these urban locations. Not all service jobs, producer service employment included, are well-paid, high-status, professional jobs and many involve part-time and low-paid work. Allen, for example, places considerable stress upon the class and gender characteristics of service-job growth and the shift towards labour-market polarization in service-based local economies, and Wood is also aware of the qualitative dimension to uneven service development. Uneven development in this case is more than the aggregate totals of job loss and job gain in different places; it is about the characteristics (the type and function) of jobs lost or created, the skills involved, and for whom – which class and which gender. In this sense there is a new unequal geography of services.

References

GERSHUNY, J. I. and MILES, I. D. (1983) *The New Service Economy: The Transformation of Employment in Industrial Societies*, London, Frances Pinter.

MASSEY, D. (1984) *Spatial Divisions of Labour: Social Structures and the Geography of Production*, London and Basingstoke, Macmillan.

4 Employment change and the role of the producer service sector

P. A. Wood

4.1 Introduction

The problems of the United Kingdom economy are well known. A rapid decline in manufacturing employment has taken place since the 1960s, only partly balanced by growth in services, while the labour force has expanded. The result has been an unprecedented post-war rise in unemployment, especially since 1979 (Cambridge Economic Policy Review, 1982) [. . .]

The spatial manifestations of these economic changes are also well known. The traditional manufacturing centres in the conurbations of the north, west and, more recently, the Midlands, have been crushingly affected, and London itself has experienced the most rapid employment decline of all in its manufacturing and port activities. The areas suffering least have been the medium-small town and rural areas, especially in the South East and in the adjacent regions of East Anglia, the East Midlands and the near South West. British 'counterurbanization' accelerated during the 1970s, and has been widely associated with the attempts of British manufacturing to compete internationally by reorganizing its levels and patterns of labour demand, both structurally and spatially (Keeble, 1976, 1980; Fothergill and Gudgin, 1982; Massey, 1983; Danson, 1982).

One theme of this chapter is that, while the incidence and geographical patterns of industrial redundancies are more immediate causes for concern (Townsend, 1982a, 1982b), it is also important, both theoretically and practically, to understand how and where new employment is being created. As Massey and Meegan (1982) have demonstrated, new types of jobs result from industrial restructuring, even though often in smaller numbers, in different places and engaging different skills from those that have been lost [. . .] A second important theme is that the analysis of differential shifts in the demand for labour cannot be confined to one sector alone, least of all to manufacturing. Developments across the whole economy, in both the corporate and competitive segments, in services and in the public and informal sectors closely interact. A perspective is required that can encompass these interactions.

The most popular model of recent employment change in Britain focuses on the role of large manufacturing firms. Job loss has occurred because of a combination of declining demand for many old-established products and severe pressure to improve labour productivity in all sectors as a result of increasing national and international competition. Rapid technical innovation has changed the nature of the production process, making it more capital-intensive and imposing different patterns of work on the remaining employees. Most commonly, within the general contraction of manufacturing employment, this has increased the share held by those with managerial and technical skills, and reduced that of skilled manual workers. New locations have been sought, expressing a growing dualism in the workforce. Investment has moved either to areas where scarce skilled white-collar workers are available or can be attracted (for example, in outer South East England and parts of central Scotland), or to areas of low wages and high unemployment, where a semi-skilled, often predominantly female labour force can be recruited to carry out largely routine, semi-skilled production activities in branch plants (for example, rural or small town areas, some in northern and western regions, where government subsidy is also available). Both of these trends thus favour areas outside the old industrial conurbations, the traditional heartlands of the unionized, male, skilled manual workforce. The job loss in these areas has therefore been accompanied by selective job creation in other areas.

This description inevitably caricatures what has been happening in fact. It relates only to some facets of recent change, especially those dominated by the manufacturing operations of multi-plant corporations in established products. However important these are in the total pattern of change, the model neglects the other trends in the pattern of labour demand which do not necessarily mirror the same tendencies. Remnants of older patterns of production, although less dominant, survive and the opportunities to arrest their decline remain to be exploited by private or public effort (for example, in coal-mining, heavy engineering, electrical apparatus, chemicals). The pattern of investment in new products and in innovative new firms, although favouring areas which already possess skilled managerial and technical workers (Gould and Keeble, 1984), is also generally more labour-intensive and requires more skilled manual workers than does routine production. Similarly, many independent firms supplying goods and services to production, even though in highly competitive markets, often engage both non-manual and manual skills in very different ways to large firms orientated towards final demand. In any case the constituent firms of multi-product corporations perform varied roles, as Taylor and Thrift have described (Taylor and Thrift, 1982). In Britain employment trends in the public sector are also particularly significant. After a period in the 1970s of relative expansion, pressures to reduce employment in administration, education, health and social welfare services have intensified more recently. Some complementary spin-off may be found, however, in the private construction and service sectors.

Two important general aspects of this complexity in labour demand change need to be acknowledged before exploring them further. The first is inevitably that the balance of change, most obviously between gross job loss and job creation, depends on macroeconomic trends. These are conventionally summarized in terms of medium-term national economic performance, whether absolutely or in international comparisons. They need also to be examined with regard to the factors attracting or repelling multinational finance into employment-creating investment in Britain (Dunning and Norman, 1983; Dicken, 1980) [. . .]

Such macroeconomic considerations are also likely to affect the balance of change between different sectors, and between corporate and competitive enterprises, the rate of adoption and success of new technology, and the resources available to the public sector. Whatever national economic fortunes emerge, however, a second aspect of changing labour demand is also fundamental; the anatomy of job loss is intimately associated with that of job creation. To neglect one side of the changing division of labour is to neglect the full significance of the other. While prediction of the macroeconomic future is difficult, further insight is still required into the principal structural shifts in the economy and the ways in which the characteristics of areas may attract or repel what employment growth is available. In considering these problems it is the contention of this chapter that the role of the formally defined service sector is of crucial significance.

4.2 The significance of the service sector

The key to the future of employment in Britain, as probably in most modern societies, lies in what is popularly called the service sector. This is not simply because in 1981 such activities in Britain employed 62 per cent of the workforce (excluding construction and utilities), and had grown by 4 per cent in the previous six years, when manufacturing employment fell by 19 per cent. Nor because most macroeconomic forecasts indicate that private sector services will continue to grow in the 1980s, while employment elsewhere falls (Elias, 1982; Moore and Rhodes, 1982). After all, recent developments in service employment disguise as many internal contrasts of growth and decline as does manufacturing change. Similarly, fundamental organizational and technical changes are as likely to confound labour demand predictions based on recent experience in services as in other sectors. Perhaps more important for the future significance of services than their current pattern of employment is the recognition that employment in manufacturing will continue to contract. What happens to service functions, whether they grow or decline, is therefore no longer of subsidiary interest. It is also clear that 'service' activities have increasingly become interwoven with production itself. Thus the employment impact of production changes cannot be properly understood without regard to changes in the supporting services, both within and outside the factory.

From a geographical point of view, the uneven distribution of service employment in Britain, especially between South East England and the rest of the country, is also a matter of growing concern, as the decline of specialist manufacturing areas has accelerated (Marquand, 1979, 1983). The cumulative effects of this trend are beginning to make a major impact on regional inequalities, both directly and indirectly through the greater attraction of new manufacturing investment to areas with a high quality service environment. The possibility that service investment may even *lead* manufacturing to certain regions is now being actively entertained (Marshall, 1982, 1985).

The neglect of developments in the service sector until recently in Britain has nevertheless been almost complete, in spite of a period of growing interest in North America (Greenfield, 1966; Fuchs, 1968, 1969; Stanback, 1979; Stanback, Bearse, Noyelle and Karasek, 1981). What attention it has received has been concentrated either on tertiary activities, especially retailing, or on the growth and locational characteristics of the 'office sector'. The latter category of activities is especially unsatisfactory as a basis for analysing the wider development of service functions. The neglect of services has been based on economists' assumptions that they are generally consumer-orientated, make only a comparatively small contribution to either national or regional trade, and are dependent for the spending power that sustains them upon the wealth created by the manufacturing sector. The supposedly low labour productivity of service production has also relegated it to a supporting role in the explanation of economic growth. The growth of service employment has therefore been attributed to increased consumer and government spending on service needs and to the low labour productivity of services compared to manufacturing. A highly productive manufacturing sector is still widely regarded as the only basis for national economic success. These assumptions, incidentally, make the stimulation of manufacturing *employment* for the revival of the depressed regions somewhat paradoxical.

Thus, most analyses of the causes for the changing geography of employment in Britain in recent years have focused on manufacturing. This is why, for many commentators, corporate sector industrial restructuring, as described earlier, provides the main dynamo of location change. Similarly, the monitoring of regional economic development has been heavily preoccupied with manufacturing employment. The work of Fothergill and Gudgin best illustrates this, on the grounds that regional variations in manufacturing employment change were most significant between 1959 and 1975, and that service employment change variations largely followed these differences, or were related to consumer or public sector expenditure (Fothergill and Gudgin, 1982, Ch. 3). As a consequence of these assumptions, the dynamics of employment creation and loss within the service sector have additionally been obscured by the poor monitoring of change.

It should nevertheless be recognized that, far from being predominantly consumer-orientated, much of the post-war growth of service employment has been in producer-related activities, including financial, legal, insurance, professional, technical, distribution and maintenance activities. Specialist white- and even blue-collar skills have increasingly been sought outside manufacturing firms to reduce the costs of their own operations. Further, around 40 per cent of jobs in the manufacturing sector itself are now in 'non-productive' support services, a figure that has grown and tends to be higher in a more successful, technically innovative firms and industries (Goddard, 1978). From the point of view of the contribution made by the workers concerned to the production process, it would appear that the decision to provide producer services 'in-house', or to buy them in from the 'service' sector is increasingly arbitrary. The distinction between manufacturing and much service employment is thus becoming increasingly misleading. As the former has fallen, the latter has grown, and the two trends are not entirely independent of each other. If much service employment 'depends' on production, as often suggested, this is true only in the same way as is employment in the formally defined manufacturing sector itself.

Estimation of the employment size of the producer-related services is, of course, fraught with difficulties. According to the 1973 Input-Output Table, about one third of the value of service output in the United Kingdom (including construction and the utilities) went to other production sectors, accounting for 37 per cent of intermediate transactions. An estimate by the author for 1981 suggests conservatively that identifiable producer service employment in Britain amounted to 18 per cent of the total, a figure that had grown during the previous six years of manufacturing decline. If an estimate of 'in-house' service employment within manufacturing is added to this, the role of producer services increases to about 30 per cent of all employment, compared with 25–30 per cent in production itself, and around 40–45 per cent in consumer-orientated services, some of which could equally be regarded as serving a 'producer' function (see Wood, 1984; and also Marquand, 1979; Robertson, Briggs and Goodchild, 1982).

The increasing 'tertiarization' of manufacturing and the growing involvement of 'service' firms in the production process have therefore been important shifts in the division of labour in recent decades, related to increasingly complex processes of production. While the pivotal importance of secondary *production* in modern economies is accepted, *employment* is increasingly being displaced away from the factory floor itself, and from the specialist production firms which make up the conventionally defined manufacturing sector. Organizational and technical changes have progressively dissolved the distinction between manufacturing and service functions. Any preoccupation simply with employment in manufacturing at the expense of service sector changes is thus an increasingly misleading diversion from the wider trends affecting patterns of job loss and creation.

A final and important elaboration is needed to the pattern of manufacturing-producer service interaction depicted so far. As the size of the service sector and its internal complexity have grown, more jobs have become based upon the service expertise offered to *other* service functions. Obvious examples include the growth of many financial, insurance, property and computer advisory agencies, the rise of the credit card industry, tourism and a good deal of building design and construction work. The variety of trends in the division of labour within the service sector itself is therefore bewildering in its complexity, spurred by corporate and technological changes in overlapping producer and consumer markets. Although we are here concerned with the more direct links between production and services, therefore, the growing internal diversity of service functions reinforces the need to increase our understanding of service sector trends.

4.3   Services and employment change

In recent years, the framework of ideas about service growth put forward by Gershuny and his associates has become increasingly influential in Britain, and has interesting implications for examination of the interdependence between production and service employment. Gershuny's principal theme is the evolution of the 'self-service economy', associated with the decline of personal service employment during the twentieth century, and its displacement by manufactured products operated by the consumer (Gershuny, 1978, 1983). In many aspects of consumption, increasingly elaborate manufactured goods, such as the motor vehicle, washing machine, vacuum cleaner and television, have replaced service labour, for example in public transport, laundries, domestic service and theatres and cinemas. Growth in consumer demand and related productivity improvement have resulted in a steady fall in the real cost of acquiring such services in manufactured form compared to employing service workers. To support this process, however, more labour has become employed in the design, selling, distribution and servicing of manufactured goods, which now embody a very wide range of skills, in addition to those of direct physical production itself.

Gershuny estimated that, in Britain by the early 1970s, only 22.5 per cent of consumer expenditure was accorded to personal service activities, half on publicly provided education, health and welfare needs. The growth of service employment to over 60 per cent of the total, although partly due to relatively low labour productivity growth in services compared to primary and secondary production, has depended also on the increasing orientation of much service employment to the process of production (what Gershuny and Miles term 'intermediate producer services') and to the domestic delivery and servicing of goods ('intermediate consumer services'). This has been an integral part of economic growth based on technical innovation during the twentieth century (Gershuny and Miles, 1983).

The satisfaction of various consumer needs through technical innovation has therefore been achieved by arranging various combinations of labour inputs, including some employed in the market economy, whether in formally defined manufacturing, producer or consumer service sectors, some working for the non-market (public) sector, and some derived from the machine-aided efforts of consumers themselves. The established patterns of labour inputs are, however, currently experiencing rapid change because of innovations, associated primarily with communications and information technology, which are having major effects on patterns of job loss and gain across the whole spectrum of employment. The division of labour which has been dominant since the 1950s, orientated to the growing production, for example, of motor vehicles, mechanical domestic appliances, electrical generating and distributing equipment, conventional air transport, and their associated public infrastructure, is being displaced by the needs of a 'new heartland technology' (Gershuny and Miles, 1983, p. 131). This will change the processes of production for these goods and support new products. In general, the numbers engaged directly in highly automated production will be relatively small, but those engaged in research and development, sales, delivery and servicing for both the production and subsequent consumption of goods will be relatively large. Huge infrastructure investment in information technology will also be needed, much of which, in Britain at least, will be provided by the public sector. In Gershuny and Miles's view, public agencies therefore have considerable power to influence the rate and form, including the location of change, quite apart from exercising regulatory powers on telecommunications design, access and control (Gershuny and Miles, 1983, Ch. 10). The new technology will, of course, also have other important implications for the style and location of work itself.

[. . .] Gershuny and Miles's perspective is of interest because of the long-term view it takes of trends in the division of labour based on detailed studies of experience in Britain and the rest of Europe. The result is a subtle analysis of the nature and role of work in the production of manufactured commodities, linking the production process itself to its supporting services, and to the ways goods are used by consumers to provide services. It allows employment changes in different sectors to be related together and to social innovation more generally. It recognizes also that the form taken by new technology, emphasizing either centralized or devolved control, affecting the pattern and rate of social innovation and the organization of working and non-working activities, depends on the representation of different private and public interests in the design process (ibid., p. 134). The most powerful pressures for change in mixed economies, however, will certainly be towards improved labour productivity to serve the needs of corporate profit. This may be particularly strong in many service activities which have traditionally been relatively labour intensive and are increasingly becoming dominated by large firms.

Such pressures on evolving patterns of consumption, private production and public policy will, therefore, generate differential patterns of job loss and creation, related to the labour force, organizational and product characteristics of service functions. For example, it is clear, as we have seen, that pressures for labour productivity increases are greatest in the corporate segment of the economy, especially in production, delivery, and increasingly in routine clerical functions, where future job losses seem most likely. On the other hand, the proliferation of specialist services favours the transfer of more labour-intensive functions to the competitive small firm segment, where tendering imposes a criterion of cost effectiveness. This has for long applied to the professional, managerial, commercial and technical consultancy activities which have expanded most rapidly in recent years. It is also becoming more common in other service areas, including such 'blue-collar' activities as building maintenance, equipment service and repair, catering, cleaning, printing, packaging, security, delivery and transportation. More emphasis is also being placed on smaller companies for specialist research and development and innovative production or marketing, often through a process of key worker 'spin-off' from the corporate sector. This may be followed by the later reabsorption of successful firms through takeover activity.

These processes of job transfer between sectors and segments of the economy in response to technical and organizational pressures on labour productivity require [. . .] detailed investigation [. . .] In general, it must be assumed that the total level of employment sustained more or less directly by production will decline as a result of these pressures, although certainly by less than that in the formally defined manufacturing sector alone. Some activities and sectors will grow, however, especially in the manufacture of new products, or the development of new support functions, such as the provision of computer software, security services or specialist printing and packaging. There is also similar scope for growth in employment in 'intermediate' consumer-orientated activities including the production of television programmes, cable communications and computer software, and in servicing new domestic equipment.

Some areas of employment have traditionally been resistant to technological displacement. Most obviously these include highly skilled information processing and exchange functions in business, commerce, government and the professions. Even here, for example in business intelligence and in education and training, innovations can now be expected that will reduce the recent rates of employment growth. This marks a further incursion of Gershuny's 'self-service' principle into areas of personal service provision that have so far been slow to adopt manufactured substitutes for personal contact. The public services in Britain, including education, health and welfare functions, although in the 'non-market' sector, have experienced recent declines in employment, mainly because of efficiency-directed changes in policy. The permanence of such politically determined trends is, of course, difficult to predict, although the impact of technical change is likely to be sustained. More certain are changes of needs within the public sector arising from demographic shifts towards an ageing population. Educational, medical and welfare priorities are likely to be affected by such shifts in the next decade and beyond.

It is likely that the skill requirements of employment will grow as a result of these organizational and technical trends. Equally likely, however, is a growing dualism in the labour market. The demand for highly trained managerial, technical and professional skills in the corporate sector will expand. The scope for other styles of entrepreneurial expertise, especially amongst workers with technical and manual skills may also increase, and although the demand for skilled workers in manufacturing will continue to fall, this may be compensated to some extent by displacement of some functions into the producer service sector. In an already polarized society, however, the position of semi-skilled and unskilled workers is likely to become relatively worse. Those employed in the corporate sector are likely to be most vulnerable to the transfer of capital abroad to low wage countries, while any expansion of the small firm, secondary labour market is most likely to be based on poor levels of pay and working conditions. All these developments suggest that labour supply attributes, especially through education and more specific training, are likely to be important factors in ensuring employment for individuals and in attracting investment to particular areas which possess reserves of such skills.

In spite of some evidence for the resurgence of the competitive small firm sector, especially in support services, and the potential for the public direction of change, the dominant position of corporate priorities and decision-making is unlikely to be challenged by current trends. In fact, the technology-led developments described here are very much by-products of the emerging patterns of corporate interest. The rising corporate power in the 'producer service' sector, already dominated by financial and marketing interests, is an integral part of modern corporate capitalism on an increasingly international scale. The elaboration of the evolving division of labour suggested in this chapter, away from the simple 'corporate' manufacturing model outlined at the beginning, does not challenge the fundamental economic power relationships underlying change. Nevertheless, the form even of corporate restructuring in different types of producer service provision (for example, banking, insurance, computer software) varies widely, with contrasted forms of concentration or dispersal of control, and the associated changes in employment distribution (Marshall, 1985) [. . .]

4.4   The spatial implications

This chapter has sought a comprehensive view of the changing division of labour in contemporary capitalism, identifying areas of employment growth as well as of decline. It has emphasized the growing domination of the producer and consumer 'service' role in employment and proposed that pressures for increased productivity, so evident in production, will also be felt differentially across the whole range of white- and blue-collar service functions. Jobs are being reallocated between increasingly interrelated manufacturing and service activities, and between the corporate and competitive segments of the economy. Although these changes are led by the need to sustain corporate profits, supporting investment in public infrastructure, communications equipment and education and training will affect the rate and pattern of economic change, consciously or otherwise, as well as providing employment in itself. [. . .]

Within this broad description, Gershuny and Miles's scenario of differential employment change contains many uncertainties, especially associated with the roles of private and public agencies. Its spatial impacts must also be uncertain. It has been surmised that the labour supply or environmental characateristics of different areas, whether attracting high-skill workers or offering a reserve of skilled or unskilled labour, may influence the form of future investment by different organizations. In these and other ways, not least the inertia of established investment patterns, the 'spatial implications' are intimately bound up with all aspects of the patterns of change so far discussed. It is clear that, whatever the pattern of future national economic growth, the balance of employment change within and between particular regions of Britain is likely to vary widely. How far can these variations be systematically considered in the context of the analysis so far?

Table 4.1 is a largely impressionistic sketch of a possible answer to this question. It takes Fothergill and Gudgin's categorization of sub-regions as its spatial base. This was derived by examining the manufacturing employment performance of all parts of Britain between 1959 and 1975, which clearly demonstrated the sub-regional nature of economic differentiation, especially between the old, heavily urbanized cores and different parts of the surrounding regions. The area categorization has been augmented to distinguish schematically between areas in the 'south' (i.e. in the South East, East Anglia and the South West) and the 'north' (the industrial Midlands, Northern England, Scotland and Wales). The table indicates a possible variety of trends in employment demand in six interrelated economic functions represented in the various types of sub-regional economy, taking into account the aggregate investment patterns across all sectors of the economy. It is not based on the analysis of actual data over any particular period of time, but attempts to indicate trends in the mid 1980s. One purpose is to suggest a framework for the further monitoring of employment change that might be more sensitive than are conventional

Table 4.1 Employment share trends in various sectors and sub-regional types

		Intermediate producer services		Intermediate consumer services	Personal services	Public investment	Total
	Production	White-collar	Blue-collar				
London	–	0	0	0	+	–	–
Conurbations	–	–	–	0	–	+	–
Free-standing cities:							
South	0	++	+	+	0	–	+
North	–	++	0	0	–	+	–
Industrial towns:							
South	–	0	+	+	–	–	0
North	–	0	–	0	–	+	–
County towns:							
South	+	++	++	++	0	–	+
North	0	++	++	+	0	–	0
Rural areas							
South	+	+	0	0	+	+	+
North	–	0	–	–	–	0	–
Total	–	+	+	+	–	–	(?)

Key:– Loss; + Gain; 0 Little change/not clear.

data sources to the technical and structural shifts in employment described in this chapter.

For these purposes, 'production' refers to trends in factory-based jobs concerned directly with the current production of manufactured goods. 'Intermediate producer services' employment includes jobs, within the factory or elsewhere, in the public or private sectors, that are ultimately orientated to the production of goods. These include, for example, workers in managerial, technical or clerical (white-collar) and all types of manual (blue-collar) *occupations* who contribute to such service *functions* as financing, planning, design, marketing, distribution, servicing and maintenance. 'Intermediate consumer services' includes a range of functions orientated to servicing manufactured goods at the place of use. They include the supply of services and materials (for example, computer software, literature, TV programmes) and repair and maintenance expertise. 'Personal services' are delivered to consumers principally on a face-to-face basis for purposes such as professional advice, education, health and welfare services, entertainment and retail purchase. 'Public investment' employment includes those concerned with providing collective infrastructure, such as transportation and communications networks and equipment, or power supply, usually through public or semi-public agencies.

The allocations in the table proceed from the assumption that growth in the share of employment is likely to occur in the white- and blue-collar intermediate producer and consumer services, with decline in production, personal service and public investment activities. The areas where employment growth seems likely to continue are especially in and around the 'free-standing cities' (Bristol and south Hampshire) and in county towns and accessible rural areas in the south. The emphasis of relative growth in these cases, however, may vary between these areas. For example, employment in production is likely to grow in the county town and rural areas, while producer services growth will concentrate in the cities and towns. Intermediate consumer services will also develop strongly in these urban areas, related to population and income growth there and in the surrounding sub-regions. Personal service employment, although declining generally, may be sustained in these areas through a combination of recreational and tourist growth and high residential incomes.

The position of similar types of area in the north is more difficult to estimate, if only because they are very varied in their characteristics. For example, the free-standing cities include areas as different as Teesside, Hull, Coventry, parts of south Wales and Edinburgh. It seems likely, however, that such cities will develop more as producer and consumer service centres for their regions than as employers of production workers, but growth is likely to be less than in the south, and total employment may not rise. The north's county towns seem likely to be more attractive than the large centres to investment in production facilities, and they may also receive a strong stimulus to producer and consumer service employment, for both local and wider demand. The remoter rural areas in the north, on the other hand, are unlikely to have the same attractions as those in the south, and employment seems more likely to become concentrated in the towns. The industrial towns in the north, having lost important elements of their existing manufacturing employment, and lacking the environmental and social attractions of their non-industrial neighbours, seem to offer little attraction to new employment, except perhaps in some aspects of relatively routine white-collar work and consumer services. In this, they are only slightly better placed than the northern conurbation areas. In both cases, and in the north's free-standing towns, the reliance upon public investment in many ways, including regional aid programmes, is likely to remain heavy.

The industrial towns in the south consist of various old-established centres in the London metropolitan fringe such as Luton, Reading and Chatham. Declining manufacturing employment here may well be partially balanced by a growth in producer and consumer services, employing established skills and cheap premises, and exploiting the markets of surrounding growth areas. Some benefit may also be felt of the decentralization from London of white-collar jobs. The position of London is, of course, peculiar. There is no sign of any levelling off in its manufacturing decline, and the most buoyant sector of the economy in recent years has been in tourist and entertainment-related personal services. Its established domination of white-collar producer service employment has begun to be challenged in recent years, especially by other areas of the South East. It seems likely to retain important elements of this sector, however, which will in turn stimulate other aspects of producer and consumer service employment in what remains by far the largest population concentration in Britain, and a likely focus for many technical innovations. The very high dependence of London on service employment is thus likely to increase further.

The geographical pattern of public investment is particularly difficult to anticipate. To some extent it will be dictated by the need to compensate for economic failure in some areas, and thus will relatively favour the conurbations and all areas of the north. On the other hand, high investment in new infrastructure will certainly be needed in the rapidly growing prosperous areas, especially of rural southern Britain.

The table suggests that the pattern of production investment is likely to continue the polarization of employment change suggested in the first section of this chapter. It also indicates, however, that trends in intermediate producer service activities, while reinforcing the favoured position of the towns and cities of the south and their rural hinterlands, may significantly modify this pattern in certain areas. These especially include London and the industrial towns around its periphery, and the free-standing cities and non-industrial towns of the north [. . .] On the other hand, producer service employment is unlikely to aid the conurbations, industrial towns and rural areas of the north, whose dependence on public investment and on consumer services is likely to continue and grow unless area development policies succeed in reviving established industries or in attracting new production investment from outside [. . .]

4.5   Conclusion

The spatial pattern of change in post-industrial Britain is unlikely to exhibit the simple dichotomies which seemed to apply until the 1960s. The sources of economic growth and especially the patterns of employment change will be unfamiliar and complex. Certainly, many entrenched assumptions about the role of manufacturing and services will need to be changed, and new perspectives on the significance of different types of work will be needed. In the past, the inherited characteristics of regions, associated with natural resources, labour reserves, markets and infrastructure, have moulded the form of capital investment they attract. Changing rounds of profit-seeking investment have shifted the geography of employment in relation to the assessed worth of such area attributes in new conditions (Massey, 1979). This, of course, remains true today, with regard to the quality of the local labour force, environmental attraction and public infrastructure investment. The rate and breadth of change is accelerating in the 1980s, however, and the form of investment, removing or creating jobs, is becoming more varied. In particular, it has been emphasized [. . .] that the variety of activities encompassed by producer services are of growing significance. Corporate and competitive behaviour in this sector, in response to technical innovation and pressures on labour productivity can no longer be neglected. The cumulative effects of intermediate consumer service employment will in addition tend to reinforce patterns of contrasted area prosperity. Public policy, including patterns of new infrastructure investment, will be under strong pressure to follow where these trends lead [. . .]

References

CAMBRIDGE ECONOMIC POLICY REVIEW (1982) *Employment Problems in the Cities and Regions of the UK: Prospects for the 1980s*, Vol. 8, No. 2, Aldershot, Gower.

DANSON, M. W. (1982) 'The industrial structure and labour market segmentation: urban and regional implications', *Regional Studies*, Vol. 16, pp. 255–66.

DICKEN, P. (1980) 'Foreign direct investment in European manufacturing industry: the changing position of the UK as a host country', *Geoforum*, Vol. 11, pp. 89–313.

DUNNING, J. H. and NORMAN, G. (1983) 'The theory of the multinational enterprise: an application to multinational office location', *Environment and Planning A*, Vol. 15, pp. 675–92.

ELIAS, P. (1982) 'The regional impact of national economic policies: a multi-regional simulation approach for the UK', *Regional Studies*, Vol. 16, pp. 335–44.

FOTHERGILL, G. and GUDGIN, S. (1982) *Unequal Growth: Urban and Regional Employment Change in the UK*, London, Heinemann.

FUCHS, V. R. (1986) *The Service Economy*, New York, National Bureau of Economic and Social Research/Columbia University Press.

FUCHS, V. R. (1969) *Production and Productivity in the Service Industries*, New York, National Bureau of Economic and Social Research/Columbia University Press.

GERSHUNY, J. I. (1978) *After Industrial Society? The Emerging Self-Service Economy*, London, Macmillan.

GERSHUNY, J. I. (1983) *Social Innovation and the Division of Labour*, Oxford, Oxford University Press.

GERSHUNY, J. I. and MILES, I. D. (1983) *The New Service Economy*, Frances Pinter, London.

GODDARD, J. B. (1978) 'The location of non-manufacturing activities within manufacturing industries', in Hamilton, F. E. I. (ed.) *Contemporary Industrialisation*, London, Longman, pp. 62–85.

GOULD, A. and KEEBLE, D. (1984) 'New firms and rural industrialisation in East Anglia', *Regional Studies*, Vol. 18, pp. 189–202.

GREENFIELD, H. I. (1966) *Manpower and the Growth of Producer Services*, New York, Columbia University Press.

KEEBLE, D. (1976) *Industrial Location and Planning in the United Kingdom*, London, Methuen.

KEEBLE, D. (1980) 'Industrial decline, regional policy and the urban–rural manufacturing shift in the UK', *Environment and Planning A*, Vol. 12, pp. 945–62.

MARQUAND, J. (1979) 'The service sector and regional policy in the UK', Research Series 29, London, Centre for Environmental Studies.

MARQUAND, J. (1983) 'The changing distribution of service employment', in Goddard, J. B. and Champion, A. G. *The Urban and Regional Transformation of Britain*, London, Methuen, pp. 99–134.

MARSHALL, J. N. (1982) 'Linkages between manufacturing industry and business services', *Environment and Planning A*, Vol. 14, pp. 523–40.

MARSHALL, J. N. (1985) 'Business services: the regions and regional policy', *Regional Studies*, Vol. 19, pp. 352–63.

MASSEY, D. (1979) 'In what sense a regional problem?', *Regional Studies*, Vol. 13, pp. 233–44.

MASSEY, D. (1983) 'Industrial restructuring as class restructuring: production decentralization and local uniqueness', *Regional Studies*, Vol. 17, pp. 73–90.

MASSEY, D. and MEEGAN, R. (1982) *The Anatomy of Job Loss*, London, Methuen.

MOORE, B. and RHODES, J. (1982) 'A second great depression in the UK regions: can anything be done?', *Regional Studies*, Vol. 16, pp. 323–34.

ROBERTSON, J. A. S., BRIGGS, J. M. and GOODCHILD, A. (1982) 'Structure and employment prospects of the service industries', Research Paper No. 30, London, Department of Employment.

STANBACK, T. M. (1979) *Understanding the Service Economy: Employment, Productivity, Location*, Baltimore, Johns Hopkins University Press.

STANBACK, T. M., BEARSE, P. J., NOYELLE, T. J. and KARASEK, R. A.

(1981) *Services: The New Economy*, Totawa, NJ, Allanfield Osman.

TAYLOR, M. J. and THRIFT, N. J. (1982) 'Industrial linkage and the segmented economy: some theoretical proposals', *Environment and Planning A*, Vol. 14, pp. 601–14.

TOWNSEND, A. R. (1982a) *The Impact of Recession*, London, Croom Helm.

TOWNSEND, A. R. (1982b) 'Recession and the regions in Great Britain, 1976–80: analyses of redundancy data', *Environment and Planning A*, Vol. 14, pp. 389–404.

WOOD, P. A. (1984) 'The regional significance of manufacturing-service sector links', in Barr, B. M. and Waters, N. M. (eds) *Regional Diversification and Structural Change* (Proceedings Canada–United Kingdom Symposium on Industrial Geography, Calgary, August 1983) Vancouver, Tantalus Research, pp. 168–84.

5 Producer services and the post-industrial space-economy

Peter Daniels

5.1 Introduction

The shift from an industrial to a post-industrial or post-affluent (Gappert, 1982) economic system is now well under way in Britain. While there remains a great deal to evaluate in detail, it is generally recognized that advanced economic systems, such as that of Britain, are undergoing some fundamental changes. Relative to the evolution of agricultural to manufacturing-based economies over the last 200 years the recent changes are rapid; they have only been manifest during the last 20–25 years. But the events are perhaps best characterized as a transition which has not been readily recognized by academic, central government and other observers whose perception of an economic system founded upon manufacturing industry has exerted an inertia which is out of proportion to its contemporary significance.

The change was spotted early by Clark (1940), who drew attention to the significance of the tertiary or service sector, but the 'belief is still widespread that society can survive . . . without much servicing outside what can be performed through do-it-yourself methods' (Gottman, 1983, p. 62). As manufacturing industry has become more efficient, capital intensive, productive and, in consequence, less labour intensive its share of national employment has declined dramatically [. . .] Of course some of the employment contraction in the manufacturing sector has been a by-product of the nation's macroeconomic condition during recent years, but this only partially disguises an underlying trend, as elsewhere (Greenfield, 1966; Stanback, 1979; Polese, 1982), which involves a gradual change of emphasis from goods producing to information-handling activities which are predominantly concentrated amongst service rather than manufacturing industries. Some care must be taken, however, in equating this with a decline in manufacturing; it has been suggested by Gershuny (1978), for example, that some services are being substituted with domestic facilities provided by durable goods such as freezers, washing machines or video recorders. This creates a demand for goods-related services (repair, maintenance, installation) provided by the manufacturers or their agents.

The contraction of the manufacturing sector has been described as de-industrialization (Blackaby, 1978; Thirlwall, 1982). This concept fits in with the classical theories of the economic development process whereby national economies evolve through a sequence beginning with the dominance of agriculture, followed by manufacturing and, ultimately, services (Clark, 1940; Rostow, 1960; Fuchs, 1968). But there is some disagreement about how best to define de-industrialization; it is most important here, however, to stress that it seems inappropriate to equate it solely with an absolute loss of jobs by manufacturing industries. Rather it represents a wider process of job loss from all industries, *including services*. Some of the latter are also losing more jobs than they create because the service which they provide is outmoded or has been replaced by modern technology.

Industrial restructuration may be the more accurate way to characterize a process in which selected industries, and their associated occupations, have steadily moved towards a more pivotal position in overall economic structure. Consequently, they now exert a significant influence on the economic potential of regions and cities, many of which are endeavouring to adjust to the post-industrial transition, within the British space-economy. The task is not straightforward because, although there has been a steady expansion of service industries, insufficient jobs have been created to replace those shed by manufacturing industries; industrial restructuration is not necessarily a panacea for dealing with major socio-economic problems such as unemployment or the deep-seated difficulties confronting the inner cities. Indeed, this may to some degree explain the low esteem ascribed to service industries (see Bacon and Eltis, 1976, for example), but this should not be allowed to overshadow their current and future importance in the space-economy where knowledge and information availability is just as important as a raw material in the production process as the more conventional physical inputs [. . .]

This chapter [. . .] is confined to an elaboration, using limited recent evidence, of an important division within service industries between producer and consumer activities, the broad regional patterns revealed by the former, some preliminary evidence about their location and related behaviour from some recent studies, and an attempt to assess their significance in the space-economy [. . .]

5.2   Some basic empirical evidence

The transition to a service-based economy has been equated with absolute employment expansion but relative, and, in some cases, absolute, decline of individual service activities, either as a result of market forces, such as in the case of transport and communication, or consequent upon public expenditure policies and their implications for employment in public administration and defence. Some 45 000 jobs in transport and communication were lost between 1978 and 1981 (just over 3 per cent of the 1981 total) and 38 000 by the latter (Department of Employment, 1983a). This compares with an increase during the same period of 128 000 jobs in insurance, banking and finance (equivalent to 9.8 per cent of the 1981 total) and 169 000 in miscellaneous services which includes a number of publicly provided services such as education and medical services which have increased their employment demand rapidly during the 1970s (equivalent to 6.7 per cent of the 1981 total). The contribution of miscellaneous services (together with professional and scientific services) to GDP has therefore improved from 21.2 per cent in 1976 to 22.8 per cent in 1981 and in insurance, banking and finance from 8.1 per cent to 9.1 per cent. The absolute change in the GDP of this sector (117.6 per cent) was also larger than for any other group. The contribution to GDP by the other service industries has remained the same or even declined and the change in the value of GDP has been much the same or lower than the GB average.

Service industry expansion has therefore been selective and has mainly taken place in those services which 'business firms, non-profit institutions, and governments provide and usually sell to the producer rather than to the consumer' (Greenfield, 1966, p. 1). Collectively, these are classified as producer (or intermediate) services and, in theory at least, are distinguishable from consumer or private services which are largely provided in response to final demand. Hence, insurance, banking and finance, together with transport and communication, can be used as surrogates for producer services in analyses of, for example, regional economic structure and change (Keeble, Owens and Thompson, 1981). But such a definition is too narrow since it neglects the wider incidence of producer service functions within the service industries as a whole. Also it is now possible to make use of the finer detail now available as classes, groups and activities within the revised Standard Industrial Classification (SIC) introduced in 1980 (replacing the previously used 1968 SIC). An attempt is therefore made here to measure the size and distribution of producer activities within the service sector, both at the aggregate national level and in relation to the Standard Regions for which the most recent data are available.

Inevitably, perhaps, it is easier to articulate the concept of a producer/consumer dichotomy within service industries than it is to translate it into its empirical and ultimately, spatial, attributes. As Greenfield (1966) observed it is difficult to find suitable measures for dividing activities into their producer and consumer components, a difficulty which arises largely from the fact that relatively few services can be readily assigned to one or the other. Census and other returns containing employment or output information do not distinguish between the proportion of workers engaged in, or output attributable to, producer functions. One solution is to introduce another category of services which can be described as 'mixed' (see Marquand, 1980) since they are neither mainly producer- nor mainly consumer-oriented. Rather than assign activities in this way, however, it may be more constructive to attempt to estimate the proportion of total employment in each service group and activity of the

1980 SIC which is devoted to producer functions. The guidelines for undertaking such an exercise are very limited, however, and the resulting estimates (Table 5.1) are first approximations based on earlier work by Marquand (1979) and more particularly by Greenfield (1966). The latter used detailed breakdowns of revenue for a small number of industries

Table 5.1   Estimated distribution of producer and consumer employment within the service sector, by industry, Great Britain, 1981

SIC (1980) Division and Class	in employment[1]	producer	consumer	% producer
		Total employees (000)		
Wholesale distribution	840	840	*	100.0
Dealing in scrap and waste metals	23	23	*	100.0
Commission agents	13	13	*	100.0
Retail distribution	2 060	*	2 060	*
Hotels and catering	938	234.5	703.5	25.0
Repair of consumer goods and vehicles	238	59.5	178.5	25.0
Distribution, hotels and catering, repairs	4 112	1 170	2 942	28.5
Railways	174	87	87	50.0
Other inland transport	404	208	196	51.5
Sea transport	66	50	16	75.0
Air transport	70	35	35	50.0
Supporting services to transport	100	100	*	100.0
Miscellaneous transport services and storage	168	151	17	90.0
Postal services and telecommunications	424	212	212	50.0
Transport and communication	1 406	843	563	60.0
Banking and finance	478	239	239	50.0
Insurance, except compulsory social security	225	169	56	75.0
Business services	831	831	*	100.0
Renting of movables	91	91	*	100.0
Owning and dealing in real estate	98	98	*	100.0
Banking, finance, insurance, business services and leasing	1 723	1 428	295	82.9
Public administration, national defence and compulsory social security	1 505	752.5	752.5	50.0
Sanitary services	372	37	335	10.0
Education	1 422	142	1 288	10.0
Research and development	121	121	*	100.0
Medical services	1 285	*	1 285	*
Other services provided to the general public	552	*	552	*
Recreational and other cultural services	430	86	344	20.0
Personal services	180	*	180	*
Other services	5 867	1 138.5	4 736.5	19.4
All services	13 108	4 579.5	8 536.5	34.9
All industries and services	21 148	–	–	21.7

[1]Employees in employment, Sept. 1981 (000s).
*Zero (0), to negligible.

Source: Estimates derived from base data in Department of Employment (1983) *Employment Gazette*, Occasional Supplement No. 1 (May), Table 4

together with an analysis of inter-industry input–output tables to derive ratios for the proportion of total employment in service industry allocated to producer/non-producer functions. This task is formidable and even more difficult when trying to identify producer services within public administration. The finer detail provided by the classes and groups listed in Table 5.1 is helpful, but still far from satisfactory.

On the basis of his analysis, Greenfield estimated that 12.5 per cent of total US employment in 1950 was in producer services, rising to 13.2 per cent in 1960. The estimates in Table 5.1 suggest that the growth trend indicated in Greenfield's data has been continuing so that by 1981 it is estimated that almost 22 per cent of employment in Britain was producer-oriented; or one in three jobs within the service sector. Slightly less than half of the producer service employment is attached to transport and communication and insurance, banking and finance although the latter has three times as many producer jobs as expected from its overall share of service sector employment. Some 25 per cent of producer service employment is attached to distribution and related activities and to other services (including the public sector). Thus, producer service employment is not insignificant in these two sectors where it represents 28.5 per cent and 19.4 per cent respectively of total employment. With almost 4.6 million workers in producer service employment it is clearly not an insignificant component of national employment.

5.3   The demand for producer services

The growth in demand for producer services can be traced to several, and sometimes interrelated, factors. Assuming that business enterprises are anxious to sustain any given level of output at an acceptable cost it may be necessary to establish whether any of the inputs can be obtained at lower cost from outside the firm. This is especially relevant for the assembly of specialized inputs which may only be required very infrequently, but are important when the demand does arise. In these circumstances it will very likely not be cost-effective to maintain in-house labour to occasionally provide the input when, because several firms may require the same input at different times, an external organization can be engaged full-time in providing it. This will lower the unit cost for the external organization of providing the input as well as to the user. It is also likely that it can also be supplied more efficiently and exactly at the time required. Greenfield (1966, p. 38) equates this with the principle of comparative advantage in that 'a firm will purchase services from other firms which may have absolute and/or relative advantage over itself in the performance of a specified function'. A good example is the recent expansion of computer services which assist other companies with the task of choosing suitable computers, provide assistance with the installation and use of computer facilities, and devise procedures and programs which best fit the requirements of each client. Computer service bureaux have also developed to provide clients with time-sharing and batch facilities centred on a major installation operated by the computer service organization.

The importance of comparative advantage will probably increase as enterprises are required to use recent advances in production, telecommunications and information technology to remain competitive (see, for example, Otway and Peltu, 1983; Hills, 1982). This will lead to changes in organizational structure and decision-making (Crozier, 1983; Simon, 1977) as well as allowing improvements in the quality or quantity of output, but the product or service must still be directed at the most appropriate segments of the market, and knowledge of this kind is obtainable through marketing and advertising research. Larger business enterprises will be able to operate departments concerned with these functions, but even they may still need to use specialized agencies to undertake studies outside the range of their own resources and expertise or because they value an independent assessment of product image or of their marketing strategy and prospects. Smaller firms will clearly have to 'buy in' this kind of specialist advice, especially if they plan to diversify or to expand market coverage. Finally, externally purchased services provided by management consultants or financial analysts are required to give firms a detached perspective on their operations, management procedures or the prospects for growth, survival or diversification. In their efforts to streamline costs or to impose as much simplicity as possible on their internal organization or the range of staff which they retain, for example, business enterprises have provided an ideal environment for stimulating the development of existing, new and as yet unrealized producer service functions.

5.4   The spatial distribution of producer services

Assuming that the demand and ultimately the growth of producer services is going to continue, it is necessary to consider whether this will have any consequences for the British space-economy. As technical and business services become more specialized, business enterprises are going to increasingly rely on imported inputs and it then follows that the supply of such services could have a significant influence on the relative development of the interacting components of the space economy; the urban places, regions, economic activities and the flows of goods, people and information which join them together. The rules applicable to the operation, structure and distribution of economic activities in a system founded upon a post-industrial economy could well be different to those associated with the industrial phase because of the growing importance of intangible rather than tangible inputs and the rather different locational behaviour exhibited by the producer services which supply many of these new types of input.

Some clues to the locational behaviour of producer services are provided in Table 5.2 where the net changes in employees in employment in the ten Economic Planning Regions between 1978 and 1981 are expressed as a proportion of the total change for manufacturing, services and all industries and services. Some 46 per cent of the net increase of 0.2 million employed in service industries was located in the South East. Only two regions, the North and Yorkshire–Humberside, recorded a reduction in the numbers employed in services. Some disaggregation of this information, but using the industry groups defined in the 1968 SIC and defining insurance, banking, finance and business services and professional and scientific services as the principal producer activities, is possible. It is apparent that insurance, banking, finance and business services have increased their labour forces in every region with the South East again associated with a large proportion (49 per cent) of the net increase of 128 000. The only other services to achieve absolute increases in almost every region are miscellaneous services, which include some producer employment such as that in research and development. The emphasis on expansion in the South East is, however, rather less pronounced (35.5 per cent of the total increase of 169 000). Employment in professional and scientific services actually contracted or remained stable in all but two regions, the South East and Scotland, so that the net change is only marginal (2000). All the other service industries show reductions in the numbers employed, but the changes in absolute terms are much smaller than those in the manufacturing sector where substantial reductions have taken place in every SIC category; mechanical engineering and vehicles losing some 300 000 jobs between them in three years. Nevertheless, industries with a large producer service component have therefore been prominent in the limited employment expansion which has taken place between 1978 and 1981 and spatial bias is a common feature.

More detailed confirmation is provided by disaggregating the estimates for producer service employment given in Table 5.1 into their regional components, by industry class, in 1981 (Table 5.3). This is not, of course, the most satisfactory scale at which to examine the data, but at the time of writing, apart from marginally more disaggregated information for the South East region, this is the only level for which recent and comparatively detailed employment information is available. Data problems are a recurring lament among those interested in the recent, let alone the historical, development of the service sector and its components [. . .] The cross-sectional information given in Table 5.3 does, however, suggest some significant inequalities in the regional distribution of producer service employment when measured against all service employment and total employment in each region.

Table 5.2   Change in employees in employment in services, by region, Great Britain, 1978–81[1]

Region	Service industry orders (SIC 1968) (000)[2]							Manufacturing	All industries and services	Per cent change
	XXII	XXIII	XXIV	XXV	XXVI	XXVII	Services			
South East	-8	1	55	11	60	-20	99	-220	-144	2.0
East Anglia	3	2	5	-1	8	-1	16	-18	-7	4.0
South West	*	-7	8	1	18	-5	16	-56	-41	1.6
West Midlands	-5	-1	13	-17	16	7	14	-216	-217	1.3
East Midlands	3	3	6	-2	17	-13	13	-84	-77	1.7
Yorkshire and Humberside	-6	-2	9	-6	4	-2	-2	-139	-158	-0.2
North West	-17	*	13	*	26	-5	16	-182	-186	1.1
North	-4	-4	5	-4	3	-3	-6	-80	-115	-0.9
Wales	-3	-3	6	*	7	-4	3	-77	-84	0.5
Scotland	-6	5	8	20	10	7	44	-119	-97	3.6
Great Britain	-43	-5	128	2	169	-38	214	-1193	-1126	1.6

[1] June 1978 to September 1981

[2] XXII (Transport and communication); XXIII (Distributive trades); XXIV (Insurance, banking, finance and business services); XXV (Professional and scientific services); XXVI (Miscellaneous services); XXVII (Public administration and defence).

*Zero (0), to negligible

Table 5.3 Convergence indices for producer service employment, by industry class and region, Great Britain, 1981

Region	Convergence index (SIC 1968)[1]				Share (%)	
	Distribution, hotels and catering	Transport and com- munication	Banking, finance, insurance, business services	Other services	Total employment	Producer services
South East	106.8	128.9	146.0	111.5	33.9	42.2
East Anglia	106.3	103.1	81.2	103.1	3.2	3.1
South West	115.3	81.9	90.2	100.0	7.2	7.1
West Midlands	97.1	73.9	62.3	85.5	9.4	7.7
East Midlands	97.1	73.9	62.3	85.5	6.9	5.5
Yorkshire and Humberside	103.8	88.3	69.8	76.7	8.6	7.2
North West	96.6	96.6	81.2	88.9	11.7	10.5
North	79.2	83.0	62.2	92.5	5.3	4.1
Wales	81.8	84.0	68.2	122.7	4.4	3.9
Scotland	90.3	97.8	84.9	110.8	9.3	8.8
Great Britain	1 167	844	1 439	1 145	21 148	4 595
(000)					(100)	(100)

[1]Region's share of producer service employment as a proportion of region's share of total employment.

Source: Calculated from the estimates in Table 5.1 using Department of Employment Census of Employment data

Convergence indices have been used to show that producer service employment has yet to achieve a regional distribution which mirrors the distribution of total employment (Table 5.3). With less than 34 per cent of national employment but over 42 per cent of national producer service employment, all the service industry classes in the South East have indices greater than 100, i.e. that region's share of employment in each class is higher than the region's share of total employment. But the degree of regional surplus varies and is largest for insurance, banking, finance and business services, in which almost 83 per cent of employment has been estimated as producer-related (see Table 5.1). This is also the class revealing the greatest range for the convergence index which reaches as low as 62 per cent in three regions: the North, the West and East Midlands. Outside the South East, only the South West region has a score for the index which exceeds 90 per cent. The ranges revealed by the other service industry classes, in which producer-related employment, although presently is less prominent, are narrower and a number of regions outside the South East also have index values greater than 100. Producer employment in Other Services is notable in this regard; the prominence of public sector employment and policies for the dispersal of civil servants from the South East to other regions [. . .] have probably contributed to the high convergence indices for Wales and for Scotland. In general, however, it is possible to conclude that every region outside the South East has less producer service employment than would be expected from its share of all employment in manufacturing and services.

It must be stressed that the spatial distribution conveyed in Table 5.3 may understate the difference between the South East and the rest of the country. An assumption has been made that the proportion of producer employment in each industry class and activity is constant irrespective of the regional location. In practice the ratio of producer to non-producer employment in the South East may be higher because, for example, of an expressed preference by organizations to locate headquarters in that region (Evans, 1973; Marquand, 1979; Dicken and Lloyd, 1981), or for research and development establishments to be located there (Buswell and Lewis, 1970; Howells, 1984). According to the Census of Employment (Department of Employment, 1983b) almost 66 per cent of employment in advertising in 1981 was located in the South East; 53 per cent of business service employment, including 71 per cent of the 45 000 jobs in central offices not allocable elsewhere (mainly national or regional head offices), and 57 per cent of the 53 000 workers employed in computer services. With reference to the latter, a study (Department of Industry, 1983) has shown that 69 per cent of the head offices of more than 1000 computer-service companies are located in the South East. Some 34 per cent of the branch offices of these companies are also located there, but over 70 per cent of all the branches are controlled by computer-service head offices in that region. Evidence of this kind confirms the earlier indications of a highly uneven distribution of producer service employment within the British space-economy [. . .]

5.5   Urban concentration

Data for Greater London can be used as a guide to the situation prevailing in other regions with major urban areas such as Leeds, Manchester and Edinburgh (Table 5.4) [. . .] While just less than half of all employees in employment in the South East in 1981 were located in Greater London and almost 53 per cent of those engaged in service industries, more than 60 per cent of producer service employment in transport and communication and 65 per cent in insurance and banking was located in Greater London with many of the latter in the central area. Therefore, while Greater London accounts for 20 per cent of all service jobs in Great Britain it is the base for more than 32 per cent of the producer service employment in banking and finance. Assuming that a similar situation prevails in the other parts of the country, then the association between urban agglomeration and the incidence of producer services is probably significant for the supply of such services and their potential contribution to economic growth.

The allocation of these urbanization/agglomeration economies must, however, be seen within the context of concentrated decentralization because much of the growth in services as a whole in the South East has

Table 5.4   Estimated share of producer service employment in Greater London relative to the South East and Great Britain, by Industry Class, 1981

SIC Division (1980)	Producer service employment (000)				
	Greater London	South East	%	Great Britain	%
Distribution, hotels and catering, repairs	218	423	51.7	1 167	18.7
Transport and communication	222	369	60.2	844	26.3
Banking, finance, insurance, business services and leasing	467	713	65.5	1 439	32.4
Other services	208	433	47.9	1 145	18.1
All service employment	2 646	5 000	52.9	13 090	20.2
All industries and services	3 513	7 168	49.0	21 148	16.6

Source: Department of Employment (1983) *Employment Gazette*, Occasional Supplement No. 1 (May), estimated from data in Table 9.4

taken place outside Greater London, especially in the Outer Metropolitan Area. In absolute terms only insurance, banking, finance and business services and miscellaneous services (SIC 1968) increased their employment in Greater London between 1978 and 1981, but in both cases the absolute increase at locations elsewhere in the South East was larger. The absolute numbers in all the other service categories decreased in Greater London only to be counterbalanced by large positive changes in the remainder of the South East. Producer service employment has participated in these locational trends, but on a more limited scale than those service industries which are more dependent on the spatial distribution of consumers [. . .]

Using employment data for metropolitan economic labour areas (MELAs) between 1971 and 1977, Marquand (1979, 1983) suggests that there are hierarchical factors which encourage the concentration of producer services in the larger cities and a tendency for under-provision to occur in smaller urban areas, especially in the regions outside the South East, East Anglia, the South West and Scotland. It is also the case that areas with a high level of dependence on manufacturing industry have a low level of producer service activity.

5.6   The significance of spatial inequalities

As producer services are in some respects the embodiment of the structural changes currently taking place in advanced economies it seems essential to know more about their role in economic development and whether, as Marquand (1983) asks, it matters if they are unevenly distributed. In so far as many organizations are able to internalize their intermediate inputs [. . .], the location and availability of possible exogenous sources may not be a significant consideration. But many firms must, if only for reasons arising from their limited size or an infrequent requirement for a particular kind of specialist input, seek to fulfil their objectives from external sources. Many small manufacturing firms are in this category and if they are to retain their comparative advantage they will require knowledge of and an easily accessible supply of producer services. Unless these are available locally (i.e. within the same urban area or region), the cost of obtaining them (travel time to meetings, telecommunications charges), the likelihood of delays caused by the inability of client and supplier to meet as often as required, may be a sufficient deterrent to limit utilization or, more seriously, to prevent use altogether and so cause firms to grow less slowly than might otherwise be the case or even to cease production because of an inability to compete with firms in those cities and regions with easier access to a comprehensive pool of producer services. Goddard (1978) has stressed that the availability at the local level of the kind of information and advice provided by producer activities such as business services is a vital factor for the present and future economic performance of peripheral areas [. . .]

The conventional view of the supply of producer services in a city or region is that they arise directly from the demand generated by manufacturing firms. When this demand declines, for reasons connected, for example, with changes in the organization of manufacturing and therefore greater internalization of service inputs (Burrows and Town, 1971; Crum and Gudgin, 1977), the supply of producer services will be adversely affected. In practice the relationship is less clearcut because, as Marshall (1982) has shown, the service sector is itself experiencing organizational changes which affect the local supply of producer services. Merger and acquisition among insurance companies, for example, has created larger, more centralized, organizations in which internal provision of accounting, marketing and some computer services via head office, has replaced the autonomy of smaller, often locally based financial and insurance companies which obtain producer services from local suppliers. The parallel among manufacturing companies is the reduced autonomy of branch plants which are less likely to use local producer services than local independent firms; Marshall (1982) found that manufacturing firms with less than 60 employees obtained more than 50 per cent of their service purchases from outside the firm and over 80 per cent of these purchases were made within the same planning region. Equivalent figures for large establishments (300 + employees) were 31 per cent and 68 per cent respectively. Imported services are provided via headquarters which, if it does require to purchase some of these inputs, will obtain them from the location, invariably in London or the South East, where it is situated. The presence of headquarters establishments in a city or region is therefore important because of the demand which they generate for locally supplied producer services (Burrows and Town, 1971; Daniels, 1984).

The significance of this has recently been demonstrated by Marshall (1983) in a study of manufacturing firms in Birmingham, Leeds and Manchester which included 63 branch plants. More than 90 per cent of the branch plants (19) with headquarters in London obtained services from within their own company compared with just over 70 per cent (22) of those headquartered in areas used for the study. Hence almost 30 per cent of the service inputs of branch plants with a local headquarters were obtained from the same area. Marshall (1982) also notes that the presence of a major producer service complex within a region ensures that a larger proportion of the demand emanating from local branches and headquarters remains within the region. The North West (Manchester) and the West Midlands (Birmingham) fare rather better in this regard than Yorkshire–Humberside, which has a far less dominant regional capital (Leeds) and a wider dispersal of producer services among a number of smaller secondary centres. Indeed, Manchester is used as a source for business services by firms in Yorkshire–Humberside and in the West Midlands.

Interregional transfer of business services which is not oriented towards

London and the South East has also been noted in a study of manufacturing and service firms in a number of other British provincial cities (Daniels, 1984). Such links are largely confined to contiguous regions, however, and are best developed among insurance, banking and finance activities (Daniels, 1984). There are also hierarchical links in the destinations of interregional business-service output and by far the largest proportion of the sales income of some producer services clearly originates from cities or regions well outside the local market area, especially for smaller firms. The significance of this for regional economic adjustment towards a post-industrial structure is that, contrary to common belief, producer service development in under-provided provincial areas can perform an export (basic) as well as import-substitution (non-basic) role.

The notion that producer services mainly exist only as a response to local manufacturing demand seems some way off the mark. Of course the link is an important one, but industrialization and the subsequent diversification/adaptation of manufacturing would not have been possible without the 'enabling' role performed by transportation, or by business services such as the financial institutions, or by professionals such as accountants and surveyors. In such circumstances it seems axiomatic that the relationship should at worst be considered symbiotic, i.e. on an equal footing, rather than 'manufacturing first, producer services (or services in general) second' [. . .]

5.7   External influences on the spatial pattern of producer services

The location of producer services in the space-economy and their potential contribution to restructuring regional economies is complicated by the pressures arising from the increasing globalization of producer service activities. Historically, most producer services have operated within the national context with the notable exception of the insurance broking and commodity trading functions of the City of London. But foreign direct investment by multinational business services has been increasing (Dunning and Norman, 1983) in an effort to capitalize more effectively upon the highly specialized technical knowledge, managerial skills or information which they have to offer. Instead of giving licences to local national companies, multinational business services are now discovering that their expertise is best provided, and protected, by retaining ownership and installing their own operational establishments at foreign locations. This procedure also offers the prospect of cost savings as a result of reduced executive travel and related overheads when providing a service from the 'home' country.

The locational choices for such international producer services invariably favour the major corporate complexes where they are able to capitalize upon good international communications both with the parent country and with other potential markets, obtain ready access to the diverse group of ancillary services integral to the corporate complex (Cohen, 1979; Corey, 1982), are readily accessible to existing or potential clients and are able to draw upon a labour pool in which the occupational skills are already likely to be available. Dunning and Norman (1983) traced some 261 US-based business services in the UK in 1976 and 82 per cent (213) operated from establishments in central London, a further 13 per cent from locations elsewhere in London, and only 5 per cent from places elsewhere in the country (mainly within the South East region from towns such as Reading). Management consultancy and executive search, advertising, accountancy, insurance, banking, engineering design, legal practices and other producer services are all represented and clearly add to the attractiveness of London and the South East as the key location for knowledge capital. This is reinforced by the location of regional headquarters of multinational manufacturing enterprises, 69 per cent (85) of which were located in London in Dunning and Norman's 1976 data. The result is a producer service complex which must also act as a magnet for national producer (as well as non-producer) activities. [. . .]

5.8 Conclusion

An assessment of the role of producer services in the British space-economy is encumbered by the paucity of constructive empirical information. It is therefore difficult to address the policy and other issues arising from the transition to a post-industrial economic system and some of the reasons for the present circumstances have been explored elsewhere (Daniels, 1983). If the distribution of employment is used as a crude surrogate for the availability of producer services in the nation's regions and cities, it seems beyond question that significant spatial inequalities exist. By exploring locational patterns, at either the aggregate regional level or more recently with reference to selected service industry subsectors such as business services, geographers have been active since the mid-1970s in showing the origins of supply-side spatial inequalities. But there is far less certainty about possible spatial variations in the demand for producer services in relation, for example, to industry sector of origin, the volume and value of transactions, the types of service required or the response of business enterprises if their requirements for specialized intermediate inputs cannot be fulfilled. By pursuing these and related questions, such as the supply-demand equation, the consequences of spatial variations in producer service activity for the evolution of the space-economy may become rather more transparent than at present [. . .]

References

BACON, R. and ELTIS, W. (1976) *Britain's Economic Problems: Too Few Producers*, London, Heinemann.

BLACKABY, F. (ed.) (1978) *De-industrialization*, London, Heinemann.

BURROWS, E. M. and TOWN, S. (1971) *Office Services in the East Midlands*, Nottingham, East Midland Economic Planning Council.

CLARK, C. (1940) *The Conditions of Economic Progress*, London, Macmillan.

COHEN, R. (1979) 'The changing transactions economy and its spatial implications', *Ekistics*, No. 46, pp. 7–15.

COREY, K. E. (1982) 'Transactional forces and the metropolis', *Ekistics*, No. 297, pp. 416–23.

CROZIER, C. (1983) 'Implications for the organization', in Otway, H. J. and Peltu, M. (eds) pp. 86–101.

CRUM, R. E. and GUDGIN, G. (1977) 'Non-production activities in UK manufacturing industry', *Regional Policy Series 3*, Brussels, Commission of the European Communities.

DANIELS, P. W. (1983) 'Service industries: supporting role or centre stage?', *Area*, Vol. 15, pp. 301–9.

DANIELS, P. W. (1984) 'Business service offices in provincial cities: sources of input and destination of output', *Tijdschrift voor Economische en Sociale Geografie*, Vol. 75, pp. 123–39.

DEPARTMENT OF EMPLOYMENT (1983a) *Employment Gazette*, Vol. 91 (Feb), p. 65.

DEPARTMENT OF EMPLOYMENT (1983b) *Employment Gazette*, Occasional Supplement No. 1 (May), pp. 2–9.

DEPARTMENT OF INDUSTRY (1982) 'Office and service industries scheme: could your company benefit?', London, HMSO.

DEPARTMENT OF INDUSTRY (1983) 'The location, mobility and financing of the computer services sector in the UK', London, South East Regional Office (mimeo.).

DICKEN, P. and LLOYD, P. (1981) *Modern Western Society*, London, Harper and Row.

DUNNING, J. and NORMAN, P. (1983) 'The theory of the multinational enterprise: an application to office location', *Environment and Planning A*, Vol. 15, pp. 675–92.

EVANS, A. W. (1973) 'The location of headquarters of industrial companies', *Urban Studies*, Vol. 10, pp. 387–95.

FUCHS, V. R. (1968) *The Service Economy*, New York, Bureau of Economic Research.

GAPPERT, G. (1982) 'Future urban America: post-affluent or advanced industrial society?', in Gappert, G. and Knight, R. V. (eds) *Cities in the 21st Century*, Beverley Hills, Sage, pp. 9–34.

GERSHUNY, J. (1978) *After Industrial Society?*, London, Macmillan.

GODDARD, J. B. (1978) 'The location of non-manufacturing occupations within manufacturing industries', in Hamilton, F. E. I. (ed.) *Contemporary Industrialization: Spatial Analysis and Regional Development*, London, Longman.

GOTTMAN, J. (1983) *The Coming of the Transactional City*, College Park, University of Maryland Institute for Urban Studies.

GREENFIELD, H. I. (1966) *Manpower and the Growth of Producer Services*, New York, Columbia University Press.

HILLS, P. J. (ed.) (1982) *Trends in Information Transfer*, London, Frances Pinter.

KEEBLE, D. E., OWENS, P. L. and THOMPSON, C. (1981) *Centrality, Peripherality and EEC Regional Development*, London, HMSO.

MARQUAND, J. (1979) 'The service sector and regional policy in the United Kingdom', *Research Series 29*, London, Centre for Environmental Studies.

MARQUAND, J. (1980) 'The role of the service sector in regional policy', *Regional Policy Series 3*, Brussels, Commission of the European Communities.

MARQUAND, J. (1983) 'The changing distribution of service employment', in Goddard, J. B. and Champion, A. G. (eds) *The Urban and Regional Transformation of Britain*, London, Methuen, pp. 99–134.

MARSHALL, J. N. (1982) 'Linkages between manufacturing industry and business services', *Environment and Planning, A*, Vol. 14, pp. 1523–40.

MARSHALL, J. N. (1983) 'Business-service activities in British provincial conurbations', *Environment and Planning, A*, Vol. 15, pp. 1343–59.

OTWAY, H. J. and PELTU, M. (eds) (1983) *New Office Technology: Human and Organizational Aspects*, London, Frances Pinter.

POLESE, M. (1982) 'Regional demand for business services and interregional service flows in a small Canadian region', *Papers of the Regional Science Association*, Vol. 50, pp. 151–63.

ROSTOW, W. W. (1960) *The Stages of Economic Growth*, London, Cambridge University Press.

SIMON, H. A. (1977) *The New Science of Management Decision-Making*, Englewood Cliffs, NJ, Prentice-Hall.

STANBACK, T. M. (1979) *Understanding the Service Economy: Employment, Productivity, Location*, Baltimore, MD, John Hopkins University Press.

THIRLWALL, A. P. (1982) 'De-industrialization in the United Kingdom', *Lloyds Bank Review*, No. 144, pp. 22–37.

6   The geographies of service

John Allen

6.1   Introduction

The geographies of service, as a title, can be understood in at least two rather different ways, both of which have shaped the content of this chapter.

The first sense of the term 'geographies' is a somewhat conventional one, in as far as it points to differences in the geographical pattern of service employment laid down by different kinds of service industry over the post-war period. Among the more significant spatial differences is that between services provided by the state and those provided by the private sector, with service employment in the former relatively evenly distributed in comparison with the latter. And within the private service industries, there are a number of different labour geographies. The pattern of employment in the leisure and cultural industries, or the retail trade, for example, is characterized by a wide spatial distribution, whereas the pattern of jobs in the banking sector or the research and development industries is spatially concentrated, in the City of London and in southern towns respectively.

Such differences are important not only because the spatial distribution of service jobs is uneven, but also because different types of service industry are laying down rather different labour geographies. The types of service jobs provided by different service industries across space is uneven; they vary in status, pay and function; and, where the labour geographies overlap, they are often unequal.

The second sense of the term 'geographies' is of a rather different kind, although equally straightforward. It points to the various ways in which it is possible to conceptualize and explain the uneven geography of the service industries. In this chapter, the approach adopted is one that takes its point of entry from Massey's (1984) argument that the geography of industry and employment is bound up with the social relations under which goods and services are produced. Changing spatial patterns of employment, the different kinds of job and functions laid down in different areas, in this sense, are the outcome of the ways in which the relations of production are organized and reorganized over space. In the first section this framework is used to explore how different service industries have responded to different national and international developments and how, in turn, these developments have altered the structure of service sector labour markets. Following this, the structure of service labour markets is examined briefly through an account of the different ways in which the service industries are structured across space. Finally, at a different level of analysis, an illustration of how the shift to services within local labour markets has taken an uneven form is set out to show the particularity of service sector restructuring.

6.2 Uneven service redevelopment

A number of different processes, grouped under two headings, are examined in this section. They are not the only processes at work in the economy, but they are among the most significant in terms of their impact upon the structure of service employment, both socially and spatially. They include the decline in state service provision and the shift towards privatization; the movement of multinational capital into the service sector and the internationalization of services; and, more generally, the shift from manufacturing to service-dominated labour markets and the increased polarization of local employment structures.

Shifting boundaries: from public to private

At a general level, what distinguishes state service provision from those services delivered by private capital is the relations of control that govern their provision. Above all, it is the absence of a financial calculation based on profitability that marks off the organization of private services from the state sector. There are, of course, exceptions. Some state services possess a degree of commodification; for example, the postal service is directly responsive to market pressures, as is rail and sea transport. Yet the bulk of state service employment in health and education, and in central and local government administrations, is subject directly to political considerations. And even the supply and location of public marketed services are subject to some form of political calculation. However, it is not the political nature of the relations of control that is crucial here, rather it is the changing *form* of that relation. Over the past decade under a market-orientated Conservative administration, three processes have, in combination, started to alter the number, type and spatial distribution of a major part of state service employment.

First, as is well known, the number of service jobs in the state sector has fallen, reversing a post-war trend that added over two million jobs to the state sector in the 1960s and 1970s. This reversal, which can be traced to the impact of cuts in state expenditure from the mid-1970s on, but especially since the end of the 1970s, also represents a kind of geographical reversal. As much of public sector service employment is relatively evenly distributed in relation to population, compared, that is, to the distribution of private service jobs, it is in local labour markets, particularly in the peripheral regions where the state is often the dominant employer, that the impact of expenditure cuts is likely to be greatest. For example in Scotland, Wales and the Northern region, where state health-care employment has been a major source of jobs, the number of health workers fell in the first half of the 1980s (Mohan, 1988). Such trends merely serve to reinforce an existing pattern of social and spatial inequality.

Connected with the reduction in the levels of state service employment is the move by the Conservative administration to replace the public provision of services with private provision. There are a number of indications of such a shift, of which the contracting out of public services such as catering, laundry and a wide range of cleaning services, including school and hospital cleaning, refuse collection and street cleaning, are among the most significant, socially and spatially. Although of limited extent, the direction of change is suggestive of a number of developments.

One such development is the movement of private capital into a number of state markets – the National Health Service, central government departments and the local authorities. Rapid growth of the contract markets and intense competition has led to changes in the dominant form of ownership and control in the contract service industries. Multinational corporations such as the Hawley Group and BET, for instance, through process of acquisition, control one-third of the contract cleaning market. (Hawley's, now ADT, took over the UK's largest contract service firm, Pritchards, in 1986; BET took over Initial Services, a major operator in the laundry industry, in 1985.) Moreover, many of the smaller cleaning companies have been taken over by the major contract cleaning companies in an attempt to extend their geographical reach across the country from the headquarters of the parent company in the South East (Ascher, 1987).

A further development is the impact that this form of privatization has had upon the pay and working conditions of a whole layer of service workers across the country. At present, the effects of contracting out have been virtually restricted to the low-paid, low-skilled and highly unionized members of the public sector workforce. As a consequence of competitive tendering the effects upon the workforce are much the same whether the contract is awarded in-house or to a private contractor – a reduction in pay levels, deteriorating working conditions and job losses. High-status service professionals in the public sector have, so far, been largely untouched by these developments. In many ways, the signs of a 'core/periphery' split in the public sector workforce, a divide between professional and managerial staff on the one hand and part-time, temporary or contract workers on the other, may have much to do with the observation that service-dominated labour markets are becoming increasingly polarized (Damesick, 1986). This point will be picked up later.

Finally, the third way in which the relations of public service provision have been disrupted is really an extension of the second, in so far as the process of privatization is consistent with the move by the state, slowly in the mid-1970s, but gathering pace after 1979, towards the market provision of services such as education, health and welfare. According to Mohan (1988), the growth in private health-care services has been rapid in recent years and carries with it its own geography; one that follows the contours of profitability. Geographically uneven in their development, private hospitals are concentrated in the south-east, at odds with the more even distribution of public health care. A similar concentration of private educational institutions in the south and south-east is also apparent.

Overall, then, the kinds of processes at work in the state service sector represent a shift towards the market and the commodification of services. In that sense, the political relations of control, although not subject directly to the requirements of capital accumulation, are for certain public services operating in a similar direction. The state, together with the expanding private service industries, appears to be laying down a new pattern of uneven development which has two distinctive features. One is the widening divide between the three southern regions and the rest of the country in terms of job growth, as the expanding industries in the service sector bypass certain cities and concentrate their activities in London and southern provincial locations. The other feature, discussed later, is the increasing polarization of jobs and skills in service-dominated labour markets, a result, largely, of the diverse yet overlapping geographies of industrial and commercial service employment. Whilst it would be wrong to imply that the state has taken a leading role in shaping these developments, it would be equally at fault to ignore the ways in which services previously dominated by public delivery are being opened up for private capital and the social and spatial implications of this political direction.

Shifting boundaries: internationalization

A different kind of opening up has been happening in private sector services since the end of the 1970s. Aside from the City of London which has performed an international role in the world's financial markets since the beginning of the nineteenth century, much of the remaining private service sector has been caught up in the process of internationalization. There are a number of different ways in which private sector services have been affected, directly and indirectly, and each possesses its own distinctive geography. The first is the penetration of multinational corporations into what has hitherto been largely protected domestic service markets, sheltered from the forces of international competition (the movement of private capital into state markets is part of this trend). The second is the increased internationalization of services, particularly among commercial and financial services, and the third is the widening of the social division of labour as both manufacturing and service firms contract out functions in response, partly, to increased competition from transnational service companies. We shall look at each development in turn to pull out the implications for service labour markets and their geography.

Among the main domestic service markets that have been opened up to international competition are the contract catering and cleaning service markets referred to earlier, and the leisure and entertainment markets (Clarke and Critcher, 1985). As the relative profitability of manufacturing has declined, service delivery in these markets has provided an alternative source of investment for multinational (and international) companies. Vendex, for example, the Dutch cleaning conglomerate which diversified from its traditional activities in the 1970s, is a major operator in the hospital cleaning market in Britain. Accor, the French hotel and restaurant group, as well as McSleep, the US hotel chain, have entered the budget end (bedrooms only, no facilities) of the hotel trade, challenging the dominance of Trusthouse Forte in the British hotel market (also known for their dominance of the restaurant trade, flight and airport catering and petrol retailing). BET, with its roots in electrical engineering, mentioned earlier in connection with their involvement in the laundry industry, are also active in the entertainments industry through their interests in Rediffusion and Thames Television. It would be possible to continue at some length, but without wishing to labour the point, the dominant form of ownership and control within a range of 'industrial' services is increasingly that of the multinational corporation, with its diverse interests often represented by individual companies trading under the umbrella of the corporate group.

Again, the issue is not just one of a change in the form of the relations of ownership, it is also about the emergence of service labour markets in which the conditions of employment bear a close resemblance to some of the worst conditions of manufacturing employment than to any post-industrial imagery. Casualized, low-paid, low-status and mostly unrewarding are some of the general characteristics of work identified by Gabriel (1988) in a study of the catering industry that, among other places, covered hospital and school kitchens, a 'gentlemen's' club and fast food outlets. Nor are these working conditions exceptional to the catering industry. They are to be found in much of the hotel, tourism and leisure industries, and in cleaning and security firms (*Labour Research*, 1986a, b, c).

More importantly, these labour markets are not on the blurred edges of the working class; they are progressively becoming a central part of the working class. And since many of the jobs in these service industries are socially structured as 'women's work', it is a working class that is progressively changing its gender, from male to female.

In the mid-1980s, for example, just under one million people were employed in the hotel and catering industry, with a further half a million in tourism, leisure and related services. In both sectors women make up the majority of the workforce, employed mainly on a part-time basis (Parsons, 1987). A similar workforce profile is evident in the cleaning

industry. Among the fastest growing sectors of the economy in employment terms, the type of labour-intensive activities performed in these
service industries are also the least likely to be affected by the process of
substitution referred to by Gershuny and Miles (1983), whereby services
are replaced by goods that enable people to 'service' themselves.

The emergence of these casualized labour markets stand in sharp contrast to the growth of high-wage, high-status service jobs in the commercial
and, in particular, the financial service industries. Although this class of
service professionals also owe much of their expansion to the growing
internationalization of services, the processes involved are different from
those which have produced the growth of industrial services. The most
notable developments are, perhaps not surprisingly, associated with the
City of London and how it has changed in response to the globalization of
industrial production and the internationalization of money markets.

It is not possible to do justice to the full range of developments that
have reshaped international finance in the 1980s, but it would appear that
two related developments have had a significant impact upon the City's
institutions and their workforces. The first is the development of international financial markets in bonds and equities, with London at the centre
of both markets. The bond market, or rather the Eurobond market, is
essentially a global loan market which has grown partly in response to the
extended geographical range of multinational corporations. The internationalization of equity markets, the world-wide dealing in company
shares, has mirrored shifts in the international loan market (GLC,
1986b). What is significant about these developments, however, is that
the internationalization of money has seen a parallel growth of international banks in London, in particular US and Japanese institutions,
which, in turn, has led to a restructuring of institutional ownership in the
City and a spur to employment growth in the financial services sector.

The second development is really an extension of this point, namely,
that the movement of foreign financial institutions into London, following
the City's altered international role, has sparked off a round of mergers
among City firms as they seek to compete with the arrival of the new
financial service conglomerates. These conglomerates are locked into the
world economy in a different way from those producing industrial services
and their growth has merely served to compound the geographical and
class divide that distinguishes the two kinds of service conglomerate.

It is not only London's enhanced financial role, however, that has
produced the concentration of high-paid service labour in the capital city,
it is also the accompanying growth of commercial services (Thrift, 1987).
As a commercial service centre, particularly in accounting, advertising
and legal services, London has always been in advance of other UK cities.
What is different today about the social and spatial configuration of
commercial firms in London is that, as with the financial conglomerates,
they are locked into an international set of relationships that separates
them from the local suppliers of business services in provincial towns and

cities. If there is a 'service class', then the commercial strata in London owe their positioning to a set of global processes that goes beyond the externalization of services by manufacturing and service firms in Britain.

This, then, takes us to the last point, namely the growth of service jobs in commercial and industrial services that has resulted from the externalization, the contracting out, of services previously provided in-house. According to Rajan and Pearson (1986), around one-half of new service jobs may be traced to this process of job redistribution between industries. And for the business service industries they put the figure even higher. Much of the job growth in these industries thus represents a deepening of the social division of labour (Massey, 1984; Walker, 1985), a development that appears to be related to the complex demands of increasingly diversified manufacturing and service firms as they reorganize their activities to maintain a competitive advantage.

Geographically, the pattern of employment in the expanding commercial services tends to be concentrated in the larger towns and cities of the south, aside, that is, from London (Gillespie and Green, 1987). This is a pattern which, interestingly, it shares with the workforce of the catering, cleaning and leisure industries discussed earlier. In a period when many of the new jobs are in these two kinds of services, the growth of services has meant an expansion of two kinds of jobs – those which are low-paid, routine and often part-time, and those which are well-paid, professional and full-time – in the same locations, a division which, it appears, is also structured along gender lines. The London labour market, with its monopoly of international services, is one of the sharpest illustrations of this labour market polarization (GLC, 1986a).

6.3   Overlapping geographies

London is exceptional for a whole host of reasons: it is a centre of government, a centre of international finance, a centre of control within the economy, and a focus for the cultural industries. Above all, it is a service city based upon the control functions of the economy, within both the private and public sectors. Other cities and towns have emerged as service-based centres in fundamentally different ways. The changing balance between manufacturing and service employment, the shift to services in many urban locations, is a result of manufacturing job loss rather than service sector expansion. In some cases, particularly in northern industrial towns, what is left is a declining public service employment base. In the larger provincial cities, in Edinburgh, Cardiff, Bristol and the like, the shift to services has been a real one, a growth in different types of service employment, public and private, high-status professional services as well as low-paid, routine service work. What emerges from all this is the pattern of uneven development noted earlier, that is, a reworked north-south divide and increasingly polarized labour markets in the larger provincial cities and London in particular.

The pattern, of course, is more complex than this. Since the 1960s many of the larger towns in the south and the south-east in particular have benefited from the decentralization of clerical service jobs from London. So, too, have parts of the north, although the crucial difference is that whereas the growth of towns around London is the result of private service firms relocating their 'back offices', the movement of jobs to the north has mainly involved the break-up of central government departments. In both cases, however, the strategic control functions, the jobs concerned with the investment and placing of work, have remained in London.

The fact that some towns and cities are becoming favoured locations for clerical 'back offices' while London retains the strategic control functions, and that the larger provincial cities are claiming the majority of both the professional strata and the casualized strata of the service labour force, is the outcome of the variety of ways in which different service industries structure their activities over space. In coming to grips with the shift to services in different urban centres, it is important to recognize that the new geography of service employment is a reflection of various ways in which industries organize their processes of production over space. Moreover, the ways in which the different spatial structures of production *overlay* one another holds the key to the kinds of polarized labour markets that are emerging in urban locations.

Before looking at some of these spatial structures and how they are changing in response to the wider processes examined in the previous section, it is also important to stress that the structures are representative of certain industries. They are representative forms. As the focus here is upon services organized by capital (the current locus of job growth), the organization of specific firms within an industry will depend upon a range of factors, including that of geography, the specific characteristics of places. We shall shift focus from industries to companies in the following section. For the moment, we will remain at industry-level.

One of the better known spatial structures of production is the 'part-process' structure in which different stages of production are located in different areas under the control and direction of a company. In this instance, each location is on a different 'rung' within an overall hierarchy of production that stretches across space (Massey, 1979). Initially developed as an illustration of the way in which certain manufacturing industries such as electronics use space, the example is also one that fits much of the insurance industry. The spatial hierarchy of labour in this case is between clerical support staff at one end, concerned mainly with the technical functions of insurance, and, at the other end, the function of high-level administration, investment analysis and insurance broking. The establishment of clerical 'back offices' in towns and cities outside of London in the 1970s on the basis of developments in the clerical labour process provided a boost to service employment in these areas, mainly for women and also of full-time jobs. In some cases intermediate-level functions such as computing, systems and accounting were located separately from the centre and the 'back offices', representing a further development of the technical division of labour across space. What evidence there is suggests that these kinds of professionals favour locations close to the provincial cities in 're-created' semi-rural settings, in areas similar to those in which the research and development industries are located.[1]

This, however, is a snapshot, a still frame of a particular period. Technological changes since the early 1980s have seen advances in computerization and telecommunications that are beginning to reshape both the internal division of labour and the spatial hierarchy of insurance firms (Cooke and Morgan, 1985). Increasingly, the direction is towards the spatial reconcentration of production, with both management and clerical labour located in a provincial centre outside of London.

In banking and in the commercial services sector the tendency, as noted earlier, is towards a greater centralization of activities in London. With the growth in the concentration of ownership and control in banking, accountancy, advertising, legal and management services, some parts of these industries have laid down a spatial hierarchy of financial and administrative controls that branches out from London to the provincial centres. This is a cloning spatial structure which reproduces the same service activities in the provincial branch offices. Control remains at the centre, in or around the capital city, and so too do the international functions. In some of the more specialized commercial service markets, such as advertising or management consultancy, local demands may also be met at the centre rather than the provincial level, provided through the headquarters of a multi-locational manufacturing or service firm (Marshall, 1985). Indeed, what is distinctive about the spatial structuring of these activities, and commercial services in general, is that the centre is a major site of production, a working hub rather than simply a site of financial or strategic control. It is in this sense that geography and class reinforce one another, with the upper commercial strata separated socially and spatially from their commercial counterparts in the provincial cities.

Of course, not all services can be provided at a distance from the market. In the act of producing some services, such as leisure or a range of personal services, the involvement of the consumer is necessary. Other services such as hotel and catering, cleaning and security, and retail sales are also provided close to their markets.[2] The spatial structure of these industries varies enormously within and between industries ranging from the local small firm or outlet, a cloned structure, to multi-industry conglomerates of the kind mentioned earlier. Despite the multiplicity of small establishments providing these services, much of the employment within these industries is accounted for by the multiple or branch outlets of major service firms and conglomerates. And within the latter kinds of organization, the relations of control over space may take any number of forms from simple ownership to franchising or licensing, or, in the case of corporate capital, from strategic to financial control.

Each of these different forms of control involves a particular spatial structuring of the relations of production; a structuring which is intended to meet the demands of spatially restricted markets to satisfy profitability. And although the calculation of profitability will differ from organization to organization, the use of space, the location of service delivery, will reflect a geographical pattern of profitability. Many of the points of service delivery therefore are located in the prosperous free-standing towns and cities.

Labour is also an important part of the locational equation. As noted earlier, industries such as cleaning and catering, hotels and restaurants, leisure and recreation, and the retail trade are labour-intensive, in a specific rather than a general sense. These industries rely upon the availability of certain kinds of labour – part-time, often temporary and usually female. The bulk of the jobs in these industries, in contrast to the commercial and financial services, make up a large part of the secondary labour market. London is one such location for this kind of labour, with its large differentiated labour market. So, too, are the free-standing towns and cities.

What is emerging, then, as indicated at the start of this section, is a set of overlapping labour geographies, with the different type of service sector occupations growing in the same locations. Although the social and spatial co-ordinates of the different groups – the high-status, professional groups and the low-paid, casualized groups – are determined by the different ways in which the service industries are structured across space, the combined result is an increase in local labour market disparities. As the growth of service production in general has tended to reconcentrate industry in the larger urban centres that have been least affected by manufacturing job loss (with the exception of London), the signs of class polarization in service-dominated labour markets are becoming increasingly visible. In so far as the spatial structuring of the private service industries follows more or less the representative types outlined, then the divisions are likely to become more marked. Having said that, none of the spatial structures identified is static; they change within and between service industries as the uses of space exhibited by service firms alter in response to changes in service production and delivery and the kinds of national and international shifts discussed earlier. In this sense, it is at the level of the firm, the internal workings of service firms and the specificity of the economic context in which they operate, that a firmer understanding can be gained of what is happening to people's jobs, how it is happening and where.

6.4   Geography at work

In this section the analysis is at a different level. There is a shift from the general to the particular, from the broad contours of uneven service sector expansion to a more detailed account of the impact of service sector expansion upon local employment structures. The focus is upon the changing structure of service sector labour markets, the general thread of this chapter, using case-study materials to illustrate one aspect – the links between geography, production change and employment change.

The aim is to show diversity rather than uniformity, to show how similar kinds of service development may take different forms across space. The two local economies, Norwich and Ipswich in East Anglia, were chosen for two reasons: first, they have both experienced strong service sector growth over the past few decades; and, secondly, because the insurance sector is a major employer in both locations and dominated by a handful of (international) insurance companies. It is the ways in which similar types of insurance capital in the two locations are forging different kinds of internal labour markets and helping to reshape local employment structures that are addressed here.[3]

Local divergence and employment structures

As referred to earlier, in the late 1960s and mid-1970s the decentralization of clerical jobs to the provinces and suburban locations gathered pace enabling insurance companies to improve the quality of clerical labour, reduce turnover, and lower office rental costs (Boddy, Lovering and Bassett, 1986). For a number of insurance companies relocation involved the introduction of new labour processes, assisted by more efficient batch-processing techniques and the gradual extension of computers into the preparation of policies and renewals (Barras and Swann, 1983). This general scenario describes the conditions under which insurance production was established at Ipswich and at a number of other provincial locations, although, as we shall see, it is only partially applicable to Norwich.

Employment in the insurance sectors of the two locations expanded significantly in the 1970s and is attributable largely to the actions of four major insurance companies. Two of the companies between them transferred some 600 staff from London to the two locations – mainly male, technical staff in the 30 to 50 year age span. Prior to 1971 one of the other insurance companies was responsible for transferring a similar number of jobs from London to Ipswich – once again, mainly male, technical staff. The bulk of the expansion in both areas, however, was largely attributable to local recruitment – mainly clerical staff and mainly female – although the number of trainees, both male and female, was not insubstantial.

Interestingly, most of the employment growth in insurance nationally has involved full-time jobs. Unlike the growth of part-time, female work in other expanding service industries in the UK (hotels and catering, retail distribution and business services), the growth in insurance has been in full-time occupations. Nationally, full-time jobs for both men and women in the insurance sector have expanded over the last decade and a half, slowing down throughout the 1980s (Rajan, 1987). The pattern is similar for Norwich and Ipswich, with both locations showing a slightly greater number of male, full-time jobs compared with the female equivalent. Part-time employment for both men and women in the insurance sector in both locations is negligible, and is restricted largely to ancillary manual and non-manual occupations.

Concealed beneath this pattern, however, is an asymmetrical structure of employment in terms of gender. In each of the four major insurance companies, basic clerical tasks (including trainee grades) accounted for over one-half of the total employment, and in one case the figure was as high as 70 per cent. Within these grades, it would appear that women are over-represented, with the majority of women concentrated in the lower technical grades. In one company there were very few women higher than the lowest rung of the managerial grades, despite the fact that recruitment at trainee level was equal by gender. The findings are consistent with Boddy *et al.*'s (1986) study which showed that gender differentiation in the insurance industry displays both a 'horizontal' and a 'vertical' segregation. Not only do women occupy different roles from men (typing, telephonists), they are also concentrated in the lower grades of the jobs undertaken by both men and women.

The gender composition and the gender differentiation of jobs, therefore, is similar in both locations. Where differences arise, however, is in relation to the structure of the internal labour markets in Norwich and Ipswich's insurance sectors.

First, in Norwich there are no significant barriers to mobility between management and clerical grades, despite the variations in hierarchical gradings between companies. In one company the clerical hierarchy ran all the way from the entry grades to the executive grades with promotion based on ability plus seniority. At the top end of the primary labour market, professional staff (computer specialists, estates surveyors, investment analysts) received 'executive' supplements. Also included in this primary market are the middle management and the clerical staff, both of whom performed disciplined and largely rule-governed jobs. Finally, at the lower end of this section, typists and non-clerical staff form a distinct sub-market with little or no connection to the clerical hierarchy. Control over work performance, turnover and work organization in this company is achieved through a 'career ladder', coupled with competitive fringe benefits. In reality, however, the majority of the company's staff have few employment opportunities outside of Norwich and, to an extent, are controlled by their own circumstances – working within a 'closed', provincial labour market. In turn, this closure, given the limited availability of managerial and professional skills in this type of labour market, encourages a company policy of career progression.

In contrast, mobility in the Ipswich insurance labour market is restricted largely to professional staff. At one end of the scale, specialist insurance staff such as brokers and underwriters are recruited nationally at graduate level and follow a separate career path from the clerical staff who are recruited locally. Promotion for professional staff is based on ability plus seniority, but linked in the case of clerical grades to job availability. In one company a ceiling on the number of jobs available for promotion among clerical staff increased turnover rates to twice that of the Norwich companies, yet this was considered quite acceptable in comparison with London clerical turnover rates. Overall, a clearer demarcation exists between 'career' and 'non-career' grades in comparison with Norwich. This division also tends to run along gender lines, with a greater number of women occupying 'non-career' jobs.

It would be tempting to conclude that the 'non-career' staff form part of a secondary section in the Ipswich labour market, but their favourable position relative to other occupations *outside of* the insurance sector in terms of pay, skill and work conditions points to a lower tier position in the primary labour market (Berger and Piore, 1980). Nevertheless, in terms of job characteristics the Ipswich insurance labour market, in contrast to Norwich, is showing signs of a polarization of staff functions between routine clerical and professional tasks. This is a product both of the greater openness of the Ipswich labour market for clerical labour (higher turnover, less retention) and the way in which technical change has been introduced and implemented in the insurance sector in Ipswich.

This last point is significant. Although the related processes of computerization and standardization have been introduced by all four companies, so that a greater integration of the production process and a clearer separation between routinized and non-standard tasks may be achieved, the impact of new technology in the two locations has been mediated by the structure of management–labour relations over time.

In the Norwich insurance sector the familiar *pyramidical* structure of the insurance job hierarchy has remained relatively intact despite the fairly widespread introduction of on-line technology. In both the major insurance companies, changes in office technology have led to a reorganization of the workforce, yet these changes have involved the reskilling as much as the deskilling of jobs. Overall, technical change has shifted the employment structure away from some clerical jobs towards data processing and systems staff. Thus the major area of substitution appears to be in clerical skills and not in the full range of 'technical' insurance skills. Volume tasks are now dealt with by computer, leaving staff to deal with the more varied and interesting non-standard tasks (claim assessments, marketing etc.). These changes, perhaps rather surprisingly, have led in recent years to a moderate increase in insurance employment in Norwich. The increased need for high-level specialist skills, flexible technical and marketing skills, and data processing staff has tended to broaden the middle sections of the pyramid. Sustaining the base, however, are a range of staff dealing with routine tasks backed up by extensive computer support *and* the trainees necessary to meet the changing skills required in an increasingly flexible and diverse marketplace.

The relative closure of the Norwich labour market has led one company to train 'in-house' its own middle management and specialists and to recruit technical staff from the local labour market. This practice has been adopted not only because there is an adequate supply of relatively immobile, well-educated, school-leavers in the local labour market, but also, it would appear, out of necessity. Unlike the other major insurance companies which dominate the financial sectors in Norwich and Ipswich, this company has virtually all of its functions, aside that is from sales, located in Norwich. Historically, the company has had a major presence in Norwich with only its investment interests and some specialist insurance business located in London. Thus the corporate structure of the company is rather atypical for an insurance company First, it is headquartered in a provincial city with bad communications to London and the rest of the country. And secondly, there is no spatial hierarchy of functions, only an internal division of labour within the company. Consequently, the company has had little choice but to recruit and train its technical, professional and managerial staff. Among its chief attractions, therefore, is an internal promotion ladder, a relatively uncharacteristic feature for a large insurance company, and one which has led to a 'top-heavy' primary labour market within the company.

This employment structure has remained intact largely because the other major insurance company in the city, a brokerage firm, is not a direct competitor. The underwriting of domestic life insurance, and to a lesser extent domestic general insurance, primarily involves claims work of a different order from that of overseas brokerage. Between the two companies there is a degree of overlap in the local labour market for clerical, typing and secretarial grades but there is little overlap between the two specialist markets. The absence of any direct overlap at this level entails little cross-firm poaching of staff or any excessive pressure to 'bid up' middle-level salaries in the local labour market. Both firms are thus able to train recruits 'in-house' without fear of losing technical or specialist staff. Moreover, the advantage of school-leaver recruitment in a closed labour market is not just a question of available numbers, but the ability to train and re-train a relatively permanent staff in the *changing skills* required in an expanding and rapidly changing technological environment and an increasingly diverse insurance market. In Norwich, outside of the insurance sector, there are few competing occupations that offer such a 'career package'.

Turning to the impact of technical change upon work practices and skills in Ipswich's insurance sector, one finds a rather different effect.

There are a number of similarities – the introduction of new technology leading to work reorganization, increasing routinization of clerical tasks, greater specialization among technical staff, and an increase in the number of data-processing staff. Yet in Ipswich this has not led to a broader pyramidical employment structure, but rather towards a *polarized* two-tier structure with a characteristic spatial form. In the two major insurance companies in Ipswich the technical division of labour has taken a spatial form, with the highly skilled professional staff located in London and a decreasing, and increasingly routinized, workforce located in Ipswich. The increasing standardization of products/policies (for example, 'packages' for commercial enterprises that cover fire, property and accident, rather than separate policies for each) and the computerization of fixed practices (draft policies, premium calculation, ledgers etc.) have led to a progressive deskilling of a range of clerical and technical functions. As in Norwich there remains a place for non-standard roles, but these are limited in number and do not lead the occupants onto higher-level functions within the hierarchy. Overall, the profile of the insurance labour market in Ipswich is showing signs of polarity with less people concentrated at the base and a greater number of systems staff giving additional weight at the top end.

Much of this can be traced to differences in local employment structures between Norwich and Ipswich. First, Ipswich is not as geographically isolated as Norwich, the labour supply is more elastic and the opportunities for well-educated school-leavers extend beyond the insurance sector to encompass an increasing range of 'high-tech' activities. It is markedly similar to Norwich in the relative immobility of clerical and data-processing staff, but there are alternative sectors competing for the same types of labour, primarily semi-skilled and unskilled, low-paid labour. The relative openness of Ipswich's labour market, characterized by clerical turnover rates double those of Norwich and the ability of companies to 'buy in' technical insurance staff, has reduced job mobility and restricted training and promotion prospects for those at the bottom end of the internal labour market. In effect, what is happening in Ipswich's insurance sector is a decline in the significance of internal labour markets and a greater dependence by firms upon the external labour market. Much has been made of this shift in the US (see Noyelle, 1987; Stanback, 1987), although its extent is bound up with the ways in which geography affects the outcome of production change.

Secondly, although Ipswich is increasingly identified as an 'insurance centre' in the region, unlike Norwich there is no symbolic connection between insurance and the city. The history of insurance within Norwich, the industry's high profile, and the parochialism that has marked employment relations in the sector has tended to emphasize locality rather than class as the locus of interest. In one sense, the insurance sector has fostered a corporate paternalism between itself, the city and the workforce (see Urry, 1980), whereas, in Ipswich, there is no historical link of dependence or identity between the insurance companies and the locality or their workforce, nor apparently any attempt to promote such attitudes; the relationship between the major insurance companies and the local population appears to be an instrumental one, untinged by any form of paternalism.

As a local labour market, Ipswich represents a rather different use of space by insurance capital from that of Norwich. Drawn into an emerging spatial division of service labour as insurance companies decentralized stages of production to take advantage of lower costs of production, Ipswich offered a relatively cheap, educated clerical labour supply. Norwich performs a similar role but on the basis of a different set of social relations. Whereas Ipswich is a relatively open labour market, the labour market in Norwich exhibits a degree of closure that has enabled its labour force to be 'remade', to be retrained to meet the changing skills demanded in the insurance world.[4] In Ipswich the insurance sector established production in the area to take advantage of an adequate, relatively stable, cheap labour supply. In Norwich these same labour characteristics provide a partial account of the expansion of insurance activities in the area. With advances in telecommunication in the 1980s, virtually all aspects of insurance production (excluding branches) are now feasible in a closed labour market in a provincial location. In Norwich this has been established by 'remaking' a captured labour force, not simply by 'using' an 'accessible' cheap labour supply. It is in this sense that space makes a difference, with geography and production inextricably interconnected.

6.5 Conclusion

Returning to the title of this chapter, the geographies of service, one of the aims has been to examine the different labour geographies of the service industries. Each section represents a different dimension, a different slice through the question of service labour and geography. The first section attempted to draw the contours of an emerging pattern of uneven service development, in both a sectoral and spatial way. The second section looked briefly at some of the spatial structures of services that lie behind this emerging pattern. In doing so, it attempted to pull out the spatial co-ordinates of different kinds of service labour and the overlap between them. In particular, the trend towards increased polarization in service sector labour markets was highlighted. Finally, at a different level, by means of case-study materials, an illustration of the specific ways in which jobs and geography interrelate was given.

There is one characteristic, however, which binds all three dimensions: the nature of the approach, the different and changing ways in which social relations are structured across space. Conceptualizing the geography of industry and employment change in this way is one kind of approach, one kind of geography. Other geographies, with the accent on the plural, offer different kinds of approach – a different set of geographies.

Notes

1   The relative power of professional service labour to choose where they live and work is an important characteristic of the market situation of this kind of service labour (see Urry, 1987). On the geography of the research and development industries, see Gillespie and Green (1987).

2   The spatial scale at which the demand for these services is met, however, is mediated by the existing organizational and spatial structure of these activities, as well as changing technological practices. Retail distributors, for example, can meet demand through a variety of spatial strategies ranging from retail warehouses, hypermarkets on out-of-town sites, multiple branch outlets acquired through expansion or franchise agreements, mail order and teleshopping to the traditional corner-shop.

3   This research formed part of an ESRC-funded project on the uneven impact of service sector expansion in East Anglia, carried out by the author in 1986/7 with Linda McDowell and Ruth Pearson.

4   The remaking of management–labour relations in a manufacturing industry, electrical enegineering, is discussed in Chapter 8 by Kevin Morgan and Andrew Sayer. In many ways, the legacy of paternalism that exists in service industries such as insurance and banking has enabled employers in these industries to draw upon and re-work existing work practices, rather than devise wholly new practices in an industry – as is the case with electrical engineering.

References

ASCHER, K. (1987) *The Politics of Privatization: Contracting Out Public Services*, London and Basingstoke, Macmillan.

BARRAS, R. and SWANN, J. (1983) *The Adoption and Impact of Information Technology in the UK Insurance Industry*, London, The Technical Change Centre.

BERGER, S. and PIORE, M. (1980) *Dualism and Discontinuity in Industrial Societies*, Cambridge, Cambridge University Press.

BODDY, M., LOVERING, J. and BASSETT, K. (eds) (1986) *Sunbelt City? A Study of Economic Change in Britain's M4 Growth Corridor*, London, Oxford University Press.

CLARKE, J. and CRITCHER, C. (1985). *The Devil Makes Work: Leisure in Capitalist Britain*, London and Basingstoke, Macmillan.

COOKE, P. and MORGAN, K. (1985) 'Flexibility and the new restructuring: locality and industry in the 1980s', *Papers in Planning Research 94*, Cardiff, University of Wales Institute of Science and Technology.

DAMESICK, P. J. (1986) 'Service industries, employment and regional development in Britain', *Institute of British Geographers, Transactions*, New Series, Vol. 11, pp. 212–26.

GABRIEL, Y. (1988) *Working Lives in Catering*, London, Routledge and Kegan Paul.

GILLESPIE, A. and GREEN, A. (1987) 'The changing geography of "producer services" employment in Britain', *Regional Studies*, Vol. 21, No. 5, pp. 397–411.

GREATER LONDON COUNCIL (1986a) *The London Labour Plan*, London, GLC.

GREATER LONDON COUNCIL (1986b) *The London Financial Strategy*, London, GLC.

LABOUR RESEARCH (1986a) 'Upstairs, downstairs in Britain's hotels', Vol. 75, No. 7, pp. 19–20.

LABOUR RESEARCH (1986b) 'Fast food, faster profits', Vol. 75, No. 6, pp. 10–13.

LABOUR RESEARCH (1986c) 'Contractors sweep up European market', Vol. 75, No. 11, pp. 15–16.

MASSEY, D. (1979) 'In what sense a regional problem?', *Regional Studies*, Vol. 13, pp. 233–43.

MASSEY, D. (1984) *Spatial Divisions of Labour: Social Structures and the Geography of Production*, London and Basingstoke, Macmillan.

MARSHALL, J. N. (1985) 'Business services, the regions and regional policy', *Regional Studies*, Vol. 19, pp. 353–63.

MOHAN, J. (1988) 'Spatial aspects of health-care employment in Britain 1: Aggregate trends', *Environment and Planning A*, Vol. 20, pp. 7–23.

NOYELLE, T. J. (1987) *Beyond Industrial Dualism*, Boulder, Col., and London, Westview Press.

PARSONS, D. (1987) 'Tourism and leisure jobs: a statistical review', *The Service Industries Journal*, Vol. 7, No. 3, pp. 365–78.

RAJAN, A. (1987) *Services: The Second Industrial Revolution*, London, Butterworth.

RAJAN, A. and PEARSON, R. (1986) *UK Occupation and Employment Trends to 1990*, Guildford, Butterworths.

STANBACK, T. (1987) *Computerization and the Transformation of Employment, Government, Hospitals and Universities*, Boulder, Col., Westview Press.

THRIFT, N. (1987) 'The fixers: the urban geography of international commercial capital', in Henderson, J. and Castells, M. (eds) *Global Restructuring and Territorial Development*, London, Sage.

URRY, J. (1980) 'Paternalism, management and localities', Working Paper 12, Lancaster Regionalism Group.

URRY, J. (1987) 'Some social and spatial aspects of services', *Environment and Planning D: Society and Space*, Vol. 5, pp. 5–26.

WALKER, R. (1985) 'Is there a service economy? The changing capitalist division of labour', *Science and Society*, Vol. 49, No. 1, pp. 42–83.

Section IV Labour and work reorganization

Introduction

The chapters in this Section have a different focus from those in the preceding Sections. All three are concerned with aspects of change in the structures of labour markets, in working conditions and in employment practices. And all three chapters, in different ways, are concerned with processes that are still working themselves out, but which collectively have already found a name or rather a number of different names.

For some, the UK economy has entered a period of 'flexible accumulation', usually denoted as some kind of 'post-Fordist' regime in which companies strive for greater flexibility from their workers, their suppliers and their production technology. Others more modestly refer to the recent changes in the organization of labour and production as a sign of increased 'flexibility' within the economy. What these labels mean is not clear, but what lies behind them is an attempt to make sense of a variety of supposedly related changes. Above all, the issue is one of conceptualization, how we grasp the particularity of changes under general concepts. As the process is a fallible one, open to criticism and revision, there is considerable difference of opinion over what the available evidence represents and how far it is possible to draw accurate generalizations.

Of the three chapters in this Section, Hudson is the only one that engages directly with the notion of 'flexible accumulation' and all the kinds of economic changes it is alleged to subsume. The other two chapters do not address this issue centrally, but what they have to say about changing aspects of work, employment and labour organization has a direct bearing on the emerging debate over flexibility in the UK economy and its potential geography.

Hudson's is a provocative study. He puts together a wide range of evidence from the 'old' industrial regions, those which bear the marks of early industrialization in the UK, to show how the changes taking place in the organization of production and work in those areas do not amount to some kind of structural transition from Fordist to post-Fordist methods of production. Rather he argues that the changes which have occurred in the 'old' industrial regions represent attempts by capital to preserve pre-Fordist and Fordist systems of production. So, for example, the enhanced ability of management to redefine their authority over labour through the introduction of new recruitment practices, new types of employment contract and new conditions of work are all taken as part of strategies by capital to preserve old modes of accumulation in an enabling political climate. The 'new' in this sense – which includes the introduction of extended shift systems and the lowering of demarcation barriers between jobs, and the shift towards a part-time and casualized workforce, together with the implementation of single-union deals – are all part of a selective reworking of capital/labour relations that is keeping alive parts of the 'old' industrial regions.

Hudson also places considerable emphasis upon the role of inward-investing multinationals in forging new work practices and employment conditions. Nissan in the North East is perhaps one of the better-known examples of a company setting up production in an 'old' industrial region and attempting to refashion labour practices in ways that are not simply a response to new or altered labour processes and technologies. In this instance, Hudson's argument overlaps with the focus of Morgan and Sayer's chapter.

Their concern is also to show how the large multinationals are among the main innovators of new forms of management–labour relations, 'bearers', as they call it, of new forms of social organization within the firm. Indeed they refer to many of the same characteristics of labour reorganization as Hudson and they too are analytically wary about subsuming these developments under some kind of broad, overarching regime of accumulation. Their study is also based upon an industry in an 'old' industrial region, the electrical engineering industry in south Wales. But here the two accounts start to diverge. Whilst Morgan and Sayer as well as Hudson refer to new kinds of management–labour practices, the kinds that Morgan and Sayer have in mind are largely to do with how management controls and maintains labour relations through the production of *consent*, the active mobilization of agreement with corporate aims. Central to this notion of management by consent is the development of social as well as technical skills among the labour force. A skilled worker in this sense is one who has developed the qualities 'of attendance, flexibility, responsibility, discipline, identification with the company and, crucially, work rate and quality'.

Development is the key word here, as these kinds of qualities, according to Morgan and Sayer, are not given but are 'made'. New entrants that establish production in a region such as south Wales meet with a complex legacy of labour traditions and practices. A process of adjustment between company practices and local labour practices takes place. But the adjustment process is not one way; it works in both directions, with the new entrants adjusting to elements of a strong labourist culture and vice versa. Coercion, the imposition of a new set of work practices, is always possible, of course, but the maintenance of such practices is likely to result from a manufactured consensus rather than a continuous assertion of managerial control over labour.

It is by no means certain, however, how far these new work practices have spread and the same, for that matter, could be said of many of the changes identified by Hudson. He, together with Morgan and Sayer, make no claim as to their statistical representativeness, although both accounts would claim that they are not restricted to the 'old' industrial regions. For Hudson, however, it is the 'old' industrial regions that are likely to experience the recent forms of work reorganization in their sharpest form, whereas Morgan and Sayer are confident that the changes they refer to are not confined to the electronics industry or south Wales. Indeed, Allen in the previous Section refers to parallel developments in the reworking of management–labour practices in the insurance industry in East Anglia.

But this kind of statement can be misleading – as both accounts are quick to point out. Even where the same sorts of labour market change or forms of work reorganization take place in more than one region, they are unlikely to be experienced in quite the same way. Variations between places, in their cultural forms, political character and economic organization, together with their specific histories, make, as they say, all the difference. They mediate the impact of such changes. In Berkshire or in Cambridgeshire, in the kinds of 'innovative' areas that Hall refers to in Section II, the absence of a strong labourist tradition would involve a different kind of adjustment, a different negotiated outcome, between a new entrant and the local social relations. Recognition of this, as Hudson implies, is just another way of talking about uneven development.

This raises a further question. If places are different in many ways, including their labour traditions, why should companies establish production in 'radical' regions such as south Wales or the North East? Why should companies in the electronics industry, for example, move to south Wales rather than to some of the areas along the M4 corridor which lack a tradition of collectivism, a culture of solidarism? Part of the answer can be found in Morgan and Sayer's emphasis upon adjustment and adaptation. Nearly all of the new entrants in their study had adjusted to a unionized environment, but in doing so they adapted unionism to their interests. Part of the 'package' of new labour practices included the introduction of single-union agreements and in some cases this was accompanied by 'no-strike' deals. In the North East, Nissan is again one of the more familiar examples of such practices. That said, although the spread of single-unionism is still limited and its geography unclear, few have missed the connection between such practices often being established by new entrants on greenfield sites in locations that do not possess the kind of radical legacies referred to by Morgan and Sayer or by Hudson.

Lane sketches much of the background that has led up to these developments and sets out the questions that a weakened trade union movement has had to face in recent years. The collapse of manufacturing employment, the disappearance of the large factory in the industrial towns and cities and the growth of multi-plant, multi-locational firms are all part of this background and so, too, is the shift from manufacturing to services. Fewer people mine coal, build ships or make cars; more work in shops, in fast-food outlets, hotels, banks and the local town hall. None of this can be taken as an indication that trade unionism is necessarily in decline or that the power of the trade unions is inevitably weakened. But it is a dispersed movement, especially in its geography. And it is the development of these more dispersed structures of unionism that lie behind what Lane calls the uneven development of trade union practices – of which single-union deals are amongst the more contemporary.

As with the signs of flexibility in the economy, however, the direction that the trade union movement is taking has yet to come clearly into focus. What is certain, however, is that the direction of change is not pre-determined. The shop steward in the manufacturing plant may be giving way to the white-collared official in the public sector or the banking sector, but this only tells us that unionism, in an era of industrial upheaval, is still with us. Precisely what kind of era we are going through, however, is the subject matter of the next Section.

7   Labour market changes and new forms of work in 'old' industrial regions*

Ray Hudson

7.1   Introduction

As the post-war 'long wave with an undertone of expansion' became transformed into one with 'an undertone of contraction' (Mandel, 1975), it became clear that momentous changes were occurring in the organiz- ation of economic activity, in patterns of work and employment, in production and consumption patterns within advanced capitalist econom- ies. They raise intriguing theoretical questions as to the most appropriate way of interpreting them and many of the answers that have been offered draw heavily, in one guise or another, on notions of increased 'flexibility'. For some, the changes denoted a 'crisis of Fordism', its imminent demise and the transition to a new 'post-Fordist' flexible regime of accumulation, which is located at the heart of the myriad observable changes (for example, Harvey and Scott, 1987). Others have focused on the more specific, though closely related, issue of the transition from 'ageing' Fordist mass production to 'ascendant' flexible production systems (Storper and Scott, 1988).

Partly because these processes of transformation and change are still going on, the extent and generality of the switch to 'flexibility' – and indeed precisely what 'flexibility' means: 'flexibility' for whom, for example? – remain a matter for debate. What I seek to do in this chapter is to explore this issue by setting some of these general theoretical claims and propositions against the detailed evidence provided by the diverse forms of recent changes in labour markets, labour processes and the organization of production in 'old' industrial regions of the capitalist world. Undoubtedly, there are some economic activities and localities that can validly be characterized as exhibiting symptoms of 'flexible production systems' or 'flexible accumulation'. The evidence available for the 'old' industrial regions does not, however, point to such a conclusion. Rather it suggests two things. Firstly, that Fordism (either in the narrow sense of a particular method of organizing production or in the broader sense of a regime of accumulation) has never established more than a tenuous hold in many of those regions. Secondly, that the changes in organization of production, employment and work currently taking place in them do not constitute a transition to a new 'post-Fordist flexibility' but

---

*This is a shortened version of a paper published in *Environment and Planning D: Society and Space* (forthcoming).

rather a selective re-working which reproduces, in modified form, pre-Fordist and Fordist methods of production. In so far as such regions remain loci of major ensembles of industrial production within the capitalist world (notwithstanding their relative, and in some instances absolute, deindustrialization over the last couple of decades), this conclusion has broader implications in understanding the transformations currently taking place within capitalism.

To put these claims into perspective – and to provide a background to the empirical evidence of the interrelated changes in labour markets, labour processes and the organization of production in them – it is necessary briefly to define what is meant by 'old' industrial regions (OIRs). The OIRs denote those areas that formed the cradles of industrial capitalism and where capitalism production grew rapidly in the nineteenth century around industries such as coal-mining, chemicals, iron and steel and related metal-processing industries (engineering, railways, ship-building etc.), organized from a very early stage in large oligopolistic conglomerates and tied into international markets.[1] Despite attempts to 'diversify' their industrial structure and labour markets, especially in the 1960s, via various national state policies, many of the OIRs remained heavily dependent upon their 'old' industries as a source of waged employment. Even so, changes in economic activities and employment within the OIRs have not been solely confined to these industries, for reasons that are set out below.

In the next section the variety of recent changes in labour markets and labour processes in the OIRs is summarized. Clearly the sorts of changes described there are by no means limited to these regions but they are perhaps most acutely experienced there, in areas where 'work' was widely, if erroneously, defined as full-time, regular, male, waged labour – 'a job for life'. It is also important to acknowledge that such changes are not experienced in the same way, or to the same extent, in all OIRs. There may well be, and often are, significant differences as well as similarities between both industries, regions and smaller localities within them, reflecting local variations in politics, culture or the practices of civil society. It is in this sense that the specificities of localities and regions can be rescued from the dangers inherent in contemplation of the unique and integrated into an understanding of the dynamics of the restructuring of capitalism as a global commodity production and exchange system. Indeed, constructing such an understanding requires this integration. This and other issues central to the theoretical interpretation of changes in the OIRs are explored in section 7.3 [. . .]

7.2 Forms of labour market and labour process change in the OIRs[2]

The most obvious effect of the changing geography of production upon the labour market in the 'old' industrial areas is the rapid increase in and current high levels of (registered) unemployment. There is a tendency to interpret the growth of unemployment simply as one aspect of a growing dichotomy between those in full-time, regular, waged employment and the long-term unemployed, solely reliant on state transfer payments. Nevertheless, this considerably oversimplifies the sorts of changes that have been occurring in these labour markets. For *related* to the shrinking number of jobs available and rising unemployment in the 'old' industrial regions, there has been a series of changes affecting the character and duration of these jobs, in employers' strategies for hiring and firing labour and in differential access to different sorts of waged labour for men and women, young and old. These issues are explored in turn.

The growth and changing character of unemployment

At the same time as unemployment has expanded there have been important changes in the character of unemployment and in who is becoming unemployed. Increasingly, female unemployment has grown in relative and absolute terms, as the 'new' manufacturing industries of the 1960s have shed labour and as the downward multiplier effects of loss of income from industrial jobs have worked through to service activities in those areas. Increasingly, long-term unemployment has ceased to be the exclusive preserve of men aged 50 years or more and became generalized over both sexes and all age groups, young and old alike, but with a growing concentration among the young [. . .]

As Osterland (1987) has demonstrated, however, even in the 1980s, it does not automatically follow that those losing their jobs in the 'old' industries have joined the register of unemployed. It may well be that many of them are re-employed within the region. In other words, the structure of the labour markets within which job losses from 'old' industries occur is important in shaping the distribution of unemployment arising directly and indirectly from these job losses. There is now growing recognition that local labour market conditions are often much more important than factors such as social class, traditionally thought of as decisive in influencing the incidence of unemployment (Ashton and Maguire, 1987). As Osterland points out, though, for those who do obtain alternative jobs, it may often mean re-employment in other companies in less skilled jobs, on lower wages and at the expense of someone else who is added to or remains on the unemployment register.

The contraction of core employment and the expansion of peripheral employment

Historically, the predominant form of work in 'old' industries in the 'old' industrial regions eventually became structured in terms of regular, waged work – a (male) 'job for life', with a progression available through a hierarchy of types of jobs within the coal-mines, steelworks or shipyards. In recent years there has been a redefinition of the extent of this core workforce and, as it has shrunk, two related changes have occurred. Firstly, there has been a growth in peripheral employment associated with work in these industries. Secondly, there have been important changes in the terms and conditions on which employment has been offered, associated with a reorganization of the labour process.[3]

Both aspects reflect a concern to increase labour productivity and in this way to increase the international competitiveness of production from plants in these regions. Because of the natural environmental basis of production and/or for technical reasons associated with the organization of production, it is often impracticable to decentralize production in 'old' industries such as coal-mining, basic chemical or steel production to small plants. Indeed in the 1950s and 1960s there were considerable productivity gains associated with the introduction of new, more automated production technologies in bigger production units and complexes in these industries (for example, see Hudson, 1983, and Lapple and van Hoogstraten, 1980). Increasing labour productivity, therefore, depends upon securing an acceptance of changed conditions of work and greater flexibility *within* big plants and industrial complexes – often under threat of their closing completely and production switching abroad, threats made against a background of global overcapacity and slow or no growth in demand for their output. One result of this has been to promote and enhance inter-plant competition in terms of labour productivity – something that workers have often acquiesced in as they see it as a way of preserving 'their' plant and community (see Hudson and Sadler, 1986).

New forms of work and conditions of employment in the shrinking core workforces of the 'old' industries

One aspect of the imposition of new working conditions is linked to the introduction of new technical conditions of production. Although there may be a general tendency to switch from a Fordist to a more flexible regime of accumulation in some economic activities, it is also important to acknowledge that in industries such as deep coal-mining there are currently strong pressures to attempt to 'Fordize' production as a way of competing with open-cast output and coal imports. This is particularly evident in the UK in British Coal's attempts to introduce the MINOS System (Winterton, 1985), both increasingly to automate production and to tighten management control of labour underground. The considerable relative autonomy that miners had over the pace of production is being eroded as the new mining technologies are being – selectively – introduced into collieries and indeed onto particular coal-faces in those collieries [. . .]

In other cases the introduction of new conditions of work is associated less with the introduction of new technology than with intensification of work with existing technology. There are several dimensions to the process of reorganizing work around a more flexible labour force. One is the introduction of new and extended shift systems (for example, see Hudson, 1986, 1988a). A second relates to the lowering or ending of demarcation barriers. For example, on Teesside ICI have negotiated an agreement with local unions whereby its shrunken core workforce undertakes maintenance work – with the additional benefit to ICI that it can then shed maintenance workers from its core workforce (Beynon, Hudson and Sadler, 1986). Elsewhere in north-east England, there have been substantial reductions in demarcation barriers within ship repair yards on Tyneside (Hudson, 1986) [. . .] A third dimension to this reorganization of work and working conditions is a move to 'one-union' arrangements in 'old' industries. In the UK, in particular, there has often been a plethora of trades unions representing the interests of workers in such industries and to some extent increased flexibility has been associated with a switch to 'one-union' deals. In 1986, for example, United Merchant Bar agreed such a deal with the Iron and Steel Trades Confederation (ISTC), the first that involved any company in which BSC had a stake [. . .]

A fourth way in which working conditions have been redefined involves wage cuts and a switch to decentralized wage bargaining [. . .] In the 1980s there has been a reluctant acceptance by workers in what are now often slump localities within 'old' deindustrializing regions of competitive forms of wage determination as part of the new flexibility that is the price to be paid for maintaining some capacity and employment in the 'old' industries [. . .] For example, Sheffield Forgemasters introduced new collective bargaining arrangements and altered pay and working conditions following a restructuring of the company into ten divisions, seven of which were based in Sheffield itself. The changes included decentralizing industrial relations to a divisional basis, unilaterally abolishing the centralized site-based shop stewards organization in a clear attempt to divide and rule [. . .]

New forms of work and conditions of employment in the core workforces of 'new' manufacturing firms

[. . .] If the 1960s' round of branch plants in the 'old' industrial regions of western Europe was particularly associated with US-based multinationals, that in the 1980s has become particularly identified with Japanese direct foreign investment (DFI), both in western Europe and North America. Quantitatively, the extent of this investment is fairly marginal as a proportion of DFI by Japanese companies. It is often more significant as a proportion of DFI in some[4] of the 'old' industrial regions but, of greater importance, it has been of great qualitative significance, especially in terms of its 'demonstration effect' to other companies. Via their strategies to recruit core workforces and to organize production within their new branch plants and emergent production complexes[5], these Japanese companies have begun radically to change the rules. It is not so much that they have introduced new practices (though they have) but rather that they have intensified existing ones and combined them in novel ways. Not surprisingly, given the high levels of registered unemployment in the OIRs, inward-investing Japanese companies have been able to exercise great care in selecting their new core workforces. In the north-east of England, for example, Nissan received over 10 000 applications for the first 240 jobs that it advertised. In these circumstances, it was able to compose its new core workforce extremely carefully, using extensive sophisticated psychological testing procedures to ensure that its new employees possessed appropriate attitudes towards work and commitment to the company. The lesson has not been lost upon other new non-Japanese companies, who have often emulated the example set from Japan. Hartlepool is some fifteen miles from Washington and when PMA (now a subsidiary of Coats-Patons) established a carpet-weaving plant there in the early 1980s it reportedly selected its initial core workforce of 24 from 3500 people whom it interviewed (Boulding, 1987). Such great selectivity is by no means confined to the UK. In the German Federal Republic, for example, in the late 1970s Daimler–Benz established a major car-assembly plant, around a dedicated line, at Bremen, an area badly affected by reductions in shipbuilding employment. By 1987 Daimler–Benz had expanded its workforce there to 13 000, carefully selected in terms of its age, ethnic composition and skill levels: the average age of the workforce was around 30 (much less on parts of the line); in contrast to many German assembly plants, there were very few southern European or north African migrants; and only skilled manual workers were recruited, irrespective of the tasks they would carry out in the plant. But like Nissan's assembly plant in north-east England, this does not represent a transition from Fordism to flexible production but rather represents one element in corporate strategies to preserve Fordist production. New plants are located in OIRs where prevailing high levels of unemployment allow the selective composition of young, physically fit workforces, committed to 'their' company, thereby achieving enhanced labour productivity and competitive production in classically Fordist dedicated-line branch plants.[6]

Japanese companies, especially concentrated in the electronics sector, have often been crucial in introducing not only innovative recruitment practices but also new working terms and conditions (Marsh, 1983) around what remains a basically Fordist production strategy in their foreign branch plants. No-union or one-union deals, often tied to no-strike agreements, have proliferated. In part this is because trades union leaders in the OIRs have extolled the passivity and other virtues of their members there as part of the global competitive struggle to secure new investment and jobs (for example, see Inward, 1987). In UK regions such as Scotland and Wales such one-union deals are the norm in the new Japanese electronics factories, while in the North East Nissan agreed such a deal with the Amalgamated Engineering Union. There are signs that some trades union leaders, who previously had been actively involved in the enticement of Japanese capital, are now beginning to appreciate the implications of their earlier stance, even though they now seem powerless to reverse a trend that they previously had encouraged [. . .] This ambivalence on the part of trades union leaders, partly borne of a fear that the choice now may be between a one-union and a no-union plant, is central to Japanese (and other) companies being able to get the sort of one-union deals that they want, often the key to and pre-condition for greatly increased flexibility over working conditions, grading and wages. But this is not part of a transition to new flexible production systems but a reflection of a shift in the balance of power between capital and labour which permits management to push through changes which allow the reproduction, in modified form maybe, of Fordist mass production.

New small firms and the growth of self-employment

From thc 1970s it became unambiguously clear that the combination of falling fixed capital investment and changes in technical conditions of production meant that the new jobs in branch plants would not replace those shed from OIRs. In these circumstances, often with considerable encouragement and more limited financial support from national states, the emphasis switched to regional self-reliance via the formation and growth of small firms. In the OIRs, especially where industries such as coal and steel were nationalized, special ad hoc state agencies were created specifically to encourage this. To some extent this switch to a small-firm strategy reflected the resurgence of regions such as north-east Italy and a misunderstanding of the possibilities for and limits to small-manufacturing-firm-based growth in the OIRs of north-west Europe and North America (see also Sengenberger and Loveman, 1987).

Although the aggregate numbers of jobs created have been extremely low, small-firm growth has nevertheless had important effects in these regions [. . .] In so far as new small firms have produced jobs, those employed as wage labour are often in a particularly vulnerable position in terms of their capacity to resist pressures to work harder and longer. They may be part of the core workforce of these companies but, even so, their position as core workers is a precarious one (especially given the very high failure rates amongst small firms). For those who have become owners of one of these new small companies for the first time, there is a switch from employee to employer with all that this signifies for their class position and, more generally, the increasing fragmentation of a working-class culture based upon a shared experience of life as wage labour.

The growing peripheral workforce

The division between a core and a peripheral workforce is not a new one (for example, see Friedman, 1977). In many OIRs the distinction between 'secure core' and 'insecure peripheral' employment has for long been a grey zone rather than a sharp black-and-white divide. Such areas have long been characterized by a male workforce possessing various complementary skills acquired via working in steelworks or shipyards. Although for some these provided 'jobs for life' with one employer, for others they were the key to a more or less uninterrupted series of contracts, allocated via informal contact networks in clubs, pubs or union offices. But what is distinctive about the last decade or so is the redefinition of the relationship between core and periphery and the increasing diversity of conditions on which waged employment is offered in this expanding peripheral workforce.

One aspect of this changed relationship is the growth of subcontracting that has occurred. In industries such as shipbuilding, subcontracting has long been an established part of the production process but it has increased markedly in recent years. For example, over the last decade the workforce of the Bremer Vulkan yard has been halved as subcontracting has increased significantly. Coal, chemical and steel companies now systematically subcontract services which formerly were performed within the company; the workforces of these subcontracting companies become part of their peripheral workforces. Some extent of the scale of subcontracting can be gauged from recent survey evidence from the West Midlands which revealed that 39 per cent of 370 workplaces surveyed had experienced the replacement of directly employed labour by contractors (*Financial Times*, 5 May 1987) [. . .]

[The] growing institutionalization of subcontracting as a planned part of production strategies has also had important repercussions in increasing competition between subcontracting companies (many of whom have recruited some of the workers made redundant because of the switch to subcontracting), especially in situations where increasing flexibility amongst the remaining core workers is absorbing some of the work that might otherwise have been put out to contract. As a consequence, wages and working conditions for those employed in the subcontracting companies have often deteriorated, especially where the companies are able to recruit 'off the cards' labour [. . .]

[The] changes in the role of subcontracting [are] related to other changes in the organization of production; [. . .] changes in the conditions on which subcontractors employ people is linked to other labour market changes. In particular, they point to a link between the growth of subcontracting and what is perhaps the most dramatic manifestation of the growing peripheral workforce: the resurgence of casualization. This is far from restricted to peripheral subcontracting companies, however [. . .]

One strategy of big companies in the 'old' industries is to re-hire former core workers on a casual basis in response to the ebb and flow of market demand; [the state-owned steel industry] has been prominent in securing this sort of deal from the major steel unions. In 1983 BSC closed its 44″ Hartlepool pipe mill, subsequently re-hiring some of its former workforce on a six-months contract to meet a specific order. Further contracts were also agreed but BSC refused to recognize continuity of employment across these, claiming that each new contract – although representing continuous employment – signified a break in service. The terms on which waged employment was on offer were also clearly laid down in an agreement which stressed the need for maximum flexibility in a 66-point schedule of working practices and emphasized that holiday entitlement and redundancy payment rights were to be waived, with every employee required to work any patterns of shifts or days that management specified (for fuller details, see Hudson and Sadler, 1985, pp. 30–5).

This sort of particularly stark instance of the recreation of casualized work revives memories of earlier phases of capitalist development in such places. But it is important to stress that this does *not* point to the emergence of *new* flexible production systems. On the contrary, it represents the re-imposition of old 'hire and fire' strategies as labour's position in the market has been seriously weakened so that workers must accept this sort of flexibility in exchange for temporary access to waged work [. . .]

The growth and changing roles of part-time work

In many service sector activities in the 'old' industrial regions, as elsewhere, the character and timing of the tasks to be performed have meant that it has been usual for employment to be offered on a part-time basis. This tendency has continued and indeed expanded. In the 1960s growing part-time employment in manufacturing reflected pressures to contain labour costs but also the pressures of labour shortages and the necessity to devise production strategies and shift-systems specifically to allow married women to combine waged work in factories or offices with unwaged work in the home [. . .]

The more recent growth of part-time work is related to but also cuts across the redefinition of core and peripheral employees [. . .] In some cases part-time employment has increased relatively and/or absolutely within a shrinking core workforce whilst in others increasing part-time work has been related to a growing peripheral workforce. The former tendency has been particularly marked in relation to part-time work in service activities. Again this can partly be related to specific national variations in state employment legislation: in the UK reducing paid employment to less than 17 hours a week enables workers' rights to be eroded and employers' costs reduced. Townsend (1986, p. 317) remarked that in the UK there is '. . . a distinct group of regions that have suffered an equally depressing loss of full-time jobs but one accompanied by an above-average recorded gain in part-time employment. This group are [sic] all associated with heavy job loss in steel, coal-mining and/or shipbuilding . . .' He goes on to note that these areas began from below average levels of part-time employment and this growth has been associated with expanding female employment. In other instances, however, part-time work has grown as part of the expansion of peripheral employment as manufacturing companies have used part-time employment among a growing peripheral workforce, recruited from former core workers for short periods (often 'off the cards') to meet temporary surges in demand [. . .]

7.3   From Fordism to flexible accumulation?

David Harvey and Allen Scott (1987) have recently argued – *inter alia* – that it is necessary to theorize and not merely eclectically to describe the bewildering diversity of expressions of labour market change that have emerged in the advanced capitalist economies in the last decade or so. It is difficult to dispute this. They go on to suggest that these changes are most appropriately understood in terms of a transition from a Fordist to a flexible regime of accumulation: that is, a change in the characteristic form of social organization from standardized production and mass consumption patterns, orchestrated via extensive state involvement in economic and social life, to a new more diverse pattern associated with '. . . the new regime . . . distinguished by a remarkable fluidity of production arrangements, labour markets, financial organization and consumption' (pp. 2–3).

As a broad macroscopic statement of contrast between the 1960s and 1980s, there is some validity in this position. Even so, it tends to use the concept of regime of accumulation at a rather more general level than does the French regulation school.[7] Lipietz (1986, p. 26), for example identifies 'two historically and theoretically linked but relatively distinct phenomena' that combine together to define 'Fordism' (or any other) regime of accumulation. These are 'Fordism as a mode of (intensive) capital accumulation' and 'Fordism as a mode of regulation of continued adaptation of mass consumption to productivity gains . . .' As he puts it, 'all this supposed a modification of the role of the state and of the forms of money management, including the substitution of credit money for gold-based currency'. Now the significance of this is that capitalist states are constituted on a territorial, usually national, basis and to a degree are in competition with one another for their territories to be centres of accumulation. Whilst there are structural limits to a particular mode of capital accumulation, national states also possess some room for manoeuvre in choosing combinations of policies to try and sustain a particular regime of accumulation. This room for manoeuvre and the resultant national variations around the central themes of a given regime of accumulation must be acknowledged.

This is not all that must be acknowledged, however. For even at national level amongst the advanced capitalist states, pursuit of a Fordist regime of accumulation was not a unanimously accepted goal within the decisive centres of state power; nor was a Fordist regime of accumulation established equally at national level in all the major capitalist states. For example, '. . . Britain, because of the resistant strength of its working class and the weight of its finance capital, which is too internationalized to be given over to this internal revolution [of intensive accumulation], has partially missed the boat of Fordism . . .' (Lipietz, 1986, p. 30).[8] Within the advanced capitalist world even at national level, then, characterizing regimes of accumulation in the post-1945 period of 'a long wave with an undertone of expansion' as unambiguously 'Fordist' is problematic. Uneven development at national level must be recognized and if this conclusion holds at national level then it will hold *a fortiori* between regions *within* these national territories. Acceptance of these conclusions raises general questions about conceptualizing change in terms of *national* regimes of accumulation, but more importantly for the present argument raises considerable doubt as to whether a transition from 'Fordism' to 'flexible accumulation' provides a suitable framework for understanding the changing conditions of labour markets, production and consumption in the 'old' industrial regions. On the one hand, as much of the evidence presented in the previous section suggests, it is by no means obvious that the starting-point for these changes is one that can be characterized as 'Fordist'. On the other hand, it is not at all obvious that all the various forms of labour market and labour process changes are in the direction of greater flexibility [. . .] and in other cases it is clear that 'flexibility' amounts to capital reasserting its power over labour via managerial strategies to reorganize production so as to preserve pre-Fordist and Fordist systems of production. It is certainly not the case that these changes are associated with emergent 'flexible' systems of production, as, for example, Storper and Scott (1988) define them (see below). This raises questions as to the circumstances in which the concept of 'flexible mode of accumulation' is a useful one. Its use may, for example, conflate and confuse different tendencies in capitalist restructuring strategies.

These various points raise some important issues. While one must acknowledge the dangers of an over-obsession with description of the myriad changes one must be equally wary of an oversimplified theoretical interpretation of them. Thus the contrast between Fordism and flexible accumulation may in *some* circumstances be an illuminating one, provided that:

1 It is acknowledged that flexible accumulation requires much tighter

specification of, for example, the strategies that capitals have used to reorganize production on post-Fordist lines (often drawing on pre-Fordist forms of organizing production and the labour process, that is, there is no general, simple and uni-directional historical sequence of modes of capital accumulation) and of the branches in which post-Fordist strategies have been constructed. Storper and Scott (1988), for example, define 'flexible production systems' as 'forms of production characterized by a well-developed ability to shift promptly from one process and/or product configuration to another and to adjust . . . output rapidly up or down without any strongly deleterious effects on levels of efficiency', with the latter presumably defined in terms of the interests of capital rather than labour. They refer to '. . . ensembles of flexible production sectors such as (a) selected high technology industries, (b) revitalized craft speciality industries and (c) producer financial services' (p. 2). Leaving aside for the moment the heterogeneous character of these often loosely specified sectors, the crucial point is that they are notably absent from the OIRs (and it remains a matter for debate as to how generalizable such 'flexible' approaches are over many sectors of commodity production).

2   It is acknowledged that Fordism as a mode of accumulation did not penetrate evenly and equally to all branches of the economy and localities; put another way, even within what from some points of view may be legitimately characterized at national level as a Fordist regime of accumulation, quite a lot of labour processes, even in manufacturing, remained and remain *of necessity* organized on a non-Fordist basis of extensive rather than intensive accumulation. Moreover, this was especially so in relation to some of the 'old' industries of the OIRs. Certainly over a broad swathe of basic chemicals, and to a lesser degree bulk iron and steel, production, there was increasing automation but hardly one that would be regarded as typical of assembly-line Fordist production.[9] Indeed, in some senses this was post-Fordism at the very peak of the success of the Fordist regime. In many other branches of manufacturing, such as special steels production, shipbuilding (despite attempts at standardized designs and products) and heavy engineering, the penetration of Fordist methods was of necessity much more limited and in many cases negligible because of the sorts of commodities they produced and/or technical conditions of production in them. This was *a fortiori* true of the coal-mining industry and the sorts of changes that are *currently* occurring in the UK in terms of attempts at automating deep-mined production or switching to more-or-less automated open-cast production [. . .] represent a continuing project to impose a quasi-Fordist organization of production in the 1980s. Thus there may well be a sense in which Fordism did have an impact on labour processes and the organization of production in industries in which it could not itself be established, but this is very different to the Fordization of all branches of production. Indeed, the really significant questions that arise from this concern the relations between production in branches organized on non-Fordist and Fordist

lines and between them and the overall process of accumulation.

3   It is acknowledged that the impacts of a Fordist mode of regulation were unevenly distributed, between localities and regions as well as classes, ethnic and gender groups, in terms of variations in lifestyles and living conditions. The precise form of these uneven distributional patterns reflected political priorities and the differing degrees of organization, power and influence of different social groups and classes. In particular, the transformation to mass consumption lifestyles in the OIRs was a very partial and uneven one. Certainly state transfer payments as part of a national welfare state system provided a floor to consumption levels for many who were unable to sell their labour-power on the market. Undoubtedly, simple, standardized, mass-produced commodities, such as packets of cornflakes or blue jeans, became widely available in retailing establishing in these OIRs. But penetration of more sophisticated consumer goods such as cars, consumer durables, 'white goods' etc., often associated with growing home-ownership and privatized lifestyles, remained both restricted in scope and uneven in *intra*regional distribution. Not least, this reflected the absence of a high-productivity, high-wage economy to provide effective mass demand for such commodities.

In summary, then, the transformation of economic and social life in the OIRs during the 1960s was at best a pale shadow of what Fordism was meant to be about, and in some regions the shadow was very pale indeed. Indeed, this *failure* to establish patterns of production and consumption characteristic of a Fordist regime of accumulation reflects the failure of national state projects reciprocally to link regional modernization with faster national growth (for further details, see Hudson, 1988a). This failure of national states to implement these policies successfully had implications at both national and regional levels – at the risk of oversimplification and, maybe, overdramatization, it ensured a crisis in, though certainly not the demise of, Fordist systems of production and the Fordist regime of accumulation. At the same time, it established some of the preconditions for the OIRs to become locations in which capitals could seek a solution to this crisis, in Fordist terms, in the late 1970s and 1980s. This raises important questions about the capacity of national states to manage the trajectory of economic and social change in their territories which is central to a regulation approach but which cannot be explored further here. A couple of simple points can be made in this connection, however.

This failure of state policies to generalize the conditions of a Fordist regime evenly over national territories reflected both the past trajectory of uneven capitalist development within these states and the growing internationalization of capitalist production at the time (the 1960s). Capitalist development in these national states had, at the risk of some overgeneralization, previously occurred in two distinctive phases, centred on two distinctive ensembles of industries, two distinctive sets of regions and two distinctive though interrelated modes of accumulation.[10] The first phase centred on extensive accumulation around 'old' industries in 'old' industrial regions, the second around intensive accumulation around a different set of 'new' industries and 'new' regions. During the tight labour market conditions of the post-1945 'long wave with an undertone of expansion', there was some de-concentration of branch plants from the second set of regions to the first as well as into formerly industrialized rural areas as big capitals re-organized production into new intranational spatial divisions of labour (see Hudson, 1987). Precisely which regions became recipients of the new branch plants depended upon cultural economic and political variations between them, as well as the political strategies of national states. These new branch plants often brought Fordist production methods to these regions for the first time. Though the extent of this innovation was limited, its longer-term significance in terms of politics and culture was considerable there. But in the short term the employment provided in the new branch plants was usually much less than that lost from the old industries and, moreover, capitals establishing these branch plants were often enticed by the availability of cheap, pliant and 'green' labour power [. . .] These sorts of labour market change emphatically did not provide the basis for a high-wage, high-productivity regional economy that could sustain a generalized transformation in lifestyles around the consumption norms of a Fordist mode of regulation. Furthermore, many of these new branch-plant jobs quickly disappeared from the OIRs as capitals were able to reorganize production in an increasing range of industries on an international scale, relocating production to more profitable locations both in the newly industrializing countries and, often more important, elsewhere in the advanced capitalist countries. In these circumstances of increasingly internationalized production, national states were less and less able to manage the location of economic activities within their national territories, further undermining their attempts to generalize the conditions of a Fordist regime of accumulation evenly over these territories. Even so, the failures of state policies in the 1960s and early 1970s to integrate these OIRs into the mainstream of Fordist production and consumption had important effects in the late 1970s and 1980s. Renewed high levels of unemployment in these regions posed persistent political and social problems. As national states drew back from interventionist policies (because of a desire to cut public expenditure as part of the fight against inflation) and put more reliance upon the market as a steering mechanism for resource allocation, the OIRs were not favoured locations for the flowering of a new enterprise culture. As Sengenberger and Loveman suggest:

> Social class structure associated with property relations, income sources and social divisions may provide why it has proven so difficult to revitalize the old, entrenched industrial regions in Europe . . . all of these regions have in common a century or more of extensive industrial production based on industries like coal or ore mining, iron and steel, or shipbuilding that produced a highly dependent working class.
> When the industrial base began to shrink and employment declined new

employment was not brought in at a rate to compensate for the dislocation. The old class of big industrialists did not do enough to reinvest, transform and modernize the economic base of these regions, *and the working-class people were too far divorced from entrepreneurship to do it themselves.* (1987, p. 101; emphasis added)

Because of a past history of extensive proletarianization, the basis for an economic and social transformation around the expansion of an 'old' or the emergence of a 'new' middle class was strictly limited; indeed, at best there have been very modest increases in self-employment and those often at the margins of the black economy. In these circumstances it seemed to some people in these regions that the only way to find waged employment was to leave and to many others that the only way to retain some waged employment was to do one or both of two things. Firstly, to agree to new more flexible forms of work in existing industries although, in fact, these 'new' forms often involved a reversion to older ones as the gains that trades unions had made in earlier periods over working conditions were eroded in the new political-economic climate. Secondly, for trades unions to accept new flexible conditions of employment as a condition for attracting inward investment in the form of branch plants. Indeed, for them to go beyond this and actively to collaborate in the competition for such investment as companies sought a solution to their problems *within* the frame of reference of Fordist production by selectively relocating into areas where the bargain between capital and labour could be redefined more in favour of the former.

In summary, then, there is no doubt that there is a great diversity in the form of labour market changes occurring in the 'old' industrial regions. Do these changes in working conditions and employment practices constitute a transition to a new post-Fordist flexible regime of accumulation, to new post-Fordist flexible production systems, in the OIRs, however? Is this the most appropriate interpretation to put upon them? Although it is perhaps dangerous to draw definitive conclusions, as these processes of change are still being worked through, the answer to these questions at this stage must be 'no'. There are certainly changes in management's capacity selectively to recruit, to compose particular types of workforce, to redefine relations between core and peripheral workers via increased use of subcontracting and to impose new forms of employment contract and conditions of work at the point of production. Undoubtedly, the climate created by the New Right political economy, reasserting the market as the pre-eminent economic steering mechanism, and weakening organized labour via a variety of legislative changes, but above all by creating massive unemployment, has been crucial in providing an arena in which such changes could be pushed through. As a result of this and parallel cuts in levels of welfare provision, the capacity of many people in the OIRs to participate in the mass consumption lifestyle of a Fordist regime is further weakened, let alone to participate in the new post-Fordist lifestyle centred around the consumption of individualized, designer commodities. Even the capacity to purchase simple, mass-produced commodities in many of these regions has been weakened. Widespread poverty has re-emerged as national governments have, to varying degrees, redefined the relation between the state and market as an allocative mechanism. In this sense, the OIRs are even further from the consumption norms of a Fordist regime of accumulation – let alone a post-Fordist one – than they were two decades ago.

Rather than constituting the emergence of a new flexible regime of accumulation in these regions, then, these related changes in production and consumption are most appropriately interpreted as part of strategies by capital to preserve old modes of accumulation in a political climate very different from the welfare state Keynesianism of the 1960s, in two senses. Firstly, they involve changes in the 'traditional', pre-Fordist industries of these regions, characterized by a mode of extensive accumulation, seeking to increase labour productivity and competitiveness within big plants and production complexes by cutting employment and redefining conditions of employment for those remaining in work in them. Secondly, they involve corporate strategies to preserve Fordist mass production of standardized commodities by carefully locating new capacity in OIRs and raising labour productivity via selective recruitment and intensification of the pace of work. This is most clearly exemplified in the archtypically Fordist car industry and in the location of plants such as Daimler–Benz in Bremen and Nissan in Sunderland. The scope that locating in such regions of high unemployment offers to managers selectively to recruit and dictate the terms on which a wage is offered helps reinforce Fordist production rather than facilitate its replacement by post-Fordist flexible production systems. In both cases then – the old 'traditional' industries and the Fordist branch plants of the 'new' ones – the common linking theme is the reassertion of managerial control over labour and the labour process. Changed labour market conditions and a back-drop of very high unemployment in these OIRs allow the relationship between capital and labour to be redefined, allow management to recover, or for the first time to impose, authority and control over labour in a *variety* of ways, depending upon particular technical conditions of production in an industry and the specificities of local labour markets (in terms of culture and politics, as well as the skill composition of the workforce and so on). But this does not constitute the emergence of a new flexible regime of accumulation in the OIRs but rather a partial reworking of old production strategies [. . .]

Certainly there is *some* evidence of the emergence of 'flexible production systems' in particular activities and locations. But the evidence of changing conditions, terms and levels of employment as the bargaining strengths of management and workers have altered in the OIRs means that the different strategies for responding to crisis in other activities are being worked through there. Recognition of this offers one way of meeting another important criticism that emerges in Harvey and Scott's paper.

This concerns the significance of locality in theorizing uneven development within capitalism. In a very literal sense, the OIRs were constructed, materially and socially, as an integral part of the initial birth and subsequent growth of capitalism as a global system of commodity production and exchange. Crucial commodities were produced and traded in and through these regions and economic and social life within them developed a sort of coherence, rooted in place, within the limits imposed by the anarchy inherent in capitalism. Harvey and Scott (1987, p. 8) rightly point to the danger of 'a fixation on the specificity of the local as opposed to a continuing concern for elucidating the generality of capitalism in its totality'. Considering the historical evolution of working, learning and living in the OIRs *without* relating this to the generality of capitalism is possible, but it is rather difficult. One cannot understand what has happened in these regions over a long period without relating this to the way the contradictions of capitalism have developed on a wider scale. Conversely, the development of the 'generality' of capitalism cannot be understood without reference to the initial emergence of capitalist production in these now 'old' industrial regions and the subsequent changes within them. So while I would concur with Harvey and Scott's insistence on the need to relate the specificity of locality to the generality of capitalism, it seems to me necessary to acknowledge and not forget these specificities. It is in this context that a recognition that in the post-war period [. . .] Fordism was *not* established as the dominant regime of accumulation [. . .] in the 'old' industrial regions becomes crucial in terms of grasping the theoretical significance of the sorts of changes in the organization of production and in labour markets that have been occurring over the last decade or so in what have increasingly become peripheral, though by no means insignificant, rather than core regions of capitalist production globally. Not least, these have in part involved projects to preserve Fordist production in sectors such as vehicles and consumer electronics and retain or restore the competitive viability on world markets of production in sectors which *cannot* be organized on Fordist (or post-Fordist) lines. The mosaic of interrelated localities, production systems and industries has taken a still more complex turn and unravelling this presents a major theoretical and empirical challenge [. . .]

Notes

1 This is, of course, a considerable simplification of the productive structure of many of these regions where, for example, textiles production formed a very important part of the industrial structure and led to a much greater incorporation of women into the waged labour force. Indeed, it was textiles production that often formed the birth place of industrial capitalism in such regions. Even so, there are advantages to be gained from focusing upon Department I rather than Department II production in these regions in terms of the argument I want to develop below.

2   It is important to emphasize that evidence of many aspects of changes in labour markets and labour processes is unavailable through official public statistics. It must, of necessity, be collected through interviews and discussions with those involved and/or observation of, say, the organization of work in a coal-mine, steelworks or car plant (which can mean an involvement with a particular plant over a period of time). In this sense, the sorts of data that are drawn on here make no claims as to being statistically representative and there are often problems in deciding how much importance should be attached to particular tendencies. On the other hand, the tendencies identified here are representative of the sorts of processes via which labour markets and labour processes in the OIRs have been and are being altered.

3   In practice, many of the changes discussed below occur in combination but are analytically separated here for clarity and convenience. Likewise, the distinction between 'new' and 'old' industries is to a degree arbitrary but it allows some important points to be drawn out.

4   For instance, cumulative Japanese investment in the Mid West of the USA now exceeds $5.0 billion (personal communication, Martin Kenney, 1987).

5   For example, Honda is constructing engine and transmission plants at its Ohio plant in the USA.

6   It would seem, however, that there may be important national variations in this respect. Kenney (personal communication, 1987), for example, suggests that companies in the USA do not display this degree of selectivity in recruitment.

7   The 'French regulation school' refers to a group of authors, including Aglietta (1979; 1982) and Lipietz (1979; 1984; 1986) much of whose work is summarized and reviewed by de Vroey (1984). De Vroey (p. 45) points out that while 'these authors draw on a similar set of concepts, like "regimes of accumulation" or "forms of regulation" . . . it would be incorrect to regard them as one homogeneous school of thought . . .' It is not my purpose here directly to provide a detailed critique or review of the strengths and weaknesses of a 'regulation' approach per se but rather to examine the extent to which changes in the OIRs may be understood in terms of a transition from Fordism to a flexible regime of accumulation and, in particular, to flexible systems of production. This does raise some questions about a 'regulation' approach, however.

8   In so far as Lipietz is correct in this judgement about the UK – and there are others who make the same point in a different way (for example, Nairn, 1977, Ingham, 1982, Rowthorn, 1983) – it raises doubts as to the validity of attempts to interpret the political economy of the UK in the post-1945 period in terms of a transition to an intensive regime of accumulation (for example, see Dunford and Perrons, 1986).

9   I would take issue here with Storper and Scott (1988, p. 6) when they claim that, 'In its classical guise, Fordism was underpinned by large and highly capitalized units of production consisting of either (a) continuous flow processes, as in the case of petrochemicals or steel production, or (b) assembly line processes (and deep technical divisions of labour), as in the cases of cars, electrical appliance or machinery.' Assuming that by 'steel' they mean bulk steel production (because a wide range of special steels have always been produced on a small-batch basis), this seemingly reduces *all* mass production to Fordism and in the process loses the specific features of the labour process and managerial control over labour at the immediate point of production that characterizes Fordism. The differences in labour process between what they refer to as 'continuous flow processes' and 'assembly-line processes' are too significant to be summarily swept away in this manner.

10   It is important to stress that in both these main phases forms of economic

organization and labour processes with their origins in earlier periods lived on; and of necessity pre-Fordist forms continued to co-exist with Fordist forms of production throughout the golden age of Fordism in the post-war period (as Storper and Scott, 1988, pp. 5–6, correctly stress).

References

AGLIETTA, M. (1979) *A Theory of Capitalist Regulation: The US Experience*, London, New Left Books.

AGLIETTA, M. (1982) 'World capitalism in the eighties', *New Left Review*, No. 136, pp. 25–36.

ASHTON, D. N. and MAGUIRE, M. J. (1987) 'Young adults in the labour market', *Research Paper No. 55*, Department of Employment, Leicester, University of Leicester.

BEYNON, D., HUDSON, R. and SADLER, D. (1986) 'The growth and Internationalization of Teesside's chemicals industry', *Middlesbrough Locality Study: Working Paper No. 3*, Durham, Department of Geography and Sociology, University of Durham.

BEYNON, D., HUDSON, R. and SADLER, D. (1987) *Planning to Close: Nationalization and the Destruction of Jobs in the North*, Milton Keynes, Open University Press (forthcoming).

BOULDING, P. (1987) *Reindustrialization Strategies in Steel Closure Areas: A Comparison of Corby, Ebbw Vale and Hartlepool*, unpublished PhD thesis, University of Durham.

DE VROEY, M. (1984) 'A regulation approach interpretation of contemporary crisis', *Capital and Crisis*, No. 23, pp. 45–66.

DUNFORD, M.F. and PERRONS, D. (1986) 'The restructuring of the post-war British space economy', in Martin, R. and Rowthorn, B. (eds) pp. 53–105.

FRIEDMAN, A. (1977) *Industry and Labour*, London and Basingstoke, Macmillan.

FROBEL, F., HEINRICHS, J. and KREYE, O. (1980) *The New International Division of Labour*, Cambridge, Cambridge University Press.

HARVEY, D. and SCOTT, A. J. (1987) 'The nature of human geography: theory and empirical specificity', paper presented to the Quantitative Methods Study Group of the Institute of British Geographers, 10 April.

HUDSON, R. (1983) 'Capital accumulation and chemicals production in Western Europe in the post-war period', *Environment and Planning A*, Vol. 15, pp. 105–22.

HUDSON, R. (1986) 'Producing an industrial wasteland: capital, labour and the state in north-east England', in Martin, R. and Rowthorn, B. (eds) pp. 169–213.

HUDSON, R. (1987) 'Changing spatial divisions of labour in manufacturing and their impacts on localities', paper presented to the Eighth Conference of Nordic Radical Geographers, Elmsta, 24–7 September.

HUDSON, R. (1988a) 'Producing a divided society: state policies and the management of change in housing and labour markets in a peripheral region', forthcoming in Allen, J. and Hamnett, C. (eds) *Housing and Labour Market: Building the Connections*, London, Hutchinson.

HUDSON, R. (1988b) *State Policies, Party Politics and Regional Change: A Study of North East England*, London, Pion (forthcoming).

HUDSON, R. and SADLER, D. (1985) 'The development of Middlesbrough's iron and steel industry, 1841–1985', *Middlesbrough Locality Study: Working*

Paper No. 2, Durham, Department of Geography and Sociology, University of Durham.

HUDSON, R. and SADLER, D. (1986) 'Contesting works closures in Western Europe's industrial regions: defending place or betraying class?' in Scott, A. J. and Storper, M. (eds) pp. 172–94.

INGHAM, G. (1982) 'Divisions within the dominant class and British "exceptionalism" ', in Giddens, A. and Mackenzie, G. (eds) *Social Class and the Division of Labour*, Cambridge, Cambridge University Press, pp. 209–27.

INWARD (1987) *Labour Performance and Productivity in North West England*, Duxbury Park, Chorley, Lancashire.

LAPPLE, D. and VAN HOOGSTRATEN, P. (1980) 'Remarks on the spatial structure of capitalist development: the case of the Netherlands', pp. 117–66 in Carney, J., Hudson, R. and Lewis, J. (eds) *Regions in Crisis*, London, Croom Helm.

LIPIETZ, A. (1979) *Crise et inflation, pourquoi?*, Paris, Maspero.

LIPIETZ, A. (1984) 'Imperialism or the beast of the apocalypse', *Capital and Class*, No. 22, pp. 81–109.

LIPIETZ, A. (1986) 'New tendencies in the international division of labour regimes of accumulation and modes of regulation', in Scott, A. J. and Storper, M. (eds) pp. 16–40.

MANDEL, E. (1975) *Late Capitalism*, London, New Left Books.

MARSH, F. (1983) *Japanese Overseas Investment: The New Challenge*, Special Report No. 142, London, Economist Intelligence Unit.

MARTIN, R. and ROWTHORN, B. (eds) (1986) *The Geography of De-Industrialisation*, London and Basingstoke, Macmillan.

NAIRN, T. (1977) *The Break-up of Britain*, London, New Left Books.

OSTERLAND, M. (1987) 'Declining industries, plant closing and local markets: a case study of the city of Bremen', unpublished manuscript, University of Bremen.

ROWTHORN, R. E. (1983) 'The past strikes back', in Hall, S. and Jacques, M. (eds) *The Politics of Thatcherism*, London, Lawrence and Wishart, pp. 63–78.

SCOTT, A. J. and STORPER, M. (eds) (1986) *Production, Work, Territory*, London, George Allen and Unwin.

SENGENBERGER, W. and LOVEMAN, G. (1987) *Smaller units of employment*, New Industrial Organization Programme, DP/3/1987, International Institute for Labour Studies, Geneva, International Labour Organization.

STORPER, M. and SCOTT, A. J. (1988) 'The geographical foundations and social regulation of flexible production systems', in Wolch, J. and Dear, M. (eds) *Territory and Social Reproduction*, London, George Allen and Unwin.

TOWNSEND, A. R. (1986) 'Spatial aspects of the growth of part-time employment in Britain', *Regional Studies*, Vol. 20, No. 4, pp. 313–30.

WINTERTON, J. (1985) 'Computerized coal: new technology in the mines', in Beynon, H. (ed.), *Digging Deeper*, London, Verso, pp. 231–44.

8 A 'modern' industry in a 'mature' region: the remaking of management–labour relations

Kevin Morgan and Andrew Sayer

In the history of capitalism new industries have been innovative not only in their technology but in their *social* organization, particularly their management–labour relations. Perhaps the most famous example is that of Henry Ford's Model T plant with its combination of assembly lines and new forms of motivation, surveillance and disciplining of the workforce. Leading multinational firms are usually the key 'bearers' of these new organizational forms, carrying them into the new areas and attempting to substitute them for traditional management–labour relations. In doing so, such firms face many risks and obstacles and these vary considerably between areas according to their social composition and prior economic history. While such firms have the advantage of being able to locate operations with different requirements in different areas, the establishment of new plants always requires *mutual* adjustment between company norms and established local practices. Workers of particular qualities are not just born waiting to be hired; they have to be *made*, both in the workplace and the community. In this chapter we shall deal only with the workplace [. . .]

In this paper we analyse how management–labour relations are being remade in a modern industry – electrical engineering – operating in a mature and reputedly radical industrial region – south Wales (Cooke, 1983). 'South Wales' is virtually synonymous with strong labourist culture and yet despite still being physically and socially moulded by its traditional industries of coal and steel the region has attracted a significant number of new electronics firms.

These firms have not merely adopted the traditional work practices of the region but are establishing – albeit often with difficulty – markedly different ones, the most conspicuous aspects of which have been single-union status for plants and no-strike agreements. In short, some of the most dramatic changes in management–labour relations are being pioneered in what many regard as Britain's most radical and traditional working-class region.

This raises a number of questions: How do technically and socially innovative firms operate in such a context? What are the problems and opportunities for capital of working in such a region? Is it a 'radical region'? In what ways has labour gained or lost and how has it responded, particularly through trade unions? And how has the working class been restructured? In this chapter we shall attempt to answer these questions on the basis of a recently completed research project (funded by the ESRC) on the electrical engineering industry in south Wales.

The chapter is in three parts. The first provides orientation by briefly outlining some theoretical points, clarifying the scope and limitations of our research and the significance of the issues. The second and major section discusses management–labour relations, comparing the practices of the newest firms with those of the older-established electrical engineering firms and the still older coal and steel industries. Finally, in the third section we attempt to relate these local events to wider processes and to assess their significance. We conclude with some comments on the theoretical implications of our work for recent and prospective research in this field.

8.1   Preliminary theoretical points

In presenting this analysis we hope to offset certain problems in socialist research. The most important of these is the neglect of management, either by treating it as uniform across space and time and wholly determined by the logic of capital or as adequately summarized by concepts such as 'Taylorism' and 'Fordism'. Management practice is neither uniform nor simple and its variations actually matter to workers by making important differences to their experience of work [. . .]

We also hope to counter some distortions which still linger on from Braverman's seminal work on the labour process (Braverman, 1974). First, deskilling and job fragmentation are not the only or always the most effective means towards the goal of accumulation. Second, management–labour relations cannot be understood purely in terms of conflict and coercion [. . .] The social relations of production involve both conflict and co-operation. On its own, coercion is an inefficient method of control: we need to understand how managers manage largely by *consent* and it is only by considering the means by which this is achieved that we can understand why workers rebel so little (Littler and Salaman, 1984). Thirdly and perhaps most fundamentally, management is not just about management of labour; even where it is, its relations with labour are also influenced by external changes in markets and products and technology (Kelly, 1982; Tomlinson, 1982). Moreover technology is not plastic in the hands of management but presents the latter with problems of application and control. The upshot of these last two points is that while controlling labour is the most important means to the end of profit it is not an end in itself; at times capitals may even introduce changes to labour processes which (inadvertently) *lessen* their control, if it is necessary for replacing an obsolete product by a new one whose prospects for realizing profits are better. So while this paper focuses on those aspects of management practice which do bear upon labour it is important to remember that management–labour relations are also affected by external influences on both sides.

The remaking of management–labour relations is accentuated where the new investors are firms in the most modern, technologically advanced sectors and where they invest during a recession. Radically different technologies are likely to fit awkwardly with established management–labour relations. However, a given set of new work practices does not follow uniquely and automatically from a new technology but must be sought out through an extended period of experimentation. In our study we found that contrary to the 'branch–plant stereotype', none of the newer entrants to the region were simply 'overspill' factories, merely adding additional capacity of a standardized character producing a standardized product (Sayer and Morgan, 1984). The newness of their production meant that establishing new types of organization was both possible, necessary, and yet risky.[1]

When this situation occurs in a recession, we have what might be called 'hot-house conditions' for the cultivation of new management–labour practices. Intensified competition forces firms to change and unemployment weakens the power of labour to resist. While new management practices and 'philosophies' do not spring up automatically in a recession, their adoption is boosted by it; previously the new management philosophy was the preserve of a few *avant-garde* management consultants, now it promises to become the new conventional wisdom of management in large firms (Littler and Salaman, 1984).

In what follows it is crucial to keep in mind that the developments in management–labour practices in south Wales (between 1974 and 1984) have occurred in a conjuncture dominated by the following four features: 1) recession; 2) a major influx of foreign, advanced capital; 3) accelerated technological change; and 4) a new management 'philosophy'.

As a final preliminary we must acknowledge the limitations of our own research. It was not a specialist study focusing purely on management and labour but a wider one looking at the nature and performance of the electrical engineering industry in south Wales. This had both disadvantages and advantages: disadvantages because we did not study individual plants in as much depth as specialist studies normally do (for example, Cavendish, 1982; Dore, 1973; Pollert, 1981; Wickham and Murray, 1983); advantages because our broader scope enabled us to set intraplant processes within the context of their external economic determinants, both in the industry generally and in the economy at large – a context largely ignored in specialist labour–management studies.

The research involved interviews with managers in 23 firms representing 79 per cent of employment in electrical engineering in south Wales, plus interviews with union officials and a few convenors. The number of firms covered and the time available meant that regrettably we could obtain little information direct from other workers. However, what information we have gained from the latter has confirmed our impressions.

We obviously acknowledge that our work is historically and spatially specific: no concrete research on management–labour relations could be otherwise. The results cannot therefore be taken in any simple sense as 'representative' of conditions in some larger entity such as 'British manufacturing'. However, while we do not expect other sectors and areas to be the same, we would be surprised if they were *entirely* different, for the changes that have occurred in south Wales in recent years have not only been against a similar economic background to those of other British regions but have actually been *linked* with changes occurring elsewhere, particularly insofar as most of the plants surveyed are part of multinational firms. In fact, as we note in section 8.3, similar processes have been registered elsewhere.

8.2   Management and labour in the electrical engineering industry in south Wales

1   The regional legacy

Past forms of industrialization can exert profound effects on a region long after the demise of its formerly dominant sectors and this structural legacy may constrain or facilitate the emergence of new, more advanced sectors. The significant characteristics of labour culture from capital's point of view go far beyond wage norms to received attitudes to work, types and extent of unionization, gender composition and racial mix, and these and many other relevant features vary enormously between different regions (cf. Massey, 1983). Such comparisons are not entirely academic, for the leading multinational firms are obliged to make them in their location decisions.

Some measure of the former dominance of the coal and steel industries lies in the fact that, together, they employed 76 per cent of the insured working population of south Wales at the time of the 1930 Census of Production. Few parallels exist, outside peripheral countries, for such an inordinate commitment of capital and labour to a narrow sectoral base of this kind, and it was not until after 1945 that the regional labour force showed signs of becoming sectorally – though not occupationally – diversified. The main features of this legacy are:

(a)   The class structure of the region was overwhelmingly proletarian and, while this stark social profile has attenuated since the 1930s, south Wales remains the nearest approximation to a single (working-) class region in Britain.

(b)   With few exceptions, external control of the region's coal and steel industries was already an established phenomenon by the later interwar years, and the consequent absence of an indigenous 'business class' helps to explain the dearth of alternative industries prior to the Second World War and the limited potential for indigenously-based regional development thereafter.

(c)   The nature of the work in the coal and steel industries allowed workers a considerable degree of automony over their day-to-day work tasks and the absence of a labour market culture tutored in 'working to the hooter' – an official euphemism for the discipline associated with factory regimes like Ford's – continued to be remarked upon even in the 1960s.

(d)   The formerly dominant industries fashioned a profoundly dichotomized gender division of labour in which women were largely excluded from wage–labour relations. The legacy of this extreme gender division is still apparent: despite the waged labour opportunities that emerged after 1945, principally in the service sector but also in 'light' industries such as electrical engineering, Welsh female activity rates remain the lowest in Britain. Significantly, with the post-war contraction of the coal and steel industries (particularly in the 1960s and late 1970s, early 1980s respectively) the gender recomposition of the employed Welsh working class has been one of the most conspicuous features of the last two decades (Williams, 1984).

(e)   The highly unionized character of the coal and steel industries lies at the root of the region's traditional labourist culture, manifested in the fact that *both service and manufacturing sectors exhibit relatively high unionized profiles* and evidenced too by the fact that south Wales remains one of the major and most consistent bases of the Labour party: so much so that it has acquired the reputation of being a 'radical region'. (Further elaboration of these points can be found in Cooke (1983).)

The implications of these preliminary remarks are clear enough. Although capital which is new to the area will attempt to reconstitute a traditional labour force to suit its own specifications, the regional legacy may imprint itself on new employers. Yet, where this regional legacy is considered too 'burdensome', alternative vistas might be to tap new sources of labour within *existing* locales (such as females) or else to seek out *new* locales within the same regions or elsewhere, where the social practices of labour are more permissive. As we shall see, both of these have occurred in the case of south Wales.

2   The electrical engineering industry in south Wales: an overview

Of the modern industries that have developed in the region in the post-war period, electrical engineering provides perhaps the most interesting example from the point of view of degree of contrast between 'traditional' and 'modern'. We have dealt with the industry's characteristics in south Wales in detail elsewhere (Sayer and Morgan, 1984), but the following salient features are worthy of summary:

(a)   The Welsh plants range from early post-war electrical engineering factories (such as Smiths, Thorn Lighting, GEC telecommunications, mostly British but including a few foreign firms like Hoover) through to the predominantly foreign manufacturers of the most advanced electronic products, such as Matshushita, Mitel and Siliconix. With only one major exception all of the firms originated outside Wales. Also notable is the fact that five of south Wales's complement of seven Japanese firms (unparalleled in Europe) are in this sector; indeed, the industry is almost entirely externally controlled.

The contrasts in both technology and social organization between the newest arrivals and the older, predominantly electrical plants are enormous. In the survivors among among the latter, process and product innovations are belatedly being made and there are signs that they are beginning to imitate the new organizational practices of the inward investors, albeit partially and with difficulty. Most of the foreign electronics firms have arrived since 1974, i.e. during the recession, and indeed leading firms have been partly responsible for exposing the weakness of the British electronics industry. In other words, although the new entrants may have roughly compensated for job losses in the older firms – in south Wales, if not in Britain as a whole – they also indirectly helped to bring them about through outcompeting indigenous firms (Sayer and Morgan, 1984). It is with this latter, recessive period, particularly since 1979, that this chapter is principally concerned.

(b)   The electronics sector has been the most resistant manufacturing sector to recession and has consistently achieved an above average growth of output. Although aggregate employment in electrical engineering in south Wales has grown marginally between 1971 and 1981 it must be acknowledged that it will never approach the peak employment levels – and therefore the social significance – attained by the coal or steel industries. Prior to the deepening of the recession in 1979, employment in the sector stood at 30 000, equivalent to some 6 per cent of total manufacturing employment in Wales.

(c)   The gender composition of the electrical engineering workforce in south Wales presents a striking contrast with that of the traditional sectors: women from 45 per cent of employees in the former but only 5.6 per cent in mining and metal manufacture (1981 ER II data). Women have been expelled from the older firms by new technology and intensification, but this has been compensated by new firms employing women as operatives.

Apart from electrical jobs, women are 'targeted' for the operator grade. The reasons are well-known: significantly higher productivity than men, even allowing for the disadvantage of women's much higher rate of absenteeism; lower wages; and less involvement in union activity. All of these characteristics are of course socially produced and as such are subject to contestation and change [. . .]

It must also be said that the 'female stereotype' is more powerful where it is ratified by female workers themselves, rather than where it is imposed only by managers and unions. For instance, even allowing for possible informal slanting of job vacancy advertising we found a considerable degree of segregation at the application stage, which suggests that individuals *self-select* according to prevailing concepts of gender when applying for jobs. In such cases, the community actively reproduces established models of gender which companies find congenial. We were also struck by the fact that this self-selection is not confined to work which is familiar to the community (for example, 'women's jobs' in wiring and soldering) but extends to types of work with no precedent (for example, semiconductor plant operatives). In short, societal reinforcement of gender stereotypes in the workplace is sometimes underemphasized in radical accounts so that it appears that company discriminatory preferences encounter more resistance than is actually the case.

The importance of gender is shown by the fact that two of the biggest industrial disputes in the industry in Wales centred on equal pay and sex discrimination. In 1976 a protracted strike for equal pay at the GEC Telecommunications in Treforest was led by women. And in 1981 women at Hoover prosecuted a successful campaign against both management *and* 'their' union who together sought to deprive them of seniority status and access to higher skilled jobs. More recently, in 1983, women at GEC-Hitachi initiated the 'walk-out' against management attempts to reduce bonus payment. This may not be simply because operators tend to be harder hit by the management offensives: as some regional union officials attested, although women are more reluctant to take action, once they do they are noticeably more combative and solidaristic than men.

Generally, we found little evidence that union attitudes towards women workers were changing in more than superficial terms. One male official we spoke to was frankly mysogynistic, and others often reproduced and cemented the 'female stereotype'. Interestingly, some also said that awareness of 'women's issues' was greater among trade unionists in London and the South East than in Wales. Clearly, from the point of view of women, the assumption that South Wales is a 'radical region' carries some ironic twists.

(d) Skills: notwithstanding the post-Braverman preoccupation with 'deskilling', the proportion of skilled workers in the British electrical engineering industry (managers, scientists, technologists, technicians) is increasing both relatively and absolutely (Brayshaw and Lawson, 1982). This is particularly evident in the electronics sectors, whether or not sectoral employment is declining (for example, consumer electronics) or increasing (for example, computers). Alongside this, there is the substantial reduction in operator grades and the less pronounced decline of craft and low-range technician grades in the wake of automatic assembly and test technologies. The overall effect is not so much 'deskilling' as a *polarization* between operator-level skills and engineer-level skills. Given its largely 'branch-plant' character, south Wales is not in the running as a location for top technical skills of this calibre and most firms there are unwilling to pay a premium to attract them for fear of triggering off wider disputes over pay differentials.

However, the status of skill as a 'location factor' is too often equated with its technical sense, based on formal qualifications and so on. Yet, there is another conception of skill that is now increasingly employed within the industry. This is rarely formally defined, but it seems to refer not so much to the technical qualifications of employees, but to their qualities as 'good company employees' in terms of attendance, flexibility, responsibility, discipline, identification with the company and, crucially, work rate and quality. This conception refers then to the behavioural characteristics of labour. The use of this concept of skill is most common in the Japanese plants: in one of these, some new, uninitiated Japanese managers misconstrued the traditional British categories of skilled, un-skilled and semiskilled as meaning good, bad and indifferent! On this concept, we found that 'shortage of skills' often meant the lack of workers who had fully adjusted to corporate standards. As we shall see, there are important spatial variations in the incidence of such behavioural skills within the region, at least in the eyes of the management.

(e)   Pay: Published information on earnings in electrical engineering is either coarsely aggregated or extremely patchy at a detailed level. However, it is clear that basic rates of pay for semi-skilled workers (usually women) are about half of those of miners and steelworkers. For example in 1983 basic rates of pay for semi-skilled workers were in the £76–£88 per week range, though bonuses are paid in some cases. At the same time the median weekly earnings for miners in Britain was £183.2 per week and for male manual workers in iron and steel £165.2 per week (New Earnings Survey, 1983).

This means that while such jobs in the new industries may be giving some women a chance to earn a wage for the first time, their rates of pay are low, not only relative to earnings in the traditional industries but in absolute terms, though they are certainly not unusual in Britain.

3   The reconstitution of management–labour practices

We referred earlier to the specific context of our analysis, notable for a number of chief tendencies: the deepening recession and the emergence of mass unemployment, especially since 1979; the acceleration of techno-logical change; and the increased emphasis on inward investments as a vehicle for reindustrialization in the UK generally and its peripheral regions in particular. Together, these tendencies have encouraged a reassertion of the managerial prerogative which has been enormously facilitated by the advent of the Thatcher government in 1979. The managerial offensive in the UK is clearly uneven within and between industries but, thus far, its most dramatic instances have occurred in the public sector industries of steel and motor vehicles (Morgan, 1983). While it assumes many forms, it is principally designed to reverse 'overmanning' and 'restrictive working practices'; impose greater disciplinary norms and, where possible, to enlist consent and identification, preferably of the *active* type, because – as Gramsci well appreciated – this is not an unimportant condition for the successful reproduction of any hegemonic system. As we shall see later, the mobilization of consent is fast becoming a key element of the new 'management paradigm', itself a backlash against conventional management practice in the US and the UK especially (Littler and Salaman, 1984).

Management and labour practices are interdependent but together they vary significantly between industries, between firms in the same industry, between plants of the same firm and even within plants between different categories of workers. Notwithstanding these variations, the following characteristics appear to be widely observed across large sections of British manufacturing industry (see Pavitt, 1980; Williams *et al.*, 1983; Brown, 1983):

(a)   management assumes little interest in the technical and social details of shop-floor production;

(b)   management and labour are relatively conservative as regards innovation and the former operates with short time horizons with respect to investment, R & D and profits;

(c)   management communicates with the workforce via a 'frontline' of shop stewards. Buoyant labour markets obscured the fact that shop stewards facilities lay largely in the hands of the employer, while the relative absence of written agreements on working practices made it easier for managements to reverse 'custom and practice' in the absence of workplace opposition:

(d)   unsophisticated recruitment methods;

(e)   multiple and complicated pay structures and (related to these) rigid job demarcation;

(f)   low productivity and low priority accorded to design and quality;

(g)   several unions per plant;

(h)   little effort to encourage worker identification with firm or plant;

(i)   disregard of workers' knowledge of the labour process in problem solving;

(j)   very hierarchical structure within management, with strong status inhibitions characterizing management–labour interactions.

These characteristics, relevant mainly to large unionized manufacturing plants, have contributed to the relative weakness of British management and the strength of shopfloor organization, especially among male craft workers. Many of these features were evident in the older British and American plants we visited, and our impressions were confirmed by shop stewards and union officials we consulted.

The main social innovations associated with the more recent entrants (post-1973) would be the following:

(a)   *Recruitment procedures*:   these are far more rigorous and tend to be more carefully tailored to the needs of the particular firms. This was even the case for unskilled and semi-skilled workers: as we shall see, this makes sense for capital, for it is hardly rational to recruit direct production workers – on whom productivity very largely depends – in a casual manner. Interviews tended to be carefully planned and thorough rather than perfunctory as was traditionally the case in British firms before the recession. Tests for dexterity and character are common and references are carefully scrutinized. Information is often sought on family background and hobbies, to use as indicators of possible attendance records and behavioural skills. One firm refused to recruit single mothers, preferring workers with stable two-parent families without pre-school-age children. Others relied more heavily on tests and probationary periods in their selection procedures, but in both cases the aim was the same: to select workers who had or would develop the necessary behavioural skills and who would have minimum distractions from the domestic sphere.

More generally, increasing importance attached to recruitment has been both allowed and necessitated by the recession. Some of the managers we interviewed in older firms noted the contrast between now and the 'heydays' of the 1960s and early 1970s when demand was high (and little affected by foreign competition) and when, at the extreme, they were 'chasing volume'. Workers would be hired (and fired) with little care, for there was relatively little pressure on them to worry about productivity and quality: they could virtually sell all they could make. The relative buoyancy of the labour market conversely meant that although they had less scope to choose from, high turnover of labour enabled them to compensate for 'excessive hiring'.

After 1974, and especially after 1979, these conditions reversed; product demand tended to be more stagnant and competition, in terms of quality at least as much as price, intensified considerably. Labour turnover fell and firms which had recruited too hastily and carelessly found themselves saddled with labour which was not only surplus to requirements but low-skilled in the behavioural sense. As one manager in an old firm put it, one of the main lessons that the recession is teaching British management is that it had for too long regarded labour as 'a cheap commodity'; in the short run, it *is* cheap and easy to buy, but treating it as such encourages complacency and lack of innovation. Extra recruitment is no longer a reflex response to increasing output: indeed all but two of the firms interviewed envisaged that they could increase output by 20 per cent with little or no employment increase, and this was not simply a matter of taking up spare capacity for they intended to limit recruitment even in the event of new capacity. In any case, the major recent foreign entrants, with their longer-term planning and profit horizons, tended not to hire labour reactively, as markets fluctuated, as did the older British and American firms, but in accordance with long-term corporate strategy.

The result of this shift into recession and of the influx of foreign firms is to make employers more reluctant to employ workers from established firms and particularly from the coal and steel industry, except where they are obliged to recruit the latter as a condition of obtaining European Coal and Steel Community Grants: such workers are otherwise generally doubly disqualified because of inappropriate technical and behavioural skills.

(b) *Flexible work practices*: the most distinctive feature of the work practices of the newer firms is their emphasis of *flexibility*: reduced demarcation, allowing wider margins of discretion over job allocation was apparent not only in comparison to the traditional coal and steel industries but also relative to the longer established electrical engineering plants. Demarcation is now under attack from recession, new foreign firms and new management 'philosophies'. Such flexibility was most pronounced in the wholly-owned Japanese plants in the consumer electronics sector. Although their productivity levels were generally still below those of plants in Japan, they had an advantage over indigenous producers not only through superior quality (and hence less time wasted on rejects and rectification) and through higher work speeds on individual tasks but through more rapid transfer of workers between tasks.[2]

This flexibility was facilitated not only by the recruitment policies already noted but by a refusal to countenance multi-unionism and by institutionalizing flexibility in written agreements: hence the General and Municipal Workers' Union in south Wales says, in its 'model agreement', that a condition of employment is that each employee accepts 'the direction of the company's management to perform *any* kind or type of work within the employee's known abilities' (GMWU, SW Region). This trend towards the flexible worker is in part responsible for the loss of job descriptions, one implication of which is that technical and behavioural skills are becoming more firm-specific and less transferable *between* firms (Brown, 1983). A parallel shift towards greater flexibility is also emerging in the higher technically skilled occupations in the shape of the multi-skilled engineer or technician, although in this case the technical convergence between different engineering skills in the industry (e.g. electro-mechanical, electronic, software) is a contributory factor.

However, as we shall see, a policy of improved flexibility cannot hope to be successful if it is pursued as an isolated objective; it requires a *package* of related policies including rigorous recruitment procedures, single-union status, simplification of pay structures, squeezing of hierarchies and new management practices.

(c) *Simplified pay structures*:   just as 'single status' is used as a device to *induce* flexible work practices, simplified pay structures (rather than higher pay) help to *sustain* them. In larger established plants (such as Hoover and GEC) the multiplicity of payment structures, together with uneven access to bonus opportunities, produced marked interjob rigidities so that workers were extremely reluctant to relinquish their 'patch'.

(d) *Managerial control*:   another distinctive feature of the new entrants is the extent to which they have circumvented the union(s) as a medium through which information is imparted to, and received from, the workforce. Among the more mature plants, management tended to communicate with the workforce indirectly via the shop stewards who, in effect, became privileged carriers of information. Management in the new entrants – many of whom believed that line supervision had been abdicated by UK managers, especially in the 1960s – accorded a strategic priority to *direct* and regular forms of communication. One effect of this is to marginalize the role and status of the union(s) in the everyday life of employees: even routine grievances, traditionally taken up by shop stewards in Britain, are processed through immediate supervisors (cf. Income Data Services, 1984).

It is no coincidence that in the most extreme of the traditional stereotypes we encountered, its management was highly centralized and far removed from the details of the shopfloor, and consequently, the union was indeed a privileged carrier of information. Significantly, during its acute crisis between 1978–82 (induced to a great extent by its neglect of product and process innovation, ignorance of direct labour productivity and recession) its major response – besides mass redundancies – was to decentralize its management structure so that it became more attuned to the direct production process [. . .]

While the older plants were beginning to appreciate the importance of behavioural skills, the new entrants recognized that these qualities were not to be 'discovered' but, rather, that they were the *result* of involved and knowledgeable management activity. While investment in advanced equipment (for example, automatic assembly and test) was a necessary condition for quality control, it was generally conceded that this was far from sufficient because of the imperative of 'building quality into products' at each and every stage of the labour process, rather than attempting to 'inspect it in' at the final state. To this end, many of the new entrants had developed 'quality circles' or 'involvement teams', the basic aim of which was to enhance the quality of output by utilizing the knowledge and skill of the workforce. The effectiveness of 'quality circles' varied but in all cases efficiency was said to depend on management communicating regular information, defining tasks, demonstrating the interdependence of tasks and training the appropriate team leaders. Significantly three of the four Japanese plants visited said these conditions were not yet met and disparaged the 'gimmicky' attempts of other firms to set up quality circles.

Further related parts of the package of new work practices have been the 'squeezing' of the vertical division of labour within plants and the harmonization and improvement of working conditions. The aim has been both to produce a reduction in the indirect labour force and a consequent increase in output per worker and to allow more direct access of management to the shopfloor. This in turn presupposes greater flexibility, simplified pay structures and improved training in order to produce the behavioural skills – particularly self-discipline and responsibility for some decisions – necessary for making the jobs of the displaced grades redundant.

The squeezing of the hierarchy is also intended to raise morale and identification with the company by reducing status differences. Improvements in working conditions and moves towards their harmonization across grades are also directed towards this end. Typical measures in the new plants include, standardization of payment methods to salaries, sick pay and holiday entitlement, shared canteens, medical check-ups and membership of private health schemes [. . .]

Divisions between primary and secondary workers are a long-established feature of capitalist firms but it is evident from our research and from other recent studies that the divisions are being made in new ways (for example, Atkinson, 1984). The older plants tended to base the division largely on technical skills and perceived status: the higher the technical skills and status, the more secure the job and the more likely is an internal labour market to exist for promotion. But, strictly speaking, such a demarcation is not wholly rational from the point of view of capital because it disregards behavioural skills and allows non-economic criteria of status (which may have more to do with distance from manual work) to influence economic decisions affecting profitability. Using such criteria, many of the direct producers whose performances is most crucial to company success (for example, operators) are categorized as dispensable. Significantly a number of the new entrants (especially the Japanese plants) adhered to a conception of core workers which embraced a variety of occupations and ascribed strategic importance to develop behavioural skills among the direct producers and this in no way penalized technically semi-skilled operators.

These, then, are the main social innovations emerging in the new electronics firms in south Wales. They are, however, just tendencies, not completed projects; progress has been uneven, even within the newer plants and we have been wary of managers presenting a progressive face in interviews. The delays in the changes in older plants cannot be wholly attributed to technological backwardness and worker resistance, for some of the innovations actually hold attractions for workers. It has also been difficult to recruit managers not habituated to the traditional management–labour relations detailed above [. . .]

However, we have still to examine the role of the unions; as we shall see, their role has not been entirely obstructive by any means.

4   Unionization

South Wales was still perceived by managers as 'one of the most heavily unionized regions in western Europe', where belonging to a union is 'as natural as breathing'. Unionization remains pervasive in electrical engineering in south Wales and, although this may legitimately be read as an index of the persistence of a labourist culture, little more can be 'read-off' from unionization (for instance, 'militancy', 'activism'). Nevertheless, all but two of the most advanced electronics plants in south Wales in our survey have accepted unions, albeit in new forms. In the case of one major US multinational, the Welsh plant was its only unionized site, worldwide, while several other firms admitted that they were breaking with corporate precedent in allowing British-style unions. More puzzling is the contrast with central Scotland where many leading companies have resisted trade unions despite the fact that much of the area has a similar industrial history to south Wales, and in 'Red Clydeside' a militant heritage[3] [. . .]

We must obviously acknowledge that we have no way of knowing how many possible entrants to Wales were deterred from locating there by unions and their reputation, but there is abundant evidence that unions have helped more than hindered those firms which have settled by providing a means to an 'ordered environment'.

Apart from the circumvention of trade unions referred to earlier, the most dramatic development in south Wales concerns the emergence of single unionism and, in a minority of these cases, this is accompanied by 'no-strike' agreements. Although single-union status was pioneered in south Wales by Sony (and the Amalgamated Union of Engineering Workers) as early as 1973, it is in the context of the post-1979 climate that their number and ideological significance has increased. The major advantage – from a management perspective – of single-union status is that it promises more flexible work practices because demarcation lines (especially at craft and technician levels) are often institutionalized in separate unions. Thus far there are at least seven single-union plants in south Wales in electrical engineering, five of them Japanese. Their number will undoubtedly increase, less through in situ renegotiation than from new entrants.

Single unionism in British manufacturing is most conspicuous in the (foreign) electronics sector and the Wales Trades Union Congress, anxious to accommodate company preferences so as to command a *spatial* advantage, has assumed a directive role in 'delivering' single status: while all unions may legitimately seek to recruit, once agreement is reached between one particular union and a company, all others are obliged to withdraw. However, competition between unions of multi-union plants to deliver single-union status has been evident. While such behaviour seems profoundly irrational from labour's point of view, once one union starts to be successful in such a strategy, others are driven to do the same to counter it [. . .]

By far the most controversial innovation as regards management–union relations revolves around the so-called 'no-strike' agreements, pioneered by Toshiba and the right-wing Electrical, Electronic, Telecommunications and Plumbing Union at Plymouth in 1981. The main ingredients of such agreements are normally: single-union recognition; equal conditions for manual and office staff; flexible work practices; an advisory board of elected staff representatives (who are not necessarily union members) empowered to discuss any issue; negotiating procedures resulting in compulsory 'pendulum' arbitration (so-called because the arbitrator must decide in one side's favour) designed to encourage moderate claims; and union resolve to settle disputes 'without any form of industrial action' (as at Hitachi). Inmos, the *state-owned* semiconductor plant, originally declared itself against any form of unionization, but relented after it won strategic concessions on the following: 'no strikes' and no actions which interrupt the continuity of production; unionization to apply only to operators, clerical workers and junior technicians (while the advisory board embraces *all* workers); and union ratification of the company's prerogative to 'renumerate its employees on the basis of *individual* performance' (i.e. *behavioural* skills).

All too often, the management–labour practices associated with new entrants are simply reduced to 'single unionism' or 'no-strike' agreements when, for management, these are merely the most obtrusive insignia of a whole series of social innovations. The 'no-strike' agreement is a brittle concord to sustain even for the most sophisticated managerial repertoires, but without the inplant innovations noted earlier, together with the solvent of growth upon which much depends, 'no-strike' agreements have little chance of being established let alone sustained.

The 'no-strike' issue has induced bitter internecine conflicts both between unions (each intent on establishing a presence in 'high-tech', but few willing to *overtly* endorse EETPU-type concessions) and within the EETPU itself. For example, shop stewards feel a conflict of interest between their role as stewards and their role as advisory board representatives; they also feel that they are used as agents of the union bureaucracy, rather than as representatives of their members. EETPU officials have tried to get their shop stewards to ratify 'no-strike' agreements but, so far, unsuccessfully.

However, most union bureaucracies appear to be adopting more corporatist forms of recruitment and liaisons with management from which the union organization at plant level tends to be marginalized. For example, in one Japanese plant with single-union status, the regional officials of the union have guaranteed that in the event of any serious problem, plant management should communicate directly with the regional office where its problem would receive priority treatment, because (in the union's view) nothing should 'interfere with continuous production'. [Note that this is in a plant *without* a formal 'no-strike' agreement, which suggests that the controversy associated with these agreements lies partly in their *formally* acknowledged character.]

This 'top-down' approach is most clearly identified with the EETPU and it is significant that a growing body of management favours this union above others: in cases where multi-union plants have become single-union sites it is invariably the EETPU which is retained. The reasons most often cited for this managerial preference were its positive attitude to profits and flexibility; its use of its own resources to train and retrain for multi-skilled grades and, because EETPU officials are appointed rather than elected, they could afford to take a firmer line with their members, thereby 'delivering' a more disciplined workforce [. . .]

New entrants – particularly from overseas – possess a distinct advantage over established firms in realizing the above innovations because labour lacks the bargaining power of existing involvement and precedent. Whereas a new union agreement in a multi-plant firm like GEC would challenge precedents in plants across the country, a new entrant can start with a *relatively* clean sheet. In delivering social innovations to the new entrants, the unions acknowledge that they have conferred competitive advantages on such plants.

In south Wales, some of these social innovations (such as flexibility, single staff status and relative job security) have been embraced with alacrity, especially by union officials. Furthermore, the promise of more secure employment within the overseas sector led, in the case of an Anglo-Japanese joint venture, to shop stewards actually inviting the Tokyo HQ to assume full control! For local communities, workforces and union organizations, overseas inward investment is perceived not in terms of a burgeoning problem of 'external control' but as a 'welcome invasion'. While this may seem a rather unexceptional response in a region afflicted by acute and long-term unemployment, it often tends to be ignored so that 'external control' is simply read as an index of the regional problem. Undoubtedly the individualistic or sectionalist desires of specific groups of workers to be associated with firms which have a track record of exceptional growth and market leadership encourages such favourable agreements with their employers, regardless of possible unfavourable consequences for the wider labour movement.

5   Local labour markets and the significance of space

The prospects for establishing the management–labour innovations of which we have spoken are affected by spatial considerations. While they are obviously affected by spatial variations in supply of technical skills, as in the contrast between south Wales and the M4 corridor, the social characteristics of the labour markets are also important: the M4 corridor being seen as a 'middle-class society' and a 'union desert' and south Wales in terms of 'steelworkers, miners and militancy'.

Although labour market differentiation would appear to offer the strongest contrast at the interregional level, managers are well aware of the contrasts *within* south Wales, especially between the valley communities of the coalfield and the coastal belt to the south and east, where many managers lived. These latter areas have long been the most favoured locations for private capital, not just for reasons of access (M4 etc.) but for *social* reasons. Companies in this area frequently emphasize its socially differentiated character compared to the more homogenized class structure of the coalfield. Absenteeism was noted to be several percentage points lower than on the coalfield and adequate supervisory and clerical labour more plentiful. It is this area which is the most frequently 'sold' by the Welsh Development Agency in its frenetic attempt to eradicate Welsh industrial history. The most obvious indication of this conscious attempt to accentuate spatial differentiation within south Wales is the WDA's recently established 'golden triangle' in Gwent (see Figure 8.1), which is considered to be more attuned to the specification of 'hi-tech' than are the coalfield communities.

These managerial perceptions of sociospatial differentiation *within* the region were not restricted to new entrants. One of the major indigenous companies, with its traditional facilities on the coalfield, is now in the process of prosecuting a policy of product diversification in which its new plants are located in the 'triangle'. Formerly, this company had expanded via in situ growth, but this had unwittingly produced the *social* diseconomies associated with the 'mass collective worker' syndrome. Now, having absorbed these lessons, it attaches great significance to small plant size as a means of securing a more motivated, flexible and manageable workforce.[4] In this case, the benefits of small plant size were combined with the perceived attractions of new labour markets in the 'triangle'. Significantly, this company, in which the mechanically-oriented AUEW is the numerically dominant union in its (multi-union) coalfield plants, has managed to establish single-union status with the EETPU in its new locations.

8.3   Conclusions and implications

Increased flexibility and reduced demarcation, increased emphasis on behavioural skills and more stringent recruitment, increased direct contact between management and workers, bypassing of unions and the introduction of single-union status – these, then, are the main, interrelated themes emerging in management–labour relations in the new electronics plants in

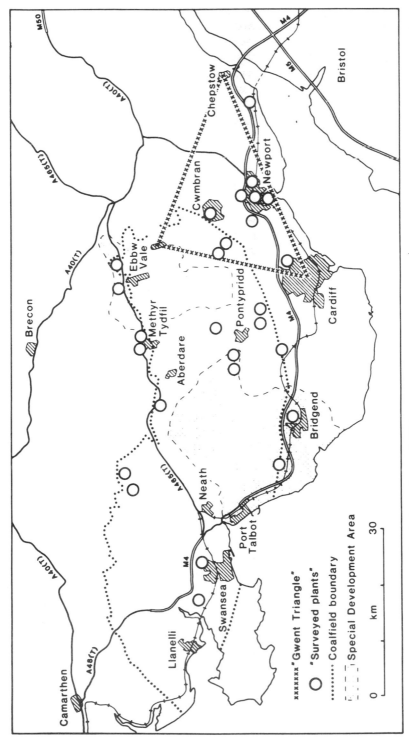

Figure 8.1   The electrical engineering industry in south Wales

south Wales. The legacy of earlier industrial development in this allegedly 'radical region' has not presented as much of an obstacle as might be expected, at least to the new entrants, given the generational change in the workforce, the different labour and locational needs of the new industry and the enabling effects of the recession. Nevertheless the new entrants have nearly all had to adapt to a unionized environment – certainly an effect of the region's history – and that minority which haven't have had to provide better work conditions to keep out unions. The speed of growth of the new entrants plus their possession of greenfield sites, has also acted as a solvent of potential problems in establishing new work practices. In the process, the nature of unionization is changing and, at the moment, unions are competing rather than uniting to face the challenge.

These developments are not incidental to the attraction of foreign firms to regions such as this, indeed it would be a serious mistake to see job creation as the only, or even the major, rationale for the attraction of foreign inward investment. In ordering the benefits likely to accrue from inward investment in Britain, the Invest in Britain Bureau claims that foreign companies bring '. . . new technology, new management styles and attitudes, the injection of capital investment, the generation of exports and new jobs' (IBB, 1983). Britain's frenetic attempt to 'capture' the Nissan car project crystallized these priorities: the major rational being that it would bring valuable Japanese management and technological expertise which would 'ripple out into British industry as a whole' (*Financial Times*, 2 February 1983). The job creation effects hardly figure as a rationale. The foreign investor is welcomed, and rationalized, primarily as an industrial tutor for *both* management and labour in Britain (*Oriental Economist*, January 1984).

It is in the longer-established plants that the past most constrains the adoption of these new practices, and here it is not so much the legacy of coal and steel but the inertia of traditional styles of British management–labour practices plus the lack of greenfield sites and the need to restructure existing production which inhibit change.

The new practices that we identified are not confined to electronics or of course to south Wales: trade unionists at a Wales TUC meeting confirmed similar developments in other sectors when we presented our findings. Furthermore, a survey by Income Data Services of four innovative firms in the brewing, confectionery, tobacco and automobile components industries also found similar results (IDS, 1984). At British Leyland (Austin-Rover) the major source of higher productivity comes *not* from its advanced production technology but from drastically new management–labour practices[5] [. . .]

This is not the first time that trade unions have had to face the challenges set by new industries, but not all the developments are retrograde from labour's perspective, though organized labour is certainly weak. Most obviously it is arguable whether the EETPU's strategy is a necessary one for gaining a foothold in such industries or a disastrous concession. As always, the answers to such questions can only be resolved through the actions of labour both within the unions and within the firms.

Notes

1 Doing things in the same old way in standardized plants producing standardized commodities is hardly a rational strategy for capital.

2 Since completing this chapter we have discovered a report by Takamiya (1981) which covers two of the Japanese plants covered in our survey. It gives further details which suggest the development of some of the kinds of radically new management techniques described in Schonberger (1982).

3 This point is further discussed in a University of Sussex Urban and Regional Studies Working Paper of the same title from which this chapter has been abridged.

4 This aversion to the 'mass collective worker' was prevalent and is very much part of the emerging conventional wisdom among management.

5 The same generally applies to the productivity advantages of Japanese firms (Abernathy *et al.*, 1983).

References

ABERNATHY, W. J., CLARK, K. B. and KANTROW, A. M. (1983) *Industrial Renaissance*, New York, Basic Books.

ATKINSON, J. (1984) *Manning for Uncertainty: Some Emerging UK Work Patterns*, Brighton, Institute of Manpower Studies, University of Sussex.

BRAVERMAN, H. (1974) *Labour and Monopoly Capitalism*, New York, Monthly Review Press.

BRAYSHAW, P. and LAWSON, G. (1982) *Manpower and Training in the Electronics Industry*, Engineering Industry Training Board (RP/5/82).

BROWN, W. (1983) 'The emergence of enterprise unionism', *Institute of Personnel Management, National Conference.*

CAVENDISH, R. (1982) *Women on the Line*, London, Routledge and Kegan Paul.

COOKE, P. (1981) 'Tertiarisation and socio-spatial differentiation in Wales', *Geoforum*, Vol. 12, pp. 319–30.

COOKE, P. (1983) 'Radical regions? Space, time and gender relations in Emilia, Provence and south Wales', BSA Annual Conference Paper, Cardiff.

DORE, R. (1973) *British Factory – Japanese Factory*, Berkeley, University of California Press.

GMWU, SW REGION (1982) *Company Agreements*.

INCOME DATA SERVICES (1984) *Group Working and Greenfield Sites*, Study 314, IDS Ltd.

INVEST IN BRITAIN BUREAU (1983) *Inward Investment: 1977–82*, Department of Industry.

KELLY, J. E. (1982) *Scientific Management, Job Redesign and Work Performance*, London, Academic Press.

LITTLER, C. R. and SALAMAN, G. (1984) *Class at Work: The Design, Allocation and Control of Jobs*, London, Batsford.

MASSEY, D. (1983) 'Industrial restructuring as class restructuring', *Regional Studies*, Vol. 7, pp. 73–89.

MORGAN, K. (1983) 'Restructuring steel: the crises of labour and locality in Britain', *International Journal of Urban and Regional Research*, Vol. 7, pp. 175–201.

PAVITT, K. (ed.) (1980) *Technical Innovation and British Economic Performance*, London and Basingstoke, Macmillan.

POLLERT, A. (1981) *Girls, Wives, Factory Lives*, London and Basingstoke, Macmillan.

SAYER, A. and MORGAN, K. (1984) 'The electronics industry and regional development in Britain', paper presented to a CURDS/ESRC Workshop on Technological Change, Industrial Restructuring and Regional Development, 28–30 March, Newcastle upon Tyne.

SCHONBERGER, R. J. (1982) *Japanese Manufacturing Techniques: Nine Hidden Lessons in Simplicity*, New York, Free Press.

TAKAMIYA, M. (1981) 'Japanese multinationals in Europe: internal operations and their public policy implications', *Columbia Journal of World Business*, Vol. 14, pp. 5–17.

TOMLINSON, J. (1982) *The Unequal Struggle: British Socialism and the Capitalist Enterprise*, London, Methuen.

WICKHAM, J. and MURRAY, P. (1983) 'Women workers and bureaucratic control in Irish electronics factories', BSA Annual Conference Paper, Cardiff.

WILLIAMS, G. A. (1984) 'Women workers in Wales', *Welsh Historical Review*, Vol. 2, pp. 530–48.

WILLIAMS, K., WILLIAMS, J. and THOMAS, D. (1983) *Why are the British Bad at Manufacturing?*, London, Routledge and Kegan Paul.

9 The unions: caught on the ebb tide

Tony Lane

Trade unionists [. . .] have been obliged to undergo a crash course in industrial economics. Schooled in the boom years when aggression was typically productive, they had little need to concern themselves with such niceties as 'market shares', 'import penetrations', 'unit costs'. But the fact that many have learned, perforce, to take these matters seriously and even to concede hard-won gains does not mean they have forgotten how to recognize an adversary. The harder-headed have adopted the maxim that 'they who fight and run away, live to fight another day' [. . .]

The re-appearance of such a day, however, is more a matter of faith than of thought. There is, perhaps, an intuitive half-conscious awareness that a return to the 'good old days' of the long post-war boom might be a long time a'coming. But there is no widespread appreciation of the possibility that certain conditions external to the workplace might have changed so dramatically as to affect future activity within the workplace. On the one hand it is obvious that the practice of trade unionism has forfeited some of its legitimacy among its own membership. On the other hand are far less obvious changes in the composition and regional dispersion of industry seriously affecting organizing capacities. This latter question will be dealt with at some length.

9.1 From town to country

Many of the underlying difficulties facing the trade union movement are not at all a function of resurgent *laissez-faire* Toryism. The Thatcher government has, wittingly or not, telescoped longer-term developments and brought things to a speedy head by adopting policies which have had the effect of accelerating processes of industrial change. Trade union leadership at all levels, from the local to the national, [. . .] often seems to take more notice of ideology than it does of material changes in its environment.

Over the last twenty years the industrial landscape, the geographical distribution of industry, has undergone a profound transformation. While to some extent checked by regional policies designed to guide the flows of industrial relocation, the fact remains that there has been a flight of large-scale industrial plants from conurbation centres. The results are to be seen in inner-city unemployment levels. In the 1960s and early 1970s when the industrial building sector of the construction industry was enjoying an unprecedented boom, manufacturing industry was decentraliz-ing: in the first instance to conurbation peripheries, in the second to the towns that formed ribbons with the larger cities and in the third and final phase to what urban geographers call 'free-standing' towns and cities, i.e. those not linked by suburban development to other towns. It is worth noting that in the course of these changes the number of plants per firm was steadily increasing and average employment per plant was falling.

Britain, unlike West Germany for example, has had a high proportion of industry clustered in and around cities. Agglomeration in West Germany has been less marked and surprisingly large plants can be found in small towns. The 'company town' phenomenon though far from unknown in Britain, appears to be more common in Germany. Whether or not the incidence of company towns in Britain is increasing is a matter for conjecture. What *is* beyond dispute is that both manufacturing and service industry is now far more widely dispersed than it was twenty years ago.

Industrial growth points have been the smaller and well-established industrial towns strategically well-placed in relation to communication networks and in the once-sleepy market towns of East Anglia, the rural southern counties, the West and South West. Overall there seem to be two trends. Nationally, more new plants and office facilities have been built south of the elliptical line stretching from The Wash to Gloucester which bends south of Birmingham and Coventry. At the regional level all areas, including those north of the South Midlands, have seen a shift of industry from town to country. Superficially at least the geographical changes which accompanied the Industrial Revolution have gone into reverse as more and more city acres revert to grass and trees (Fothergill and Gudgin, 1982).

The changes we have noticed so far – the decrease in plant size, the increased number of plants per firm and the relocation of plants away from urban areas – all have implications for trade union practice and working-class politics. Especially important is the industrial decline of the city.

City trade unionism

Although the pattern has now changed, trade unionism in most of the larger towns and cities was until recently dominated by manual workers concentrated in perhaps a handful of industries. These industries were in turn either dominated by a small number of large firms where trade unionism was well-entrenched or operated in an economic environment conducive to trade union militancy. Whichever way it was, towns had acquired large workplaces which were well-organized and became exemplars for trade union practice in other workplaces in other industries. Thanks to a lengthy period of near full employment in the years after 1945, workers started to change jobs more frequently and in doing so passed on the word about methods and amounts of payment, working conditions, union tactics.

The informal networks were supplemented by other and more organized sources. The AUEW had introduced quarterly meetings of shop stewards in the districts as early as the 1930s. In the TGWU in the '60s and '70s more and more district communities were being formed and membership of them [becoming] much less dependent upon the patronage of full-time officers. In the GMWU, after the Pilkington strike had rocked the union from top to bottom and David Basnett succeeded Jack Cooper, people were no longer afraid of their own shadows and began to organize openly. And then on top of these developments within the major unions there was the extraordinary growth of education programmes from the late 1960s: these brought people together who would never otherwise have met to exchange experiences.

Much has changed since these developments reached their apogee in the mid-'70s. The dock industry, an important exemplar, organizing centre and training-ground for activists had been all but wiped out in Liverpool, Hull and London's East End; the heavy engineering industry has been battered in Manchester, Coventry, Tyneside and Clydeside; the steel industry has been decimated in Sheffield and South Wales; the West Midlands foundry, car and car components industries have suffered huge job losses. These were the highly organized industries with long traditions of struggle, the universities of up to three or even four generations of trade unionists. It must surely be significant that in the TGWU on Merseyside today [1982] the liveliest branch is composed of unemployed people and those on MSC schemes.

In today's cities the odds are that the largest employers are in the public sector: the local councils, hospitals, universities and polytechnics. With highly sectionalized workforces, elaborate status hierarchies and little muscle, these cannot be the leading cohorts of the future. On the contrary and as the recent health workers dispute has plainly demonstrated, they are critically dependent upon secondary support on a scale not ordinarily given.

The surviving industries

The obliteration of some of the big battalions, the drastic reduction in scale of the remnants and the flight into the free-standing towns of a growing proportion of the more modern industrial sectors raise a host of problems. But before elaborating on this, let us notice that the cities have not been stripped bare of private industry. The retail trade, though declining in numbers employed, is collectively a large employer of wage labour. But like the catering and leisure industry which also employs large numbers, it is notoriously a union organizer's nightmare. Workers in these industries are scattered, do work which is more individual than collective and experience personalized authority relations. In short, such workers have few opportunities for learning about combination and experiencing solidarity.

Manufacturing industry has not, of course, disappeared from the city. Small firms abound, although a recent report commissioned by the Department of the Environment suggests that for every new starter there is likely to be a casualty. The larger plants remaining in the cities are almost invariably branches of multi-plant companies, are housed in old buildings and belong to industries that show few signs of growth. These are firms in traditional industries which face saturated or near-saturated markets: in Liverpool it might be the biscuit industry, in Bristol tobacco, in Birmingham chocolate, in Leeds clothing. In these industries the more dynamic survivors have invested heavily in new plant and equipment and become far more capital-intensive.

A typical remaining large-scale city plant has a long tradition of female employment and trade union organization but no history of militancy. A combination of part-time and seasonal employment for many of the women, the reservation of the best paid and most strategic jobs for the men and paternalist personnel policies produced quietest trade unionism. But things in such plants are quietly changing. Feminist currents are plainly intruding and automation has eliminated distinctions between full- and part-time employment. In the biscuit and confectionary industries the remaining female workers are now full-time. Surviving establishments of this sort might potentially provide a new vanguard for city trade unionism though much hinges on an insurgent feminism. It is pleasingly ironic that a male-dominated trade union movement might be partially dependent on feminism for its renaissance. It is certainly instructive that the only recently effective struggles against redundancy have involved women workers.

Plainly *all* is not lost in the cities. Nevertheless, the fact of the dispersion of industry around and well beyond city boundaries must mean that the old pattern of leaders and laggards in ratchet relation will be transformed. Here we must bear in mind that many of the firms with plants in the high technology sectors with growth potential are widely scattered and often in remote areas.

What the city has provided has been quick and easy communication via an elaborate network of informal meeting places and formal organizations. The city, too, has a large and diverse population and this bestows on the individual a certain social invisibility, an immunity from the sort of scrutiny and social censorship that is more evident in the small town. The city, then, because of its diversity and scale, has provided both a range of organization and a high degree of personal 'protection'. It is not, therefore, by accident that major campaigns start in cities and ripple outwards with diminishing effect. The more distant and isolated the workplace the less the likelihood of involvement in the big issues. It is surely significant that on those occasions when trade unionists in the smaller towns take part in such things as demonstrations, they are far more likely to send contingents to the city than to organize a local event.

9.2   Suburban and rural industry

Such new and large-scale workplaces as have been created in the last twenty years or so have almost invariably been built in green fields on city perimeters. While many of these plants have been accompanied by new housing estates, the traditional city phenomenon of a conjunction between place of work and place of residence has not been repeated on the same scale. The typical city-perimeter plant – say BL's Longbridge or Ford's Halewood – draws its workforce from a large catchment area: from adjacent housing estates, from the old city centres and inner suburbs, from outlying towns. Symbolic here is the statistical category 'travel-to-work-area' used in employment returns.

With trade union representatives as scattered as their constituents, the opportunities for the formation of informal social and political networks are greatly diminished. While linkages with the city remnants are maintained, they are usually tenuous. It is true that many of the newer perimeter plants have seen the development of effective in-plant trade union organization and have often been pacemakers in the annual rounds of wage negotiationis. It is true also that they have trained some workers in trade unionism who have subsequently moved on to work and organize in other establishments. In short, they have replicated some of the functions of the old city-based organizing centres. Their *relative* isolation, however, has prevented them from becoming substitutes.

The second phase of industrial relocation from city perimeter to satellite or ribbon town need not detain us since in its effects it does not materially differ from the phase just dealt with. Of much more importance is the more recent phase wherein relocation has been in free-standing towns and semi-rural areas.

The move into the country has not necessarily meant the establishment of non-union plants. While it would be reasonable to expect lower levels of unionization in these areas, in-going plants, especially those of larger companies with established recognition agreements and elaborate industrial relations systems, will often have stitched up recognition deals for outlying plants before they have even opened their gates. In those cases, and there have been more than a few, trade union organization has been created in advance of a population of trade unionists! [. . .]

Trade unionism from above

It may be taken for granted that trade unionism imposed from above is unlikely, in the short run at least, to be very tough-minded. But then of course most workers taken on in new workplaces in rural areas will not have experienced off-the-peg trade unionism and will have had to build their own organizations. To the extent that they have done so they will not have found much in local political tradition to provide ideological sustenance and personal support. Most of the free-standing towns with an industrial tradition have largely forgotten any radical tradition they may have had. As for the old market towns radical expression was often furtive and almost underground [. . .]

The lack of a radical tradition in these towns (which contain the bulk of the electorate in rural constituencies) is not trade unionism's only handicap. There is also the physical isolation from the better organized centres and an intimidating socio-cultural ethos of arrogant middle-class conservatism [. . .]

Regardless of whether or not tweedy fantasies have been indulged, we can be quite sure that a new rural plant belonging to a multi-plant firm has been provided with carefully designed labour processes. Equipped with supervisory workers long-experienced in the habits, ruses and dodges of urban workers, firms can establish from scratch their ideal job descriptions and work rhythms. Where union organization exists in such plants, it may not amount to very much: its shopfloor leadership is likely to be very inexperienced and easy meat for a management drafted in from the city.

At first glance the problems for effective trade unionism of the new rural plant might not seem very great. After all, it might be said, exactly the same conditions often applied to new plants built on city perimeters and in satellite towns. All of that is true of course – but what is different is the physical and social isolation of the rural areas. The normal working of social processes meant that little *conscious* effort was needed to bring the city-perimeter plant into the orbit of vanguard trade unionism. The same can hardly be said for the workplace buried in the countryside.

9.3 The multi-plant firm and its consequences

The death of city-based plants and the survival of those in the countryside is not the only aspect of industrial change to affect trade unionism. Perhaps equally important is the organizational structure of the large firm. While it is common knowledge that throughout the twentieth century there has been a steady increase in the proportion of net manufacturing output accounted for by the 100 largest firms, rather less notice has been taken of the operational structure of these large firms. Popular imagery which associates giant workplaces employing tens of thousands with the large firm could not be more mistaken. The typical large firm of today might have as many as 100 plants, employ as few as 15 in the smallest and little more than 1000 in the largest.

The large firms have grown larger by expanding into a wider range of activities and by multiplying the number of plants under their control. Firms in high growth industries have expanded by adding on plants to produce familiar products. Firms in low growth industries, usually through merger, have either moved into product lines adjacent to historic activity (for instance, breweries into hotels and gambling) or diversified into fast growing sectors of other industries (for instance, Imperial Tobacco into snack and frozen foods). Over the last few years the average number of plants per firm has decreased and so, of course, has the average number of persons employed per plant. Nevertheless, the multi-plant, multi-product firm continues to dominate manufacturing industry.

While practices as between firms and industrial sectors vary, the most common method of coping administratively with such sprawling empires has been to resort to a divisional structure. Each broad product area has its own group of plants, its own board of directors and its own industrial relations/personnel set-up. Some firms, the best-known being GEC, have gone even further by designating *plants* rather than divisions as profit centres. Now with this sort of industrial structure, no intellectual gymnastics are required to see the centrifugal effects this must have had on trade union bargaining. It is unlikely in the extreme that any of this was designed deliberately as an instrument of confusion and divide and rule but it has certainly had that effect.

These developments have patently contributed to a switch from industry-wide to company, divisional and plant bargaining. In the short run and in the past fractionated bargaining may well have lent itself to the workers' economic advantage. Considered from a different perspective it has undoubtedly hindered the construction of solidarity and the production of politically relevant knowledge.

Combine committees

From the trade unionist's point of view the multi-plant firm raises a host of not readily resolvable problems. The wide dispersion of plants over considerable distances, with location in areas differing in their labour movement traditions, means that within the divisional structure of any one firm uneven development of trade union practice as between plants is the norm. Attempts at forming combine committees always fall foul of this problem – and doubly so where combine committees organize on an inter-divisional or inter-company basis [. . .]

These circumstancs are compounded by internal union organization. Full-time officers in most unions have, so to speak, a portfolio of companies within a given geographic area for which they are responsible. It follows that the employees of a multi-plant company operating in a number of regions must have contact with a number of full-time officers. Constraints of time, resources and variations in outlook as between these officers ensures that they neither meet nor exchange information on a regular and systematic basis. The only point of convergence is through the national officer responsible for the company concerned – who suffers from precisely the same constraints.

As if to make bad worse, some unions are hostile to combine committees, some are indifferent and positively none are encouraging to the point where they provide appropriate resources. Naturally, these interunion variations are important: firstly because different sections of workers are organized by different unions, secondly because there is no guarantee that process and white-collar workers are organized by the same union and thirdly because identical grades of workers might be organized by one union in one plant and another union in another plant.

The lack of official support for combines is critical. Without that backing combines must be dependent upon such funds as shop stewards committees and branches can muster: these are bound to be indaequate. An *efficient* combine committee would need, in addition to a substantial travel fund, to produce its own newsletter and maintain a continuously up-dated data bank. The absence of anything approaching this leaves plants' inhabitants isolated, disunited and hard-put to mount effective resistance in a period when there is a desperate need for a coherent defensive strategy.

First-hand contact with the workplaces of a multi-plant company can be a depressing experience. Even in the better organized plants stewards often have little knowledge of company structure, of product range, of investment and depreciation, of the productive capacities of other plants. Intelligence is rarely systematically gathered and as a consequence much energy may sometimes be spent in checking out the latest rumour. Contacts with stewards in other plants are infrequent and relationships often tinged with barely concealed suspicions and rivalry. As between plants it is almost a case of dog-eat-dog in a period of retrenchment.

In general, though not always in the particular, it is unreasonable to pin any blame on the stewards. The fact is that they have simply not been trained to handle all relevant matters. Highly-skilled and well-schooled in the city plants in handling local day-to-day issues, they had little apparent need when the boom was on to acquire the skills needed for strategic planning [. . .]

9.4   A crisis of legitimacy?

By no means all of the unions' problems can be attributed to changes in the industrial environment. In one form or another there is plenty of evidence to suggest that trade unionism in general is not nearly as popular with its own members as a healthy movement ought to be [. . .]

It would be going too far to suggest that amongst the trade union rank and file there is an articulated critique that amounts to a consistent argument. There is nothing so substantial. And yet the drift of complaint is pretty clear for it is registered in a moral vocabulary . . .

In the early 1960s George Woodcock, whom recent history incredibly has forgotten, exhorted the movement in a memorable speech at the TUC to make up its mind about its purpose: it had to decide whether it wanted to be the collective entrepreneur of labour, adopt the jungle ethics of the market and practise business unionism, or whether it wanted to play a significant part in the creation of a new society constructed on a morality of equity instead of greed. The unions failed to make up their minds then and have continued in that failure subsequently. This central ambiguity confuses people. On the one hand the unions proclaim their commitment to equity and draw widely on a moral vocabulary. On the other hand there are many instances where it is clear enough that sectional interest has prevailed and little attempt is made to hide the fact [. . .]

9.5   Conclusion

Some years ago, when but recently retired from the general secretaryship of the National Union of Mineworkers, Will Paynter expressed reservations about the shift of power within the trade union movement toward shop stewards. Paynter's anxieties had nothing to do with an erosion of 'bureaucratic centralism' or with a personal loss of power. What concerned him was that such developments might give full reign to activity narrowly based on localized sectional interest. Looking at the problem as a *socialist*, Paynter was pondering the classic dilemma: while short-run economic gains might be made through vigorous bargaining at plant level, gains made there would make it increasingly difficult for unions operating across a range of industries to devise national policies with progressive import. Non-industrial unions would find their fragile organic unity being dissolved and would come to resemble loose confederations bound together by little more than a common purse. Such a *tendency* has of course always been present, but so long as collective bargaining tended to be national *and* industry-wide it could be held in check and hold out the possibility of generating from within the unions' longer-term industrial policy.

It is now clear that in his private musings Will Paynter identified a very serious problem for the trade unions, for there is no doubt that the multiplication of actual and potential bargaining centres has exacerbated sectionalism. This in turn has done much to produce that lack of political direction of which the rank and file implicitly complain. But before the trade unions can begin to address themselves to these sorts of questions they must rid themselves of the belief that the shift to local and company bargaining was a response to rank and file demands for democracy. In reality, rank and file demands for democratization of collective bargaining gained in strength as the structure of industry itself underwent major change. As in all previous phases of its development, trade unionism simply adapted itself to the contours of its environment.

On the assumption that the *worst* of the current recession for British industry is over [. . .], the unions *should* by now have a fairly clear picture of how what is left is organized and regionally distributed. Armed with that analysis the large general unions – TGWU, AUEW and GMWU – need to take themselves by the scruff of the neck and shake themselves into the shape necessary to cope with what effectively is a new environment [. . .]

Reference

FOTHERGILL, S. and GUDGIN, G. (1982) *Unequal Growth: Urban and Regional Employment Change in the UK*, London, Heinemann.

Section V Uneven development: a new phase?

Introduction

This final Section steps back from the detail of changes in particular parts of the economy and attempts to take a wider view. All three chapters deal with the economy as a whole and with a wide range of changes within sectors of economy. All three link the fortunes of UK cities and regions to their place within the wider international division of labour. And all three also begin to draw in to the consideration of economic change, the contemporaneous and interrelated shifts in social structure and in the political sphere.

All three, moreover, agree about the basic spatial changes which have taken place in the UK economy over the post-war period, and about which changes have been most distinctive and significant. Each chapter, however, deals with those changes in a different way. In part this is because their aims are different; in part it is because they adopt contrasting theoretical approaches. Martin develops a grand, overarching theory based on the approach of the regulationist school, but using a concept of socio-institutional structure instead of their 'mode of regulation'. His argument is that the 'post-war expansionary regime' had, by the early 1970s, been undermined both from without and from within, and that we are currently witnessing the emergence of a regime of flexible accumulation. This thesis thus builds upon an approach which tries to pull together the disparate aspects of 'flexibilization' discussed in the last Section. The contrasts between the periods involve not only the whole organization of the economy but also social structure, politics and state intervention. And it is as a result of some combination of all these that the periods are also contrasting in the forms of their 'space-economies'.

Cooke develops, as the centrepiece of his chapter, the concept of 'spatial paradigms' which have as their main bases technological paradigms. And the sequencing of technological paradigms is of key importance in the periodization of the economy. The focus on the relation between technological change and spatial change is thus shared with Martin. Beyond that, however, there are differences. On the one hand, Cooke tries to specify some actual mechanisms through which economic change might feed through to spatial change, in particular by specifying 'middle-range rules' which operate within the broad necessities (in capitalist economies) of profitability and competition. On the other hand, while he clearly links the changes of recent decades to changes beyond the immediately economic, and in particular to state politics, Cooke does not bind everything in a formal framework like the regime of accumulation/socio-institutional structure of Martin.

In the chapter by Massey, the main focus is on the conceptualization of uneven development. However, she argues, doing this adequately requires precisely linking it to the social organization of production and to wider characteristics of and changes in economy and society. The key concepts deployed to make this link are spatial structures of production and spatial divisions of labour.

A common element which runs through the three chapters is that each embodies an element of critique of approaches which bear some relation to their own.

Martin takes on a number of approaches before developing his own. He argues that long-wave theory might be questioned on its characterization of cycles in relation to the UK (in other words, an empirical criticism) but also raises the frequent questions of the theory's adequacy in terms of explanation and its characterization of the international level. He also argues that, in spite of some attempts, the socio-institutional context is still under-recognized in long-wave theory. Mandel's (1980) arguments in this direction are criticized for an unwarranted distinction between endogenous and exogenous causes of change. The socio-institutional structure may, argues Martin, have its own dynamic which may, or may not, at different times be favourable to the prevailing regime of accumulation. This concept of socio-institutional structure which he derives from the work of Gordon *et al*. (1982), he then pairs with the regulationist-school concept of regime of accumulation. This, he argues, provides a more general social framework for changes in production than that implied by the regulationists' 'mode of regulation'.

Cooke examines the 'organized-disorganized capitalism' thesis and finds it wanting in a number of respects. He challenges it first on empirical grounds, arguing in particular that the characterization of organized capitalism relies on features (for instance mass production and the nature of state regulation) which were neither ubiquitous nor permanent. Moreover, he argues, this in turn has further implications. Firstly the 'tension' between leading edge and other sectors had spatial implications, leading to very different formations in regions not themselves dominated by the putatively nationally dominant regime. (This is a point which recalls that of Hudson in the last Section, though the latter might perhaps not agree with all of Cooke's characterizations of sectors.) Further, argues Cooke, the differently organized sectors did not just exist side by side; they were interrelated.

It might be noted that all this raises the question of what 'dominance' means. Clearly it cannot mean 'universal'. Neither Lash and Urry (1987) in their characterization of organized capitalism nor Martin in his regimes of accumulation would claim that it does. Nonetheless it behoves such perspectives to address the question. Cooke's querying of the characterization of organized capitalism can be addressed equally to Martin and to the regulationist school.

Cooke's criticism of 'disorganized' capitalism as a conceptualization of the current era is of a different nature. Here the query is whether 'disorganized' is the correct term. Is it disorder or a new order which is the more adequate conceptualization? Cooke argues for the second.

Massey's main critique concerns the conceptualization of uneven development. This, she argues, if it is to have any grasp on the underlying dynamics of society, cannot be content with quantitative indices, but must be tied in to the fundamental relations of power and control in society. Her own chapter focuses on the economic sphere and argues for a conceptualization of uneven development which begins from an analysis of the spatial organization of the relations of production. This, she argues, highlights the fact that uneven development can vary not only in degree but also in nature. This contrasts with a conceptualization which concentrates on distributional measures. The significant issues for the future, on this argument, may not be whether or not the north-south divide, for instance, has got 'worse' in terms of some quantitative measures, but what are its underlying dynamics.

Massey argues that a new spatial division of labour began to predominate in the United Kingdom from around the mid-1960s. And indeed, with different emphases, all three chapters take this position. For all of them, there has been a major shift in the form of uneven development. Moreover, despite their different emphases all argue that this shift has taken place through a series of phases, of attempted adjustments and strategies of modernization. For all of the chapters, too, the 'indices' of uneven development point to an increasingly unequal geography, at national level between regions, and at a smaller spatial scale within regions and within local areas. Such spatial polarization both reflects the increasing inequality in society as a whole and exacerbates it. If this is, indeed, a historical turning-point, as all these three chapters argue, then it is one in which uneven development – uneven re-development – is an integral part.

References

GORDON, D. M., EDWARDS, R. and REICH, M. (1982) *Segmented Work, Divided Workers: The Historical Transformation of Labour in the United States*, Cambridge, Cambridge University Press.

LASH, S. and URRY, J. (1987) *The End of Organised Capitalism*, Cambridge, Polity Press.

MANDEL, E. (1980) *Long Waves of Regional Development*, London and Basingstoke, Macmillan.

10   Industrial capitalism in transition: the contemporary reorganization of the British space-economy

Ron Martin

10.1   The restructuring of industrial society: a new historical divide

With the benefit of hindsight we know what the structural changes and crises of the 1920s and 1930s ushered in: a new order of state-managed economic accumulation that, following the Second World War, gave western capitalism a quarter-century of renewed, indeed unprecedented, growth and prosperity – the Keynesian-based, long 'post-war boom'. But in the early 1970s that long expansionary phase came to an abrupt end, to be replaced by what is now widely referred to as the 'great slow-down' or 'second slump' (Mandel, 1978; Matthews, 1982; Maddison, 1987).

Outwardly this slow-down can be viewed as the product of several successive economic 'shocks': the collapse of the Bretton Woods Agreement in 1971, two major oil-price hikes in 1973 and 1979, the rapid acceleration of inflation during the 1970s, and two severe recessions in 1974–75 and 1980–82. However, many social scientists, including human geographers, economists, social and political theorists, and even cultural analysts, are now united in the conviction that these 'shocks', though crucial, have been bound up with and compounded in their impacts by a more fundamental underlying process of socio-economic 'restructuring' (O'Keefe, 1984; Newby *et al.*, 1985). According to this viewpoint, the economic stagnation and instability since 1973 should not be seen simply as a recessionary interruption, albeit a protracted one, to the post-war boom; nor should the recovery that appears to be currently emerging be regarded as marking a 'return to normal'. Instead, the growing contention is that western capitalism is currently passing over another historical divide akin to that of fifty to sixty years ago, that we are witnessing once more a transition to a new order or phase of socio-economic development.

Of course, this is not to deny that the socio-economy is continuously evolving, or that many of the changes presently under way are but the latest expressions of much longer-term trends. However, in addition to the indisputable elements of continuity in economic evolution, the history of structural and social change in the advanced industrial nations also indicates that the process of development is far from smooth and incremental. Echoing the turmoil and upheavals of the inter-war decades, what stands out from the past fifteen years or so is the accelerating pace, profound nature and marked shift of direction of change. In Britain, western Europe, North America and other advanced industrial nations, in fact across much of the world economy generally, the industrial, socio-political and spatial forms of economic organization that provided the basis of post-war development are losing their former role as the leading sources of growth and accumulation. Previously dominant industries, technologies, methods of production, skills, class divisions, state policies and even institutional arrangements are all in decline, and are being superseded by new industries, new technologies, new production methods, new skills and class divisions, and new policies and institutional configurations. Rather than simply marking a temporary inflection of the economic trajectory of the post-war decades, the intense and wide-ranging reorganization since the early 1970s would seem to herald a significant break from it.

Geographically, the result of this reorganization has been a far-reaching restructuring of the patterns of uneven urban and regional development built up over previous decades, a succession of regional 'role reversals', and a marked widening of spatial socio-economic inequalities. Although the detailed specifics vary from country to country, the broad trends are similar, and are now well known. At the urban level the precipitate decline of industrial activity in the older cities has left them, and especially their inner areas, economically, socially, physically and fiscally debilitated. Alongside increasing problems of inner-city unemployment, a dramatic shift of jobs into services and the rapid expansion of financial, commercial and cultural functions have led to a pronounced dualization of the urban labour market and to sharp spatial juxtapositions of poverty and prosperity. As national and local governments in the advanced countries seek desperately to regenerate and revive their declining older urban areas, the historical role of cities in the economic accumulation process seems to be changing in fundamental and irrevocable ways (Harvey, 1985, 1987a; Rees and Lambert, 1985; Smith and Feagin, 1988).

At the regional scale, once-leading areas of manufacturing production, such as the north and the West Midlands of Britain[1], the North East–Mid West of the United States, northern France and the Ruhr in Germany, have 'deindustrialized' into 'sunset' or 'rust-belt' regions (Bluestone and Harrison, 1982; Sawyers and Tabb, 1982; Summers, 1984; Martin and Rowthorn, 1986). Meanwhile, the geographical locus of capital accumulation has shifted to 'newly industrializing' rural areas, such as the 'Third Italy', and to new, high-technology-orientated complexes in buoyant 'sunrise' or 'sun-belt' regions, such as the southern states of the US, the south-eastern regions of Britain, and the southern parts of France and Germany (Castells, 1985; Markusen *et al.*, 1986; Hall *et al.* 1987; Aydalot and Keeble, 1988). And all of these spatial manifestations of economic reorganization within western capitalist societies are in turn inextricably bound up with a major restructuring of the international division of labour associated with the rapid ascendancy of the 'newly industrializing countries' (NICs), particularly in South East Asia, and with a dramatic intensification of international competition and capital mobility (Frobel *et al.*, 1980; Saunders, 1981; Beenstock, 1983; Bradbury, 1985; Peet, 1983, 1987). The cheap-labour advantages of the NICs have enabled their industries to capture increasing shares of the domestic and export markets of the advanced nations, while at the same time the low-cost and expansionary economic environments in the NICs have proved increasingly attractive to western-based multinationals which have shifted capital, production and hence jobs to these more profitable sites.

Yet if all these economic, social and spatial realignments do justify the widely made claim that industrial capitalism is currently in transition, they simultaneously raise a key issue around which considerable debate and lack of consensus exists, namely how this transition should be theorized and explained. My intention in the remainder of this chapter is to derive such a synoptic framework with which to characterize the British case.

10.2   Interpreting the current transition: in search of a framework

There have been several conceptualizations of the socio-economic reconfiguration under way in Britain and other advanced capitalist countries. Some see it as marking the passage between the downswing phase of a fourth (post-war) Kondratiev long wave and the beginnings of the upswing phase of a new, fifth Kondratiev (Mandel, 1980; Freeman, 1984; Hall, 1985; Marshall, 1986). Others view it as a crisis of legitimation and rationality of the Keynesian welfare state, as the emergence of a structural incompatibility between market capitalism and interventionist social democratic politics (Bowles and Gintis, 1982; Offe, 1984), and the rise of a new economic liberalism (Nell, 1984; Gamble, 1988). Still others interpret the current upheaval as representing the end of an epoch of 'organized capitalism' and the rise of a new epoch of 'disorganized capitalism' (Offe, 1985; Lash and Urry, 1987; see also Cooke Chapter 11 in this volume); while others have suggested that we are witnessing a shift from one 'regime of accumulation' based on Fordist principles to another regime of post-Fordist or 'flexible' accumulation (Piore and Sabel, 1984; Harvey, 1987b; Moulaert, Swyngedouw and Wilson, 1987; Jaeger and Ernste, 1988). Yet a further interpretation is that a change of socio-technical 'paradigm' is occurring, from one based on 'modernization' to another identified with 'post-modernization' (Cooke, 1987). Although different, these perspectives often overlap, all are historical and structural in orientation, and each can be given both orthodox (liberal) and radical (Marxian) interpretations.

A new long wave of economic development?

Given the dramatic post-1973 slow-down, culminating in the early 1980s in an economic crisis unparalleled since the slump of the early 1930s, it is perhaps not surprising that the notion of long waves, forst formulated by Kondratiev (1935) and Schumpeter (1939), has been revived. Modern long-wave theorists posit a chronology of four historical growth cycles, each of forty to sixty years in duration. However, although major changes in growth momentum have occurred in Britain and other advanced industrial nations over the past two centuries (see Table 10.1), the case for systematic long-term rhythmic waves in economic activity remains unproven. Indeed, in Britain's case the pattern appears to have been more one of long-run secular decline in the rate of economic growth, at least across the first three long waves. Further, when viewed in this context, the rapid expansion during the post-war boom or upswing phase of the fourth wave, was (as in many other countries) quite exceptional, and the much slower growth rate during the slow-down after 1973 can arguably be seen as in a resumption of this long-run downward trend in growth performance that has progressively left Britain trailing its main competitors, particularly from the 1870s onwards (Gamble, 1981; Matthews *et al.*, 1982).

Nevertheless, the belief that since the early 1970s western capitalism has been in the throes of a 'long-wave' trough, a period of 'creative destruction' which prepares the way for a new wave, to use Schumpeter's argument, has gained wide currency. The neo-Schumpeterian long-wave theorists, such as Freeman (1984, 1986) and Hall (1981, 1985 (reprinted as Chapter 2)), see this trough as marking the maturation and degeneration of the leading technologies and associated industrial sectors – electrical and electronic systems and products, motor vehicles, mass production techniques – which formed the basis of the fourth wave that began in the 1930s and 1940s. The economic and spatial restructuring resulting from this downturn is regarded as setting the stage for a new long-wave up-swing whose dynamic will be based on the constellation of new technologies and innovations – micro-electronics, telematics, information processing – that has been rapidly evolving over the past decade or so. In Hall's view this transition between the fourth and fifth technological long waves accounts for the contemporary uneven geography of socio-economic restructuring in Britain. The regions that led the fourth, post-war wave – such as the North West and West Midlands, and many of the major cities – are precisely those that have experienced the most rapid deindustrialization since the early 1970s. The new high-tech industries and activities, on the other hand, have begun to emerge out of quite different spatial concentrations of innovation in the southern parts of the country. As Hall (1981, p. 357) puts it, 'tomorrow's industries are not going to be born in yesterday's regions', but 'in that broad belt that runs from Oxford and Winchester through the Thames Valley and Milton

Table 10.1 'Long waves' of economic growth: the United Kingdom in international context

	First wave 1780 to 1840s		Second wave 1840s to 1890s		Third wave 1890s to 1940s		Fourth wave 1940s to 1980s	
	1780–1820	1820–50	1850–70	1870–90	1890–1913	1913–50	1950–73	1973–84
United Kingdom	2.6	2.4	2.3	2.0	1.8	1.3	3.0	1.1
France	(nd)	1.7	1.1	1.4	1.9	1.1	5.1	2.2
Germany	(nd)	2.0	2.0	2.4	3.2	1.3	5.9	1.7
Denmark	(nd)	1.9	1.8	2.2	3.1	2.5	4.0	2.1
United States	(nd)	4.5	4.1	4.5	3.9	2.8	3.7	2.3
Japan	(nd)	(nd)	(nd)	2.4	2.5	2.2	9.4	3.8

Upswing and downswing phases of GDP growth (Average annual compound rates)

1 'Long-wave' chronology based on Mandel (1980), van Duijn (1983), Marshall (1986).
2 Growth phases chosen to correspond as closely as possible with long wave chronology and calculated from Maddison (1982, 1987); Dean and Cole (1962).

Keynes to Cambridge'.

Few would question the formative role that the present technological revolution is having, but the neo-Schumpeterian long-wave perspective affords only partial insight into the current transition. It fails to explain why a new 'technological system' is emerging, or why it has arisen in particular geographical areas, or to give sufficient attention to the factors shaping its diffusion to, and implications for, other regions. It also fails to take account of the wider international framework, the shifting patterns of international economic hegemony, within which phases of development take place. In addition, this approach has yet to recognize fully the importance that socio-institutional context plays in conditioning the emergence and development of a new technological system (Perez, 1986). A new technological paradigm will have characteristics that are likely to differ fundamentally from earlier dominant technologies, in terms of skill requirements, management strategies, firm structures, infrastructural investments, consumption norms, government policies and so forth. Only if the required restructuring of this socio-institutional environment occurs will a new coherence be established that permits the productivity and profitability gains of the new technologies to be realized.

A much greater emphasis on the role of the socio-institutional structure features in the various Marxist perspectives on long waves. In Mandel's (1978, 1980, 1984) 'asymmetric' theory, each of the four historical long waves has been associated with – in fact propelled by – a new and radically different type of technology, machine system and labour process (successively, craftsworker production, machine production, assembly-line production and continuous-flow production). Once a given labour process becomes established, for a while it generates a rising rate of profit and accelerating capital accumulation. But with increasing diffusion and 'vulgarization' of the new labour process throughout the economy, the endogenous 'laws of motion' of capitalism ultimately create problems of over-accumulation, above-average increases in the organic composition of capital and thence declining profit rates and a consequential slackening of capital accumulation: in short, the expansionary phase eventually itself generates the onset of the depressive downswing phase of the long wave. And as the downswing phase becomes entrenched, so there emerges a growing incentive for capitalists to search for a new technological and social organization of the labour process in order to restore profitability.

It is at this point that Mandel appeals to the crucial role of 'exogenous' social, institutional and political factors: whereas the upper turning-point is endogenously determined by the logic of the laws of accumulation, the lower turning-point, from stagnation to expansion, depends on the autonomous radical restructuring of the socio-political and geographical environment, for example: the erosion of trade-union power, the break-up of established skill divisions, the redrawing of class relations, and the overthrow of previously dominant political ideologies and state policies. The outcome of the depressive phase is therefore not predetermined, but

rich in historical contingency. The radical transformation of technology
and the labour process needed to induce a new expansionary economic
upswing is, however, dependent on the successful resolution (for capital)
of the social and political conflicts generated by this restructuring. According to Mandel this schema, suitably adjusted to take account of the
specific corporate, political and international developments of the post-war
period, explains the current upheaval in the advanced industrial societies,
both the slowdown after the early 1970s and the social and political
turmoil of the present decade as capital and national states strive to
achieve a new social, technological and spatial 'fix', to borrow Harvey's
(1982) terminology.

A new social structure of accumulation?

Among the many criticisms that can be levied at Mandel's long-wave
framework (see, for example, Maddison, 1982; Blackburn *et al.*, 1985;
Marshall, 1986), one stands out. In his attempt to assign key significance
to the socio-political matrix in shaping the rhythm and course of economic
development, Mandel may well have over-stated the degree of exogeneity
of social change and transformation. The contribution of Gordon and his
co-workers is of relevance here (Gordon, 1980; Gordon *et al.*, 1982). In
contrast to the neo-Schumpeterian and Mandelian version of long waves,
Gordon explains long-term cycles in economic development as outcomes
of life-cycles in what he calls the 'social structure of accumulation'.

This concept is based on a simple proposition: that the process of
capital accumulation and economic development cannot take place without
a stable and favourable social and political environment. This environment
constitutes the social structure of accumulation. It consists of all the
institutions and institutional arrangements, both general and specialized,
that impinge upon economic production, investment, consumption and
employment. Thus it embraces, for example, the money and credit
system, the form of state activity (the pattern of state spending, intervention and regulation), the nature and degree of labour organization, the
structure and rules of operation of labour and product markets, the social
and technical organization of labour processes and work practices, and
the accepted structures and conditions of those international institutions
that influence the organization and operation of the national economy.
Long swings in economic development are then seen as in large part the
product of the success or failure of successive social structures of accumulation in facilitating economic growth.

According to Gordon, a social structure of accumulation alternately
stimulates and constrains the pace of capital accumulation. A period of
expansion is built upon the construction and stabilization of a favourable
social structure of accumulation, which promotes investment and rapid
economic activity. After a certain lapse of time, however, this expansion

itself is likely to set off forces that undermine the institutional basis of the growth process: accumulation either runs up against limits imposed by the existing institutional structure or begins to destabilize that structure. In the first instance the institutions themselves produce the constraints; in the second the disruption of the institutions produces the constraints. In either case, continued rapid growth becomes increasingly problematic within the existing set of social and institutional arrangements and as a consequence accumulation slows. The problem is that social and institutional structures exhibit considerable inertia, and are likely to be reformed and reshaped only after a prolonged period of economic stagnation or during severe economic crisis. Only when a new institutional environment is constructed is the restoration of economic growth possible. The form that the new structure takes will be substantially influenced by the character of the social and political conflicts during the crisis phase, which in its turn will have emerged in part out of the inherent rigidities and latent constraints of the previous structure. Each new social structure of accumulation is virtually certain to differ in significant ways from its predecessor, thereby generating a succession of 'stages of capitalism'.

This framework contains a number of suggestive elements. In particular, the socio-political environment is allowed to play a much more endogenous role in determining the evolution of economic development. The result is not a new 'economic determinism' as Mandel (1980, pp. 51–2) has claimed; the importance of 'exogenous' factors and historical contingency is not denied. What is hypothesized is that there may be an internal dynamic to the social and institutional structure itself, a dynamic which impinges at first favourably and then unfavourably on capital accumulation. A given socio-institutional structure fostered by and functional for a specific pattern of accumulation is likely eventually to become a source of rigidity and hence dysfunctional for that economic system, precipitating instability or even crisis in the latter. Thus Gordon argues that the end of the post-war boom in the early 1970s was caused in part by the breakdown of the 'social accord' on which it was constructed. The forms of labour organization, wage determination, macroeconomic management, corporate organization, technical division of labour and international monetary regulation that had underpinned the boom after 1945 had, by the early 1970s, become subject to 'diminishing returns' and increasingly unworkable: the accord no longer provided the environment for a regime of continued, profitable accumulation.

A transition from Fordist to flexible accumulation?

In fact an increasingly prominent interpretation of the present conjuncture is that it represents a shift in 'accumulation regime', from the post-war 'Fordist' paradigm to a post-Fordist regime of 'flexible accumulation'. The concept of accumulation regime is taken from the theory of capitalist development advanced by the French 'regulation' school (for example,

Aglietta, 1979; Lorenzi *et al.* 1980; Boyer and Mistral, 1983), where the term is used to denote the structural characteristics of economic growth, especially the methods and organization of production (production norms) and the patterns of consumption demand (consumption norms). The respective roles of the various market mechanisms, institutions and customs that link production and consumption, and thereby ensure the reproduction of a given economic system, are designated the 'mode of regulation'. The essential elements of the latter are held to be the wage relationship (the sets of laws, customs and institutions that control the use of wage labour) and the system of monetary management. This while the mode of regulation clearly resembles Gordon's social structure of accumulation, it is perhaps less general in scope. According to the 'regulationists', the history of industrial capitalism has been one of a succession of accumulation regimes and their related modes of regulation, the change from one regime to the next being promoted by the exhaustion of the productivity possibilities of the existing form of labour mechanization. Such a productivity crisis highlights the limitations and constraints of the mode of regulation, and if productivity and growth cannot be revived within the parameters of the existing regulation system, then there will be pressure to experiment with new forms of productive and social organization, until a new accumulation regime and type of regulation are established.

The beginnings of the so-called Fordist regime of accumulation can be traced back to the early decades of this century when the features of monopoly and mass production first began to appear as new structural components of the economies of the United States, Britain and elsewhere. But is was not until after the Second World War that this regime became fully developed. Inevitably it has taken different specific forms and has proceeded to varying extents in different countries; however, these experiences all share a number of common elements. On the production side, Fordism involved the rise and diffusion of serially integrated production processes, from the assembly-line to continuous-flow, semi-automated forms of mechanization, incorporating highly prescribed tasks, a detailed division of labour and specialized, dedicated machinery, making very large batches of standardized products at very high levels of productivity (Aglietta, 1979; Blackburn *et al.*, 1985). To be economically viable this production system required on the consumption side the growth, social acceptance and maintenance of mass-consumption norms. Traditional production and consumption patterns continued alongside these developments, but decreased in relative importance as the mass-production paradigm became more generalized.

This 'Fordist' type of accumulation was regulated by the continuous growth of purchasing power brought about by rapidly increasing wages (permitted by rising productivity levels but also pushed upwards by the growth of strong unions), by state monetary and fiscal policies favouring the expansion and the maintenance of aggregated demand, and by the development of a supportive welfare system. Since the size of the domestic market presents a major limit to the development of mass production at the national level, this regime became associated with a progressive search for market opportunities on a world scale, with the proliferation of world trade and global capital flows and the creation of corresponding international regulatory mechanisms and institutions.

By the early 1970s, however, this structure of accumulation and regulation had begun to encounter several internal and external obstacles. The technical and social rigidities of mass production ('hard automation'), mounting problems of labour militancy and worker morale, and rising costs of production slowed down productivity growth and eroded competitiveness. As economic momentum declined and problems of excess capacity increased, so a major wave of deindustrialization and industrial rationalization began as one form of response to the crisis. Another was the internationalization of production as firms sought to regain Fordist production advantages by shifting capacity to cheap labour Third World countries. A third response was the unsuccessful attempt by western governments to manipulate a recovery, for example through wage controls, using the instruments of a Keynesian mode of economic regulation that clearly was fast being undermined by far-reaching changes in the economic and social structure on which it had been predicated.

It is within this breakdown of the Fordist regime that the beginnings of a new one seem to be stirring. Although in its nascency, the hallmark of this new regime – labelled 'neo-Fordism' by some (Blackburn *et al.*, 1985; Jaeger and Ernste, 1988) but 'flexible' accumulation by others (Piore and Sabel, 1984) – is flexibility: of production technologies, labour processes, products, labour markets and patterns of consumption. Within production, the focus of innovation is on flexible specialization and flexible integration, and on small-batch processing and product customizing – what some have called internal 'economies of scope' – shifts facilitated by the development of an array of computer-aided and computer-controlled design, tooling, machining and stock-handling systems, and the 'electronicization' of office machinery and information processing. This flexibilization of production, and the new forms of 'soft automation' on which it is based, are being paralleled by the de-rigidification and redrawing of skill boundaries and work practices, by new systems of labour utilization, management and organization, all of which carry major implications for the operation of labour markets. These developments are not confined to manufacturing. The new information technologies have already begun to transform existing service activities and to stimulate the growth of new ones, both producer and intermediate consumer services, as well as increasing the scope for their 'personalization'. On the consumption side, product differentiation, niche markets and quickly changing fashions are all being actively promoted by business and the advertising media, while consumption itself has been boosted by a dramatic explosion of credit and 'plastic money'. At the level of state regulation, the widespread decline of Keynesian demand management in favour of policies to improve the flexibility of the supply side of the economy, to enhance the adjustment of markets and to foster innovation and competition, signals a commensurate effort to de-rigidify the forms of state intervention previously built to support the Fordist regime and instead to promote the 'flexibilization' of the socio-economy.

Of the major interpretive frameworks that I have briefly reviewed here, the two concepts that would seem to me to offer the most useful framework for describing and explaining the current transition are those of accumulation regime and the socio-institutional structure of accumulation, and it is in these terms that I now turn to an examination of the British experience.

10.3   The re-organization of the British space-economy

During the late 1970s, in the midst of what Gardner (1987) calls the 'decade of discontent', a general atmosphere of anxiety surrounded the stagnation of the British economy, a disillusionment sufficient to evoke such prognoses as the 'British malaise' (Mackintosh, 1977), the 'British disease' (Allen, 1976), and even that of 'Britain dying' (Kramnick, 1975). All of these analyses seem to imply that the British economy had stopped growing, and that British society was becoming ungovernable. And perhaps with good cause: what had come to an end was a period of prosperity unparalleled in the country's history, a phase when economic growth had been higher even than during the mid-Victorian boom, when Britain enjoyed its world supremacy. Between the early 1950s and the early 1970s, labour productivity and real wages doubled or more than doubled. Such was the buoyancy of the economy that rapid growth, rising prosperity and full employment shielded society from the social costs and political tensions of the old 'problem' industries (shipbuilding, iron and steel, coal and heavy engineering) that had suffered structural decline during the inter-war crisis. In Britain, as in other major industrial countries, this unprecedented period of expansion and boom was founded on what was for a quarter-century a particularly favourable combination of accumulation regime and socio-institutional structure, both domestically and in the wider international arena.

The post-war expansionary regime

Some of the key characteristics of this regime and associated socio-institutional structure in Britain are summarized in Table 10.2. The post-war regime had its origins in the technological, economic and social

Table 10.2   The post-war expansionary regime, late 1940s to early 1970s

Characteristic	Key features
	Accumulation regime: monopolistic
Industry	Monopolistic; increasing concentration of capital; steady growth of output and productivity, especially in new consumer durable goods sectors; secular expansion of private and especially public services.
Employment	Full employment; growth of manufacturing jobs up to mid-1960s; progressive expansion of service employment; growth of female work; marked skill divisions of labour.
Consumption	Rise and spread of mass consumption norms for standardized household durables (especially electrical goods) and motor vehicles.
Production	Economies of scale; volume, mechanized (Fordist-type) production processes; functional decentralization and multinationalization of production.
	Socio-institutional structure: collectivistic
Labour market	Collectivistic; segmented by skill; increasingly institutionalized and unionized; spread of collective wage-bargaining; employment protection.
Social structure	Organized mainly by occupation, but tendency towards homogenization. Income distribution slowly convergent.
Politics	Closely aligned with occupation and organized labour; working-class politics important; regionalist.
State intervention	Keynesian-liberal collectivist; regulation of markets; maintenance of demand; expansion of welfare state; corporatist; nationalization of capital for the state.
Space-economy	Convergent; inherited regional sectoral specialization (both old and new industries) overlaid by new spatial division of labour based on functional decentralization and specialization: regional unemployment disparities relatively stable.

developments of the inter-war period. One of its leading features was the rise and spread of mass production and a progressive concentration of industrial capital into large monopolistic enterprises: between 1950 and 1970 the share of the largest 100 firms in manufacturing net output doubled to more than 40 per cent, while merger activity increased seven-fold (Hannah, 1976). The fastest rates of output growth were in the new industries of electrical engineering, vehicle manufacture, and chemicals and petroleum products. The spread of mass-consumption norms, rising incomes and the expansion of demand, both at home and abroad, for new, standardized, consumer goods, encouraged both the adoption of mass flow-line and sequential fabrication production methods – especially in industries such as motor vehicles, electrical household products and certain foodstuffs and clothing – and the growth of large and often multi-plant and multi-region firms capable of exploiting the economies of scale afforded by the growth of volume domestic and export markets. And alongside this expansion of manufacturing was a corresponding growth in the range and output of personal, business and public services.

The early 1950s marked the high point of Britain's role as a specialized 'workshop' economy: in those years the country ran a surplus on manufacturing trade equivalent to 10 per cent of GDP, a figure never equalled, before or since, in British history nor surpassed elsewhere. By 1970 this surplus had fallen by half, while the deficit on services (in excess of 10 per cent of GDP in 1950–52) had also been halved. These trends were mirrored in the movements of employment. From the late 1940s, the number of industrial jobs steadily increased to reach an all-time peak in 1966, and although numbers fell thereafter, this decline was more than offset up to the early 1970s by the growth of service employment, especially within the public sector. Throughout the period there was a progressive feminization of the employment structure, due particularly to the growth of women's jobs in the service industries but later also to the fall in men's jobs in manufacturing. There was also a recomposition of many of the latter, as the diffusion of more capital-intensive and mechanized methods of production eroded older craft occupations and created sharp divisions between narrowly defined skill groups.

The national socio-institutional structure that both underpinned and was moulded by this regime of economic growth was essentially collectivistic. The degree of organization and demarcation within the labour market increased steadily over the 1950s and 1960s, as did the membership and strength of the trades unions, and the incidence of industry-wide, collective wage-bargaining, all stimulated by tight labour market conditions and the growth of large industrial plants. Under these circumstances, and given its monopoly power, unionized labour extracted an increasing share of net output, a rising real wage that fed domestic consumption demand. Both the social-class divisions and the contours of political allegiance were organized mainly along occupational lines, although there was some homogenization of the social structure and a slow convergence of incomes. All this in turn was supported and regulated by an accomodative Keynes-Beveridge liberal-collectivistic form of state economic management and political legitimation (see Thompson, 1984), characterized by a commitment to full employment, the maintenance of aggregate demand and an extensive social welfare and education system, imperatives regarded by both of the major post-war political parties as emblematic of 'one-nation politics' (Martin, 1988a). It was also a form of state activity that supported and intervened in large sections of industry, either directly by means of nationalization and public ownership or indirectly through investment subsidies and location controls, and which accorded a political role to both sides of industry (capital and labour) in the formulation and implementation of economic policy.

The organization and development of the British space-economy under this economic and social system involved several elements. Under conditions of rapid growth and prosperity the 'regional problem', the pattern of uneven spatial development moulded during the inter-war crisis decades, based on the division between a sectorally specialized and industrially depressed northern and western periphery on the one hand, and a more economically diversified and dynamic Midlands and South East on the other, was considerably reduced: although the unemployment rate in the peripheral depressed regions remained twice that in the south and east, unemployment everywhere was at an unprecedently low level. There were, however, two important shifts in the regional distribution of industry and employment over the period. First, the Midlands and South East regions saw the continued growth of the new consumer and durable goods industries that formed the basis of the long post-war boom, and both areas increased their shares of national manufacturing employment; in fact by the mid-1960s the South East had emerged as the country's major geographical concentration of manufacturing industry. Reflecting their high output growth, both of these regions functioned as national wage-leaders, setting the pace of wage growth which was then diffused to remaining parts of the space-economy by union comparability bargaining along established intra- and inter-industry wage contours.

But, secondly, from the late 1950s onwards a partial spatial decentralization of manufacturing activity from the growth areas to the northern regions and from the major cities to suburban locations began, promoted in part by the government's redistributive regional policies, and in part by the search for cheaper labour and sites. This process contributed to the convergence of industrial structure across the regions, but simultaneously it generated a new functional spatial division of labour involving a relative geographical shift of lower-skilled final production and assembly activities to the north, while increasing the concentration of corporate headquarters, research and development, and similar high-order functions in the south (Massey, 1984). A further consequence was that certain areas in the northern regions became much more dependent on branch-plant activity, much of which was controlled from corporate head offices located in the southern half of the country. In combination, therefore, by the early 1970s these developments had added a new twist to the 'regional problem': it was no longer simply definable in terms of unemployment differentials, engrained though these still were; there were now also important new spatial inequalities in the range and quality of employment opportunities, and in the degree of potential vulnerability to external corporate strategy.

Processes of change and the crisis of the post-war regime

By the early 1970s it had become clear that this post-war regime was beginning to be undermined from within and without. Five intersecting processes or forces have combined over the past decade and a half to break up the social, economic and political structures of the post-war period, and have been spear-heading the formation of a new regime and socio-institutional structure of accumulation. The first of these is the wave of rapid and intense deindustrialization of the nation's manufacturing base that has destroyed nearly 3 million manufacturing jobs (a reduction of 36 per cent) since 1971. The second is the wave of technological innovation, based primarily on micro-electronics and information processing, that began in the early 1970s and which is generating a number of new industries and services while dramatically transforming the operation of existing ones. The third development has been the accelerating growth of the service sector, a new phase of tertiarization that has created some 3.3 million jobs since 1971, many of these in banking, insurance and finance. The fourth new development is political, and relates to the re-orientation and reconfiguration of government policy and state intervention away from the post-war Keynesian social democratic model. Fifthly, Britain's economic performance, industrial competitiveness and its position and role in the international economy and division of labour have been subject to fundamental pressures from changes in the global economy, including expanding competition from overseas, particularly Japan and the NICs in South East Asia, structural changes in international monetary relations and institutions, our membership of the European Community and the slow-down of western capitalism.

It should not just be thought, however, that these destabilizing disturbances to the post-war 'Fordist-collectivistic' regime are simply exogenous in character; for in part they have arisen from processes inherent in the post-war regime itself, from its organizational characteristics and its latent and emergent rigidities, In Britain, as in most other advanced industrial countries, the enormous output and labour productivity gains achieved by mass-production methods, aided by state-managed economic stability, the social accord between capital, labour and government, and the expansion of home and foreign markets, began to show distinct signs of exhaustion from the mid-1960s onwards, as the technical limits of such methods began to become apparent, as market saturation began to be encountered, and as growing problems of capital-labour conflict increasingly interrupted accumulation.

Thus, throughout the 1970s the combination of rising wage inflation, stagnating growth, falling profits and an increasing under-utilization of productive capacity fuelled a progressive process of deindustrialization, expressed in terms of a sustained shake-out of labour, rising unemployment, a rapidly declining manufacturing trade surplus and growing numbers of company bankruptcies. This crisis in turn soon exposed the latent shortcomings and rigidities of the Keynesian approach to state intervention. Reflecting its very origins and objectives, Keynesianism had one basic inherent limitation: as a method of short-run cyclical regulation of aggregate demand it neither took into account nor sought to influence the long-run structural development of the socio-economy. But the problem was precisely that by the early 1970s various structural developments in the post-war economy had dramatically reduced the power of Keynesian demand management to regulate accumulation and the conditions of mass production and mass consumption: one of the key components of the socio-institutional structure that had engendered the development of the Fordist or monopolistic regime of accumulation no longer appeared capable of maintaining that regime.

In retrospect it can be argued that the success of Keynesianism during the quarter-century after 1945 was historically specific, the product of a unique and particularly favourable set of national and international circumstances, and that it eventually became the victim of the very form of capitalist development it had helped to underwrite. It had led to a continually expanding state sector, and to a cumulative growth in public spending and debt; it had helped to foster the concentration and centralization of capital, and the corresponding organization and collectivization of labour; in other words, Keynesianism had fostered developments which made the joint tasks of managing economic growth and balancing class interests, of accumulation and legitimation, increasingly more difficult, and which encouraged the emergence of endemic inflation, a problem that it proved ill-equipped to control. In addition, of itself Keynesianism provided neither the stimulus nor the strategy for modernizing or restructuring the economy; if anything, by moderating the cyclical contractions of economic activity and by encouraging the formation of large structural units of labour and capital, it tended to reduce the impetus and restrict the scope for restructuring, encouraging economic and social inertia instead. By 1976 national financial bankruptcy looked imminent, and in line with its negotiations with the IMF the Labour government of the day was forced to concede that the case for Keynesian interventionism was no longer tenable. That disavowal marked the beginning of a far-reaching counter-revolution, the start of a fundamental shift towards a new, monetarist-based, less collectivistic form of state policy and political philosophy: by the close of the 1970s the life-cycle of Keynesian orthodoxy had reached its final stages, and with it many of the economic, social and spatial features of the post-war accumulation regime.

The emergent regime of flexible accumulation

It is out of the growing crisis of the old regime that the new, flexible regime of accumulation has been unfolding. There are several dimensions to this flexibilization of the bases of economic growth (Table 10.3). The first has been a new phase of deindustrialization of unprecedented intensity and generality. Over the past decade capital has been rationalized and 'slimmed down', enormous numbers of workers expelled, and work practices and arrangements restructured across almost every industrial sector in the quest to improve productive efficiency and competitiveness. In many cases this has been accompanied by an acceleration in the multinationalization and internationalization of production, and in predatory (hostile) takeovers, as firms have switched activity between locations and abroad in scarch of higher profits, lower costs and new markets (Cowling, 1986). All this is aimed at breaking old commitments, whether these be to productive capacity and methods, labour or locations, and at increasing the 'mobility' of capital in the widest sense of the word.

The second source of flexibility is technological innovation. The significance of the current technological revolution is threefold. One feature is its pace and pervasiveness: being based on the generation and transmission of information of all kinds and in various ways, its impact is not restricted to any one sector of the economy or sphere of social activity. Secondly, it is contributing to a dramatic shortening of product life-cycles, with profound implications for the responsiveness of investment and production. And, thirdly, the new technologies are beginning to play a pivotal role in transforming the modes of production, marketing and distribution within a growing number of existing industries and services, radically raising the flexibility and performance of their operation. Within manufacturing, although the economies of scale of production for mass markets remain important, the new methods of computer-controlled production, flexible machine systems and robotics are creating a new equipment and process technology (EPT) that is available equally to small and large enterprises, and which offers the possibility of changing products and product features quickly and efficiently. These post-Fordist developments in 'flexible factory automation' and 'flexible specialization' are beginning to make it possible to produce a broad range of differentiated, even quite distinct, products for different niches of domestic or global markets without sacrificing the scale economies that come from long production runs of standardized items (see Jaikumar, 1986; Valery, 1987). Though still in their infancy, flexible manufacturing, economies of scope – the ability of firms to produce varieties of customized products at low cost (Levitt, 1985) – and just-in-time (JIT) manufacturing and sourcing systems (Estall, 1985) seem certain to form increasingly important components of British corporate investment strategy.

Likewise, a trend towards greater flexibility of labour utilization is also under way (see Atkinson, 1984; Atkinson and Gregory, 1985; Morris, 1987). A re-division and re-segmentation of the workforce is taking place whereby, on the one hand, temporary, part-time, contracted self-employed and home-based workers are increasingly being used by manufacturing firms to provide them with numerical flexibility in their labour require-

Table 10.3 The emergent regime of flexible accumulation, mid-1970s onwards

Characteristic	Key features
	Accumulation regime: flexible
Industry	Rationalization and modernization of established sectors to restore profitability and improve competitiveness; growth of high-tech and producer service activities, and small firm sector.
Employment	Persistent mass unemployment; generalized contraction of manufacturing employment, growth of private service sector jobs; partial de-feminization (in manufacturing); flexibilization of labour utilization; large part-time and temporary segment.
Consumption	Increasingly differentiated (customized) consumption patterns for new goods (esp. electronics) and household services.
Production	Growing importance of economies of scope; use of post-Fordist flexible automation; small batch specialization; organizational fragmentation combined with internationalization of production.
	Socio-institutional structure: competitive-individualist
Labour market	Competitive; de-unionization and de-rigidification; increasing dualism between core and peripheral workers; less collective, more localized wage determination.
Social structure	Trichotomous and increasingly hierarchical; income distribution divergent.
Politics	De-alignment from socio-economic class; marked decline of working-class politics; rise of conservative individualism; localist.
State intervention	Keynesianism replaced by free-market Conservatism; monetary and supply-side intervention rather than demand stabilization; de-regulation of markets; constraints on welfare; self-help ideology; privatizing the state for capital.
Space-economy	Divergent; decline of industrial areas (pre- and post-war); rise of new high-tech and producer services complexes; increasingly polarized spatial division of labour; widening of regional and local unemployment disparities.

ments, as these vary with changing levels of output demand and changes in production methods. Including its counterpart in the service sector, where it is equally important, this segment of employment is growing faster than any other: it has increased by 16 per cent since 1981, and now accounts for more than a third of the total workforce. One quarter of men and half the women in work are in this 'peripheral' category (Leadbeater, 1987). In contrast to this segment is the group of permanently employed 'core' workers, many of whom are being required to have multiple and transferable skills, to be functionally flexible with respect to production tasks within the firm. In manufacturing this functional flexibility is bound up with the technological flexibilization of the production process and with the introduction of new systems of work organization, such as small teams and work cells, in place of the sequential flow-line arrangements and sharply defined skill hierarchies of the past.

The renewed expansion of the service sector, itself a major restructuring force, is another element of flexible accumulation. There is an important difference between the present phase of tertiarization and that which characterized the 1950s and 1960s. Unlike that earlier period, when the public services were an important area of growth, the current boom in service activity is based entirely in the private sector. Within the latter, business, financial, research and development, and professional services stand out as particularly buoyant. This can be traced to three developments: an increasing preference by manufacturing firms to externalize and buy in specialist business and research services rather than provide them in-house; the national and international boom in financial trading and international money markets; and the spread of new computerized methods of information processing and data handling, which are creating new niche-type, customer-tailored service activities and new service 'professionals' but also reducing the skill base and relative position of many other white-collar office and clerical workers.

This flexibilization of production, accumulation and service provision is both forging and being forged by corresponding changes in the socio-institutional structure, away from its predominantly collectivistic 'Fordist' form towards a more competitive-individualistic type of organization. The decline of the older basic industries and the post-war consumer durable goods sectors, all heavily unionized, and the shift of employment towards the less unionized service and high-tech industries, are resulting in a de-unionization of the labour market: union membership has declined by nearly 3 million (21 per cent) since the late 1970s, falling most rapidly in the industries and geographical areas traditionally most unionized, and growing but slowly if at all in the most dynamic and least unionized industries and areas of the country (Beaumont and Harris, 1988; Massey and Miles, 1984; Millward and Stevens, 1988). In conjunction with the 'discipline' of persistent mass unemployment, recent restrictive employment legislation, and the thrust of new technologies within production, this decline has considerably weakened the power and bargaining strength of organized labour, and is de-institutionalizing the wage-setting process and enabling employers to push through new, strike-free, single-union and 'Japanese-style' systems of industrial relations (Bassett, 1986). Furthermore, these different developments have become the cause of a growing split between different types of union and worker, particularly between those attached to older, declining industries and occupations, and those associated with newer industries and more technical and professional jobs. As Jane Jacobs astutely observed several years ago, at a time of creative destruction and economic transformation the primary conflict is perhaps not so much between capital and labour, as 'between people whose interests are with already-established economic activities, and those whose interests are with the emergence of new economic activities' (Jacobs, 1969, pp. 248–9).

These changes are themselves part of a wider reconfiguration of the social and class structure. In addition to the major divide that has now endured for almost a decade between the employed and the unemployed, there is a growing trichotomization of society (Therborn, 1986) into: a wealthy, securely employed, professional, technical and managerial upper tier with rapidly rising incomes; a middle segment of reasonably well-paid, stably employed workers, increasingly divided according to enterprise, sector and hierarchical position; and a bottom layer or 'under-class' of marginalized, low-paid workers and the unemployed. As a result, the income distribution has widened sharply, with a growing differential between the upper and lower pay groups. At the same time, the rapid rundown of traditional industries, occupations and jobs, and the break-up of the mass industrial cultures of the post-war period on the one hand, and the rise of new technical and service classes, with different values and attitudes, a different sense of community, and different ideological viewpoints on the other, are dramatically redefining the contours of social and political differentiation. Above all, there has been a major re-alignment of popular politics away from the social democratic consensus of the post-war period around a new politics that is much more conservative-individualistic and less committed to collectivism and extensive statism.

As articulated by the Thatcher governments since 1979, this political shift has become a programme for restructuring Britian, economically, socially, spatially and ideologically, around a new consensus of 'free market individualism'. The thrust of state policy has shifted from welfare to enterprise. The aim has been to reverse the post-war drift towards collectivism and creeping corporatism, to redefine the role and extent of state intervention in the economy, to curb the power of organized labour, and to release the 'natural, self-regenerative' power of competitive market forces in order to revive private capitalism, economic growth and accumulation. Gone is the Keynesian commitment to the macroeconomic goal of full employment and microeconomic policies to control wages, to be replaced by a new macro-level objective of controlling inflation by means of restrictive monetary measures and a new microeconomics of supply-side flexibilization. The aim has been to purge the economy of the endemic inflation of the 1970s and to promote a fundamental restructuring of industry, work practices and social attitudes.

From its inception, 'Thatcherism' has been a doctrine for remodernizing Britain's economy by exposing its industries, its people and its regions to the rigours of international competition. This, it was hoped, would help to promote the shift of resources out of traditional and inefficient industries and processes into new, more flexible, more competitive, high-technology sectors, production methods and work practices (Martin, 1986). The main foci of the government's own economic intervention have been the privatization and rationalization of the post-war nationalized and public industries (which are believed to be 'immunized from the process of spontaneous change that competition and fear of bankruptcy imposes on the private sector'), the deregulation of labour and money markets, the reduction of taxes, and the promotion of innovative small firms ('the heart of the enterpirse spirit'). On the social front the government has been no less anxious to achieve a major 'cultural revolution' consistent with the pursuit of a free enterprise economy: to instil the virtues of self-reliance, individualism, wealth creation, financial independence, property ownership and entrepreneurship; a new consensus of 'popular capitalism'. Thus, as such, this new 'enterprise politics' has deliberately sought to wrest British society away from the economic, industrial and social structures of the 'Fordist' regime, towards a new fabric conducive for and generative of 'flexible' accumulation (Jessop *et al.*, 1987). Of course, this objectives and the policies employed to secure it, are not without their contradictions and costs; nor have they gone uncontested. But while this agenda is far from finished, it is now widely acknowledged that the changes in policy and ideology that have taken place since 1979 have already so influenced business and public attitudes towards economic activity and state intervention that a return to the methods and policies of the old Keynesian-collectivistic model is most unlikely, even after the specific phenomenon of 'Thatcherism' itself has passed.

The geography of flexible accumulation

Whereas the development of the post-war space-economy up to the early 1970s was generally convergent, since then and especially during the 1980s it has been markedly divergent. The pattern of uneven development has been one of increasing spatial division, at a variety of geographical scales. To a large extent these divergent geographies and widening spatial inequalities reflect the different roles of different areas and localities in the old and emergent regimes of accumulation, and their differential capacity to adjust to this shift of regime and to the changing international division of labour of which it is a part. No area of Britain is immune from the pressures and imperatives of the economic and social flexibilization that is in train. But the specific form and implications of the process clearly differ in significant ways between different social groups and geographical areas.

Certain groups, such as unskilled and conventionally skilled workers, the unions, inner-city residents, public sector employees, and labour in old line industries and regions have borne the main disruptive effects and costs of adjustment, as measured by extensive job losses, mass unemployment and slow wage growth. On the other hand, the highly skilled, technical, professional, scientific and private sector white-collar groups, those working in high-technology activities, business and producer services, and high-earning residents in southern parts of the country, have been the chief beneficiaries, faring considerably better as regards earnings growth, job opportunities and wealth accumulation. At a broad spatial level, these unequal experiences of economic transition have mapped out a widening divide between the 'north' and 'south' of Britain (Martin, 1988a)[1]. There is a clear inverse relationship between deindustrialization and tertiarization: those regions that have suffered most from the decline of manufacturing employment have gained least from the expansion of jobs within the private service sector (Figure 10.1). While virtually no part of the country has escaped the pressures on the manufacturing sector, deindustrialization has been overwhelmingly concentrated in the north and west of Britian, not only in those regions with a long-established industrial base and long history of structural weaknesses, extensive labour organization and productive rigidities, namely the North, south Wales, central Scotland and all of the old industrial conurbations, but equally in what had been prosperous manufacturing regions during the post-war 'Fordist' regime, that is the West Midlands, the North West and Yorkshire-Humberside (Martin and Rowthorn, 1986).

Figure 10.1 Mapping Britain's economic transition

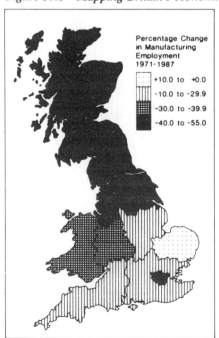 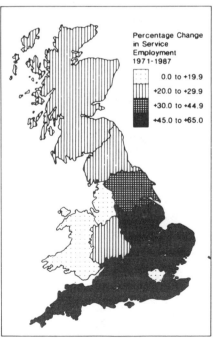

(a) The geography of deindustrialization   *(b) The geography of tertiarization*

Source: Department of Employment

In contrast, those regions that were less industrialized, more diversified economically or which had come to contain a high proportion of corporate headquarters, have suffered a much less intense and thereby less disruptive process of industrial decline and restructuring. For example, between 1979 and 1986 three-quarters of the job losses associated with deindustrialization have been concentrated in the 'north', but the 'south' has received more than two-thirds of the 860 000 new jobs in services. Thus the South East (with the important exception of parts of the Greater London subregion), the South West and East Anglia regions, being less dependent on and therefore relatively unburdened by the inflexibilities of historically mature and heavily unionized industries, have proved not only somewhat less vulnerable to deindustrialization, but by the same token more favourably placed to lead the new regime of development. The existence of a more diverse, more flexible and more technical labour force has been one crucial factor in accounting for the south's new growth advantage. Another has been the long-established concentration of corporate, financial and political power in the South East, and of course London particularly, a dominance of key importance in articulating and shaping the present economic transition of Britain. London and its surrounding region monopolizes the national banking, insurance, business consultancy and financial markets, all functions that are not only sources of high growth in their own right but also sectors that are exerting considerable influence on the creation, expansion and geographical distribution of new economic activity and employment more generally. A third structural advantage in the south has been the highly favourable nexus of private and government research establishments and defence-related industry, some of the origins of which can be traced back to early developments dating from the inter-war years, and around which the current wave of technological innovation and enterprise has clustered.

Given these favourable characteristics, it is not too surprising that the South East region now contains the largest single geographical concentration of the country's leading industries and services (see Table 10.4). This specialization in high technology and producer services helps to explain the south's better relative economic performance over the past decade. It also accounts for the distinctly higher levels of per capita gross domestic product in the South East, and the increasing agglomeration of high-earning technical, professional and managerial groups in the region (see Table 10.5).

It has been in the south of Britain, therefore, the South East especially, but also the South West, East Anglia and to some extent the East Midlands, that the new 'enterprise politics' prosecuted by the Thatcher governments has struck its most receptive chord. Since the mid-1970s the widening of the regional socio-economic divide has been accompanied by an increased spatial polarization of political support. While de-industrialization and social restructuring have reduced the size of the traditional working class and allegiance to social democratic values, and have there-

Table 10.4 Regional distribution of some leading industries and services, Great Britain, 1984

Region	Percentage share of GB employment		
	Manufacturing sectors[1]	Producer services[2]	Research and development
South East	41.1	49.3	54.9
East Anglia	2.5	2.7	7.1
South West	9.3	7.0	7.2
East Midlands	5.8	4.3	4.3
West Midlands	10.7	7.6	4.6
Yorkshire and Humberside	2.8	5.9	2.2
North West	11.8	9.2	7.0
North	2.7	3.4	3.0
Wales	3.8	2.8	1.7
Scotland	7.7	7.3	7.2

[1]Office machinery, data processing equipment, electrical and electronic engineering, aerospace equipment, instrument engineering.
[2]Banking, finance, insurance and business services.
Source: Department of Employment

Table 10.5 Aspects of the new spatial division of labour, by socio-economic class, Great Britain, 1981

Region	Relative to Great Britain average			
	Share of regional total employment		Share of regional manufacturing employment	
	Professional & managerial	Unskilled & semi-skilled manual	Professional & managerial	Unskilled & semi-skilled manual
Outer South East	124	84	141	80
Greater London	110	87	119	87
South West	101	104	101	104
East Anglia	104	94	107	91
East Midlands	91	105	92	102
West Midlands	92	109	90	106
Yorkshire and Humberside	88	111	84	111
North West	92	110	88	112
North	79	116	72	108
Wales	89	107	74	118
Scotland	86	110	78	105

Source: Census of Population, 1981

fore helped to underpin a national shift to the political right, the net effect spatially has been the steady retreat of the Labour vote back to its historical heartlands in the industrial-urban north and to its shrinking secondary socio-spatial bases in the conurbations of London and the West Midlands. By contrast, fuelled by its leading role in the new regime of accumulation, the south of Britain has become the primary stronghold of the new politics of competitive individualism and 'popular capitalism'.

Hence thus far, for much of northern and urban Britain, the transition to a new regime of flexible accumulation has been overwhelmingly synonymous with efficiency-orientated industrial rationalization and reorganization, and with the large-scale loss of jobs and skills. Since 1979 total employment has fallen by almost a million jobs in the 'north' of Britain (Scotland, the North, North West, Yorkshire–Humberside, West Midlands and Wales). In the 'south' (South East, East Anglia, South West and East Midlands) flexibilization has meant much more than expansionary creation of new sources of economic accumulation and new jobs: in this part of the country total employment has increased by more than half a million since 1979. But while this broad divide between the 'two Britains' is unquestionably the main dimension in the present geography of socio-economic inequality across the country (Martin, 1988a), the transition to a new regime has simultaneously opened up stark contrasts at the local level (Champion and Green, 1988; Cooke, 1986; Massey, 1988).

There are several areas in the 'south' with problems of economic decline and unemployment comparable to any of those found in the most depressed northern localities. Equally, within the 'north' there are numerous localities where industrial renewal, high-technology development and expansion of provincial financial centres and consumer services (including new, giant shopping complexes) are forming the basis of an economic renaissance. The fact is that both the dynamic 'south' and the less prosperous 'north' have acquired their own internal social and spatial divides. Like regional differentials, inter- and even intra-locality inequalities have widened dramatically as a result of the contemporary restructuring process. There are now sharp divisions between 'newly industrializing' rural zones and economically stagnant urban areas; between buoyant service-based localities and depressed manufacturing towns; between the deprived and unemployed population entrapped in the inner cities and an increasingly affluent, securely employed and succesful new middle class living in suburbia or in 'gentrified' and 'yuppified' metropolitan areas; between those working in the high-paid, high-tech jobs and those in peripheral occupations and low-paid service employment. It is in terms of these local disparities, which can be found right across the country, that the uneven impact of destabilization and restructuring caused by economic transition is being most keenly felt, and where the challenge of adjustment has stimulated a host of new policy innovations, a new 'economic localism', and a corresponding debate over the form that this policy localism should take (Martin, 1988b).

10.4   The renewal of Britain?

What I have tried to argue in this chapter is that Britain, in common with other advanced industrial nations, is passing over another historical divide, another *fin de siècle*, which can best be interpreted as a transition to a new accumulation regime and new associated socio-institutional structure of accumulation. The compelling imperative driving this transition, within both the private and public domains of the socio-economy, is the renewal of the conditions of economic growth, of prosperity and employment. At one level all the signs suggest that a new phase of expansionary development is now established. Since 1981 Britain's economy has experienced a sustained average growth in total output of 3 per cent per annum (4 per cent in manufacturing), a rate comparable to that of the post-war boom and well above that achieved by any other European country during the 1980s. After their stagnation in the 1970s, and dramatic collapse between 1979 and 1981, manufacturing output, productivity and profitability have now recovered to pre-1973 levels. There has been a huge accretion of overseas investments, the public sector borrowing requirement has been turned into surplus, inflation has been reduced to its lowest since the 1960s, and for a majority of the population the real standard of living has improved considerably.

But the form and the distribution of this growth are different from the post-war boom. National prosperity is now sustained far less by manufacturing and increasingly by service and financial activity. Many of the social groups and geographical areas that dominated the previous accumulation regime have now lost economic and political power to a different set of social groups and areas that are at the forefront of the new regime. Above all, we seem to have entered a phase of accumulation that demands considerable economic, institutional and social flexibility, a mode of growth that requires the rapid rundown and elimination of uncompetitive industries, jobs and skills, a continual redirection of economic and human resources, a considerable shift of power from labour back to capital, and the prioritization of economic efficiency above social equity. Certainly thus far the consequence of this type of renewal seems to be the sharpening of social and spatial inequalities.

Note

1   In what follows, Northern Ireland is excluded from the discussion because of incomplete data comparable to those available for the UK Standard Regions. Other related data indicate only too clearly, however, that in terms of many socio-economic characteristics Northern Ireland is the most depressed part of the United Kingdom, and is thus a major component of the 'northern' half of the divide.

References

AGLIETTA, M. (1979) *A Theory of Capitalist Regulation*, New Left Books, London (Revised edition: Paris, Calmann Levy, 1982).

ALLEN, G. C. (1976) *The British Disease: A Short Essay on the Nature and Causes of the Nation's Lagging Wealth*, London, Institute of Economic Affairs.

ATKINSON, J. (1984) *Flexibility, Uncertainty and Manpower Management*, Report, Brighton, Institute of Manpower Studies, University of Sussex.

ATKINSON, J. and GREGORY, D. (1985) 'A flexible future: Britain's dual labour force', *Marxism Today*, April.

AYDALOT, P. and KEEBLE, D. E. (eds) (1988) *High Technology Industry and Innovative Environments: The European Experience*, London, Routledge and Kegan Paul.

BASSETT, P. (1986) *Strike Free: New Industrial Relations in Britain*, London and Basingstoke, Macmillan.

BEAUMONT, P. B. and HARRIS, R. I. D. (1988) 'The north-south divide in Britain: the case of union recognition', (mimeo.), Department of Economics, Queens University of Belfast.

BEENSTOCK, M. (1983) *The World Economy in Transition*, London, George Allen and Unwin.

BLACKBURN, P., COOMBS, R. and GREEN, K. (1985) *Technology, Economic Growth and the Labour Process*, London and Basingstoke, Macmillan.

BLUESTONE, B. and HARRISON, B. (1982) *The De-industrialisation of America*, New York, Basic Books.

BOWLES, S. and GINTIS, H. (1982) 'The crisis of liberal democratic capitalism', *Politics and Society*, Vol. 11, No. 1.

BOYER, R. and MISTRAL, J. (1983) *Accumulation, Inflation, Crises*, Paris, Presses Universitaires de France.

BRADBURY, M. (1985) 'Regional and industrial restructuring processes in the New International Division of Labour', *Progress in Human Geography*, Vol. 9, No. 1.

CASTELLS, M. (ed.) (1985) *High Technology, Space and Society*, London and Beverly Hills, Sage Publications.

CHAMPION, T. and GREEN, A. (1988) 'Local prosperity and the north-south divide: winners and losers in 1980s' Britain', Report, Institute of Employment Research, University of Warwick.

COOKE, P. (1986) 'The changing urban and regional system in the United Kingdom', *Regional Studies*, Vol. 20, No. 3.

COOKE, P. (1987) 'Britain's new spatial paradigm: technology, locality and society in transition', *Environment and Planning A*, Vol. 19, No. 1.

COWLING, K. (1986) 'The internationalisation of production and deindustrialisation', in Amin, A. and Goddard, J. B. (eds) *Technological Change, Industrial Restructuring and Regional Development*, London, George Allen and Unwin.

DEAN, P. and COLE, W. A. (1962) *British Economic Growth, 1688–1959*, Cambridge, Cambridge University Press.

ESTALL, R. C. (1985) 'Stock control in manufacturing: the just-in-time system and its locational implications', *Area*, Vol. 17, No. 2.

FREEMAN, C. (ed.) (1984) *Long Waves in the World Economy*, London, Frances Pinter.

FREEMAN, C. (1986) 'The role of technical change in national economic development', in Amin, A. and Goddard, J. B. (eds) *Technological Change, Industrial Restructuring and Regional Development*, London, George Allen and Unwin.

FROBEL, F., HEINRICHS, J. and KREYE, O. (1980) *The New International Division of Labour*, Cambridge, Cambridge University Press.

GAMBLE, A. (1981) *Britain in Decline*, London and Basingstoke, Macmillan.

GAMBLE, A. (1988) *Free Economy, Strong State*, London, New Left Books.

GARDNER, N. (1987) *Decade of Discontent: The Changing British Economy Since 1973*, Oxford, Basil Blackwell.

GORDON, D. M. (1980) 'Stages of accumulation and long economic cycles', in Hopkins, T. and Wallerstein, I. (eds) *Processes of the World System*, London and Beverly Hills, Sage Publications.

GORDON, D. M., EDWARDS, R. and REICH, M. (1982) *Segmented Work, Divided Workers: The Historical Transformation of Labour in the United States*, Cambridge, Cambridge University Press.

HALL, P. (1981) 'The geography of the fifth Kondratieff cycle', *New Society*, 26 March.

HALL, P. (1985) 'The geography of the fifth Kondratieff', in Hall, P. and Markusen, A. (eds) *Silicon Landscapes*, London, George Allen and Unwin. (Reprinted as Chapter 2 in this volume.)

HALL, P., BREHENY, M., MCQUAID, R. and HART, D. (1987) *Western Sunrise: The Genesis and Growth of Britain's Major High Tech Corridor*, London, George Allen and Unwin.

HANNAH, L. (1976) *The Rise of the Corporate Economy*, London, Methuen.

HARVEY, D. (1982) *The Limits to Capital*, Oxford, Basil Blackwell.

HARVEY, D. (1985) *The Urbanisation of Capital*, Oxford, Basil Blackwell.

HARVEY, D. (1987) 'Flexible accumulation through urbanisation: reflections on "post-modernism" in the American city', *Antipode*, Vol. 19, No. 3.

HARVEY, D. (1988) 'The geographical and geopolitical consequences of the transition from Fordist to flexible accumulation', forthcoming in Sternlieb, G. (ed.) *The New American Economic Geography*, Rutgers, Rutgers University Press.

JACOBS, J. (1969) *The Economy of Cities*, New York, Random House.

JAEGER, C. and ERNSTE, H. (1988) 'Europe: a way beyond Fordism?', (mimeo.), Department of Geography, Zurich, Swiss Federal Institute of Technology.

JAIKUMAR, R. (1986) 'Post-industrial manufacturing', *Harvard Business Review*, November–December.

JESSOP, B., BONNETT, K., BROMLEY, S. and LING, T. (1987) 'Popular capitalism, flexible accumulation and Left strategy', *New Left Review*, Vol. 16, No. 5, September–October.

KONDRATIEV, N. (1935) 'The long waves in economic life', *Review of Economic Statistics*, Vol. 17, No. 6.

KRAMNICK, I. (1975) *Is Britain Dying?*, Ithaca, NY, Cornell University Press.

LASH, S. and URRY, J. (1987) *The End of Organised Capitalism*, Cambridge, Polity Press.

LEADBEATER, C. (1987) 'In the land of the dispossessed', *Marxism Today*, April.

LEVITT, T. (1985) 'The globalisation of markets', in Kantrow, A. M. (ed.) *Sunrise . . . Sunset: Challenging the Myth of Industrial Obsolescence*, New York, Wiley.

LORENZI, J. H., PASTRE, O. and TOLEDANO, J. (1980) *La Crise du 20e Siècle*, Paris, La Decouverte.

MACKINTOSH, J. P. (1977) *The British Malaise: Political or Economic?*, Southampton, University of Southampton Press.

MADDISON, A. (1982) *Phases of Capitalist Development*, London, Oxford University Press.

MADDISON, A. (1987) 'Growth and slowdown in advanced capitalist countries: techniques of quantitative assessment', *Journal of Economic Literature*, Vol. XXV.

MANDEL, E. (1978) *The Second Slump*, London, New Left Books.

MANDEL, E. (1980) *Long Waves of Capitalist Development*, Cambridge, Cambridge University Press.

MANDEL, E. (1984) 'Explaining long waves of capitalist development', in Freeman, C. (ed.) *Long Waves in the World Economy*, London, Frances Pinter.

MARKUSEN, A., HALL. P. and GLASMEIER, A. (1986) *High Tech America: The What, How, Where and Why of the Sunrise Industries*, Boston, George, Allen and Unwin.

MARSHALL, M. (1986) *Long Waves of Regional Development*, London and Basingstoke, Macmillan.

MARTIN, R. L. (1986) 'Thatcherism and Britain's industrial landscape', in Martin, R. L. and Rowthorn, B. (eds).

MARTIN, R. L. (1988a) 'The political economy of Britain's north-south divide', *Transactions of the Insitute of British Geographers*, Vol. 13, No. 4. (Reprinted in Townsend, A. R. and Lewis, J. (eds) *North Versus South: Industrial and Social Change in Britain*, London, Paul Chapman.)

MARTIN, R. L. (1988b) 'The new economics and politics of regional restructuring: the British case', in Albrechts, L., Moulaert, F., Roberts, P. and Swyngedouw, E. (eds) *Regional Planning at the Cross-Roads*, Newcastle, Roger Booth.

MARTIN, R. L. and ROWTHORN, B. (eds) (1986) *The Geography of De-Industrialisation*, London and Basingstoke, Macmillan.

MASSEY, D. (1984) *Spatial Divisions of Labour: Social Structures and the Geography of Production*, London and Basingstoke, Macmillan.

MASSEY, D. (1988) 'A new class of geography', *Marxism Today*, May.

MASSEY, D. and MILES, N. (1984) 'Mapping out the unions', *Marxism Today*, May.

MATTHEWS, R. C. O. (ed.) (1982) *Slower Growth in the Western World*, London, Heinemann.

MATTHEWS, R. C. O., FEINSTEIN, C. H. and ODLING-SMEE, J. C. (1982) *British Economic Growth 1856–1973*, Oxford, Clarendon Press.

MILLWARD, N. and STEVENS, M. (1988) 'Union density in the regions', *Employment Gazette*, May.

MORRIS, J. (1987) 'New technologies, flexible work practices and regional socio-spatial differentiation: some observations from the UK', (mimeo.), Cardiff Business School, University of Wales Institute of Science and Technology.

MOULAERT, F., SWYNGEDOUW, E. and WILSON, P. (1987) 'The geography of Fordist and post-Fordist accumulation and regulation', in Association de Science Regionale de Langue Française, *Coloque International Espace et Périphérie*, Lisbon, LNEC.

NELL, E. J. (ed.) (1984) *Free Market Conservatism: A Critique of Theory and Practice*, London, George Allen and Unwin.

NEWBY, H., BUJRA, J., LITTLEWOOD, P., REES, G. and REES, T. L. (eds) (1985) *Restructuring Capital: Recession and Reorganisation in Industrial Society*, London and Basingstoke, Macmillan.

OFFE, C. (1984) *Contradictions of the Welfare State*, London, Hutchinson.

OFFE, C. (1985) *Disorganised Capitalism*, Cambridge, Polity Press.

O'KEEFE, P. (1984) *Regional Restructuring Under Advanced Capitalism*, London, Croom Helm.

PEET, R. (1983) 'The global geography of contemporary capitalism', *Economic Geography*, Vol. 59.

PEET, R. (ed.) (1987) *International Capitalism and Industrial Restructuring*, London, George Allen and Unwin.

PEREZ, C. (1986) 'Structural changes and assimilation of new technologies in the economic and social system', in Freeman, C. (ed.) *Design, Innovation and Long Cycles in Economic Development*, London, Frances Pinter.

PIORE, M. and SABEL, C. (1984) *The Second Industrial Divide: Possibilities for Prosperity*, New York, Basic Books.

REES, G. and LAMBERT, P. (1985) *Cities in Crisis*, London, Edward Arnold.

SAUNDERS, C. (ed.) (1981) *The Political Economy of New and Old Industrialised Countries*, London, Butterworth.

SAWYERS, L. and TABB, W. K. (eds) (1984) *Sunbelt-Snowbelt: Urban Development and Regional Restructuring*, New York, Oxford University Press.

SCHUMPETER, J. (1939) *Business Cycles: A Theoretical, Historical and Statistical Analysis of the Capitalist Process*, Maidenhead, McGraw-Hill.

SMITH, M. P. and FEAGIN, J. R. (eds) (1988) *The Capitalist City*, Oxford, Basil Blackwell.

SUMMERS, G. (ed.) (1984) *De-industrialisation: Restructuring the Economy*, London and Beverly Hills, Sage Publications.

THERBORN, G. (1986) *Why Some Peoples Are More Unemployed Than Others: The Strange Paradox of Growth and Unemployment*, London, Verso.

THOMPSON, G. (1984) 'Economic intervention in the post-war economy', in McLennan, G., Held, D. and Hall, S. (eds) *State and Society in Contemporary Britain*, Cambridge, Polity Press.

VALERY, N. (1987) 'The factory of the future', *The Economist* (Special Survey), May–June.

11 Spatial development processes: organized or disorganized?

Philip Cooke

11.1 Introduction

If the 1960s were characterized by relatively stable patterns of economic development, broadening of welfare state services and political settlement between the contending class organizations, the 1980s are indisputably characterized by their reverse. Not only has development, as measured by output and employment indices, slowed, it has declined absolutely and relatively in some advanced economies such as the UK, declined absolutely in many less-developed countries such as Mexico, Chile or Tunisia, yet continued to rise at an accelerating pace in newly industrializing countries [NICs] such as South Korea, Singapore and Taiwan (Belassa, 1984). Welfare spending is in retreat under monetarist hegemony in the advanced countries as structural crisis imposes limits upon growth (Offe, 1984a). And to the extent that there really was a definable class settlement in the post-war UK, USA and continental European countries, this has either broken down completely, as in Thatcher's Britain, or received severe though perhaps, as yet, not debilitating shocks in certain northern European countries. To employ the language of a long-established Germanic analytical tradition, the 1960s probably marked the high water mark of 'Organized Capitalism' while the 1980s signify the onset of 'Disorganized Capitalism' (Urry, 1985b; Offe, 1984b; Urry and Lash, 1986).

While there are important questions to be raised about the validity of broad-sweep, long-range theorizations such as these, which despite their conceptual superiority to such theories as 'Industrial Society' and 'Post-Industrial Society' nevertheless share their time-scale, and may well run the risk of appearing somewhat archaic shortly after coming to fruition (Giddens, 1979), it is clear that some rather dramatic changes in the pace and direction of economic and social change have occurred over the past two decades. Many of these are picked up by theorists of the 'Disorganized Capitalism' school [. . .]

11.2 Organized and disorganized capitalism

The clearest statement of the distinctions between these two forms of capitalism is presented by Urry (1985b). In terms of time-scale, the organized phase begins in the late nineteenth century with the ending of the Long Depression that occurred in the developed economies of that time. The pace and scale of organization varied from country to country but all had in common the following features. Industrial and financial capital concentrated, centralized and became more bureaucratized. A scientific stratum grew to service capital; employers and trade unions organized collectively and exerted pressure on the state, which itself grew and promoted national interests rigorously both internally and externally, especially in the form of imperialism.

In spatial terms, concentration produced distinctive spatial divisions of labour, regions tended to be sector-specific with extractive and heavy industries predominant amongst those that were most organized. Regional economies were labour-intensive and supported large industrial cities which served them financially and commercially. Collective organizations of capital and labour were themselves regionally organized and regions tended to form direct trading links with markets overseas, especially colonial ones [. . .] Regional representation within national politics was strong and distinctive.

The 'disorganized capitalism' thesis is that these structures had been transformed in the advanced economies by the period between the mid-1960s and early 1980s [. . .] [T]he general and spatial features of this phase are as follows. Concentration and centralization have transcended national boundaries as the world economy has grown. White-collar work, especially that of the scientific/professional stratum has exploded whereas traditional blue-collar occupations have been eroded through a combination of deindustrialization and automation. Corporatist forms of interest mediation have become vulnerable or have broken down at the level of the nation-state; increasingly wage-bargaining is becoming localized. Multinational firms are no longer easily regulated by the state, and have 'capitalized' the Third World, a process involving the 'decapitalization' of manufacturing in the advanced world. Class politics are in decline and are being augmented by internationalist social movements pursuing issue-based political goals.

Spatial change involves the removal of regional economic distinctiveness and a greater reliance everywhere on service-dominated labour markets. Plant sizes have peaked in employment terms and there have been sizeable shifts of productive output and employment from metropolitan to small urban and rural locations. Population density decline in cities is associated with a decline in their tax-base combined with a failure by the state to take a leading role in the replacement of fixed investment in the urban fabric (the inner-city problem). Much of the labour-intensive employment base of cities and older regions has either disappeared permanently or been exported to low labour-cost countries now participating in the 'new international division of labour'.

Disorganization derives from the breakdown of old modes of state regulation of the economy, the openness of world trade in credit and commodities and the global scope and development of multinational enterprise. Moreover, this has coincided with a profound restructuring of the world economy consequent upon the long period of economic crisis experienced in the west with the ending of the post-war boom in the late 1960s/early 1970s. In most western societies the spread of the state's involvement in economic and everyday life has been turned back; there is a profound disaffection with the capacity of the state to remedy market-failure and a widespread ideology to the effect that state intervention and expenditure are responsible for the inflationary surge which weakened the western economies in the 1960s and 1970s. The leading economic philosophy of the moment rests on the injunction that salvation relies on a return to market principles and a weakening of the social-democratic faith in planning.

There are two criticisms that can be advanced of these formulations. The first concerns the characterization of the 'organized' phase as being ineluctably one in which capital concentration and centralization predominated. Clearly, it would be foolish to argue that this did not occur but it is far from being a ubiquitous tendency. In some advanced economies such as Italy and France but not Germany the domestic market for mass-produced goods remained small, and in most, mass production was closely tied to export markets. The rest of production was often the province of small and medium, non-corporate organization. Moreover state regulation was not as pronounced as is implied by the 'organized capitalism' thesis because of economically liberal regimes, and the political weight of small agricultural interests and of small-scale capital. Furthermore, the impact of organized labour upon capital or the state, outside a few concentrated industries should not be overstated – the regionalized system of labour organization in France and [the USA], but, again, not Germany, for example, reduced labour's perception of the need to organize industrially or represent its interests through the state. This is not to say that 'organized' characteristics did not emerge, at some points, notably during and after the interwar Great Depression and in France and Italy after the war, but that they were by no means permanent features of the economic order (Piore and Sabel, 1984).

This tension between the leading edge of concentrated mass production, tied often to a centralized finance system and the rather overshadowed, but nevertheless important, smaller, craft-led sector of industry and localized services had spatial connotations too. New regional mixtures arose in areas where extractive and heavy industry had yet to make inroads, such as the West Midlands for motor vehicles and electrical engineering or outer London for vehicles and domestic appliances in Britain; Paris and Bavaria for the same new industries in France and Germany; and the Mid West and California in the USA. However, the individual companies responsible for production in such sectors did not concentrate at the same rate even in single countries – the contrast between Ford and GM being a vivid illustration – and in Europe, where the 'GM path of amalgamation' predominated, full concentration was not achieved in some cases until the end of the 'organized capitalist' phase in the late 1960s. By then, many of the industries which *are* good examples of 'organized capitalism', coal, steel and chemicals, had lost political and economic power to the new consumer sectors, and had long been in a condition of employment, though not always output, decline. A further feature of the industries of the third technological revolution (Mandel, 1975) is that they were, and remain, heavily dependent for componentry upon the small-to-medium-sized company sector, were normally subject to seasonal fluctuations in the market which casualized the workforce to an unusual extent, and possibly as a result were often quite late in accepting unionization of the workforce.

So, the criticism here is not that there are no common features of 'organized capitalism' to be found across some sectors and many advanced economies from the 1880s to the 1960s, but that the universality of these features is overstated. The organization of capital, the relationship between finance and industrial capital, their relationship to the state and to labour varied over time and space, both internationally and interregionally. Moreover, although mass production became the dominant ideological tendency, or *technological paradigm*, it was far from the only, or necessarily major form of production, either of goods or services. Indeed in both employment and output terms, mass production in large corporations remained the junior partner in the period under consideration, such that even in the 1970s in the home of mass production, the USA, 70 per cent of engineering production came from small firms in small production runs (Piore and Sabel, 1984).

The second line of criticism concerns the degree to which contemporary capitalism can be considered 'disorganized'. While it is certainly true that the introduction of floating exchange rates in the early 1970s destabilized the fixed currencies of the major trading nations and made international transactions a more hazardous business, by the 1980s finance capital had re-equipped, especially through the application of new technology to speed up the rate at which trading information could be acquired, and its capacity to 'read the market' is now vastly enhanced. Even when a highly de-stabilizing crisis such as that surrounding the less developed country debt-burdens of the 1980s emerged, international banks were able very quickly to relieve the crisis by re-scheduling loans and restructuring debts. In other words, world finance may well operate in a more uncertain environment now than hitherto, but that hardly adds up to disorganization.

Moving to the industrial sphere, the argument is rather similar in the sense that multinational corporations, especially the very largest of these, seem relatively little affected by the [. . .] economic recession, have the capacity to restructure functionally and over space and are penetrating ever-deeper into the under-capitalized world, including the state socialist countries as market places or production platforms. Clearly, many western corporations have had a shock, particularly from the competitive surge in numerous producer and consumer goods sectors from Japanese corporations. However, competition for markets (including labour markets) has seen even the largest western multinationals such as GM or Ford adjusting their strategies, absorbing important lessons in product-quality, work organization and, not least, relationships with the [. . .] small-to-medium-sized sub-contractors on which they depend, in order to re-assert their competitive position in the world and domestic market place.

It is important not to view this process as controlled in any strategic or centralized manner on an inter-corporate basis as Smith (1986) notes with reference to British Leyland:

> In view of the fact that the management of BL had to undergo a long and costly process of learning it would be misleading to describe the restructuring of the company as being a deliberate and well-ordered national or local manifestation of a process orchestrated by and/or on behalf of 'international capitalism'.

The 'disorganized capitalism' thesis might well agree with this but the key question is whether as a result of the widespread restructuring that has occurred in a rather 'bunched' fashion over the past two decades, over most industrial and financial sectors, disorder or a new order has emerged.

Spatially speaking, there are growing signs that a new order is emerging both on a world scale, and more evidently on an interregional scale, especially in the UK. Looking at the world scale first, let us take two important manufacturing sectors, and then briefly look at an interrelated set of service sectors – producer services.

Motor vehicles

Motor vehicles production is an important element of the world-economy, in many respects a harbinger of new production techniques, labour relations and forms of international economic integration. It has passed through three phases of development, each with its centre of gravity in a different continent. The first was the achievement of mass production by American producers in the first decade of the twentieth century [. . .] Notwithstanding the dependence of mass production upon subcontracting relations, the world followed suit and sought to replicate the new technological paradigm. The 'American Plan' was ultimately embraced in Europe in the post-1945 period although individual nations pursued different paths and a diversity of products resulted.

European recovery heralded the second phase, and its temporary hegemony was built on the diversity of its products. The small car penetrated a segment of the US market neglected by home producers, forcing US producers to respond in kind under the impetus of the energy shocks of the 1970s. As this occurred, European producers moved up-market and opened up a new luxury market segment in the US. In the 1970s Europe was easily the world's greatest source of motor vehicles and its greatest exporter. Once again, the leader was being emulated and overtaken, driven by the dynamic of competition.

Out of this phase of the development of the industry a new leader in a new continent emerged – Japan. Initially protected by tariff barriers and dependent on licensing European technology, Japan adapted US and European technology and management practice, building massively upon the dualistic nature of the production relations characteristic of mass production, with its raft of small suppliers keeping it afloat [. . .] Quality control and intensified subcontracting gave the Japanese a price and quality edge which makes them now the world's leading vehicle exporter [. . .]

So the world order has changed, [. . .] with competition providing the motive force for such shifts. Productivity, price, quality, distribution, parts, servicing and so on are key elements in the competitive, but, to the extent that it involves emulation, relatively orderly struggle for domination. In the process, other parts of the world space-economy have been integrated in new ways. Mexico has become a major supplier of componentry for the US car industry, though not a major assembler of vehicles. Elsewhere in Latin America, Brazil and Argentina achieved full production with less than 95 per cent local content as a result of earlier investments by Germany and the US. In Asia India, Taiwan and South Korea are substantial producers though tied technologically to Japan, and in the Indian case to the UK to some extent. The picture, therefore, is of increasing world economic integration and the *reorganization* of spatial production relations, at a rapid pace, without undue signs of disorganization, precisely because of the power of multinational enterprise (Jones and Womack, 1985).

Microelectronics

Much of the same pattern is discernable in the most internationalized sector of all – microelectronics. Intense competition has produced a number of locational shifts on a world scale. The one-way flow of US investment into Western Europe has been complemented by a lesser flow from Japan in the same direction and an increased flow by both into the US. The peripheral parts of Western Europe have become important offshore locations for US and Japanese investors to penetrate European and Middle-Eastern markets. US and Japanese capital has established significant production centres in the Newly Industrialized Pacific countries of Asia, some of the more advanced of which have developed integrated producer-user complexes (Lin, 1985). Low-skill, assembly-only work has moved to less developed industrializing countries in Asia and the Caribbean. Competition between, primarily, the US and Japan is forging a new economic order amongst diverse countries in terms of their market standing, skill levels, local entrepreneurship and labour-cost advantages. The labour-cost variable is decreasing in importance as automation grows in the production process, but foreign direct investment is not being withdrawn from NIC locations because of the emergence of substantial markets for finished products, especially personal computers, in those countries.

This ordering process even extends to the differentiation of functions within what were originally offshore 'export platforms'. Thus Taiwan and South Korea are becoming world export leaders in computer terminals and monitors, Singapore concentrates on supplying disk drives while Taiwan, South Korea and Hong Kong are expanding as exporters of finished personal computers. Meanwhile, R & D, marketing and testing, along with a considerable amount of basic production remains in the innovation complexes of the US, Japan and Western Europe, with Japan the leader in standard componentry, the US and Western Europe stronger in the production of special components (Ernst, 1985).

Producer services

Internationalization of producer services has become more important as the internationalization of manufacturing has itself burgeoned. The real estate, accounting, legal, consulting and insurance services required by banks and industrial corporations can be supplied cheaply and effectively by means of large corporations subcontracting such requirements out to specialist companies who themselves become internationalized in the process (Daniels and Thrift, 1985). Until relatively recently much of the activity of such companies focused on the domestic market, but by the 1980s world competition for the international producer services market had brought about a transformation in company practice. Following and slightly modifying Reed's (1983) analysis, the new world order now consists of the following:

(i) Supranational Centres – London, New York;

(ii) Supernational Centres – e.g. Frankfurt, Paris, Zurich, Tokyo;

(iii) International Centres – e.g. Brussels, Chicago, Hong Kong, Sao Paulo;

(iv) World Regional Centres – e.g. Los Angeles, Milan, Montreal, Seoul.

The first category deals in the full range of international services – commodity exchange, currency clearing, securities dealing, specialist services (insurance, legal, accountancy, etc.); the remaining categories either specialize more in some than others, or serve a more restricted part of the globe (Thrift, 1986).

Thus, it is reasonably clear from the foregoing discussion that three features have emerged from the undoubted break in the pattern and organization of world capitalism over the past two decades. First, international competition for expanding markets and market niches has led corporations, and even much smaller companies (see Frobel *et al.*, 1980) to engage in production as well as trading activities in wholly new areas of the world in order to gain market advantage. Secondly, the emergence of new producers, imitating, synthesizing and emulating the performance of lead-countries who were first to innovate in manufacturing or service sector activities has brought a significant spatial restructuring of the world economy – the rise of the Pacific Basin, relative decline in the older industrialized economies [. . .] [T]hirdly, such change, rapid as it is, seems capable of producing not a disordered mélange, but new specialisms, a marked degree of hierarchy and a relatively well-defined new economic order based upon the financial and technical power of successful competitors.

Such characteristics, now being mapped out on a world scale, are also replicated in the internal space-economies of particular countries. In the UK there is now a relatively well-established hierarchy of financial and technical power whose apex is in London and the South East where corporate financial and manufacturing headquarters, research and marketing facilities predominate. In the semi-periphery of Britain are to be found a mixture of restructured, established manufacturing industry, regional consumer and producer services and some new industries in the computer and defence sectors of the economy. And on the periphery we find the branches of London and overseas-headquartered companies, deindustrialized localities and proportionally large numbers of public-sector service workers. This, too, is a reasonably well-ordered hierarchical system of financial and technological power, replicated in comparable, though not identical, ways in other advanced, national space-economies (Lipietz, 1985; Soja, 1985; Massey, 1984).

11.3   Spatial paradigms: the re-ordering process

In a recent critique of Massey's (1984) industrial restructuring thesis [. . .], that is, the thesis that spatial divisions of labour derive from the overlaying of historic rounds of investment (and disinvestment) upon specific local space-economies, Warde (1986) has pointed to what he sees as three difficulties with this 'geological metaphor'. First, he argues, the 'transformation rules' which govern the deposition of layers of investment in space are not specified. Second, the connection between sequences of restructuring and particular social-class effects is unclear. And third, the range of local social effects other than those having to do with social class is inadequately explored

[. . .] [T]hese problems [. . .] can be [. . .] address[ed], in part from the foregoing discussion of organized and disorganized capitalism. With respect [. . .] to the question of the 'transformation rules' [. . .] it is important first to consider the appropriateness of the concept 'rules' [. . .] They may only be identifiable post hoc, rather in the way that Smith

(1986) referred to the British Leyland experience in the 1980s, as distinct from being available in recipe form ready to be applied. Nevertheless, the idea that capitalists behave intentionally in their investment and disinvestment decisions is clearly a reasonable one, and one which warrants exploration.

Inevitably, decision rules of the kind we are concerned with here take a hierarchical form. [. . .] [F]irst, in a capitalist economy, what, in Marxian terms, is referred to as 'the law of value' has to be observed if a company is to survive and be in a position to develop. Even in a socialist economy with finite sources of surplus there has to be, as there indeed is, a method for allocating resources in the least wasteful manner – [. . .] Similarly, in those parts of the capitalist economy – state services, for example – not normally subject to the law of value, questions of 'value for money' arise when resources become limited, as UK residents are only too aware. So, the first rule is fairly straightforward: it is that outputs should at least balance, preferably exceed and continue exceeding at an increasing rate, inputs measured in cost terms.

However, countries differ culturally in the ways such rules are specified. Japanese capital has longer time horizons over which profitability may be measured on capital advanced than British or American companies. Different political regimes can render their producers artificially profitable by the imposition of tariff barriers: again Japan is a case in point, and the wave of protectionist legislation in the west in the 1980s is also significant.

A second rule is that of competition – between countries of whatever political stripe – and within capitalist countries. The rule – defeat the opposition in the market place – clearly underpinned much of the discussion of the earlier part of this chapter, and is a crucial motivating force in the economic development process. While [. . .] it [. . .] ought to lead to chaos and disorganization it appears from contemporary experience to [. . .] lead to the emergence of new ordering processes [. . .]

The third [. . .] rule [. . .] concerns technology. In the contemporary period of restructuring, this factor, set within the context of the two rules discussed above, is the principal dynamic of economic change. To understand this, it is helpful to introduce the concept of 'technological paradigm' (Dosi, 1983; Soete and Dosi, 1983). The concept is useful in specifying change in the *nature* of competition. Development occurs as participants strengthen or weaken due to their capacity to implement managerial and technological 'breakthroughs' of a transformative kind, i.e. their ability to impose a new technological paradigm, just as the American car industry did in the 1900s, the European in the 1970s, and the Japanese in the 1980s. Each emergent technological paradigm threatens the existing technological trajectory which, in turn, may fight back – steam ships leading to better and faster sailing ships; Concorde leading to Jumbo Jets – and defeat it or not, as the case may be.

Clearly, the technological paradigm concept is a complex unity of ideological, social and political factors as well as technological ones [. . .]

Now, what is often overlooked [. . .] is that technological paradigms have spatial connotations, and [in so far as] these spatial connotations consist of different though complementary elements to those of techno- logical paradigms, one may [. . .] speak of the transformation rules of the spatial development process taking the form of *spatial paradigms*.

Within the macro-rules of value, competition and technology, there are what might be termed middle-range rules which firms can adopt to respond to new technological paradigms. Those were clearly enunciated by Massey and Meegan (1982) as:

(a)   rationalization – i.e. reducing the labour force;

(b)   intensification – i.e. speeding up the labour process;

(c)   technological change – i.e. automating production processes.

These need not be thought of as exhaustive of the restructuring rules available to companies – for example, changes in management practices, changes in ownership relations such as joint ventures, and changes in relations with suppliers, can be added as significant forms of restructuring in response to a new technological paradigm. Nevertheless, the three middle-range rules noted above are useful in analysing changing relation- ships between firms and the labour they employ. And once this relation- ship is considered, questions of a socio-spatial nature enter the argument in important ways. Moreover, once these elements are introduced, the role of the state, especially with regard to its spatial planning function becomes an integral element of the re-ordering process. This can be referred to as the development of a new spatial paradigm.

11.4   Social paradigms: ordering 'de-maturity'

In this section I will try to address the two other criticisms made by Warde (1985, 1986) of Massey's (1984) 'geological metaphor'; namely, the lack of a clear analysis of the relationships between restructuring sequences and, first, specific social class effects and, second, specific non-class social effects. The critique is that Massey's consideration of the impact of inward investment on different spatial class formations (specifically Cornwall and South Wales) is descriptively valuable but inadequately explained. Its value lies in its demonstration of the manner in which the arrival of new industry undermined classic proletarian bases of identification in heavy-industrial South Wales while, paradoxically, helping to form the basis for collective working-class organization in Cornwall where such a class base had either been long-eroded by the loss of its industry's competitive edge in minerals, or never truly coalesced into a class force because of its dispersion, isolation and existence in a more deferential, agricultural social setting. With respect to non-class social effects, such as those of gender or ethnicity, the critique is comparable and even though an explanation as to why new industry often employs women in former heavy industry areas is offered by Massey, that is cheap labour, this does not capture, for example, the undoubted sectoral variation in female activity rates in new industries in declining regions. Moreover, other non-class questions are not explored.

These points constitute a substantial agenda of research questions for those engaged in socio-spatial studies over the next few years. All that will be attempted here is to point to some possibly important factors that should be taken into account in undertaking such studies [. . .]

Perhaps the clearest way to exemplify the manner in which wide-ranging economic restructuring, of the kind being considered in this chapter, creates relatively ordered socio-spatial relations out of the social disorder that appears to attend technological paradigm shift is to contrast two post-war periods of restructuring. The first of these occurred during the 1960s and early 1970s, the second has been developing through the 1980s.

The first restructuring period is associated, politically, with the Labour governments' commitment to modernization of British industry. It was a period when the UK was gearing up for an initially abortive attempt to join the European Economic Community, in a context of loss of empire and the first signs of revived market penetration from competitors whose economies had been devastated by the Second World War. The competitors [. . .], especially Japan and the German Federal Republic, had in important ways followed the American pattern of mass production of standardized products aimed at volume markets in consumer goods. The UK response was politically led along similar lines. The Industrial Reorganization Corporation was set up to encourage mergers and take-overs which would enhance economies of scale, productivity deals were agreed with trade unions, redeployment of workers took place from old declining industries to newer ones, regional assistance helped redeployment to some extent, but more importantly, it assisted capital to shift production to new plants where new kinds of worker could be employed. This is the restructuring of which Massey (1984) writes. It was associated with a degree of social convergence over space as unemployment and income levels evened out a little between classes and regions (Urry, 1985a; Massey, 1985), there was a marked degree of feminization of the labour market with regions where female activity rates had been low catching up, and there was some de-skilling of work as craft-jobs were replaced in many industries by new labour-saving technology.

[. . .] [T]his earlier period of restructuring was associated with the principle that regions with a high representation of members of the working class should themselves be modernized, enabling that class to reproduce itself albeit in modified form in situ. This was made possible by the co-incidence of a restructuring process which, although driven primarily by the need to reduce the overall amount of 'living' labour in production, nevertheless remained, by contemporary standards, relatively labour-intensive. The places which benefited least from this process were the older industrial conurbations, the manufacturing base of which in old, medium-sized and inefficient plants, was sacrificed to the construction of a new spatial division of labour. Inner-city areas were particularly negatively affected by these changes. They lost mostly male jobs in mechanical and electrical engineering, and, perhaps because these consumer industries (especially the latter) were experiencing the competitive squeeze most, these were the industries where low-paid jobs for women increased in greatest numbers in the regions. These jobs were overwhelmingly in the lowest, operator, grades.

The present period of restructuring is very different in its socio-spatial effects from the earlier one. To begin with, it is predicated on the failure of the previous round of restructuring to modernize the UK economy in the right way. It has now become clear that investment in technical change aimed at making labour-cost savings alone has mainly had the effect of putting the UK in price-sensitive competition with newly emergent industrial economies in south-east Asia and elsewhere, a competition which can scarcely be won due to the labour-cost advantages enjoyed by such countries. The real competitive game is non-price competition, based on product quality, innovativeness and value for money. Getting into this game means giving political priority to changing large parts of the UK's industrial culture because it requires the adoption of quality-control criteria which both government and UK industry perceive as best achieved by 'dead' rather than 'living' labour. Moreover, the consumer, confronted with choice from more technologically advanced countries, now demands a more differentiated product than the standardized car or TV set of yesteryear. Areas, and social classes in them, associated with the older forms of product and production process are now seen as something of a drain on the capacity of firms to engage fully in the new competitive contest.

This problem [. . .] is emphatically not simply a physical environmental phenomenon but rather something which:

> refers to the condition of many old established, highly urbanised and diversified urban areas which are suffering from a general maturity of the economic and environmental structure: physical congestion, high land rents and labour costs, union aggressiveness and high social resistance to change, bureaucratisation of industrial and management practices. (Camagni, 1985)

In such regions and urban concentrations, locational advantage is lost to newer locational settings. Often, tertiary sector employment continues to grow quite rapidly, especially for women, but cannot offset manufacturing job loss. It is the problem being faced by the North American 'Snow-belt', many larger UK cities, not least London, and older industrial regions of Europe such as Wallonia, Lombardy and the Ruhr. In stereotypical terms it is the socio-spatial expression of what is sometimes known as 'the crisis of Fordism' (Lipietz, 1984).

Such locations are not necessarily being entirely vacated by capital in the 1980s. Rather there are signs of a restructuring which is jettisoning much of the low-skill operative labour – often female – taken on by manufacturing industry a decade or two earlier, and its replacement by new technology. For example, in the UK engineering industry there was a 43 per cent fall in operator staff between 1978 and 1984 compared with a 36 per cent increase of professional engineers, scientists and technologists (Cooke and Morgan, 1985). It may be presumed that, to the extent that the earlier restructuring brought mainly operator jobs to problem regions, the latter will have been hit disproportionately by the job-shedding aspects of the contemporary restructuring, but are unlikely to have benefited greatly from the upsurge in demand for highly qualified labour. There is limited evidence (Morris, 1976) that some peripheralized plants increasingly use their low-skill labour as a casualized, semi-employed reserve brought in on a short-term contract basis. This practice, which used to be the norm in core engineering factories before trade unionization became strong in the post-war years, is also being resorted to in highly competitive sectors such as motor vehicle manufacture (Smith, 1986).

Weaker unions, new technologies which enable flexible management and manufacturing systems and require flexible work and labour market practices from lower order employees, consumer demand for less stereotyped products, the need to get away from *mature* social formations, the diminished need for 'living' labour with ordinary skills combined with the growing demand for creative, highly qualified labour adapted to the newly flexible production environments, are all working to re-organize the social composition of those in work and the characteristics of those out of work. The latter, by and large, have skills which have become redundant, the former are increasingly bifurcated into a well-paid, middle- to upper-middle, professional service class and a working-class [. . .]

Such changes as these are clearly complex, differentiated by industrial sector and by geographical space. Economic revitalization is often to be found taking place in regions which do not display a mature general environment. The problem of the mature socio-spatial formations is to 'de-mature' (Abernathy, Clark and Kantrow, 1983) through environmental rejuvenation and new firm formation in which older social practices such as robust collective organization by workers are weakened. In barest outline these are some of the social class, and non-class social, forms entailed in the re-ordering process associated with technological and spatial paradigm shift. They include [. . .] the expansion and contraction with associated occupational differentiation of operative workforces; the tendency towards driving out of 'living' labour from the production process but the absorbing of increasing amounts of subjectively auton-omous living labour into the conceptual and control sides of that process; the breaking up of class-conscious pools of employed workers as technical change renders Fordist structures out-dated; and the selective incorpora-tion, dis-incorporation and re-incorporation of workers along gender, age, and, probably, ethnic lines as the rules of the competitive struggle and the relative strengths and weaknesses of organized labour in different spatial locations change, particularly in an era of rapid technological transformation.

11.5 State planning and spatial paradigms

In liberal democracies the interests of capital and labour are represented in the political process. Over time the balance may tip away from the interests of capital sufficiently for the labour interest to be able to be expressed in clear policy forms, but, for the national state [. . .] to remain capitalist this balance may not be allowed to shift so far in favour of labour for the interest of capital to be completely neglected. What occurs is a process of *transmutation* of interests such that capital's interest in maintaining its capacity to accumulate is assisted in ways that also, in the short term at least, enable the interests of labour too to be furthered (Cooke, 1983). In what follows I will talk solely of industrial capital and industrial labour to try to illustrate the micro-rules of spatial transformation whereby socio-spatial relations enter a new spatial paradigm as capital enters its new technological paradigm.

For illustrative purposes I will discuss changes in the UK space-economy in the 1960s and 1980s, highlighting the role of state planning in the process.

Recognition in the 1960s that the UK was losing market-share in numerous manufacturing sectors to overseas competitors led to a move within the state to establish quasi-autonomous economic planning machinery [. . .] An ideology of 'modernization' through state intervention in the macro-management of industrial development was accepted by both the main political parties and the higher echelons of the state bureaucracy, and underpinned changes in the functional and spatial organization of British industry. The key to 'modernization' was perceived as lying in the achievement of labour-productivity gains through economies of scale bought by investment (mergers, takeovers) in mass production. The aim was to improve UK standing in volume markets for the standardized products mass production could yield. At this time the involvement of labour in strategic thinking about modernization was echoed in the manner in which firms delegated shopfloor authority to union stewards who became privileged mediators in the sphere of factory industrial relations.

Modernization required spatial restructuring too. The spatial planning machinery was overhauled in the 1960s in ways which assisted the industrial modernization process. At the regional level a substantial boost was given to peripheral regions by the extension of assisted area status to localities suffering from the decline of Victorian industries. Regional aid was a political demand from the labour side, assisted initially by capital, but later embraced, for example, by the Confederation of British Industry, in the light of the significant aids to capital embodied within the legislation. Even though aids to labour were also included these were short-lived. Regional policy is thus a good example of the political transmutation of demands from divergent interests – 'bringing work to workers' and helping firms to modernize simultaneously. At the city level there was also a strong modernizing ideology at work, though favouring dispropor-tionately the interests of commercial and financial capital. A great wave of city-centre rebuilding, with associated residential redevelopment cleared much old, smaller industry from city centres, industry de-centraliz-ed to the peripheral regions, and later to semi-peripheral growth towns beyond the conurbations. Industry found new, cheap, often female labour pools in previously male-dominated industrial or agricultural labour mar-kets, and was able to cut labour costs both by de-skilling the labour process and employing more women than hitherto.

Thus the technological paradigm and spatial paradigm rules coincided around *modernization, economies of scale, state development planning* (economic and spatial) and *decentralization of production*. In retrospect, it is clear that this strategy was unsuccessful, mainly because, as has recently been noted, British manufacturing investment was devoted to cutting labour costs by introducing labour-saving machinery rather than to seeking innovative, quality-conscious product and process designs such as those that competitor nations were developing (Cooke and Morgan, 1985). As Britain made inroads into the standardized markets, the Newly Industrializing Countries began to compete in ways Britain could never match – the technological and spatial paradigms had been realized too late.

In the 1980s a new technological paradigm has taken root and with it, taking its own, though complementary form, has emerged a new spatial paradigm. The technological paradigm is still underpinned by an ideology of 'modernization', but the rules for its implementation have changed dramatically. In place of the faith in 'planning' is a revived faith in 'the market' as the key motive force. British industry is being urged to re-discover the entrepreneurial spirit, classically thought to be embodied in 'the small business'. Managerial ideology has turned away from the labour market and production rigidities inherent in the huge mass-production plants towards the medium-sized, flexible manufacturing plant buying in an increasing amount of its production content from subcon-tractors. Standardized markets have become fragmented [. . .] as customer tastes have become more sophisticated. Unionization is anathema to the new paradigm, indeed casualization of labour and the increased use of small, subcontracting businesses, union-free and flexible, as in the Japanese model is becoming widespread. Moreover, the decentralization strategy of the 1960s is no longer the norm, rather re-concentration, often back to refurbished urban plants, even in the inner city, perhaps in an Enterprise Zone, is not unknown (Cooke, 1986).

The spatial paradigm is already present, enveloping the new technological paradigm rules of the 1980s. Regional assistance has been more than halved, many peripheral areas have lost regional aid status altogether. The days when regional development agencies constructed large advance factories have disappeared, now they construct small incubator units, and liaise with private capital to provide seed-corn for new enterprises. Unemployed workers from closed branch plants in the periphery are enjoined to move to the prosperous metropolitan region, amongst those unemployed are many women now augmenting the redundancy statistics as closures and technological restructuring render their low labour costs superfluous [. . .] Inner-city land is being recycled for up-market residential and small-business entrepreneurship while ethnic ghettoes remain residualized by the withdrawal of expenditure on the renewal of the urban fabric. Established ideological pillars such as Green Belt protection of the urban fringe, and the construction of new environments in New Towns are crumbling or have been consigned to the private sector. Meanwhile islands of growth in the favoured, semi-rural settings of the under-unionized Home Counties develop, often on a raft of hidden state subsidies from the Ministry of Defence procurement budget (Lovering, 1985). From the 'convergence' years of the 1960s when unemployment and social welfare indices showed a diminution of disparities between the rich and poor communities of Britain, we have moved into an era of socio-spatial polarization as entrepreneurship is rewarded and communality is penalized.

So the technological paradigm and spatial paradigm rules move into synchronization around *entrepreneurship*, *economies of scope*, *market-reliance* and *reconcentration of production*. In the process, class organization, in the sense of trade union collectivism, is being attacked in most of its strongholds, gender equalization is in retreat as opportunities for working women are eroded in full-time factory work in favour of part-time service work, and the efforts of localities are stifled by the centralization of political and public economic power in the higher reaches of the state.

References

ABERNATHY, W., CLARK, K. and KANTROW, A. (1983) *Industrial Renaissance: Producing a Competitive Future for America*, New York, Basic Books.

BELASSA, B. (1984) 'Adjustment policies in developing countries: a reassessment', *World Development*, Vol. 12, pp. 955–72.

CAMAGNI, R. (1985) 'Industrial robotics and the revitalisation of the Italian North-West', paper presented to an International Seminar on 'Technologies Nouvelles', Brussels, April.

COATES, D., JOHNSTON, G. and BUSH, R. (eds) (1985) *A Socialist Anatomy of Britain*, Cambridge, Polity Press.

COOKE, P. (1983) *Theories of Planning and Spatial Development*, London, Hutchinson.

COOKE, P. (ed.) (1986) *Global Restructuring, Local Response*, London, Economic and Social Research Council.

COOKE, P. and MORGAN, K. (1985) 'Flexibility and the new restructuring: locality and industry in the 1980s', *UWIST Papers in Planning Research*, No. 94, Cardiff, University of Wales Institute of Science and Technology.

DANIELS, P. and THRIFT, N. J. (1985) 'The geographies of the UK service sector: a survey', *Economic and Social Research Council Changing Urban and Regional System Working Paper 1.*

DOSI, G. (1983) 'Technological paradigms and technological trajectories: a suggested interpretation of the alternatives and direction of technical change', *Research Policy*, Vol. 2.

ERNST, D. (1985) 'Automation and the worldwide restructuring of the electronics industry: strategic implications for developing countries', *World Development*, Vol. 13, pp. 333–52.

FROBEL, F., HEINRICHS, T. and KREYE, O. (1980) *The New International Division of Labour*, Cambridge, Cambridge University Press.

GIDDENS, A. (1979) *Central Problems in Social Theory: Action, Structure and Contradiction in Social Analysis*, London and Basingstoke, Macmillan.

JONES, D. and WOMACK, J. (1985) 'Developing countries and the future of the world automobile industry', *World Development*, Vol. 13, pp. 393–408.

LIN, V. (1985) 'Health, women's work and industrialisation: women workers in the semiconductor industry in Singapore and Malaysia', paper presented at the International Sociological Association Conference on 'Regional Impacts of the New International Division of Labour', Hong Kong, August.

LIPIETZ, A. (1984) 'La mondialisation de la crise generale du Fordisme, 1967–1984', *Les Temps Modernes*, November.

LIPIETZ, A. (1985) 'Le national et le regional: quelle autonomie face à la crise capitaliste mondiale?', *CEPREMAP Paper*, No. 8521, Paris, CEPREMAP.

LOVERING, J. (1985) 'Regional intervention, defence industries and the structuring of space in Britain: the case of Britain and South Wales', *Environment and Planning D: Society and Space*, Vol. 3, pp. 85–108.

MANDEL, E. (1975) *Late Capitalism*, London, New Left Books.

MASSEY, D. (1984) *Spatial Divisions of Labour: Social Structures and the Geography of Production*, London and Basingstoke, Macmillan.

MASSEY, D. (1985) 'Geography and class', in Coates, D., Johnston, G. and Bush R. (eds).

MASSEY, D. and MEEGAN, R. (1982) *The Anatomy of Job Loss: The How, Why and Where of Employment Decline*, London, Methuen.

MORRIS, R. J. (1976) *Class and Class Consciousness in Victorian Britain*, London and Basingstoke, Macmillan.

OFFE, C. (1984a) *The Contradictions of the Welfare State*, London, Hutchinson.

OFFE, C. (1984b) *Disorganized Capitalism*, Cambridge, Polity Press.

PIORE, M. and SABEL, C. (1984) *The Second Industrial Divide: Possibilities for Prosperity*, New York, Basic Books.

REED, H. C. (1983) 'Appraising corporate investment policy: a financial centre theory of foreign direct investment', in Kindleberger, C. and Audretsch, D. (eds) *The Multinational Corporation in the 1980s*, Cambridge, Mass., MIT Press.

SMITH, D. (1986) 'Factory and community: the restructuring of South West Birmingham', in Cooke, P. (ed.).

SOETE, L. and DOSI, G. (1983) *Technology and Employment in the Electronics Industry*, London, Frances Pinter.

SOJA, E. W. (1985) 'Regions in context: spatiality, periodicity, and historical geography of the regional question', *Environment and Planning D: Society and Space*, Vol. 3, pp. 75–90.

THRIFT, N. J. (1986) 'The fixers: the urban geography of international commercial capital', in Henderson, J. and Castells, M. (eds) *The Regional Impacts of Global Restucturing*, Beverly Hills, Cal., Sage.

URRY, J. (1985a) 'The class structure', in Coates, D., Johnston, G. and Bush, R. (eds).

URRY, J. (1985b) 'From organised to disorganised capitalism', paper presented at an International Sociological Association conference on 'Industrial Restructuring, Social Change and the Locality', University of Sussex, April.

URRY, J. and LASH. S. (1986) *The End of Organised Capitalism?*, Cambridge, Polity Press.

WARDE, A. (1985) 'Spatial change, politics and the division of labour', in Gregory, D. and Urry, J. (eds) *Social Relations and Spatial Structures*, London and Basingstoke, Macmillan.

WARDE, A. (1986) 'Some political effects of restructuring in Lancaster', in Cooke, P. (ed.).

12 Uneven development: social change and spatial divisions of labour

Doreen Massey

12.1 Uneven development

The concept of uneven development, if it is to have any purchase on the structure and dynamics of economy and society more widely, must refer to more than the fact that there are more jobs in some places than others, or even that there are better jobs in some places than others. Such measures are interesting, and they are important, but they do not in themselves link that inequality to its causes in the deeper structures of the organization of society. In order to do this, uneven development must be conceptualized in terms of the basic building-blocks of (in this case, capitalist) society. In this chapter those are taken to be classes, and the focus will be quite narrowly on the relations within the economy, as these are assumed to be the primary foundation of class structure.

The term 'relations' is important, and is actually much more appropriate than 'building-blocks'. For the classes are not structured as blocks which exist as discrete entities in society, but are precisely constituted *in relation to* each other. Capitalist is defined in relation to worker, and vice versa. Carling (1986) argues for 'the reinstatement of societies as sets of relationships among individuals (and things)' in order to undermine 'the deeply ingrained habit of seeing societies in terms of hierarchies, pyramids, diamonds, heaps, layer cakes, jellies, blancmanges and other party pieces of social stratification' (p. 30). Where I disagree with him is that the prime focus should be on relationships between *individuals*. Much more important – certainly from the point of view of the analysis here – are relationships between classes and class-strata. Where I agree is that the focus should be on relationships.

Different classes in society are defined in relation to each other and, in economic terms, to the overall division of labour. It is the overall structure of those sets of relationships which defines the structure of the economic aspect of society. One important element which any concept of uneven development must relate to, therefore, is the spatial structuring of those relationships – the relations of production – which are unequal relationships and which imply positions of dominance and subordination. It is on this that the chapter will focus.

The notion of groups/classes being mutually defined by the relationships between them goes beyond the obvious case of capitalist and worker. It is not possible to have work which is predominantly 'mental' or 'intellectual' (in spite of the frequently applied epithet of 'knowledge-based society') without manual work. Steve Bell's cartoon in which yuppies float off into the sky calling 'we don't need dustbins' makes a powerful point. They are wrong. They do. And they need people to empty them.[1] Similarly, it is not possible to have supervisory work without there being activity to supervise. It is not possible to have assembly without the manufacture of components. Thus, the different functions in an economy are held together by mutual definition and mutual necessity.[2] They are the basis of the (economic) division of labour in society and of the unequal relations of wealth and power.

Those unequal class relations do not, as the saying goes, exist on the head of a pin. They are organized spatially. And it is contended here that this spatial organization must be an important element in any exploration of the nature of uneven development.

One way of approaching this is through the conceptualization of the spatial structuring of the organization of the relations of production. Some spatial structures of the relations of production involve the geographical separation, within one firm, of headquarters and branch plant. Although the precise form will vary (branch plants can, for instance, have varying degrees of autonomy), what is at issue here is the stretching out over space of the relations of economic ownership and of possession (the functions of control over investment, of administration and co-ordination, and of the hierarchy of supervisory control over labour). Such 'managerial hierarchies' have become longer and more complex with the development of capitalist production, and indeed with its increasing geographical spread. Or, again, a spatial structure might involve the geographical separation of the work of strategic conception from that of execution. A classic example here would be the separation of research and development from direct production. Or a production plant may be one in a series within the technical division of labour within a firm, each plant performing only one part of the overall production process. Here the relations between the plants will be planned within the firm rather than determined by the external market. (Market relations are also conducted over space – exchange relations between firms within or between sectors – and these too may involve systems of unequal power relations, and of domination. Relations between small and large firms come to mind, but unequal power may also exist by virtue of other characteristics which structure the apparently equal relations of market exchange. Highly contrasting degrees of oligopolization between retailing (highly concentrated) and the production of final consumption goods (often very fragmented between firms) in the UK has long meant the dominance by the former over the latter.)

Now, the potential variety of actual spatial structures is in principle infinite. Indeed, later sections of this chapter indicate that one of the characteristics of the current structural changes in the economy may well be the spawning of new types. But the point, at least here, is not to categorize or to produce a typology. Still less is it to produce stereotypes. It is, rather, to stress the importance of analysing the spatial ordering of the relations of production. For these different dimensions (of internal corporate structures, of the relationships of economic ownership and possession, of the technical division of labour) are dimensions along which run relations of power and control, of dominance and subordination. They are also dimensions which develop in systematic ways with the evolution of capitalist society.

So, interregional or inter-area relations, as they are so often called, are actually these relations of production stretched out between areas (at any scale of analysis from the very local to the international). To different degrees they are the relations of class power and control. These relations exist between functions within the overall division of labour. Regions or local areas may be specialized in the performance of a small number of functions and these in turn may be those to which attach power, and strategic control over the operation of the economy, or they may be those which are relatively powerless, subordinated. Most often, there will be a mixture.

But, further, the performance of particular functions within society is part of what defines groups within the class structure. One of the bases of the definition of classes and social strata is their place within the overall relations of production. The location of headquarters in one re-gion/country/local area and of branch plants in another will be reflected in the social compositions of those places. So will the location of the functions of research and development as opposed to shop-floor manufac-turing, or of financial functions as opposed to more direct production.

Perhaps more importantly, and to return to the opening theme, to say that one area has all the high-status, white-collar jobs and another all the less well-paid, manual work, while important, is only to capture one element of the full meaning of uneven development. For that distribution of distinct occupational (and social) groups is itself one reflection of a perhaps more fundamental structuring of inequality between those areas – that carried by the organization between them of the relations of production (Massey, 1984).

All this immediately has two further implications. First, if these divisions of labour which are stretched out over space (spatial structures) consist, as we have said they do, of mutually defining elements, then the functional (and social) characteristics of some areas define the functional (and social) characteristics of other areas. If one region has all the control functions, and only control functions (to give an extreme example), then other regions must have all the functions which are controlled, the subordinated functions. This clearly has political and policy implications. Second, it means that as far as the characteristics we are considering here are concerned, any local area (region/country) can only be understood when analysed in relation to the functions in the wider division of labour which are performed within it, and in the context of its place within the wider system of relations of production. These characteristics of 'a local area', in other words, must be conceptualized in terms of the evolution of the wider structures of capitalist economy.[3]

There are other reasons why it is useful to conceptualize uneven development in terms of spatial structures, the spatial organization of the relations of production. For distinct spatial structures are likely to have different implications for the dynamics of growth in their constituent areas. The geographical separation of control functions and production (headquarters and branch plant) is an example. It may result in the flow of profits for subsequent investment from branch-plant region to HQ. It may imply much higher local multipliers for business services in the latter region than the former, since many such services are related to the functions of control and strategy rather than to direct production. That in turn will lead to a greater coherence between parts of the economy in the control regions than in the areas of branch plants. There may also, of course, be different income multipliers because of the likely higher salaries in the former regions than the latter. Workers in the branch-plant economy will have to negotiate either with a management which is local but does not have strategic power, or with a management based outside the region. And so on.[4] In cases where the branch plant is also simply one part in the technical division of labour within a company (a part-process structure), the local effects may be even more dismal. Not only is the level of local multiplier effects to the business-services sector likely to be restricted, but so also is the whole range of technological multipliers. Components will be brought in from another plant within the company (and the output, likewise, might simply be shipped off to yet another). These really are 'cathedrals in the desert' and their propulsive effects on local economies are likely to be minimal. (A plant producing similar physical output but not as part of a wider corporate structure might have different local effects, and one which was embedded, say, in the quasi-market relations of subcontracting might have different ones again.)

So, different spatial structures imply distinct forms of geographical differentiation, both in terms of the patterns of social differentiation between areas and in terms of the structures of interregional relations. What this means is that uneven development does not vary only in degree, as some of the arguments about it, and measures of it, would imply; it varies also in its nature. There can be different *kinds* of 'regional problem'.

There are, then, certain internal necessities to a spatial structure. The distinct elements within it are held together in a mutually defining tension. There are also likely implications: different spatial structures are likely to have different impacts on local areas. But it is also important to note what is *not* necessarily implied by a spatial structure. First, the fact that a spatial structure of production implies a particular division into functions within the overall relations of production says nothing about which groups in society (defined outside of occupational categories) will actually perform those functions. That is determined by its own set of causal relations only contingently related (though, indeed, probably related) to the logic of the spatial structure. Secondly, a division into functions does not necessarily imply the social value which will be accorded to the performers of those functions, their precise social status or, for instance, their monetary reward. All this, again, is contingent although, also again, it is likely to be related to the definitions of the functions themselves and to the nature of the groups performing them. Thirdly, and finally, a spatial structure in itself does not say anything necessarily about its actual geography, in the sense of the particular places in which its constituent parts will be located. Once again, however, and as we shall see in a later section, although there may not be necessity in the *form* of their interrelation, all the elements above may influence each other.

Finally, the overlapping and interweaving of all these spatial structures is the basis for a spatial division of labour. In the mid-1960s a new spatial division of labour became dominant in the United Kingdom, in which control functions were concentrated, even more than before, in London, scientific and technical functions were clustered in the south-east (with some outliers in other places) and direct production, while present throughout the country was a higher proportion of economic activity in the regions outside of the south and east. That new spatial division of labour was the outcome of a whole series of changes affecting different parts of the economy in different ways. It was contributed to by shifts in the balance between sectors and the reorganization of, and development of new, spatial structures. It was the combination of spatial structures which produced a new spatial division of labour over the country as a whole. One question which the rest of this chapter will address is how much that scenario has changed in subsequent years.

12.2   New directions

That period of economic and spatial reorganization of which the full establishment of this new spatial division of labour was a part lasted from the mid-1960s to the mid-1970s. Its ending coincided with further shifts both in the economy as a whole (at national and international levels) and in the political climate (see Massey, 1984; and Cooke, Ch. 11 in this volume). It had been a period in which geographical reorganization, and national economic and regional policy, were dedicated to 'modernization' (Massey, 1984). Moreover, it was a form of modernization which in turn could be interpreted as an attempt to prolong the life in Britain of what has been called Fordist production, broadly defined, and the social relations which went with it.

The old, basic (pre-Fordist – see Hudson, Ch. 7 in this volume) industries, such as coal and shipbuilding were 'rationalized', resulting in major job losses and the creation of additional labour reserves in the 'peripheral' regions. Older means-of-production industries in manufacturing saw capacity closure and technical change, resulting in employment declines, especially for male skilled and semi-skilled workers, in the conurbations and nineteenth-century industrial areas. New means-of-production industries, especially in electronics, expanded employment. There was growth of R & D and technical occupations, particularly in the south-east, and also of assembly jobs, mainly for women, in all parts of the country, including some decentralization to 'the north'. Consumer goods industries grew slowly but did expand, especially those owned by big capital, and continued their longer-established decentralization of employment, including in particular, jobs for women, to peripheral regions. Among services it was the public sector which grew most. While employment in the central state exhibited the classic divide, with high-status jobs concentrated in the south-east (mainly London) and some decentralization of lower-status and less well-paid employment to the regions, local authority employment both professional and manual, and that in health and education, was geographically more evenly distributed in its growth. Finally, in private sector services, it was producer services which showed the fastest rate of employment growth overall. Once again, the higher-status professional and higher-technical jobs were concentrated in the south-east.

The decentralization of manufacturing branch plants to the regions was in some sectors associated with technical change, and with an increasingly sharp technical division of labour within production. In other sectors, such as clothing, the move north or west was much more simply a means of cutting labour costs in the face of growing competition in a reorganizing international division of labour. Services, too, began to decentralize, but again it was only the mass-production parts which left the south-east.

As an attempt to use spatial reorganization to enable survival in a world where rules were changing, it failed. In those manufacturing sectors where competition was increasingly coming from the Third World, a move to the UK regions was insufficient. And if the decentralization of certain public sector establishments can be interpreted in terms of trying to cheapen the costs of collective provision and thereby prolong the life of the current mode of regulation, it too failed. In public sector services, locational change is inherently unable to reduce costs to any great extent because most of those services, and precisely those which grew most quickly in the late 1960s, such as health, education and social services, are inevitably tied to the geography of the population which they serve.

The dominant dynamics reshaping UK economy and geography since the mid-1970s have been different. Not only has the wider economic context changed, so also has the political and ideological prism through which it has been viewed by the prevailing government. Many of the same processes have continued, but in a different tempo or in a different way, and the balance between the processes, and the way they have meshed together, has been distinct from in the earlier period.

At a descriptive level, a number of important changes can be picked out. There have been further cuts in the basic industries of the old Development Areas – coal, steel, shipbuilding – though in a different social and political context from that of the '60s. The decline in manufacturing employment, under way since 1966, sharpened dramatically during the recession of the early 1980s, though easing somewhat again thereafter. Geographically, the impact of this decline was highly differentiated, the bulk of the jobs being lost in the regions outside the South East, South West and East Anglia (see Martin, Ch. 10 in this volume). The long-term growth of service sector employment also continued, but again there were marked changes both in its importance and in its character. In part because of the faster decline of manufacturing, the shift from manufacturing to service employment speeded up. But the nature of the growth in service jobs changed too: since the 1970s it has been overwhelmingly private sector services which have dominated employment growth. Not only is the geography of services as a whole different from that of manufacturing, but the geography of the two parts of the service sector is also highly contrasting (see Allen, Ch. 6 this volume). Since the late 1970s service sector employment growth has been overwhelmingly in London and the South East. The most important sectoral elements of this private service growth have been in business services and banking, insurance and finance, as part and parcel of the emergence of London and its region as a world city.

One process which certainly came to an end in the mid-1970s was the decentralizatio. of manufacturing employment. The combination of investment, modernization through cutting labour costs, and geographical shift was abandoned in the face of accelerated decline. Whatever the effect of regional policy in the 1960s and early 1970s, it declined thereafter as the supply of potentially mobile investment dried up. Much of the decentralized employment has itself been subsequently lost. In other sectors which had been important underpinnings of the new spatial division of labour, the pattern of employment changed. 'Electronics' as a sector failed to become a major employer – indeed its employment nationally went into decline. Its internal structure of employment also changed. While the job losses mainly occurred among direct production workers, the numbers of professional and scientific workers continued to grow. Given the contrasting geographical distributions of these groups of workers, with the latter being more concentrated into the south-east, once again the geographical impact of these sectoral changes was highly differentiated.

But if the process of decentralization from the south and east is no longer important, the regions of the north and west are still subject to the arrival of branch plants and to branch-plant status. Now, however, they arrive as part of a different process, more often coming directly from abroad. Most importantly of all, the medium of branch-plant status is shifting from manufacturing to service industries. Leyshon, Thrift and

Twommey (1988) give evidence of this in parts of financial services, and Allen's discussion (in Ch. 6) of the penetration of multinational corporations of hitherto protected domestic markets hints at the process for a wider range of services, including contract catering and cleaning, and leisure and entertainment. Daniels' Table 5.2 gives a good indication of the variety of shifts under way. While services as a whole continued their centralization in the South East and South West (with an outlier of expansion in Scotland), the different constituent sectors behaved very differently. There were losses all round in public administration and defence, a continued growth with a (relatively) even distribution across the country in miscellaneous services (which includes education and health), further concentration (again except for Scotland) in distribution (in marginal decline) and professional and scientific services (marginal growth), and evidence of at least some regional decentralization in insurance, banking, finance and business services.

Finally, the last years of the 1980s indicate some new changes on the horizon, in particular a pushing out of growth from its established bases to colonize new areas. There has been a rediscovery by certain service sector industries, preceded by the property developers, of selected parts of the inner cities, and some re-working of the north–south divide as growth spreads into some of the more southern, and the more rural, areas of 'the north'.

12.3   Spatial structures

What insight can be gained about these changing patterns by employing the concepts of spatial structure and spatial division of labour?

At the level of occupational structure in the UK as a whole, the changes in direction which took place around the late 1970s seem to have reinforced many of the broad shifts which were already under way. Managerial and professional strata have continued to expand as a proportion of the economically active population; skilled manual workers have continued to decline quite rapidly and semi-skilled and unskilled manual workers together declined more slowly. The long, slow growth of clerical and sales workers, however, virtually ceased. The geography of the social structure also continued to move broadly in the same direction as previously, although there are some incipient changes, hinted at in the end of the last section, such as the invasion of certain inner-city areas by higher-income groups. But, most obviously, managers, administrators, professionals and technicians continued to concentrate in the south and east of the country.

In very broad terms, then, the spatial division of labour looks very similar, indeed is being reinforced. However, the balance of spatial structures underlying that spatial division of labour has changed somewhat since the late 1970s. There are a number of ways in which this can be illustrated.

First, as far as manufacturing is concerned, the regions of 'the north' remain very largely dominated by branch-plant structures. Indeed that subordinate status was reinforced during the '80s. But in some ways the nature of the branch plants has changed: the spatial structure of which they are part is different. A higher proportion of them are responsible to ultimate headquarters outside the UK. In part, this is because of the decline of British-owned manufacturing within the UK; in part it is because of new inward investment by foreign companies, the Japanese multinationals being the best-known. Further, although many of these branch plants are clearly part of production, or part-process, hierarchies, dependent on inputs from other plants in the same firm but based elsewhere, the way those hierarchies work may be changing. If it is true that just-in-time systems, for instance, are being adopted by more companies, then these branch plants are less likely to be the classic 'cathedrals in the desert' of the 1960s. Increasingly, they may demand that components suppliers locate in their vicinity (Crowther and Garrahan, 1987; Oberhauser, 1987; Shoenberger, 1987).

In other words, the 'branch-plant status' of much northern manufacturing remains, yet there is some evidence of two ways in which it may be being transformed – and transformed because of a change in the type of spatial structure into which the branch plants are inserted. The plants are more subject to ultimate control from outside the UK (which may be conceived of as negative) yet they may have rather larger technological multiplier effects locally (usually assumed to be positive). Such a scenario accords with the writing on neo-Fordism which foresees a process of spatially decentralized concentration setting in. It has to be said, however, that this possibility must be treated highly tentatively. Almost all the – anyway fragmentary – evidence comes from the car industry (as it also did, of course, for Fordism).

There is a further way in which these spatial structures are being reworked and their local impacts thereby changed. This is the move towards increased subcontracting and casualization, both of which change the form of the social relations of production, either directly with the workers concerned or with other firms (see Hudson in Ch. 7 of this volume). Here the increased importance of short-term market relations in comparison with either long-term contracts or planned relations within firms is leading to dichotomization of working conditions in manufacturing companies.

Secondly, and equally still only on the horizon in the late 1980s, is the related possibility that the vertically integrated corporations argued to have been key to the period of Fordism may become rather less important, while more vertically disintegrated, or quasi-integrated, structures may become more important (for example, Christopherson and Storper, 1986). There is, again, little systematic evidence yet of this in the UK, but there are two developments which could be seen in this light. The first is the increase in an independent technical services sector, including both R & D and such activities as software production. The second is the rise of a similarly independent (independent, that is, from manufacturing) sector within financial and other business services. Both of these phenomena are concentrated into (parts of) the south-east of England.

What they are evidence of is, with the increasing complexity and growth of this part of the division of labour, the externalization of certain functions from manufacturing. Thus new parts of the social division of labour, new sectors, are formed out of what were once parts of the technical division of labour within manufacturing-based corporations. What were once planned relations within firms are replaced by market relations between them (even if operating partly in 'non-market' terms – quasi-integration).

If these things are happening, then some aspects of the spatial structures which underlie the spatial division of labour within the UK are changing. One element of this is a shift in balance towards a sectoral division between north and south, with financial, technical and professional service firms, as a separate sector within the social division of labour, concentrated in the south, and away from domination of north by south through the part-process hierarchies of the technical division of labour. It is a shift in balance which would also result from the changing relative importance of different sectors in the economy, in particular the continuingly increasing importance of services in relation to manufacturing, and the declining relative importance of electronics.

We shall see later that the picture is actually much more complex than this; but consider the implications of the argument so far. Such a re-emergence of an element of sectoral division between north and south would more than anything else be likely to fuel even further the self-feeding cycle of the growth in the south-east. That process was already present in the 1960s and '70s. The presence of control functions in London and the south-east is an important reason for the concentration of business services in the same region. It is HQ which deals with those relations. Moreover, the presence of business services, once established, is a further condition for the establishment and growth of other firms, especially small ones where buying-in such services is necessary (Daniels in Ch. 5 of this volume). The presence of the City assures a greater availability of venture capital in the South East than in other regions (Mason, 1987). Even the higher house prices (a product of the concentration of growth, and of the higher incomes of these groups) means it is easier to raise initial capital. Higher incomes generate further growth through generalized demand. The finance sector generates demand for electronics hardware and software, for services such as design, for property development and construction (Leyshon, Thrift and Daniels, 1987). And so on. It was already a virtuous circle which was further strengthened as financial and business services became the key growth sectors of the economy. In electronics, the tendency to cluster already operated both through firms wanting to be 'in on the scene' in a technical sense and through their needing to have access to the main pool of highly qualified labour. With vertical disintegration or quasi-integration, however, there is evidence that the tendency for agglomeration of this upper-echelon type of activity may be increased precisely as a result of the increased importance of market relations and thus of the need to be 'in on' the important social networks (Christopherson and Storper, 1986, p. 317).

To the extent that this scenario is correct, it has a further effect, for it reinforces a picture of increasing separation between the economies of the north and the south of the country. North and south are locked in very different ways into *international* spatial structures and the international division of labour. On the one hand there is the metropolitan region of the south-east of England, with London as one of the three prime world cities at its heart. It has for centuries been true that the financial City of London looked more outward to the world economy than 'homeward' to the UK economy. But it is more true today, and increasingly true of the economy of much of the South East region. Indeed, Leyshon, Thrift and Daniels (1987) believe that 'the City constitutes one of the pivots, or perhaps *the* pivot of the economy of the South East of England' (p. 80). The finance and service sectors which are based in the region, and which are a growing part of its economy, are increasingly internationalized. London and the South East are the first and often only point of entry to the UK for the globalized business service sector (Daniels, Ch. 5 of this volume). There has been a massive influx of foreign companies into the financial sector in London to the extent that it is non-UK institutions which are in the lead in the increasing international centrality of the City. The economy of London and parts of the south-east is in many ways more in competition with and linked to other international metropolitan regions and world cities than it is with the rest of the UK.

In contrast, the factories of the north are linked into, and in competition with, similar factories in similar regions in Europe, and also to some extent the Third World. The foreign investment in the north links the region into the world network of branch plants of production, not global financial systems.

And it is not just in terms of spatial structures and systems of competition that north and south are differently linked into the changing international division of labour. The same is true of labour markets. The elite strata of the south and east are increasingly part of international labour markets – indeed 'a spell abroad' may be an expected part of the climb up the career ladder.

And yet, of course, north and south *are* linked. One of those links, however, is much the same as the way in which the economy of London is linked to other parts of the world. It is the location of *control*. If the south is spawning its own economy relatively unconnected to the north, much of the economy of the north is still subordinate to London. Moreover, there are also increasing signs of an expansion northwards of some of the newer and fast-growing service sectors in the south. Although some decentralization of business services did occur in the 1960s and '70s it was very limited, and was more often from London to the region around it than from south to north. There is no *major* interregional decentralization now, in the late '80s, but there is evidence of some. Within the whole range of financial services, for instance, some elements have remained highly centralized in London and the south-east while others have shown definite signs of spreading their spatial structures out to major regional cities. Investment banking, accountancy and the commercial property sector are examples of the latter (Leyshon, Thrift and Twommey, 1988). This tentative relative decentralization to the regions (or rather, to certain cities within them) can take a number of forms including, in a few sectors, indigenous growth. Important, however, has been the expansion into the regions of large firms based in the south-east, either through the establishment of branch plants or through the acquisition of local companies.

In that sense, what is happening now in some service sectors reproduces what happened in manufacturing in the 1960s and the first half of the '70s. The north's economy continues to be structured around branch plants and subordinated to control functions located in London and the south-east, and increasingly also ultimately abroad. As the national employment structure is increasingly dominated by services, so services are reproducing the branch-plant relation between the south-east and the rest of the country.[5]

However, these are not the same spatial structures as in the manufacturing decentralization of the '60s, and the nature and the impact of the branch plants within them are also therefore different. So, too, are the interregional relations of dominance and subordination which they imply.

Take the example of certain parts of the financial sector. If spatial structures are thought of as the organization of the social relations of production, in their broadest sense, over space, then the spatial structures produced by the financial sector's establishment of branch plants in regional cities are sometimes quite different from those typical of the manufacturing decentralization of previous decades. Firstly, very different kinds of functions are involved, and therefore relations between functions. While there will certainly be a geographically structured managerial hierarchy, with ultimate control – and top management – remaining in London or the south-east, the London and regional offices are likely to differ in the type of function they perform. One typical scenario is that the office in the world city will be the transactional centre, and regional offices will be responsible for business generation and sales outlets within their designated regions (Cooke, Ch. 11 of this volume). Secondly, and relatedly, in some parts of the finance sector the nature of the functions means that the *reason* for regionalized offices is to perform an agency function in relation to a particular geographical market. This would be the case, for instance, with investment banking, where some relative decentralization has occurred. The point of such a branch plant is precisely to 'relate' to the local area rather than only the central headquarters. Its function is to find local investment outlets. Finally, there is evidence that the branch plants of City firms tend to have more autonomy than do the branches of manufacturing companies. Moreover, this autonomy may be expected to increase as the regional branch office integrates itself further within the local market. These, then, may be branch plants of a different type from the range of types already recognized within manufacturing.

Their impact on the local region is likely to be correspondingly distinct. Leyshon, Thrift, and Twommey (1988) have carried out an analysis of this. They point out how different the local impacts can be from those associated with branch plants in spatial structures more typical of manufacturing in the 1960s and '70s. The clearest contrast is that these branches have 'agency impacts', that is, their provision of finance or producer services may help encourage other local economic growth. This is particularly true for that sub-sector which provides perhaps the sharpest contrast to the 'normal' imagery of a branch plant – investment banking. The establishment of branch plants (even through acquisition) might be important in upgrading provincial financial centres and in counteracting the regional bias, mentioned above, in the availability of certain forms of investment capital.

Secondly, the establishment of such branches was found to have direct multiplier effects, particularly in the property and land market and on the construction industry. For such establishments need property to assert their status and little suitable building was either available or in suitable condition on their arrival in provincial centres. This, then, is an element of the 'rediscovery' mentioned earlier of the inner areas of certain northern cities.

In principle, the fact that they are branch plants and therefore in subordinate positions within managerial hierarchies, is, ironically, likely to mean that the multiplier effects of these offices, through purchases within the local economy, might be low. In this they might be more like the classic manufacturing branch plant. This could be compounded by the recent process of conglomeratization and internalization of services within these sectors in recent years. Even here, however, the greater degree of branch-plant autonomy might have an effect, and indeed Leyshon, Thrift and Twommey do suggest that local direct multiplier effects are likely to include the purchase of ancillary services.

They also point out that the impact will be different from that of the classic manufacturing branch plant in terms of the type of employment generated, for a very high percentage of the jobs will be in the professional and managerial groups. And this, in turn, will mean that the income multipliers within the local economy from their salaries will also be greater.

There seems little doubt, then, that these spatial structures are very different from those of the '60s, and that they have correspondingly distinct local impacts. Nonetheless, Leyshon, Thrift and Twommey are restrained in their assessment of the overall effect, which they summarize as 'ambiguous'. In spite of the effects enumerated above, it is also 'undoubtedly true that the growth of the offices of large multinational financial and producer service conglomerates within the provincial cities of the north have themselves [sic] contributed to the extension of corporate control over financial and producer service activity. In this sense, the growth in the office networks of these large firms ... can be seen as a way in which the influence of the City of London is being extended throughout the regional economies' (p. 46). Moreover, it must be stressed that this is not a major phenomenon. In all the listings of world financial centres of different ranks, no city in the UK other than London ever makes an appearance. The gap between London and the rest remains a huge one. Furthermore, it is only some regional cities within the UK which are seeing the establishment of many such branch functions. In effect, as far as the financial system is concerned, a considerable reorganization of the urban hierarchy is under way.

Finally, that kind of spatial structure, where relations of dominance and subordination may be more muted and local effects more positive, is by no means typical of service industries, nor even of the financial sector. Allen (Ch. 6 of this volume) points to the very different structure in other parts of banking and commercial services and to part-process structures within insurance. Each of these will have different effects on the economies of the branch-plant cities. Even more negative will be the impact of the expansion of catering and cleaning services where they are increasingly taken over by multinational conglomerates and in particular where this is taking place in a context of privatization and/or 'contracting out'. As in the case of manufacturing mentioned earlier, the impact here is the reduction of wages and the deterioration in working conditions to levels well below those of the large-firm branch plants of the 1960s. In these cases, the implications for the north of being a branch-plant economy of London and the south-east are worse in the service industries than in manufacturing.

So, it would seem that the new spatial division of labour which was established in the UK in the '60s in very broad terms continues its dominance. Since the later 1970s, however, there have been some shifts in its constituent spatial structures. As ever, and as they were in the '60s, the spatial structures generating a spatial division of labour will be a mixture (Massey, 1984) but since the late '70s that mixture may have changed somewhat in its balance and in its components. Correspondingly some of the effects within local regions may also have changed. If it is possible simply to summarize the evidence examined here, it indicates that the effects in the late '80s are more likely to produce polarization within local labour markets. Finally, there are the effects on relations between regions: the economies of London and the south-east increasingly integrated into the international spatial structures of financial and commercial services, the economies of the north bound into the very different global structures of manufacturing corporations. The south-east embarked on its own process of cumulative growth, the north still tied in, though in ways which are perhaps increasingly complex, to structures of control based in London. It is the ability to grasp these wider relations, that tie local and regional economies in various and changing ways into the evolving structures of capitalist production – the ability to go beyond uneven development as a set of surface distributions – which is provided by an approach through the concept of spatial structures.

12.4   The geography of social structures

The concept of spatial structures thus provides a way in to the analysis of the economic relations between regions, the geography of the social relations of production which underlie any particular form of uneven development in capitalist societies. It also provides a basis for examining the geography of social structure, the geography of class.

If class is understood to be importantly (though not solely) defined by place within the relations of production, then the geography of those relations and the places within them, which spatial structures illuminate, begins to define a geography of class. It is not a deterministic relation, as was pointed out in the opening section and will be illustrated below, but if class is in any way based in production, then this is a way in.

We shall explore just one set of examples here. The fastest growing occupational groups in the economically active population of the UK are those which fall under the headings managers, administrators, professionals and technicians. In particular, it has been the last two groups (professionals and technicians) whose growth has speeded up in recent years (an interesting reflection, in itself, on the difference between Wilsonian modernization, when managers and administrators expanded faster, and Thatcherism). We shall concentrate here on the upper echelons of these groups. What they mainly represent, in descriptive social terms, is a relatively high-income, high-status and non-manual stratum within society. There is a continuing debate about its precise class definition and character, which cannot be addressed here. The question here is what light can be shed on these groups, and on their geography, through an analysis of spatial structures of production.

The first thing to be said is that in fact this broad grouping contains within it a mixture of different groups, each of which has its basis in distinct parts of the division of labour. Managers are distinct from technicians and specialist professional workers (Massey, 1984), public sector employees from those in the private sector. They belong in different parts of the division of labour.

For that reason they also occupy different positions in spatial structures of production. And indeed they have different geographies. All are clustered into the south and east of the country, but managers are more specifically concentrated in London itself, with a very clear hierarchical ordering, the top echelons being in the capital, lower orders forming a larger proportion in the regions. What evidence there is indicates that scientific and technical strata are less focused on the metropolis and more spread through the less urban parts of the South East region as a whole and its surroundings (Massey, 1984). These, then, are distinct geographies of different types of strategic control over British economy and society.

Moreover, there have been changes in the balance between the different elements of this group and in their class character. The 1960s and the early 1970s were the era of 'big is beautiful', of public sector growth and of manufacturing. Lash and Urry (1987), indeed, argue that this was the period of *formation* of what they call the service class in the UK, and they stress the significance of its public sector base. It was, precisely, a product of Wilsonian modernization. Today, the emphasis is less on the construction of complex corporate managerial hierarchies, and more on 'flexibility' and the promotion of the small firm. This in no way means that real control over society has been dissipated, still less democratized, but nonetheless the slackening growth of the purely managerial may be a reflection of the change of emphasis. Similarly, the typical scientist of the 1960s worked in a big corporate R & D lab (Steward and Wield, 1984); the equivalent employee in the late 1980s would be more likely to work in a smaller firm, certainly a smaller unit, and to combine with their scientific and technical functions some elements of management and even of ownership. This marks a change in their class position.

A contrast between the Southampton region and Berkshire is instructive here. In their study of the electronics and electrical engineering industry in the Southampton city region, Witt, Mason and Pinch (1988) demonstrate the connection between the *timing* of the growth of the sector in the region, its *place within the spatial structures* of the industry, and its *social character*. The growth of the industry in this region was early, occurring mainly in the late 1950s and the 1960s. It was also mainly a product of the in-migration of already operating companies, either through the establishment of new production branch plants or research and product-development establishments, or through the relocation of independently owned companies. It was, in effect, a product of a very early wave of decentralization of electronics mainly from its initial base in London. Local entrepreneurship played only a minor role. Moreover, most of the scientific and technical workers (which form a high proportion of the total) work either in big R & D labs or on sites which also have manufacturing functions (p. 30).[6]

The proliferating studies of Berkshire present a rather different picture. Here too, growth began in the 1950s, and was based around branches of major, often multinational, companies (Morgan and Sayer, 1988). Recently, though, 'local' entrepreneurship has become more significant . . . 'there has been an increase in small indigenous hi-tech firms, often set up by previous employees' (Barlow and Savage, 1986, p. 160). The class character of the scientific and technical strata appears to be changing, and with it the spatial structures of which they are part. No longer so often employees buried in corporate structures and, although undoubtedly an elite, with their work subject to 'proletarianization', they are now increasingly combining the power which comes from their monopoly over technical knowledge with some of that which derives from ownership and control. All of this is integral to their place in the emerging spatial structures of this region outlined in the last section.

The groups which have been growing fastest of all have been the wide range of private sector 'professionals' associated with business, and especially financial, services. Thrift, Leyshon and Daniels (1987) have documented the explosive growth of this group, its changing class character and increasingly international outlook. But what all these groups share, simply as a product of their position within the unequal division of labour within society, is participation in and possession of strategic levels of power and control over the economy as a whole.

None of this, however, says anything necessarily about which groups in society (defined outside of production) fill these different elite positions within the various spatial structures. That is contingent to the division of labour itself; it is not necessarily implied by it. However, to take just one characteristic, even the most cursory of glances at the statistics demonstrates that these positions are filled overwhelmingly by men. The reasons vary, but in no case do they follow simply from class relations or the demands of capital.[7] Cockburn (1985) has analysed the case of those who in this schema are called (scientists and) technicians. She argues that the design and development of the means of production has always been a peculiarly crucial and powerful function within class societies (p. 26) and she documents the mechanisms by which it has always also been a part of the production system that men, as opposed to simply 'capital', have fought to dominate. She looked at three industries, and reported 'the significance of the role we have found women playing in all three new technologies is simple: they are *operators*. They press the buttons or the keys . . . What women cannot be seen doing in any of these three kinds of workplaces is managing technology, developing its use or maintaining and servicing it' (p. 142, emphasis in original).

Another characteristic of this group is the degree of autonomy which it has within the workplace, the degree of control over the labour process (Massey, 1984). But this too has implications. One of them is that people work extremely long hours. Cockburn adds to the already considerable evidence on this, and to its implications. Many of them 'worked very long and irregular hours. Family commitments must come second. Such work is clearly predicated on not having responsibility for childcare, indeed on having no one to look after, and ideally someone to look after you' (1985,

p. 181). Leyshon, Thrift and Daniels (1987) document a similar lengthening of the working day among City workers (p. 60). It is not inherent in the class structure or the technical division of labour that it should not be women who become technologists and have men at home doing the housework. It is, however, in fact men who are the technologists and that fact itself has an impact on the nature of the functions performed, and on how they are performed (Murgatroyd, 1985). Argues Cockburn, 'holding on to the heights of technological advantage is more and more important to them as women chip away at the foundations of other male citadels. Men can ill afford to lose their historic position as the world's engineers just at the point when they can no longer feel themselves secure in the status of family breadwinner and head of household' (p. 235). In 1984 in the British electronics industry 95 per cent of scientists and technologists, 96 per cent of technicians and 98 per cent of craft-workers were men. And for good measure so were 97 per cent of managers (EITB quoted in Cockburn, 1985, p. 225).

But if one contingent characteristic of these spatial structures (i.e. which social groups actually fill the variety of positions within them) has not changed much in recent decades, other characteristics *have* been modified. In particular, the relative privilege of these groups within UK society has considerably increased, in both income and status terms. There are a number of bases for this. In relation to the finance sector, and the City in particular, Leyshon, Thrift and Daniels (1987) document the impact on London salaries of the internationalization of the labour market.[8] The fact that in this case wages were forced up, rather than wages elsewhere being forced down, reflects again in part the power of these strata in the labour market. Big Bang and internationalization together produced major skill shortages. Skill shortages, exacerbated by low levels of training in the UK, and by a seepage of qualified people to the even better-paid financial sector, have also pushed up wages among the technical strata. Finally, all these groups benefited hugely through the redistributive government policies, from poor to rich, during the 1980s.

So far, then, what has been established is a deepening of the technical division of labour in electronics in such a way that spatial proximity between research and production is not always necessary,[9] and in some 'high tech' sectors and parts of finance and business services a deepening of the social division of labour through externalization from manufacturing such that the need for spatial proximity may be greater within and between those sectors, and between them and the headquarters of major companies, than it is, again, with direct production itself. Secondly, many of these positions are filled by men, a fact which adds to the status given by the division of labour itself. Thirdly, the income and status of these groups have been considerably increased by other means. What has emerged is a set of spatial structures in which the spatial clustering of these groups, and their distance from the rest of the economy, is a prime characteristic.

There is, however, a further contingency to be structured into the discussion. For the actual geography of a spatial structure in terms of where the different elements in the division of labour will actually be located, is not given by the spatial structure itself. It is contingent, that is, dependent on a whole set of other causal systems not necessarily implied by the spatial structure itself. The location in the outer south-east of such a high proportion of these elite, white-collar strata, however, provides a fascinating example of the interaction of all the characteristics summarized above, and one in which spatial form and social form interweave and affect each other. In fact there is a whole range of factors behind the growth of this area, including nearness to London as a centre of control and of international linkages, the presence of Heathrow and good communications generally, and initially for the electronics industry the concentration there of government defence and research establishments. There is also the fact, referred to above, that the structure of these activities at the moment means that, once established, an area is likely to grow through the tendency to clustering. But another element which consistently shows up in research as being important is that the area itself has status.

The question then is, why? The development of the division of labour provides the possibility for these groups to be located separately from direct production. The high status which they have both striven for and been awarded perhaps inclines them to operationalize this possibility, to assert their separateness from the shop-floor and to locate in an area with cachet. But that does not explain why certain areas and not others should be seen in this way, nor indeed why separation from production should be seen as a status asset. References to 'high amenity areas capable of attracting a highly-qualified, highly-paid, highly-mobile workforce' (Hall, in this volume, quoting Berry, 1970) and to 'psychic income' merely assume what is to be explored, and assign cause by simple inference from effect. The area *must* be 'high amenity' because that is where these people who have choice ('highly-paid, highly-mobile') choose to go. In fact, of course, such preferences are not innate; they have to be constructed. This is demonstrated in a very simplistic way by the most recent development of all, the rediscovery by the young and rich of the central city. In London some part of this is due to the pressures of the combination of the long hours demanded on the dealing floors and the commuting times now required if home is to be really 'out of town' (Leyshon, Thrift and Daniels, 1987). But a glance at the literature indicates that these areas are now considered 'high amenity' and that another innate preference has been discovered – that for living by water in the form of rehabilitated canals and docks (renamed, 'quays').

So what *is* the attraction of the outer south-east? There is much evidence to suggest that it is mainly about self-assertion and class. It has been argued, for instance, that location in such areas enables self-definition through association with the trappings of some vision of 'the gentry' (Thrift, 1988). It is a means of asserting social arrival. Secondly, however, all this raises the question of whether the 'urban-rural shift' was urban-rural at all. Rather, it seems to have been from industrial (meaning manufacturing) to non-industrial. The beginnings of what may be a rediscovery of the urban, the boom of world cities (London's population is growing again) are some evidence of this. Keeble's work (1976, 1980) used manufacturing, not urban population, as a variable; Fothergill and Gudgin's work is precisely about *industrial* cities (Fothergill, Gudgin, Kitson and Monk, in Ch. 3 of this volume); and Lloyd and Reeve (1982), for instance, point out that there are many small towns in the north which are not getting service growth or middle-class in-migration. They give examples: Shaw 80.5 per cent employment in manufacturing, Littleborough 99.2 per cent. What really does seem to be at issue is distancing from manufacturing production and from the physical *and social* context that goes with it. The invasion of the Docklands by the private sector middle class is very different from the public sector gentrification of other parts of inner London in the 1960s and 1970s. It involves completely clearing the area or re-fashioning it. It was a bold thing to move in early and the brave pioneers were often offered special incentives. Once established as 'acceptable' places, of course, such areas, whether they be Docklands or the M4 corridor, embark on another element of the virtuous circle of growth, but this time based on class. Thirdly, however, the particular groups examined here must be set in a wider context. The South East is home also to a broad range of other groups, which form part of the basis for the social character of the region, and which in turn forms part of the attraction of the region to the groups being analysed. They range from employees of the central state to workers in the whole gamut of cultural industries. And in particular they are there because of London, the capital city.

Everything points to the importance of class dynamics in a social sense as a factor in the emerging locational pattern of the currently dominant sectors and strata in the UK economy. Lash and Urry (1987) make two points which go to the heart of this. First, they argue that the main causal power of these strata is 'to restructure capitalist societies so as to maximize the divorce between conception and execution' (p. 177). Secondly, they argue that 'British professions followed the gentry model of "status professionalism" rather than the bourgeois one of "occupational professionalism"', and they note 'the spatial significance of London in this process of status professionalization which affected not only the old professions but new ones as well, such as engineering' (pp. 184–5). The increasing importance of these strata and their changing composition, especially since the late 1970s, has demonstrated the significance of both these points.

But if spatial structures are geographical systems of mutually defining elements, as argued in the first section of this chapter, then this clustering of certain functions in the overall division of labour has other implications. Most obviously, the existence of clusters in particular functions necessitates the existence also of areas deprived of those functions – in this case, within the UK, the northern regions of the country. Indeed, the evidence is that the concentration of this group in the south-east, and their increased relative incomes, is a prime element in accounting for one of the more obvious descriptive indicators of the north–south divide – that of salaries. While the bottom 10 per cent of incomes in the different regions of the country do not vary much, the variation in the top 10 per cent of *male non-manual* earnings is considerable, with the income levels of this decile in the South East being far higher than those in other regions (Massey, 1988). Further, the fact of this spatial clustering itself has social effects. Most obviously, it has resulted in labour shortages for these groups in the South East, thereby increasing salary levels still further. Yet at the same time those (far smaller numbers) in regions in the north who have the same skills either remain on lower income levels, or cannot find work and/or cannot afford to move south either to find work or to increase their salaries. In this way, the cumulative dynamics of the initial spatial concentration are reinforcing the income advantages of the already privileged in the south, and even producing geographical inequalities within the group as separate northern and southern circuits develop, those in the former on lower incomes and unable to move in even should they want to, those in the latter in increasingly powerful positions in the labour market, moving increasingly rapidly from job to job, bargaining themselves up the income scale, and seeing their wealth grow still further as house prices continue to rise.

We have then, changing divisions of labour, both technical and social, with a particular social content and consequences, which have enabled – and apparently in some measure been the cause of – new spatial structures, the location of which in turn has further moulded the social character of the constituent groups.

An interesting issue arises here. Marshall (1987) in his account of the long historical rises and falls of British regions (long waves of regional development) argues that the upswing of each new long wave sees the rise of new social and political forces, and moreover that these have been regionally based, in the areas where the long wave has had greatest impetus. He points to the Manchester free-trade movement in the first half of the nineteenth century, and the social imperialists of the West Midlands in the late nineteenth and early twentieth. There is no sense in which the pre-eminence of the outer South East and its outliers constitutes the same kind of phenomenon at the end of the twentieth. Nor, it should be stressed, can such political characteristics in any way be directly derived from spatial structures, nor from the social structures with which they are associated. However, although there is in no sense a 'movement', this region is clearly one the imagery of which is used in political discourse. It is the heartland of Thatcherism. Other regions are urged to 'follow its example', and become more 'entrepreneurial' (Massey, 1988). Moreover its location around London gives it a special pre-eminence.

This time, the long wave has its greatest impetus in the region around the capital city, and the combination of the forms of dominance provides an even wider basis for a form of regionally based 'supremacy'. It is certainly the constellation of class forces based in this region which is currently dominating the social form taken by what has been called 'the fifth Kondratiev' in the UK.

12.5 Uneven re-development: reproduction over time

The structures of uneven development are constantly evolving. While the mid-'60s saw the establishment of a new spatial division of labour, the years since the late '70s have seen some changes in the underlying spatial structures. What seems to be clear, however, is that, although change is continuous, there are also periodic bouts of more thorough-going transformation. In other words, there is structural change in types of uneven development as well as in other aspects of the economy. Moreover, each is integral to the other. (Decentralization in the '60s was part of an attempt to save existing forms of industrialization and a particular place in the world economy; the rise of the outer south-east is part of the assertion of a newer dominant international role.) There is, in other words, a relationship between the periodization of an economy and its regionalization (in the most general sense) – its forms of uneven development. And it seems clear that the major shift towards a new spatial division of labour, which began in the mid-'60s, is continuing today. If it began as part of an attempt to install one technocratic, social-democratic view of modernization, it is being perpetuated, probably reinforced, by the economic and political changes since the late '70s.

What the changes we have been discussing produce is a shifting kaleidoscope of local and regional variation. Both geographical surface and the demands of industry are constantly changing. To give an example of the former, recent evidence would seem to indicate that some regions of the north and west are no longer seen as having reserves of mainly female labour, as they were in the 1960s and '70s at the height of manufacturing location there. That characterization of the local labour reserves was a result of the women of those regions being seen as 'green' labour and hence potentially vulnerable. Now, however, decades of unemployment, and of desperation for jobs, and the existence of a new generation of males without trade union experience, indeed often without experience of paid work at all, have transformed the male labour markets of these regions from being heartlands of trade unionism to ones where it is possible to introduce completely new forms of labour relations. The male labour of those regions may now also be viewed by industry as a vulnerable reserve.

'Geographical surface' and 'the demands of industry' always interact. Morgan and Sayer (Ch. 8 in this volume) give an example of such mutual adjustment precisely from the sphere of management-worker relations. 'General processes' only ever exist in the form which they take in particular circumstances. The new spatial structures and their social forms discussed in the last two sections take shape in the context of previously laid down spatial structures and social forms. Each has an impact upon the other. The arrival of vastly increased numbers of white-collar, high-income employees into the outer south-east has transformed the prospects of an older working class already living there. Either they have been able, through employment or through housing, to benefit from the influx or they have been marginalized. Just as the concentration of upper-income groups has had some effect on the character of those strata (see last section) so also it has affected those on below-average incomes. The experience of living on a fixed (for example, state) income in London or the South East is very different from that in the north. Apart from the fact that the inequality is more visible, and probably that there are fewer supportive organizations, prices are higher, and housing is very difficult to find at an affordable price; the money goes less far. The South East is the richest region in average terms, but it is the most unequal.

The conjunction of wider processes within a particular area can also set off other dynamics. The price of land has a long history in London of contributing to the difficulties of the manufacturing sector in the capital city, but the current conjunction of forces is particularly acute. The combination of the heightened international competition which was afflicting, at a national level, many of the sectors which figured prominently in the London economy, with pressures both on its labour supply and on its costs through increasing land and property prices, imposed difficulties which were not present in other parts of the country. Indeed, there is evidence that that kind of local impact now occurs also beyond London; Barlow and Savage (1986) give evidence from Berkshire.

Both these last two points have concerned conflicts of interest, or at least different interests, within particular areas, and both have been well studied. Characterizations of local areas may well vary between groups, and may often be conflicting. However, one issue which seems not to have been researched is the labour market for graduate women in the outer south-east. The dichotomy between 'male professional workers' and 'local workers' is frequently commented upon (for example, Barlow and Savage, 1986). But what of female (would-be) professional workers, of whom given the social structure there are likely to be many? In their study of Bristol, Boddy, Lovering and Bassett (1986) note a growing presence of younger women in certain technical and professional posts, but their overall conclusions are not hopeful for the quality of employment opportunities for women. They also point out that most jobs for women (low-paid ones) are in sectors generated by the spending-power of highly-paid men. In other words, the wider implications of high, local income multipliers, discussed in the last section, may be further to fuel the growing polarization within local labour markets, given the low pay and conditions in other service sectors. It may be that the combination, discussed in previous sections, of spatial structures of production and the social character of the groups within them, is producing within the outer south-east yet another form of 'patriarchal region' within the wider spatial division of labour.

'Spatial division of labour' is not an explanatory concept in the sense that it embodies an explanation of any particular form of uneven development. In this it is like any other concept of division of labour. A longer perspective on history indicates that the reasons for uneven development taking any particular form will change over time. It is certainly not the case that 'labour-force characteristics' are always the dominant consideration (Warde, 1985). Indeed, patterns of industrial location are not to be explained simply by lists of 'factors'. There are broad parameters, the maintenance of capitalist accumulation chief among them. But the way in which that operates to produce a particular spatial division of labour will depend on a whole host of things. Of supreme importance in explaining the shifting character, over two centuries, of uneven development in the United Kingdom have been the changing relation of the economy to the international division of labour, the (related) changing sectoral structure of the economy, and the dominant modes of technological and industrial organization. It is the structuring together of all these which will influence the kinds of spatial structures developed, the balance between them, and their overall resultant in a broad spatial division of labour. Further, as we have seen, it is also more than this. As well as the maintenance of capital accumulation, the form of uneven development will also reflect battles over the maintenance of class power (which, though clearly related, is certainly not the same thing) and will be refracted also through a wider level of politics, including the political interpretation of what *are* the requirements of capitalist accumulation. Since the late '70s, for instance, the strategy has been to emphasize and enable a particular dual role for the UK within the international division of labour: a combination of banking centre and low-cost-production location. It is this, and the ascendancy of particular class strata, which lies behind one of the most important dimensions of uneven development in the UK today.

Notes

1   Given the stage of development we are currently at, and the direction of this development.

2   An assumption is clearly entailed here that all the work done in a society, all the functions performed, are included in the characterization of the overall division. This raises two important issues. The first is that the system under consideration must be conceptualized as in principle international. The divisions of labour in which the economies of the regions of the UK are involved are frequently global in reach. The second issue is that the overall division of labour

in society includes much work which is unpaid and therefore lies outside that which is normally considered to be 'the economy'. Thus, the 'economic' position of 'family breadwinner' implies another position (performer of domestic labour) which will probably fall outside the paid sector. Thus, it is correct to call for the inclusion of the reproduction of labour in the approach (Warde, 1985, 1988), something which, unfortunately, this chapter does not attempt to do, but this cannot be achieved simply by adding on further 'aspects' of local areas.

3   Which is not the same as saying that this is the only conceptualization which must take place – see later.

4   There is a much fuller discussion of these potential implications, and of the contrasting impacts of different spatial structures, in Massey (1984), especially Chapter 3.

5   The rather inadequate statistics imply that in some sectors (only) Scotland may be a partial exception.

6   However, the study did not include the independent R & D sector.

7   In relation to recent debates (see McDowell, 1988) it therefore seems better, as Cockburn (1985) and Walby (1985) argue, to keep the dynamic of patriarchal relations, however defined, analytically separate from that of capitalist relations. It also means that it may not be enough to ask simply about 'the effects on women' of industrial restructuring. 'The effects on women' do not only derive from the actions of capital but also from the effects of men's struggle to maintain their supremacy.

8   This impact of geographical change on salary levels must be one of the few times when international comparisons have forced wages to *rise*. (It happened at the same time as workers in branch plants in 'the north' were seeing their wages and conditions undermined by international comparisons – another example of the different ways in which north and south are locked into the international division of labour.)

9   Though it may be: see Boddy, Lovering and Bassett (1986).

References

BARLOW, J. and SAVAGE, M. (1986) 'The politics of growth: cleavage and conflict in a Tory heartland', *Capital and Class*, No. 30, pp. 156–82.

BERRY, B. J. L. (1970) 'The geography of the United States in the year 2000', *Transactions, Institute of British Geographers*, Vol. 51, pp. 21–53.

BODDY, M., LOVERING, J. and BASSETT, K. (1986) *Sunbelt City?: A Study of Economic Change in Britain's M4 Growth Corridor*, Oxford, Clarendon Press.

CARLING, A. (1986) 'Rational choice Marxism', *New Left Review*, No. 160, pp. 24–62.

CHRISTOPHERSON, S. and STORPER, M. (1986) 'The city as studio; the world as back lot: the impact of vertical disintegration on the location of the motion picture industry', *Environment and Planning D: Society and Space*, Vol. 4, pp. 305–20.

COCKBURN, C. (1985) *Machinery of Dominance: Women, Men and Technical Know-how*, London, Pluto Press.

CROWTHER, S. and GARRAHAN, P. (1987) 'Invitation to Sunderland: corporate power and the local economy', paper presented to the Conference on the Japanisation of British Industry, UWIST, Cardiff (mimeo.).

HAMNETT, C., McDOWELL, L. and SARRE, P. (eds) (1988) *Changing Social Structure* (Restructuring Britain, Open Text 2), London, Sage/The Open University.

KEEBLE, D. (1976) *Industrial Location and Planning in the United Kingdom*, London, Methuen.

KEEBLE, D. (1980) 'Industrial decline, regional policy and the urban-rural manufacturing shift in the United Kingdom', *Environment and Planning A*, Vol. XII, pp. 945–62.

LASH, S. and URRY, J. (1987) *The End of Organized Capitalism*, Cambridge, Polity Press.

LEYSHON, A., THRIFT, N. and DANIELS, P. (1987) 'The urban and regional consequences of the restructuring of world financial markets: the case of the City of London', Working Papers on Producer Services, No. 4, Department of Geography, University of Liverpool.

LEYSHON, A., THRIFT, N. and TWOMMEY, C. (1988) 'South goes North? The rise of the British provincial financial centre', paper presented at the Annual Conference of the Institute of British Geography (mimeo.).

LLOYD, P. and REEVE, D. (1982) 'North West England 1971–1977: a study in industrial decline and economic restructuring', *Regional Studies*, Vol. 16, No. 5, pp. 345–60.

MARSHALL, M. (1987) *Long Waves of Regional Development*, London and Basingstoke, Macmillan.

MASON, C. (1987) 'Venture capital in the United Kingdom: a geographical perspective', *National Westminster Bank Quarterly Review*, May, pp. 47–59.

MASSEY, D. (1984) *Spatial Divisions of Labour: Social Structures and the Geography of Production*, London and Basingstoke, Macmillan.

MASSEY, D. (1988) 'A new class of geography', *Marxism Today*, May, pp. 12–17.

McDOWELL, L. (1988) 'Gender divisions', in Hamnett, C., McDowell, L. and Sarre, P. (eds) Ch. 5.

MORGAN, K. and SAYER, A. (1988) *Microcircuits of Capital: The Electronics Industry and Uneven Development*, Cambridge, Polity Press.

MURGATROYD, L. (1985) 'Occupational stratification and gender', in The Lancaster Regionalism Group, *Localities, Class and Gender*, London, Pion.

OBERHAUSER, A. (1987) 'Labour, production and the state: decentralization of the French automobile industry', *Regional Studies*, Vol. 21, No. 5, pp. 445–58.

SCHOENBERGER, E. (1987) 'Technological and organizational change in auto-mobile production: spatial implications', *Regional Studies*, Vol. 21, No. 3, pp. 199–214.

STEWARD, F. and WIELD, D. (1984) 'Science, planning and the State', Unit 16 of D209 *The State and Society*, Milton Keynes, The Open University.

THRIFT, N. (1988) 'Images of social change', in Hamnett, C., McDowell, L. and Sarre, P. (eds) Ch. 1.

THRIFT, N., LEYSHON, A. and DANIELS, P. (1987) 'Sexy, greedy: the new international financial system, the City of London and the South East of England', paper presented to the Urban Change and Conflict Annual Conference (mimeo.).

WALBY, S. (1985) 'Theories of women, work, and unemployment', in The Lancaster Regionalism Group, *Localities, Class and Gender*, London, Pion.

WARDE, A. (1985) 'Spatial change, politics and the division of labour', in Gregory, D. and Urry, J. (eds) *Social Relations and Spatial Structures*, London and Basingstoke, Macmillan.

WARDE, A. (1988) 'Industrial restructuring, local politics and the reproduction of labour power: some theoretical considerations', *Environment and Planning D: Society and Space*, Vol. 6, No. 1, pp. 75–95.

WITT, S., MASON, C. and PINCH, S. (1988) 'Industrial change in the Southampton city-region: a study of the electronics and electrical engineering industry', Working Paper, Urban Policy Research Unit, Department of Geography, University of Southampton.

Index